The Idiot and the Odyssey
Walking the Mediterranean

Joel Stratte-McClure

Praise For "The Idiot and the Odyssey: Walking the Mediterranean"

"The whimsical author, a serial hiker in the midst of a mid-life crisis, embarks on an epic undertaking with determination, a sack full of Homeric quotes and Buddhist wisdom. You'll be glad you came along on a journey of discovery that is both entertaining and inspirational. Onward!"
Tony Rocca, author of "Catching Fireflies"

"Stratte-McClure goes way beyond sharing an amazing personal adventure with us. He delivers an endless stream of wit and wisdom with such selfless honesty that we are compelled into self-examination. Every stressed corporate exec should read this! His creative energy is infectious and guaranteed to inspire innovation. Life changing!"
Mitch Waite, founder and creative director, IntuThink

"In this midlife 'coming of age' quest, we're invited to join Stratte-McClure on his extraordinary journey – trekking the Mediterranean through each creek and cranny as he weaves his observations of the physical world with his own inner contemplations. Readers are treated to meanderings filled with encounters, adventures and mishaps amidst a backdrop of musings abundant with wit and wisdom. An amazing and amusing read!"
Elizabeth Billhardt, photographer/author of
"Coastal Pleasures: Perusing the French Coastline"

"With the Mediterranean as his muse, Joel Stratte-McClure embarks on travels intended not only to broaden the mind, but also to serve as a springboard for reconnecting with the wisdom of the past. An Odyssey that meanders from Greek philosophers to personal demons, a reflective, amusing and open-minded attempt to reconstrue existential questions we ask at the age of 20, some thirty years on."
Jill Harry, editor of New Riviera Magazine

"Contemplative and entertaining, *The Idiot* traverses a very contemporary Mediterranean shoreline – though Greek gods and goddesses pop up along the way. Much more than a guidebook, Stratte-McClure's tale is saturated with history and humour. This mid-life meditation will appeal to adventurers and armchair travellers alike."
Linda Phillips Ashour, author of "Speaking in Tongues"

"Like slow food, the Herculean hike around the Mediterranean by Joel Stratte-McClure – no idiot, for sure – seems an improbable ambition. Yet, inspired by Odysseus, Chinese philosophy and his own mid-life crises, the account of his adventures is a triumph of travel writing – entertaining, witty, perceptive and informative. An enchanting read."
Marion Kaplan, photojournalist/author of "Focus Africa"
and "The Portuguese - The Land and Its People"

"Joel Stratte-McClure maintains it would be unreasonable to think anyone can achieve Nirvana after walking less than 5000 kilometres. Wrong! I felt enlightened from the first page to the last of this inspiring and motivating book as I faithfully accompanied the author on every step and stumble of his remarkable journey. And it's a delight to see pesky French women finally taken off their pedestal."
Margaret Kemp, editor at large/critic of Bonjour Paris

"Joel Stratte-McClure's *The Idiot and the Odyssey* is a wonderful book. By turns whimsical and profound – and more than occasionally laugh-out-loud funny – it defies all the conventions. It is at once an adventure story, a work of history, a philosophical treatise and an unflinchingly honest memoir."
Harry Stein, screenwriter and author of "The Girl Watchers Club:
Lessons from the Battlefields of Life"

"*The Idiot and the Odyssey* mixes an enjoyable walk with a little Greek mythology in a breathtakingly beautiful part of Europe. It encouraged me to get off the golf course and out of the pool to explore by foot a land steeped in history and natural beauty. I even felt that Bogart, the author's yellow Labrador, was there in spirit."
Des Baum, low-handicap golfer, master swimmer
and founder/president of Covico (Antibes, France)

"If, as the Greek physician Hippocrates said, 'Walking is man's best medicine,' then Joel Stratte-McClure's book proves it. Everyone who accompanies him will be healthier in mind and spirit. Slow down and read *The Idiot and the Odyssey*."
Alex Belida, media critic, former foreign correspondent for
the Voice of America and author of "Regrets Only: An Africa Journal"

"Perhaps our perception of the world does not depend on the places we visit but the gait of our travelling. I never thought that, in an era obsessed with speed and technology, somebody could thrill me with his amusing observations, experiences and ruminations while tracing on foot the same route I travelled by car in 1968 to visit my aging grandfather at the other end of the Spanish coast. This is the best guide to the Mediterranean since Homer's *The Odyssey* and as informative as James Michener's *Iberia*."
Princess Beatriz de Orleans Borbón from Spain.

"An amazing read. With each step we learn more about life as we do not necessarily know it. We forget about the physical strength defined in the author's trek and are captivated by his soul, which is defined with every step of the way."
Tevia Celli, founder and owner, Body & Soul Workout and The Daily Core (West Hollywood, California)

"This amazing account of human stamina and daring do, where mythological references merge with the author's experiences, creates a brilliant correspondence between past and present. Woven seamlessly in this tale are courage, curiosity and personal reflection, often against a historical or cultural context that shuns all pretence. The trek illuminates the human adventure, comprehension of the self and understanding of 'the other'."
Constantine Christofides, Professor at the University of Washington and the Institute for American Universities in Aix-en-Provence, France.

"This wonderful story of a journey through a fascinating part of the world, through time and history, is best of all a story of people. I learned much about the Mediterranean that was new to me and it gave me a new vision of the coast of France that I thought I knew so well.
Russ Collins, founder and editor, ProvenceBeyond.com

"I always knew Joel could tell a good story, but this is a real feat (although I don't quite remember the Moroccan incident in 1970 as he does). As a bookseller, I'm already looking forward to the next volume."
Henrietta Dax, owner of Clarke's Bookshop (Cape Town, South Africa)

" A deeply amusing , and in an affecting way, a quietly heroic book. The spirit of the writer caught me."
Cratis Hippocrates, former Group Learning and Development Editorial Manager, Fairfax Media Group, General Manager, Open Universities

"A remarkable book that is equal parts travel guide, history book and charming memoir. Beautifully written, *The Idiot and the Odyssey* is a siren song to our peripatetic Australian psyche. Heracles would be ever so proud!"
Susie Dobson, president, Australians in Film (Hollywood, California)

"Reminiscent of *The Great Railway Bazaar* by Paul Theroux but on foot, this is a book you can savour, take to bed and roll around in your mind to learn about life's journey. Packed with information, loaded with humorous encounters, stuffed with life-changing revelations, this meandering walk is worth living vicariously. A great gift to inspire employees, friends and wives."
Charles Eisenhour, commercial director, Pepe Jeans (London)

"Having revelled in the sun, storms and special characters of the Mediterranean, I can attest to Stratte-McClure's insightful clarity. Without being tedious or sanctimonious, he introduces people and places as stereotypical, fantastic and ridiculous as could only be true in the Mediterranean. From one audacious and adventurous minga to another, I compliment him on his stable stride in an unstable but captivating region."
Ethan Gelber, Lonely Planet author and president of BikeAbout the Mediterranean

"A great book. Concept clearly explained, curiosity quickly alerted, classical mythology very effectively utilised with a clarity that will hold the ignorant as well as the cognoscenti. And light of touch as well as erudite."
Michael Knipe, former foreign correspondent of The Times of London

"A brave and unique story from a naturally talented writer, weaving with commendable, self-deprecating humour hard-won lessons drawn from the author's colourful life, with those gained on this amazing hike around the Mediterranean, all of it laced with erudite seams of wisdom from Homer's *The Odyssey*. This deserves a prize for originality and sheer daring."
Francis O'Hara, author of "Be My Guest"

"Reading *The Idiot and the Odyssey* provides a hugely entertaining perspective of the world's oldest and greatest journey, conjured millennia ago by Homer. The book is a reminder that the Mediterranean, even today, is a wild and fascinating place."
Tony Perrottet, author of "Route 66 AD: On the Trail of Ancient Roman Tourists"

"Reading *The Idiot and the Odyssey* made my feet hurt but my imagination soar. It sparked a long-dormant wanderlust that inspired me to hastily stuff a backpack and head for the Mediterranean. Then practicality set in and I realised the task is far too Herculean for a mere mortal. Luckily Joel Stratte-McClure, who must have been infused with the power of the gods, was up to the challenge and let me vicariously feel like an adventurer through his awe-inspiring exploits."
Adam Rifkin, writer/director, (Look, Detroit Rock City, Mousehunt)

"This book puts the soul into walking, capturing the spirit of place and enabling you to feel that you are on every step of this adventurous journey. It provides real insights to the people, the culture and lifestyle found around the shores of the Mediterranean. Inspiring as it makes travel fun."
Peter Robinson, radio personality and editor of San Francisco Books & Travel

"The brazen tale of this eccentric author smacks of attitude both audacious and foolhardy, yet he emerges, through his hilarity and touching humanness, wiser and more virtuous. A marvellous narration, one breathing ancient literature into a modern and real theatre, it connects myth with geography, history with legend and life-affirming purpose with the old bugaboo, the concept of impossible Quest. I'm so confident that *The Idiot and the Odyssey* will become a classic that it's already required reading for my advance placement students."
Gerald Rodgers, English curriculum coordinator,
Santa Maria High School District (California)

"A delightful, soulful memoir-cum-guide of the birthplace of modern civilisation. Veteran journalist Stratte-McClure takes readers along the sometimes rugged and often-urban coastline of the Mediterranean and, with his well-honed reporting skills, peppers the adventure with wise words from our greatest philosophers, history lessons of coastline sites, colourful descriptions of the characters he meets and tales of his own rugged life. It makes you want to put on your hiking boots and hit the path yourself. In search of what? As Stratte-McClure understands more clearly with each day of his years long trek, that is the eternal question."
Dana Thomas, former Newsweek correspondent and author of
"How Luxury Lost Its Luster"

"Joel Stratte-McClure's didactic but sensitive voice simultaneously describes and contemplates the Mediterranean landscape he traverses and the individuals who inhabit it. He combines a knowledgeable guide's eye of historic and cultural detail with a tourist's awe of the fascinating scenery and people. Homer would love it!"
Vince Tomasso, Classics Department, Stanford University

"From the turquoise-tinted water and zillion dollar yachts of Saint-Tropez to the intrigue of the Kasbah in Tangier, Joel Stratte-McClure takes the reader on a delightful spiritual journey around the Mediterranean that is filled with nudists and Buddhists, the obscenely chic and the exotic. *The Idiot and the Odyssey* is such a terrific antidote to the middle age melancholia that if Homer could do a sequel, Odysseus would probably jump ship to join Stratte-McClure's MedTrek instead."
Craig Unger, Vanity Fair contributing editor, author of
"The Fall of the House of Bush" and Fellow at the Center on Law and Security at New York University's School of Law

"Homer and Lao Tsu may be the author's go-to guys, but as I read this enchanting book I was reminded of Cervantes. The humorous adventures, the piquant observations, the dreamlike buoyancy of memories jostled by travel - Joel Stratte-McClure is Don Quixote with his head screwed on right."
Jeff Wheelwright, Author of "The Irritable Heart: The Medical Mystery of the Gulf War"

"Like travel writer Paul Theroux's *Happy Isles of Oceania: Paddling the Pacific*, journalist Joel Stratte-McClure's *The Idiot and the Odyssey* invites us along on a wonderfully entertaining pilgrimage around a legendary sea, undertaken by a recently-divorced middle-aged man hunting for fresh adventure, renewal and the meaning of life. The fleet-footed McClure finds his share of all three, and a dream experience of a lifetime. It's worth every ebullient, blistering step!"
Tom Moore, editor-in-chief, Reader's Digest Australia

"Joel's fascinating account of his trek round the Mediterranean foreshores from Monaco to Morocco is part wry observation, part history, and part rumination and reflection. It makes you wish you could have been with him as he walked."
Lucienne Joy, former radio announcer and author of "Ulterior Motives"

The Idiot and the Odyssey

Walking the Mediterranean

Joel Stratte-McClure

FAST TH!NKING

The Idiot and the Odyssey
Walking the Mediterranean

Published by
Fast Thinking Books
A division of ETN-COM

J.M.F. Keeney: Chairman and Editor-in-Chief

P+61 2 9418 7100
F +61 2 9428 2607
Level 3, 448 Pacific Hwy
Artarmon NSW 2064
www.etncom.com
www.fastthinking.com.au

ISBN 978-0-9775866-5-3

Designed by Nick Dale.
Edited by Tim Mendham.
Printed by KHL Printing, Singapore.

Publisher's Note

The Idiot and the Odyssey:
Walking the Mediterranean

One of my most magnificent blunders as a publisher was the initial rejection of this remarkable book. Why did I do that? I was hurried, engaged in other projects, moving too fast to adequately focus.

Months passed and I picked up the manuscript again during a weekend at the farm, well away from the city bustle, where one can think at leisure. Discovery was at hand. Of course, by then I had to dive into the book world's equivalent of a feeding frenzy: many a publisher and agent had already seen what I had failed to.

The Idiot and the Odyssey is much more than another travel-by-foot book, as good as it is in that less-than-a-category. No doubt the avid trekker will enjoy the challenges of the walk itself. Stratte-McClure is no slouch when it comes to scaling hills and wryly recording the rigours of long walking.

But *The Idiot*, as I came to call it, is much more than that. The sub-themes which I awoke to that weekend are what lift it above and beyond the norm.

As an oblique introduction to Homer's *Odyssey*, it probably has no peer – a non-academic unfolding of Odyssean tales and quotes inspired by the trek's landscapes and personal memories. I can see it inspiring many to read or re-visit this pillar of western culture; it certainly got my copy back on the nightstand. The young, who think Homer's work a dusty ancient thing, will be inspired to look anew.

For the armchair traveller, there is a fine if random series of impressions of historical sites and architecture and accompanying anecdotes, drawn from years of tramping this part of the world, constant reading and observation – the author worked as a journalist for 30 years in the region, and seems to have met nearly everyone famous or infamous during that time.

And then there is the continual thread of contemplation on alcoholism, from the often hilarious recollections of boozing years to the last decades of sobriety in its fullest sense, and meaning.

The counterpoint to the extremes of excessive drinking comes from a steady flow of gentle observations and quotes on Buddhism, especially the walking meditation principles of a Zen monk under whom the author practiced, along with the Dalai Lama and assorted others.

A good part of the walk is solitary and this brings forth countless ruminations, some profound, others of deep amusement: the crush of divorce; the value of friends; parenthood; mortality; bankruptcy; life as an expatriate of over 30 years. And a number which recount life tales of the wild and debauched in the 60s, 70s and beyond.

But above all there is a comfort here: we feel as though we are walking alongside the narrator in a relaxed conversation sharing insights and the delights of the trail.

So here is a book like a prism – shards of light glancing off in different directions, different colours and tones, but always grounded by the challenges and serenity of a coastal walk over 4400 kilometres from the extremes of Algeria to Rome, the long way. What unites it all is the author's jubilation and the partnership one feels; as he considers his own life, he teaches us things, naturally, undogmatically, and nudges the best in ourselves to come forth.

J.M.F. Keeney
Chairman and Editor-in-Chief
Fast Thinking Books / ETN Communications
editor@fastthinking.com.au

Sydney, September 2008

Dedication:
To the Mediterranean Sea and my companions on the path.

Contents

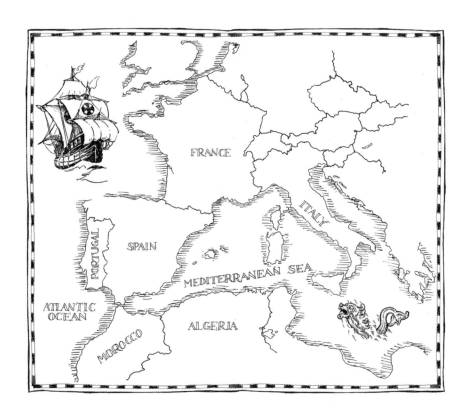

Preface

What am I doing here?

I've trekked more than 3000 accident-free kilometres along the sandy, rocky and rugged coasts of France, Spain and North Africa. But now I'm staring up at the sky from the bottom of a cliff on the edge of the Mediterranean Sea.

I've survived the fall but my head is bleeding, my ankle is badly twisted, my hand has a deep gash, and my entire body is shaking. Just above me a herd of Moroccan goats, whose curiosity brings them closer and closer, is unleashing an avalanche of rocks. For some mysterious reason, all I can think of is that goats were symbols of fertility in ancient Greece.

I vaguely hear my son screaming from the cliff top.

"I'm still here," I say weakly, almost in a whisper, to him and to me. "I'm still here."

But my walk around the Mediterranean may have ended ahead of schedule.

What *am* I doing here?

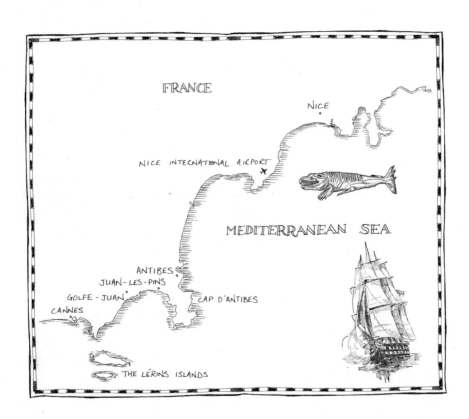

FRANCE

NICE

NICE INTERNATIONAL AIRPORT

MEDITERRANEAN SEA

ANTIBES
JUAN-LES-PINS
GOLFE-JUAN
CANNES
CAP D'ANTIBES

THE LÉRINS ISLANDS

Part One

The French Riviera: Getting on the Path

1. Do Not Delay Me, For I Love the Sea Ways

"Sing in me, Muse, and through me tell the story of that man skilled in all ways of contending, the wanderer, harried for years on end, after he plundered the stronghold on the proud height of Troy." — The Odyssey

Call me Homeric, philosophic or poetic. Or accuse me of embarking on a foolhardy quest, a lark, an escape, an act of maniacal ego or even some sincere spiritual soul searching. But there are actually several legitimate reasons that I'm launching a walk around the Mediterranean Sea.

I'm in the middle of a melancholy divorce, mired in an emotional and spiritual cesspool and greatly in need of a cosmic uplift. As a jaded journalist, even exotic assignments smack of déjà vu and I'm desperately seeking an extended adventure on unexplored turf. I also love to hike and this multipurpose expedition – which I call a MedTrek not only because it's about the Mediterranean, but also because it's meditative and, hopefully, medicinal – will enable me to reflect, stay in shape, forge new friendships and perhaps have a life-changing adventure or two. It will almost certainly improve my mood and, after 15 years without a drink or drug, keep me clean and sober. Maybe.

It's also now or never. This is the only time I'll have the physical strength, financial resources and free time to fulfil my childhood dream: to hike around the world's largest inland sea in my own version of *The Odyssey*, Homer's epic about the dramatic homeward voyage of Odysseus after the decade-long Trojan War that began in 1194 BC.

Incidentally, the name Odysseus from the Greek word *hodos*, or road, can mean 'a guide, one showing the way' or 'one who is hated'. And the man the Romans called Ulysses was nothing if not well-travelled and, occasionally, despised. His perilous voyage took him throughout the eastern Mediterranean and the account of his exploits resulted in the world's first dramatic travel narrative. Sometimes I think I can hear him laughing at my proposed exploits.

Why am I following in his footsteps? I've strolled around Walden Pond in Massachusetts, trekked in the Andes and climbed the Himalayas. Yet a significant mission requires a more substantial target. What could be more pleasurable than a footloose look at life on the Mediterranean and the twenty-something countries on its shores?

The journey will give me a chance to become more intimately acquainted with *The Odyssey* and I'm bound to run into some of Homer's goddesses, heroes, sea nymphs, warriors and villains. Maybe I'll even find out if there's any truth to the adage "The goal is the path, the path is the goal" written by Lao Tsu, who lived a few centuries after Homer. And, as I seek the answers to numerous existential and eternal questions, it never hurts to get additional instruction in life lessons.

Or maybe it will be a total fiasco. No mentors, no myths, no magic. The whole affair could turn out to be a cosmic joke perpetrated by Zeus, the father of gods and mortals who, said Homer, "grants us this or that, or else refrains from granting, as he wills; all things are in his power".

But I'm not completely cut off from reality. I recently met a Tibetan lama and told him that I plan to continue studying 'The Path' of Buddhism while walking around the Med and coming to terms with the existential agony and angst of my divorce and professional monotony.

"Enjoy your walk without thinking of arriving anywhere," the sage old monk told me. "Take your time. In your case, spiritual progress could take thirty lifetimes. So could a walk of that distance."

"That's very encouraging," I replied. "Thanks for the tip."

I'm eager to get going on New Year's Eve, the day before my Mediterranean journey begins, when I visit the Picasso Museum perched on the weathered stone ramparts overlooking the sea in Antibes in the south of France. I gaze at "Ulysses and the Sirens", Pablo Picasso's vivid 12-foot high allegorical painting from 1947 that features my cunning and crafty hero bound to the spar of his ship as he withstands the mind-blowing song of the tempting Sirens. Picasso's kaleidoscopic portrayal of misshaped mountains, fish and sea maidens pointedly reminds me that this expedition has been beckoning since I was a kid.

My favourite book was a large-print tome called *Myths and Legends of the*

Ages, a collection of Greek and Roman tales. I was seriously besotted by ancient stories about the Golden Fleece, the return of Ulysses and the Trojan Horse. I've recently had the book rebound (though some of the pages still have chocolate ice cream stains on them) and have read and reread various translations of the works attributed to Homer, underlining verse after verse about the legends of the Greeks during the Bronze Age. I'm equally enthused about more recent but nonetheless still ancient Mediterranean history. Like the Peloponnesian War that began in 460 BC and the era of Alexander the Great, the short and stocky Macedonian who cut the Gordian knot and was tutored by Aristotle.

About to set off on a journey inspired by a multitude of myths and a literary white rabbit that will lead me into a Mediterranean wonderland, I imagine myself a contemporary Odysseus tied to the mast as my sailors, wax in their ears, row past seductive Sirens to meet, as Homer recounted, the vagaries of the "Ocean, who is the source of all." Incidentally, at 50 I'm a bit older than Kirk Douglas was when he portrayed Ulysses in a 1955 film.

Listening to the waves crashing on the rocks below, I don't know if I'll be gone as long as Homer's persistent hero. He travelled for 20 years, a victim of divine and meteorological whims, before he finally made it back to Ithaca to find his wife Penélopê and son Telémakhos. Or have "bright molten tears run down my cheeks" and learn that there is "nothing like the sea for wearing out the toughest man alive." But I'm convinced, after living and raising two kids on the French Riviera for the last 20 years, that the Mediterranean is my fabled siren and the MedTrek my intended destiny.

Staring out the museum window over the bright azure sea takes me far beyond the seemingly infinite sapphire horizon. My mind's eye transports me first to the cliff-hanging village of Bonifacio on the southern tip of Corsica where I once admired the purported remains of the "Lady of Bonifacio" dating from 6570 BC. Then I mentally dart across the sea to Carthage, the seaside city-state in contemporary Tunisia founded by Queen Dido in 814 BC that's one of my preferred archaeological sites on that country's 1300-kilometre coastline. Finally I time travel to a hotel beneath Mount Etna in Sicily where my daughter Sonia was conceived in 1981.

I have to admit that the Mediterranean is, if nothing else, a bit daunting. It's nearly 16,000 kilometres in circumference, according to an 1857 atlas astute enough to measure such things. The Greeks called it Mesogeios, or 'Middle Land', and the Romans named it Mare Nostrum, which means 'Our Sea'. The word 'Mediterranean' is a derivation of the Latin for 'middle' and 'earth'. Perhaps because the sea is surrounded by three continents, or perhaps because, to many back in those days, it was literally the middle of the earth – the centre of the then-known world.

Although the Mediterranean probably does not have a beginning or an end, it seems appropriate that the Côte d'Azur city of Antibes, a cradle of Greek civilisation in the fourth century BC and just a few minutes from my home, is my starting point. One of the largest pleasure boating harbours on the Mediterranean, Antibes is known for the dolphins and sharks at its Marineland, its flourishing flower production, the Bacon (pronounced Bah-cone) fish restaurant and, for me at least, the 50-metre pool where I've been swimming with a masters team for two decades.

Incidentally, my aquatic teammates know that I'm a sprinter rather than a long-distance kind of guy and are a bit sceptical about my ambitious project. During one of our recent post-workout lunches they snickered when I mentioned, over *salades Niçoises*, that the journey will instruct me about balance, clarity, serenity, a higher power, good and evil, sun block, global warming and doing nothing. But one of them cut me a little slack.

"Well, at least you're not swimming around it!" said Des Baum from South Africa. "And fortunately it's not the Pacific!"

Nothing like some unconditional support!

Actually, I'm not the first person to realise the strategic importance of this port. The Greeks kicked things off 2400 years ago when voyagers from Massalia, as Marseille was called at the time, used Antipolis, as Antibes was known, as a trading post with the Ligurians, a surly tribe that occupied the mountainous territory a few miles back from the sea. This was during the period when, according to Socrates, Greek male-dominated poleis or city-states ringed the Med like 'frogs around a pond' and aristocrats from Hellas spread Greek culture as they sailed their trade routes.

It's easy to understand why Antibes was an inviting place to land both then and now. Besides the natural allure and physical attraction of the coast there are scores of surprises and treasures in the lavender-and-thyme scented *arrière pays*, or back country. My top picks are the 30,000 mysterious Bronze Age rock engravings found in the Vallée des Merveilles, or the Valley of the Marvels, in the Alpes-Maritimes. I also frequently visit medieval perched villages like Gourdon, Peillon, Bariols or Utelle and often embark on canyoning or kayak trips down the gorges of the Estéron and Vésubie rivers. A rock-climbing expedition up the Baou de Saint Jeannet provides an overview of the region's botanical beauty and floral wealth, from hillside fields of scented roses to ornately landscaped Belle Époque gardens, which complement the sand, sea, sky and sun as reality and symbols of the Cote d'Azur.

Near the Picasso museum, where the artist painted for a few months in the late 1940s, is the town's archaeological museum. Its plethora of ancient treasures includes the reconstruction of a Roman ship as well as Etruscan, Greek and Roman amphorae and artefacts that illustrate a whopping 4000 years of history. A visit there excites me about the rainbow of religions, languages, literature, history, cultures, cuisine, climate and countryside that I'll encounter on the MedTrek.

And there's something else. The word 'museum' is derived from the nine Greek muses who were the daughters of Zeus and inspired arts and sciences.

I swear I hear them murmur: "Come with us. We'll shelter and protect you, and your readers, in this land of chicanery and chance."

Chicanery, indeed. The aura of deception and distrust associated with many Mediterranean locations, including the wheeling and dealing on today's French Riviera, probably sprang from the time when Antibes, built behind steep stone ramparts, was a centre for trade. The Greeks, who controlled commerce at the time, didn't trust those wily Ligurians enough to let them through the city's only gate and conducted all of their trade outside the town's wall. Not a good way to do business and probably why the Greeks went broke.

The Romans and barbarians followed the Greeks, but a number of invasions sent Antibes downhill for centuries until it became a border post on the Franco-Savoyard frontier in the 1300s. When it was understood that the city could play a key military role, Antibes again became prominent. Since then, during various reigns by everyone from the Grimaldis (who ultimately settled in Monaco) to Napoleon Bonaparte (who ultimately was exiled and died on the island of Saint Helena in the South Atlantic Ocean), wheeling and dealing has been rekindled.

Street criminals, known as 'rats' in French, are still in ample supply, but Antibes has generally cleaned up its reputation and had its share of noteworthy celebrities. Napoleon lived here in 1794 and was imprisoned for a time in the still-standing 16th century Fort Carré. Author Graham Greene, who was constantly heckling and needling local politicians, lived in an unassuming apartment near the port until shortly before his death in 1991.

Just steps away from the Picasso Museum is the Place du Safranier where Nikos Kazantzakis, who wrote *The Odyssey: A Modern Sequel* and *Zorba the Greek*, lived. A plaque on the door at 8 rue du Bas-Castellet reads "I fear nothing. I expect nothing. I am a free man." A copy of his 33,333-line version of *The Odyssey*, finally published in the late 1930s as a continuation of "the sufferings and torments of renowned Odysseus", is in my backpack.

It turns out that we're not the only adventurers who've found inspiration and guidance in *The Odyssey*. Alexander the Great frequently read Homer after his father told him "Macedonia is not large enough to hold you."

As I begin my own journey, I tell myself "I fear nothing. I expect nothing. I'm almost a free man."

2. Did Odysseus Have Trouble with His Pedometer?

"A journey of a thousand miles starts under one's feet." – Lao Tsu

Although I relish walking alone, my odyssey is not an anti-social undertaking. A month before the departure date, I invited friends to symbolically join me for the first fifty kilometres. The overwhelming response had me imagining myself a seaside Pied Piper, a Mediterranean Johnny Appleseed. But as the take-off approaches, the actual trekkers are few and far between. In fact, they're almost non-existent. Probably because few people are willing to get up at the crack of dawn on New Year's Day to go for a long walk.

I have only two companions. One is Bogart, my aging yellow Labrador Retriever who, born and raised on the Riviera, has been running, walking, swimming and wandering around France with me for over a decade. The other is Delphyne, a Franco-American acquaintance who claimed, exactly as Homer recorded in *The Iliad*, she "knew the things that were and the things that would be and the things that had been before".

"If you need a spiritual guide then you've got to take me along!" Delphyne emailed enthusiastically when she heard about my midlife project, which I hesitated to call a midlife crisis. "I haven't done much hiking, but I'll keep your psyche inspired."

I encouraged her to join me. After all, who could turn down a potential spiritual goddess and the offer of an inspired psyche at this stage of the journey? Certainly not someone terminating a 20-year marriage and approaching the next stage of life.

It's a dry, quiet and slightly chilly morning as we begin our stroll along the dark and grumbling shore. This is definitely not what Homer frequently called "a rosy-fingered dawn" on what Kazantzakis christened "the pearly sea". The Mediterranean coast is hardly at its bathing-beauty best on the first day of January. The sandy beaches along the ramparts just beyond the two Antibes museums are covered with winter debris, including seaweed and bottles, plastic and trash. I pick up bits and pieces of litter, including an empty Champagne bottle, to improve the state of the seaside.

In the distance, the snow-covered Alpes-Maritimes look calm and pristine as seven cormorants fly in formation above us at the roundabout near the Josse Hôtel. Delphyne insists they are a good omen. She has obviously read her Homer because in *The Odyssey* a compassionate sea nymph appears on Odysseus' raft in the form of a cormorant.

"These birds are descendants of Odysseus's helpful feathered friend," Delphyne tells me.

As we begin to round the rocky Cap d'Antibes, there's a lot less litter. I'm not worrying about making good time, walking a particular distance or even breathing properly. The pace, I figure, will take a few days to establish. Today I'll just try to focus on taking it easy and making some interesting detours.

Delphyne proclaims that the distinctive blue-green colour of the water is another good omen and stops at a bench by the sea, she says, to "meditate myself into the right frame of mind for the MedTrek". She wants 30 minutes of "quiet time", which gives Bogart and me a chance to climb to the Garoupe lighthouse, the most powerful beacon on the coast with a beam that shoots out 40 miles.

Olive-black clouds obscure Corsica, the island that de Maupassant called "a mountain in the middle of the sea" where some claim Homer's savage and cannibal Laestrygones giants once lived. Near the lighthouse, a small chapel called the Sanctuary de la Garoupe is open and, passing between two wrought-iron gates, we step inside. Standing amidst frescoes and dozens of votive offerings, including oddities like a tattered black sailor's cap and a broken walking stick, I light a candle at the wooden statue of Our Lady of Safe Homecoming. This Black Madonna is known as the patron saint of sailors. Hopefully, she might look especially kindly on seaside walkers.

After praying for a safe journey and patience with my fellow travelers, I'm struck with an exuberant full-bodied tingle.

"Ahhh ommm!" I softly utter to Bogart and the sea below us. "We're actually doing this! We're about to walk around the Mediterranean."

Bogart, the frequent herald of my adventurous outings, doesn't fully understand. He looks at me like this is just the start of any walk, rather than a truly momentous occasion. He apparently has no clue that the coins I leave in the chapel are meant as an offering to both Tyche, the cornucopia-holding Greek goddess of good fortune and luck, and Hermes, the patron of travelers and wayfarers who always wore winged sandals.

"The Greeks always left offerings to the gods at sanctuaries," I explain to my bemused Lab. "And they often included things like gemstones, statuettes and even votive casts of diseased body parts that had been cured by a god. So leaving some coins is really nothing much. The gesture might keep us out of trouble and prevent us from being turned to stone."

Afterwards, we sneak into the Parc Thuret gardens, despite their being closed for the holiday, and I suck in the invigorating winter aroma produced by the scent of the sea breeze blended with the bouquet of pine, cedar and eucalyptus trees. Unfortunately we can't get into the twenty-five acre Villa Eilen Roc, which was designed in 1867 by Charles Garnier, the architect of the opera houses in Paris and Monaco. We skip that enchanted forest to return to the seaside sidewalk, fetch a now fully-meditated Delphyne and continue walking in front of villas with exotic-sounding names like Mer et Pins and Maloko.

Most of the residences on the Cap d'Antibes are elegant, cared for, distinguished and obscenely chic and expensive. But Maloko looks like a crumbling government office in Kinshasa, the capital of the Congo that I visited frequently as a journalist in the mid-1970s when the country was called Zaire and led by the devilish Mobutu Sese Seko Kuku Ngbednu Wa Za Banga. Mobutu's mythical name, which is translated as "the all-powerful warrior who, because of his endurance and inflexible will to win, goes from conquest to conquest, leaving fire in his wake and arising from the blood and ashes of his enemies like the Sun which conquers the night", would probably have been music to the ears of the Greek gods.

It's too early to drop into Bacon where owner Etienne Sordello and his chefs create luscious *bouillabaisse* and serve 100-euro lobster dinners. Actually, I tell Delphyne, my best meal at Bacon was free. Sordello and I dove for sea urchins, caught a dozen of the prickly critters, then surfaced, returned to the restaurant, sliced them open and ate them raw.

The spiny creatures feed on algae and are considered a real delicacy if you're a sea otter or a sushi fanatic in search of an aphrodisiac. They are filled with delicious coral-coloured gonads and roe that resemble the consistency of a ripe fig or salty caviar. Their taste, helped along with some olive oil and lemon, has the fresh bittersweet seawater tang of a raw oyster. A delicious and succulent, albeit messy, meal.

"Won't it be fun to catch our own fish and cook fresh vegetables once we get beyond civilisation?" I enthusiastically suggest. "Just think! In Morocco, where there're no towns or villages for miles, we'll have to live off the land and sea!"

Delphyne, whose earliest namesake was a dragon woman and guardian of the sinews of Zeus in Greek mythology, looks a bit sceptical. "Well, I'm not sure I'll make it to Morocco but I certainly wouldn't mind a lunch at Bacon," she says. "Can't we just wait here until it opens?"

"I thought we could grab some sandwiches and picnic on the sea," I reply. "Let's see where we are at noon and stop then."

"Noon?" she exclaims. "My pack already feels like I'm lugging boulders. I'm not sure I can make it until noon."

I pull a persimmon out of my pack, slice it open and hand half of it to Delphyne.

"Here, this will give you some additional stamina," I say. "The Greeks used to call this the 'fruit of the Gods' and its scientific name, *Diospyros lotus,* is often translated as 'the wheat of Zeus.' You might recall that it's mentioned in *The Odyssey* and that those who ate it forgot about going home and instead stayed to feast on it with the lotus-eaters. So watch out!"

I met Delphyne, a highly-paid executive with a multinational cosmetics company, when she provocatively emailed me a few months ago. She wanted to become a writer and asked me to be her literary mentor.

"Why me?" I emailed back.

"I've read every word you've published," she wrote. "Let me buy you lunch at La Jarre on the ramparts in Antibes!"

We wound up meeting at a nondescript Chinese restaurant in the old part of town. Lithe, blonde, in her early 30s, wearing a warm smile and a tight cashmere sweater, Delphyne was a lot more appetising than my moo shoo pork. She was also smart and (you probably hate this word as much as I do) sensitive.

Our friendship blossomed as I helped her publish an article on female execs coping with sexual harassment on European business trips. But despite my tattered marriage, I tried to keep things purely professional and ignore the ego boost I got from Delphyne's endless compliments about my mind, body and spirit. I never for a moment thought we might get romantically involved because, I told myself, there's no way that this young trophy girl could become my ultimate spiritual soulmate, my physical muse and the answer to all the prayers I'd never had time to make. If nothing else, my years on this earth had taught me not only that love is blind but also that there's no fool like a middle-aged fool. A mid-life crisis? Moi? Not quite yet.

Anyway I've never hiked with Delphyne and, of course, you never really know anyone until you walk together for a few days.

Despite her avowed spirituality and professed psychic powers, I'm already a little sceptical about subjecting Delphyne to the uncertainties and demands of a long hike that requires a modicum of physical stamina, mental flexibility and emotional tolerance. Bogart was used to being my partner and fitted the bill, but I'm not sure if Delphyne, despite our friendship, can cope with either the distance or my own idiosyncrasies.

Walking with a dog is a lot easier than with another mortal. Odysseus might have left his hound, Argus, at home when he set off for the Trojan Wars, but Bogart and I are constant companions. And while I remain a clumsy American alien in a nation that prides itself on cultural knowledge and social refinements, Bogart has become a truly multicultural canine. I might be embarrassingly distinguished by my accent, my penchant for punctuality and fabricated stress that, within an instant, enables me to become obsessively fixated on, and tormented by, an imagined problem entirely of my own making. Bogart, on the other hand, is a majestic cohort and breezes through the rigours of French life as though he's a mongrel mix of Descartes, Pascal and de Gaulle.

His French birthright, of course, gave him a head start on me, the permanent foreigner sitting on the multicultural sidelines. He leaped into the lead when he became completely bilingual ('sit' or '*assis*', 'fetch' or '*va chercher*', it's all the same to him) and mastered many of those distinctive ingrained French traits, like arrogance, discretion, finesse, politesse, and stubbornness.

And face it. Dogs are still a big deal in France. Probably the most insightful remark I ever made about the French was during an appearance on a segment of the *Today* show, an American morning television program being shot at the Gare de Lyon in Paris in the late 1980s. They'd flown me north from Nice simply to inform host Jane Pauley that the best thing Americans visiting France can do is leave their bikini tops at home and bring their dogs. I added that the worst thing they could do is to tell any canine-obsessed Frenchman that "Your dog is ugly!" because they take it very personally. This is still remarkably sound advice to give any American planning a trip to France.

After living with the French for over three decades, I'm positive they're different from the rest of mankind, at least when it comes to dogs. For starters, pooches are treated better than people. Only dogs, not children nor adults, can walk on the grass in Paris, which, along with the lousy weather, is one reason I fled the capital for the Riviera once I had kids of my own.

But there's no reason to contest the importance of canines in this culture. That's why I have two (Bogart and Humphrey, an American Cocker Spaniel) and frequently travel with them because they open a lot of doors. Although I'm worried how his paws will fare on rockier shores, Bogart will almost certainly win me more French friends and favours than Delphyne. And if actor George Clooney could get away with sleeping in a double bed in Hollywood next to Max, his potbellied pet pig, then I wasn't too worried about accusations of bestiality on my journey around the Mediterranean.

Maybe the dog's the god in this story. After all, Homer said gods "liken themselves to all kinds of strangers, go in various disguises from city to city, observing the wrongdoing and the righteousness of men". And to the Greeks, gods were as real as your next-door neighbour. But could a god be a dog? Or vice versa?

There's a description in *The Odyssey* about a god who "first took on a whiskered lion's shape, a serpent then; a leopard; a great boar; then sousing water; then a tall green tree".

Being a dog, then, is probably not too difficult a task.

A lone male swimmer is preparing to wade out into the dark, uninviting water at La Garoupe beach, where Gerald and Sara Murphy used to rake the sand and bring their compatriots, the F. Scott Fitzgeralds and the Ernest Hemingways, for dips back in the 1920s. Fitzgerald, in *Tender Is The Night*, described "the ghostly wash of the Mediterranean" and, perhaps imitating Homer, characterised the sea "as mysteriously coloured as agates and carnelians of childhood, green as green milk, blue as laundry water, wine dark".

The swimmer's girlfriend is attentively watching him strip down to take the year's inaugural plunge and I have to restrain Bogart from joining him.

"*Bonne année,*" I yell as he's about to dive into the water. "You're starting the year off right."

"It's definitely purifying," he replies in English with a distinctive Dutch accent. "And a nice little jolt on New Year's Day. I usually do this in Holland where the water's much colder."

Then he screams something that sounds like "whoopee" and swims a few strokes towards Africa.

Otherwise, it's eerily quiet. There are few cars in the large parking lot and not a single yacht is anchored in the popular bay. The two best seafood spots, Keller Beach and Le Rocher, are tightly shuttered and the nearby hotels are closed for the winter. As we walk on the smooth cobblestone-and-rock trail that winds around the end of the Cap d'Antibes, we have an unobstructed eastward view of Antibes, Nice, Cap Martin, Cap Ferrat and the Italian coast.

That part of the Riviera is definitely a destination for vacationing lovers. In fact, there are few outings more romantic than a slow meander along the coast, cliffs, coves, capes and *corniches* between Antibes and the Italian border. All the charisma of the Côte d'Azur – the light, the sea, the views, the gardens, the scents, the nostalgia, the legends – are included on a delicious ramble with mouth-watering surprises around every curve (and there are many curves). Amazing, I think to myself as I selfishly consume the enticing panorama, in a few years I may have walked around the entire Mediterranean only to perhaps discover that some of its main attractions are in the home stretch through seaside harbours in Beaulieu-sur-Mer, Saint-Jean-Cap-Ferrat, Villefranche-sur-Mer and Nice.

The Antibois and other locals frequently walk this two-mile path around the cape to relax, sit by the sea and, in the summer, cool down with a dive or swim off the jagged rocks. But now, less than an hour into a hike that could take me years, I'm neither relaxed nor cool. I'm embarrassed to admit that I'm obsessed with my pedometer, compulsively calculating the distance of each step in centimetres. I've convinced myself that knowing exactly how many steps it requires to round the Med could significantly contribute to posterity. And I don't want to err and provide any misinformation to anyone following in my footsteps.

I think I've got it figured out. But as I jump from one stone to another, the fragile digital instrument slips, smashes on the rocks, then drops into the sea. I scurry down to the water but can't even see the pedometer, much less retrieve it. Then I get completely drenched by a breaking wave.

"*Merde!*" I shout as I futilely attempt to wipe the saltwater off my wire-rimmed titanium glasses. (The unbreakable, bendable lightweight titanium frames are a key hiking commodity.) "It didn't even make it through the first day. And this fish-cold brine is freezing! I don't know how that Dutchman could get all wet."

"Look, if you're going to worry about something as insignificant as a broken pedometer and getting wet you probably won't last very long," Delphyne calmly instructs me. "Do you think Odysseus cared about losing a pedometer or a touch of cold water? Let's just keep walking."

Homer explained in *The Iliad* that "a companion's words of persuasion are effective". He's right and so is Delphyne. I'm getting off on the wrong foot (in more ways than one) and should try to heed her well-intentioned advice. But my feigned tranquility doesn't last long. I'm again frustrated when our path is blocked by the Eden Roc Hôtel, one of the best-known celebrity haunts on the Côte d'Azur, and one of the few hotels that can still get away with demanding, and actually getting, cold hard cash for its outlandishly priced rooms.

The hotel's equally outrageous security fence and a sign declaring 'Propriété Privée' ('No Trespassing') force us to hike out to the street where we stumble on a bronze plaque, half hidden by a hedge. It proclaims, in French, that Jules Verne once lived and wrote here. This, I tell Delphyne, is what makes walking different from other modes of travel. I must have driven and jogged by this spot dozens of times and never noticed the monument to one of my literary heroes. I've always loved the magical and mythic worlds Verne created in *Mysterious Island* and *Twenty Thousand Leagues Under the Sea*. But I had no clue, until now, that he'd lived here. My mood brightens immediately.

We pass the front gates leading into the opulent Eden Roc and run into the Naval and Napoleonic Museum located in a former battery called Le Grillon. There are two giant Louis XIV bronze cannon at the entrance. Inside are scale models of sailing ships and soldiers, a bust of Napoleon sculpted in 1810 and even a document bearing Bonaparte's signature.

"This is really remarkable," I say enthusiastically. "In just an hour we've met Picasso, Kazantzakis, Verne and Bonaparte. Who cares about the stupid pedometer or the water temperature? I owe you an apology for being so stressed out."

By the time we round the Cap to Juan-les-Pins we've hiked nine kilometres. But, as the cormorants fly, we are less than one kilometre from our starting point. That's the kind of added distance that will increase the time it takes to make the entire circumnavigation of the Med.

"I won't bother to calculate how long, if this continues, it will take us to get around the sea," I tell Delphyne, though I simultaneously figure out that at this rate the 16,000-kilometre distance will become 144,000 kilometres.

It's not yet midday but Delphyne's already beginning to tire.

"I'm not even sure that I can make it to Cannes, much less around the sea," she says. "This knapsack is killing me and my feet hurt. Why didn't you tell me to carry a lot less?"

"Actually I did tell you that you could get by with a quarter of the things you packed," I gently remind this woman who may adore me but seems to be testing me with every step and remark. "But you said 'Better safe than sorry.'"

Not that I'm travelling particularly light. I'm carrying a spare pair of shoes, small first-aid kit, flashlight, tiny collapsible umbrella, baseball cap, poncho, a moderately detailed local map, gloves, a swimming suit, sun block, some extra clothes, the authoritative Michelin Green guide to the French Riviera, the Kazantzakis book and another version of *The Odyssey* by Derek Walcott, a collection of old photos of Cannes, lots of water and some tangerines. I'm so certain about the direction I'm going that I didn't bring a compass and don't plan on carrying camping equipment until I get beyond civilisation.

Trying to distract Delphyne from her earthly pain, I tell her I found myself at the annual summer jazz festival here in 1970, when I'd finished hitchhiking around Spain and Portugal and thumbed a ride to Cannes. Hundreds of us were standing below the window of the once-elegant Belles Rives hotel chastising Aretha Franklin for not coming back on stage for an encore.

"Give us some R-E-S-P-E-C-T," we chanted over and over, as though we were passionately protesting the Vietnam War. But she didn't.

Juan-les-Pins, still the preferred teenage party locality on the Riviera with popular clubs like Pulp and Village, is replete with sandy beaches, glitzy stores, a slot machine-filled casino and a renovated boardwalk featuring sculptures, statues, fountains and elegantly shaped stone benches. But everything's closed as we walk along the promenade and a drunk, just coming out of his New Year stupor, extends a hand towards us.

"There but for the grace of Zeus and other gods," I always whisper to myself when I stumble upon somebody in worse shape than me. Homer, who in fact may have been a number of poets rather than one sole storyteller, felt that "all strangers and beggars are from Zeus, and a gift, though small, is precious". I figured he, the gods, the dog, Delphyne and the beggar would presumably all support my next proposal.

"Why don't you give him some of your water?" I suggest to Delphyne as I hand the *clochard* a power bar, wish him *"bonne année"* and watch him stroke Bogart like he's a long-lost relative. "That'll help him sober up and lighten your load."

"Absolutely not," sniffs the first spiritual goddess of my MedTrek, seemingly certain that this guy is not an immortal in disguise. "I didn't carry my pack this far just to give things away. And why give it to someone I don't even know and will never see again?"

"Because you're only as decent as your latest social encounter," I soothingly say to Delphyne. "And you keep things by giving them away. You know that. It's one of the first lessons on the spiritual curriculum."

She pretends not to hear.

I hesitate to quote a phrase from one of the meditation books that I read every morning. I don't tell Delphyne that "Whenever you meet a problem, help if it is in your power to do so. Then there is no worry." Nor do I mention that even Homer contended that "rudeness to a stranger is not decency, poor though he may be".

Okay, it's true. I do have a handy spiritual phrase for every occasion and I've learned *The Odyssey* by heart. But I fear this is not the time to trot out a particularly apt axiom. So I gently say, "Is that so?" to Delphyne and get a slurred *"Merci et bonne année à toi"* response from the drunk.

While hiking I often encounter handicapped, physically challenged, ill, very elderly or homeless persons. It usually happens at the end of a long day when I'm on the verge of collapse and in self-pity mode. But the chance meetings, like this one, invariably make me grateful, both that I'm walking and able to walk.

One of the things I hope to do on the MedTrek is integrate the people I meet along the way into my experience and somehow let them know that I'm hiking on their behalf. Talk to them. Give them water. Smile at them, at least. Carry their images in my head, maybe. Giving away some food seems like a step in the right direction.

I'm hardly the first to ponder the chivalrous concept of sharing steps.

"We walk for ourselves and we walk for those who cannot walk," said Thich Nhat Hanh, the meditative Vietnamese Buddhist priest who has a monastery called Plum Village in southwestern France. "We walk for all living beings, past, present and future. Walk for yourself and you walk for everyone."

A little philosophical but it makes sense. I'm picking up litter. I'm giving away food. And I'm walking on behalf of the people I meet, the people I've known, my ancestors and you, the reader. What's next?

As we pass the Bijou Plage restaurant on the outskirts of Juan-les-Pins, I mention to Delphyne that I'd planned to throw a surprise party here for everyone walking with me on the first day out. I spent two hours here last week sampling the *bouillabaisse*, *aioli* and fresh fish. Remarkably, the Bijou cuisine is prepared under the aegis of Satoshi Kubota, an imported Japanese chef.

The New Year's Day luncheon would have been great fun but since it's just the three of us, and Bogart doesn't really do fish, I'm still more in the mood for a picnic on the seashore. The long, curved sandy beach continues to Golfe-Juan and, prompted by a mosaic portraying debarking troops, I mention that Napoleon landed here in 1815 after he escaped from the isle of Elba.

"That explains why this garish six-storey apartment complex has been named for him," I tell Delphyne as I buy lunch at a boulangerie.

We stop to picnic on a bench at the port and Delphyne notices that the salesgirl forgot to put our warmed pizzas into the bag with the baguette. I walk back to retrieve them and it's apparent that this little bit of back-stepping tries my patience.

"If you're going to worry about something as insignificant as forgotten pizzas and a two-minute walk in the wrong direction you probably won't last very long," Delphyne gently instructs me. "Do you think Odysseus cared if the pizzas were cold? Just sit down and eat."

She's right again.

As we relax and eat our first lunch of the year, I have a MedTrek epiphany. Eureka! The purpose of the entire walk, the point of this whole exploit, hits me. I'm destined to become a Mediterranean tour guide! I'll not only be perhaps the first person to hike the entire Mediterranean seaboard but I'll bring my own appreciation to the "soundly beaten" track, as Evelyn Waugh called it.

Then and there, I pronounce to Delphyne and Bogart that after my current circumnavigation I'll lead tours around the Med.

"My educational MedTrek training period will be followed by a real job with long-distance hiking clients when I'm in my 60s, 70s and 80s. Maybe even in my 90s," I tell them. "It'll give me a chance to share all the beauty and truth we discover with someone else."

Bogart looks like he loves the idea and Delphyne seems to think it makes sense.

"Well, at least you won't need a pedometer the next time around," she smiles cattily as she removes a shoe to examine her own bright red heel. "And by then you might be experienced enough to tell people what to carry instead of letting them break their spines and wreck their feet with heavy packs."

Uh, oh! Even soothsaying women in love can get blisters and become complaining, cynical and critical. I obviously should have spent more time preparing Delphyne for the physical trials of the trip. My mistake. And a valuable lesson when I welcome future companions.

"Looks like you've got a little problem of matter over mind," I joke. "But if you don't mind, it won't matter. You'll be fine in a day or two."

I silently wonder if I should be walking around the sea with Delphyne, even if she is a goddess. Maybe, while still enjoying a period of abstinence coinciding with post-marital depression and reflection, I should listen to Homer, who said that "there is no more trusting in women", and just travel with Bogart. After all, he never complains about the directions I choose or the food I want. And he listens to whatever I want to talk about.

Sacré bleu! Maybe the dog is a god. Or maybe I'm becoming French.

3. Technology and Sex Amidst the Sand, Sea, Sheiks and Sun

"A beautiful accomplishment takes a long time, ultimately involving lifelong consideration."
– Deng Ming-Dao, Chronicles of Tao

From our bench, we can see road signs pointing north towards Vallauris, the centre of pottery making on the Riviera and another place where Picasso once lived and worked; Sophia Antipolis, a forested high-tech office park that's about a 15-minute drive from the coast; and the scented city of Grasse, the mother village of the area's perfume industry that, with its frescoed façades and mosaic fountains, is a sweet-smelling hillside town (think Willie Wonka & the Vanilla Factory) full of flower, fruit, flea and vegetable markets. More significantly, the scenic Route Napoleon begins here, wends its way past Vallauris and fragrant Grasse, and continues through the Maritime Alps to Grenoble. Bonaparte and his armies marched north from this very spot in 1815 and today this is one potential starting point for anyone hiking from the Mediterranean to Paris, which Bogart and I did in 1991.

Sophia Antipolis, a combination of the Greek words for wisdom and Antibes, is a miniaturised, gallicised Silicon Valley indicative of a remarkable 20th century transition on the Riviera, or the Côte d'Azur, as local political leaders insist on calling it. I describe this cultural and scientific transformation to Delphyne as we approach the least pleasant aspects of the day's hike, the seaside *voie rapide*, or speedway, between Golfe-Juan and Cannes.

"There are few destinations as fabled as the legendary and romantic Côte d'Azur," I begin pedantically, competing with the stink and sound of late morning traffic with the feigned authority of a pan-Mediterranean tour guide. "This stretch of colourful coast between the Italian border and the jet-set capital of Saint-Tropez is seductively sprinkled with poetic evocations of an artistic, cultural, culinary, historical and literary past."

That's probably a bit too gushy and guide bookish for the tours I plan to lead but, hey, you've got to start somewhere. And I've got a few years to perfect my spiel.

A woman approaches us on the very narrow sidewalk and we exchange glances.

"*Bonne année*," I say politely.

"*Merci, monsieur*," she smiles back. "*A vous aussi*."

This typical French greeting is a polite exchange on New Year's Day. It's absolutely no big deal. But I can feel Delphyne seething as we continue walking. She is, apparently, extremely jealous, or maybe mildly envious, of this twenty-something French babe in a sleek silky black blouse that she probably picked up for only a bit less than $1000 at Dolce & Gabbana.

"Do you have to say something to everyone we run into?" she asks. "And do you have to look at every woman you see?"

"I'm just being polite," I respond. "It's a nice thing to do. It's normal. It's politesse. Do you think that Odysseus would have survived if he didn't look at people and greet them?"

I don't mention it to Delphyne, who seems to have inherited a jealous streak from the wary and vindictive Greek goddess Hera, but France is a great country for looking at women. Probably the best in the world, with the possible exception of Italy, for the Occidentally inclined. I know that this sounds politically incorrect and chauvinistic, but French women expect to be looked at. A stare that might get you slapped, or even accused of sexual harassment, in the United States is still considered simple politeness, or politesse, in France. It really is. Especially down here on the Med. When my French female friends return to Nice from New York, where they insist that men don't know how to look at women, they seem to relish the head-to-toe ogle by French males.

I've seriously studied full-blooded French women, from the intricacies of their toilette to the way they sensuously glance at themselves in the mirror before leaving the house, and continue to marvel at an instinctive flair that gives even the most *petite femme* a commanding physical presence coupled with an unassailable social composure.

I learned along the way that the key to their seductive stylishness and finesse is not only genetic, cultural and historical but is also acquired. Don't tell anyone I let you in on this but every French woman's success, stature and sensuality is partly due to instruction provided throughout the country by *La Patrouille d'Amour*, or The Love Patrol. The goal of this little-known French government organisation is simple: safeguard and enrich the distinctly French tradition of feminine-inspired romance by encouraging winking in streets, embracing in gardens, caressing in alleyways and cuddling in courtyards.

When I was living in Paris, where the somewhat secretive Love Patrol is headquartered just off the rue Saint Denis, I heard through the grapevine that the institute wanted some foreign input to help them ensure that all French women are aware of the myriad possibilities for romance beyond the top of the Eiffel Tower, the cavernous corners of Notre Dame and the candle-lit restaurants near the Pantheon. I'd just written a guidebook to the city and an anonymous emissary from *La Patrouille d'Amour* asked me to provide an inventory of my favourite offbeat romantic spots in the capital. I came up with a list that is still being sent to women throughout the country and, apparently because of it, French women now instinctively seem to smile and wink at me, though things frequently go downhill if we progress beyond that point.

Incidentally, even if you're not French, you might want to know that my recommendations included the tomb of Abelard and Heloise, perhaps the greatest lovers of all time who had a scandal-provoking affair around 1120, amid the maze of alleyways and crypts in the sculpted Père Lachaise cemetery. I also suggested a tryst in the secluded Arènes de Lutèce, once a circular stage for gladiatorial antics, in the fifth arrondissement and assured The Love Patrol that the most romantic garden in town is the tiny park at the end of Ile Saint Louis, the smaller of the two islands in the Seine, where lovers can step down to the quay for some philandering under the willow tree.

Want more?

I let them know that the city's most romantic fountain is La Fontaine des Medicis, a narrow deep reflection pool lined with urns and vases dominated by a statue of the Cyclops Polyphemus gazing with envy at a pair of young lovers, in the Luxembourg Gardens. And that the most romantic view of the city is from the vine-covered Place de Calvaire in Montmartre, though I added that "the more ambitious will want to squeeze up the narrow 237-step stairway to the top of the Basilica of Sacre Coeur".

Despite these romantic suggestions Delphyne knows, or should know, that I'm too emotionally raw to be at all interested in a purebred French woman. For one, despite the way they look, they constantly seem to be having a *dépression nerveuse* or a *crise de foie* or a dramatically sentimental love affair. And they always use expressions like "*tu me fais mal*", which I translate as "You are the bane of my existence and make my life miserable whenever I see you and you open your mouth." I'm not alone. An unpublished study by *La Patrouille d'Amour* characterised 72 percent of French women as "*tu me fais mal-ers*". Whether the figure is right or wrong, French women are usually too much for me.

Most of the serious women in my life, including my first wife, have been Franco-American—a mixture of the American spirit of adventure and the French sense of finesse and fashion—or Franco-something. Princess Caroline of Monaco, half-Monegasque (which is just a few steps away from being half-French) and half-American, embodies this breed best, though England's snobby Princess Michael of Kent once condemned her mixed heritage because Caroline is "the daughter of a movie star, for God's sake".

And yet, I recently learned I wasn't meant to marry even a half-French woman. And right now I'm not thinking about any women at all, which makes Delphyne's attitude a bit rankling, though maybe she's just testing me again.

I return to safer subjects like Sophia Antipolis and technology. During the past three decades this popular European tourist destination has become a haven for well-known multinational high-tech companies. The Côte d'Azur is even referred to as Telecom Valley by the high-tech jetset. And many firms consider it a springboard for business throughout the Mediterranean, Europe, North Africa and the Middle East.

How's this for an amusing statistic? The annual revenue from high-tech companies in the South of France is equal to the $5-6 billion spent each year by the 8-9 million tourists. And you thought this was just a place for lazybones, retirees and thieves!

Besides leaving chilly Paris and finding the right place to raise my kids, another reason I settled here was actually because of the region's high-tech attitude. In 1984 I launched a newsletter about Sophia Antipolis called *Sophialet* and also wrote about the *technopole*, which is what the French call a scientific industrial park, for international business magazines and newspapers. Sophia Antipolis, covering the royal family in Monaco and reporting on annual events like the Cannes International Film Festival became my local bread and butter.

So what have I learned? That the high-tech movement on the Mediterranean is sometimes fancifully linked to the same aesthetic flavor that inspired artists like Matisse and Picasso. Some contemporary French philosophers contend, and far be it from me to disagree, that the long-established artistic tradition in this part of the country creates an appropriate setting for the innovation necessary to develop state-of-the-art technology. The climate and environment are often even credited with making employees less stressed and businesses more productive.

That's not all. Politicos in the South of France are promoting a high-tech sun belt throughout the entire Mediterranean basin. They imagine a vast High-Tech Route, a Silicon Crescent, around a sea still more renowned for its sun than its science. Fat chance, I've always thought. But such vision probably can't do any harm. And I'll certainly discover if there is a High-Tech Route during my walk.

"Forget the lures of women and the flesh on the Riviera," I tell Delphyne. "Today, brains matter, even more than climate, geography or history. Science, silicon and software are replacing sand, sea, sun and sex."

"Of course people are happier working in a warm climate," Delphyne replies. "But has all this technology had any impact on the Riviera's sexual mores, laid-back lifestyle and quality of life?"

I take the bait and silently ponder the Riviera's much-touted sociological qualities and the libertine attitude towards sex down here as we near the end of the horrendous *voie rapide*. Napoleon and his hungry, smelly armies also marched from Golfe-Juan to Cannes but the road then was not the noisy raceway it is today. I'm carrying a tattered photo album that contains weathered shots of Cannes and other Riviera sites in the 1920s. The contrast with the scene this morning is so stark that I dread to think what someone from Napoleon's time, much less an ancient Greek like Odysseus, would have thought were they to time-travel to the 21st century. Even Bogart seems intimidated by all of the cars whizzing by on this long thin stretch of blacktop. His baleful, slightly accusatory expression suggests that we drop into city hall and lodge a formal complaint.

More than just the highway has gone downhill in the past 15 years. The Clinique Californie, where my son Luke was born, has gone out of business. And there's some French and Arabic graffiti on the concrete wall dividing the railway tracks from the seaside villas, including one owned by a Saudi sheik detested by locals because his garish mansion blocks hiking access along the sea.

After passing in front of this grotesque Arabia-sur-Mer, we enter a fish farm factory and meet Denis Charvoz, the owner of Cannes Aquaculture.

"You're walking around the sea? I don't think anyone's ever tried that!" Denis says, explaining that his fish are kept in net-surrounded areas about 200 metres off the coast and fed through a network of pumps and pipes. Then the fish are brought to the factory to be cleaned, packaged and later become food themselves. Ah, the circle of life.

Denis, obviously an entrepreneur, offers us the first gift of the MedTrek: a large, fresh sea bass that he wraps in a plastic bag.

"You'll definitely need this and a bit of local olive oil to keep going!" he says as he hands it to me. "It's part of the Mediterranean diet that will keep you strong and healthy. Man can live on fish alone. Just try it! And when you're walking, keep your eye out for bluefin tuna and bottle-nosed dolphins. They're as ancient as the Greeks but their numbers are declining."

"What a kind New Year gesture," Delphyne tells him. "This will bring you good karma through next Christmas."

I, too, consider this a good omen because it portends, to me anyway, that most of the fish I'll be eating along the sea route—including the tiny red mullet, sardines, sea bass and tuna that I hope to catch and fry myself over fires on the sand—will be fresh.

It turns out that this isn't our only karmic offer of the day. As we approach the peaceful Pointe Croisette just before Cannes, a brunette hooker in a red Renault Cinq blinks her headlights at us. You can fix a French prostitute's price by the make of her car and, as you might imagine, a Renault Cinq is pretty basic. But I'm amazed. A backpacking duo and a dog? On New Year's Day? What is she thinking? Perhaps we're the only potential clients she's found and she'll take what she can get. This does not include us, but I know the encounter would have just tickled Odysseus, who ran into all sorts of women during his wanderings.

"I guess sex is still alive and well down here," I tell Delphyne. "And in just a few months most of the women on the beach will be topless."

Skyrocketing skin cancer stats notwithstanding, it's still strictly *à la mode* to go topless on the Riviera. Not only on beaches but even while swimming laps in the public pools. I occasionally get somewhat distracted when I meet a topless female at the flip turn when I'm working out. But even gardening is permissible without a top. My seventy-something neighbor is forever weeding her yard naked from the waist up in the company of her nonplussed Brittany spaniel.

We wander into a camp of Gypsies, or *Gitans* as they're known in France, crowded into one of the seaside municipal parking lots. I've always wondered how these migrating tribes, a frequent winter sight down here, afford satellite dishes, camping cars, trailers, computers and mobile phones. And is it really sane, I restrain myself from mentioning to the longhaired father of one brood, to let children run around shirtless on a nippy afternoon?

All day I have been muttering "*bonne année*" to everyone I pass. It's forbidden in France to say "Happy New Year" before January 1 but, paradoxically, fine to keep wishing people "*bonne année*" or "*meilleur voeux*" or "*bonne chance*" well into February. The French usually don't send Christmas cards but it's not unusual for a New Year "*meilleur voeux*" to arrive in mid-January. Go figure!

"And a Happy New Year to you," the Gypsy father, perhaps considering me his first unwitting mark of the year, replies in English. "Want to buy a carpet that was hand woven by my wife's aunt's mother in Romania? It's authentic. It really is."

I don't want to kick the year off with an argument about whether the rug is actually authentic, which it almost certainly is not, but I'll be the first to acknowledge that this *Gitan* is the real McCoy. His most distinguishing feature is not his greasy black hair or the jig-sawing scar across his right cheek, but rather shrunken dark beady eyes above a disfigured hawk-shaped nose that would have left Edmund Rostand, who so colourfully described Cyrano de Bergerac's prodigious snout, scratching for adjectives.

"No, I'm travelling light this year," I reply in French, without mentioning his ominous protuberance or going into any detail about my walk. "But take this fresh fish. Cook it for your family. The Mediterranean diet'll be good for the kids."

As soon as I retrieve this gracious offering from my pack he impatiently snatches it from me and rips apart the plastic bag with his mangled thumb and three short grimy fingers (one is missing). He quickly examines the dorsal fin on the bony bass and, after a perfunctory snort, tosses it to one of his daughters. Then the Gypsy makes a crack about my accent. "You talk like a Spanish cow," he says with a fish-eating grin. "You must be an immigrant, a *ros bif* maybe?"

Ros bif, or roast beef, is French for British.

I'm used to the French remarking on my accent and am not particularly upset to be mistaken for a Brit or even for being criticised by a member of Europe's largest minority. After all, this nomad is entitled to stay here because every town in France with a population over 5000 by law must have a field or parking lot reserved for Gypsies.

"Yes, I'm a *gadjo*, but American not English," I tell him.

He's not at all impressed that I know that *gadjo* is the word for a non-Gypsy guy in Romany, the language of the *Gitans*. I also know that most Gypsies, especially the younger and politically active ones, now prefer being called Roma, which means "man" in Romany. And that the Roma live by a code called *marimé*, a set of laws that govern their social and personal behavior.

I've been getting heat for being a foreigner, or simply just for my foreign accent, by all sorts of folks since I arrived in France. About almost everything. Take my daughter Sonia, who has both French and American passports, and the problems she once had in school. It could have been the Montessori method or the school. It could have been the teacher. It could have been my daughter. It could have been the weather. But no. As the French say, and this is one of their favourite aphorisms, "There are not 36 solutions."

"It's because you're American," I was told by Ludmilla, the stern headmistress who, in the same breath, said how sorry she felt about this desperate circumstance, referring to the unfortunate fact that I had been born in North Dakota instead of Nantes. "Your lack of culture, your lack of education, even your ridiculous accent has unfortunately been passed on to the next generation. You have destroyed your daughter. Take her home to *les Etats-Unis*."

I tremble at the thought of the curse that I might have passed on to my kids and wonder if my diseased gene will be transmitted to their progeny. Yikes!

But I also face the facts and admit that Ludmilla and the Roma aren't entirely wrong about my French. I speak it well enough and fast enough to be considered bilingual. And a few French women have said they find my manner of speech charmingly seductive. But, hey, I can't roll my Rs. And if I'm completely honest, my accent does make all of those North African immigrants, who so irritate the French, sound like Robespierre. No one north of Tunis, where I'm actually complimented on my accent and command of the language, has ever mistaken me for a native.

In addition, I take pride in combatting the French government's campaign to purify their language by banning English expressions and 'Franglais'. I like using phrases like *le shoot out*, *l'air bag*, *le weekend*, and *email* to keep the French on their toes. I even say "C'est hunky-dory" in response to "*Ça va?*" And I refuse to be taunted when French kids ask me to say words containing a problematic 'R' – like 'Arthur' or '*représailles*', which means reprisals.

Since I've lived in the south of France—where kids and dogs are treated equally, where everyone speaks in some kind of Provençal patois, where I'm generally accepted despite my genetic flaws—I've also tried to solve the language problem through the increased use of my hands. Down here, generous gesticulations are the key to communication. Sure, sometimes I make mistakes. I confuse one handy symbol with another. The other day, walking with my dogs, I made a combination shrug, twitch and hand movement to indicate to a teenager that he'd dropped a pack of Gitanes cigarettes. He failed to catch the drift, or was especially diplomatic, and pointed to the nearest doggie toilet.

No one, ever, has suggested that I'm French. And no, I don't plan to become French, even though my current permit lets me legally reside here until 2013 and Bogart is an official member of the animal-friendly Brigitte Bardot Foundation. I still really enjoy being an alien in someone else's country because it gives a biting edge to day-to-day life. And although I've assimilated to a degree, I have not, as Taoist author Deng Ming-Dao suggests, "reached a spiritual stage where cultural references become meaningless". Sometimes I feel as clueless as I was the day I arrived in Paris in 1970. And it doesn't bother me a bit.

So I just smile at the Gypsy and, catching a glimpse of surfers and windsurfers in wetsuits darting over the waves just offshore, continue on my way.

We walk past the sprawling Palm Beach entertainment complex towards central Cannes, which got its name from the cane reeds, or *cannes*, that grew in the marshes when the town was founded at the foot of Le Suquet hill in the tenth century.

The most delightful aspect about strolling onto the Croisette, the city's croissant-shaped seaside promenade, on a holiday afternoon is the enticing smell of the fish cooking at all of the beachfront restaurants. Right near the De Gaulle Rose Garden, I stumble upon the second most delightful thing: perhaps the cleanest toilets I've seen during my entire time in France. Only after living here for decades would clean toilets make an impression that rivals the smell of cooking fish. I cheerfully tip the caretaker and, of course, wish him *"bonne année"*.

Toilets are not the only things I've been keeping an eye on as I developed a love/hate relationship with this race of over 60 million people.

Take the French as neighbors. The odds are that 97 times out of one hundred a French neighbor will immediately say to you, the new foreigner on the block or in the apartment building: "Oh, you must come by for drinks." You, the newcomer, will immediately think the French, perhaps all of the French but especially your new neighbours, are not cold and distant but really friendly. A year later the same French person, who has now pointedly ignored you on a day-to-day basis, will repeat: "Oh, you must come by for drinks." You will by now understand that this is not an invitation. It's politesse. Either you'll accept the idea of politesse or, like one American woman I know, just say "Look, please don't keep inviting me for drinks. I don't want to have drinks with you. You don't have to exude politesse with me."

To live with the French, it's essential to understand the difference between politesse and sincerity. The distinction ranks up there with the importance of discretion. Master it and you will thrive. That's why I think that, in an amusingly paradoxical way, the French have grown on me, and me on them.

I returned to one Paris neighbourhood after a five-year absence and visited the wizened, stooped concierge in the 17th century building that housed *The Paris Metro*, a magazine I helped edit and publish in the late 1970s until we went bankrupt. I thought, as anyone might, that Madame Yolanda would be happy to see the once overly confident entrepreneur who, realising that a first-class relationship with a concierge was the key to a peaceful if not profitable business, always used to bring her bottles of wine or Cognac as a *bonne année* present. I thought she might recall that, though I skipped out on a few months rent when we bit the dust, I once bought her a dress at La Samaritaine department store (okay, I admit it wasn't Dior or YSL) and gave her stacks of French Francs for simply bringing us the mail and locking the massive gate of our *hôtel particulier* every night. Wrong again.

"What do you want now?" she said to her long-lost tenant as I approached with a broad smile, open arms and lips pursed to kiss the loose skin drooping from both of her saggy cheeks.

To really understand what she said you must shout *"Qu'est-ce que vous voulez encore?"* in your deepest and most threatening voice, as if you'd just caught someone going through your garbage. This incident, I pointed out, provided me with the definition of that trusty French phrase *"plus ça change, plus c'est la même chose"*. Or, as I prefer to put it, 'things can always get worse'.

But ultimately I've been accepted here.

After living in Africa for three years, I turned up at the café that I used to frequent on the rue des Archives in Paris. Would they ask me for war stories or wonder what happened to my girlfriend? Did they care about the animal sounds and jungle smells of the Kenyan bush? Were they concerned about apartheid? Had they worried about me?

"Did you have a nice weekend?" asked the nonchalant waiter, who expected to be a nonchalant waiter there all his life. His question gave me the feeling that I had finally established myself as an American alien in France.

Plus ça change, plus je ne sais pas trop. Or "The more it changes, the less I understand". Which is perhaps why I'm undertaking this existential walk. Odysseus, who would have loved the waiter's comment, would understand.

The Croisette – with tall palm trees, wide sidewalks, majestic hotels, street vendors peddling everything from antiques to watercolours, and a nearby chic walking and shopping street called the rue d'Antibes – is typical of the perfectly relaxed Mediterranean environment necessary for the fabled leisurely afternoon promenade. Some of the older people are a little bit snooty about the roller bladers, skateboarders, bikers and mobile phoners. But there's a genuinely laid-back feeling, though the New Year crowd somewhat resembles the hordes that arrive for the International Film Festival each May. Appropriately, the inflated Santa Clauses mounting the façade of Hôtel Carlton seem straight from a Hollywood movie back lot.

As the three of us approach the Palais des Festivals where the film festival is held, Delphyne and I sit in two chairs on the Croisette and Bogart curls up at our feet. Until a decade ago, little old ladies sold tickets to anyone taking a seat here. Now the chairs are free, but they weigh a ton to avoid theft. We both stare over the mirror-like water at the Esterel mountain range in the distance. That's where we'll walk tomorrow.

Beyond are wonders like the limestone *calanques*, or escarpments, near Marseille. Then there's the Camargue, which the Michelin guide calls "the most original and romantic region of Provence and possibly of France". And even further is the Costa Brava, the savage Spanish coastline that gets its name from the steep rocks, fierce waters and glorious bays. Beyond that is the Cabo de Gata-

Nijar Natural Park, where parts of *Lawrence of Arabia* were shot amidst the cacti, wind and Jordan-like hills. And across the Straits of Gibraltar is the wild terrain of northern Morocco.

Unworried about my accent or the fact that I'm a foreigner, I'm enthusiastic about tackling the seaside path. I don't want to be delayed like Odysseus who, trapped for seven years in the clutches of the nymph Kalypso, sat each morning on the rocky shore of the island of Gozo near Malta and "broke his own heart groaning, with eyes wet scanning the bare horizon of the sea". Kalypso had offered him eternal youth and immortality. But even that wasn't enough, especially when the gods got involved and Zeus instructed Hermes to order Odysseus home.

"Now the command is: send him back in haste," Hermes told Kalypso. "His life may not in exile go to waste. His destiny, his homecoming, is at hand, when he shall see his dearest, and walk on his own land."

When Zeus gives a command, it's not ignored. And Odysseus knew that, despite constant allures and obstructions, he had to stay on the road, and that, despite ill winds or no wind, a cold gray sea or a bright blue one, the path was the goal. I knew it as well.

4. Quick, Get Me to a Monastery!

"All men have need of the gods." – The Odyssey

Cannes has been chic since the 1830s when Lord Brougham, launching a trend enthusiastically pursued by the British aristocracy, took up his winter residence here to escape the harsh climes of London. But the city's current reputation is largely due to its renown as host of the International Film Festival for the past six decades.

"Of course it's a zoo," jokes Roman Polanski, a frequent Cannes habitué whose film *The Pianist* won the coveted Golden Palm award in 2002. "But don't we love all of the animals?"

The Festival initially took place in the original Palais des Festivals on the Croisette near the Hôtel Carlton, which Delphyne and I just passed. But in 1983 the event moved to the new sprawling $60 million Palais des Festivals ("My God, it's an Egyptian tomb," said Liza Minnelli when she first saw it) near the city's main port. And that's where it is held now, exactly 20 kilometres from the start of the MedTrek.

We stop to investigate the imprinted palms—hands, not trees—of movie stars placed in concrete squares around the Palais. This is the Riviera equivalent of Grauman's Chinese Theater in Hollywood, which is not too far from Beverly Hills, Cannes' twin-sister city in California. On the other side of 'the bunker', as the indefatigable Liza Minnelli also dubbed the sprawling monstrous modern complex, the port is chock-a-block with tall-masted sailboats, foreign-flagged kazillion dollar yachts, bedraggled fishing boats and a fleet of functional ferries. The latter transport passengers to the two nearby Lérins Islands, named after a prominent Ligurian warrior, in the bay. One of the islands, Ile Saint Honorat, is populated solely by monks in a monastery.

It's only three o'clock but Delphyne decides to return to Antibes by train.

"I've had it for the day!" she exclaims as we lay on our backs on the public beach near the Palais. "But I really enjoyed myself and hope you liked having me along."

"I wouldn't have started the MedTrek without you," I reply.

The patch of sand we're on not only stands apart from all of the nightmarish pebbly beaches on the Riviera, it also doesn't cost anything to get some space in the sun here, unlike the many private hotel beaches on the Croisette that charge sunbathers a fortune for mattresses, towels, showers and the use of a bathroom.

"I'll join you down the road tomorrow," Delphyne adds. "Why don't you let me take Bogart back with me. He's as exhausted as I am."

"You both did a great job and should be proud of yourselves," I tell her. "I'll walk another hour or so and catch the red sunset over the Esterel. I'll give you a call when I stop for the night."

"Well, have fun playing Thoreau," Delphyne jokes as she and Bogart trudge towards the train station a few blocks from the beach.

Perhaps relieved by their departure, I suddenly feel tempted to abandon the hike for the day. Maybe I should slow down, step back, and ponder my challenging mission. Maybe now, before I go too much further, is the time to pause and answer a few basic questions. "Am I meant to hike alone around this sea or find a guide in the guise of a goddess?" "Is Delphyne destined to become part of my future or just my first hiking crony?" "Am I capable of putting my brain in my back pocket and meditatively walking a step at a time without pretending to be a philosophical Montaigne, a profound Thoreau or a stoical Seneca?"

The responses to these inquiries, as well as more personal and profound uncertainties, will invariably be delivered throughout the duration of my quest. But I decide to check into the monastery to begin to figure things out.

Why not? I like monks because they are, in so many ways, my kinda guys. Early to bed and early to rise, they lead quiet, structured and disciplined lives. Silent and humble, they pray, meditate, chant and are ecologically minded. Okay, so they don't have a Delphyne and a dog to distract them from their purpose, prayers and chores. But that's a minor difference. The fact is that whenever I stay in holy places, as I do a couple of times each year, I feel at peace. No matter what type of mood I'm in when I arrive, I calm down quickly, get a soothing sleep, sense no stress, receive some spiritual instruction and invariably feel, as the French love to say, "*bien dans ma peau*", or comfortable in my own skin. It's been that way since I spent my first night at a Buddhist monastery in Japan over 30 years ago.

I take the last monk-run ferry of the day to the Abbaye de Lérins just four kilometres off the coast. I'm sure that Brother Jean-Marie, the monk in charge of the inn and dining room, will have a room for me. After all, accepting pilgrims is the true nature of his Cistercian order founded in the 11th century and Odysseus himself was constantly given food and lodging, by everyone from kings to swineherds.

Jean-Marie, whom I met when I first stayed at the monastery in the late 1980s, might enjoy hearing about my plans to hike the Med. And, for the record, this is where I came for a week when I learned that my wife planned to leave me for a 24-year-old bouncer at an Antibes discotheque. But more on that, and how it turned my life upside-down, later.

As the sun sets during the 20-minute ferry ride out to the island, we're one of the few boats on the sea. It's not always this quiet. The water is often lousy with luxury yachts, fancy sailboats and other expensive floating clutter during the summer months. Despite the seasonal din, I used to sail over with friends for a quick lunch at Chez Fréderic, a delightful seafood restaurant that was the only non-monastic industry on Saint Honorat for over 75 years. But a few years ago the current abbot decided that the expensive lobster at Fréderic's, and the crowd that ate it, was too up-market for a community of monks. It's been replaced by a more humble café called La Tonnelle that offers basic homemade sandwiches and drinks. The owners invite the monks over for dinner each July just before Bastille Day.

The restaurant isn't the only thing that's changed. The monks also created their own ferry company to service the island, banning other commercial boats from their dock. And the small Sisters of Bethlehem convent was politely asked to leave in 1991. The rival ferry firms sued the monks, but the sisters circumspectly tossed in their towels and changed their habits, moving to the hills behind Nice.

"We might all be Christians but the Cistercians just didn't get along with us, or perhaps we didn't get along with them," a former nun whispered to me during one of my retreats. "And this is a very small island."

The monastery is not the only attraction on the two Lérins Islands. There's also a fortress on the larger Ile Sainte Marguerite that was reputedly where Alexandre Dumas' mysterious prisoner in *The Man in the Iron Mask* was jailed back in 1687.

Both islands, just half a kilometre apart, are a nature lover's delight with sweet-smelling eucalyptus groves and plantations of lavender, rosemary and thyme; very rocky beaches with only an occasional sandy cove; and shaded paths that, at this time of year, have more pheasants and partridges than visitors. There are no cars on Saint Honorat, just two tractors that plough the fields and a small city-owned garbage truck. Nor are there any fast-food joints. But there are a couple of vending machines and a quaint, slightly touristy, gift shop that sells CDs of chanting monks, jars of the monk-made honey, and bottles of the monks' wine and their too-potent liqueur, Lérina, which is sometimes used to heighten the monastic experience. Wonder if that's why the nuns had to leave. Wine, women and chanting are not a far cry from wine, women and song.

I'm not the first pilgrim here by any means and I marvel at the history of the place. At the end of the fourth century, Honorat was seeking an isolated refuge with seven of his disciples and founded what was to become one of the most famous and all-powerful monasteries in the Christian world. As the monastery and different chapels were gradually constructed, the abbey earned itself a place in history books. Saint Patrick was here in the early 400s and in 660 Saint Aygulf founded the Benedictine order. Seven chapels were built during the past 1600 years and a still-standing fortified monastery was constructed in 1073 by Aldebert, who made sure it was sturdy and steep enough to protect the monks from sacrilegious invaders. On one visit I swam out to sea, inspected the outer walls, and guessed that a good rock climber could scale them. Presumably the attackers were not renowned for their rock-climbing skills.

But it wasn't all smooth praying. Five hundred monks were reportedly massacred in 782 by Saracen pirates on one of their raids and the monastery closed down completely in 1791 after the French Revolution. The island frequently changed owners for the next 50 years until the bishop of Fréjus acquired it in 1859.

Honorat was not the only member of his family to adapt to island life. His sister, Marguerite, founded a convent on the other island after her brother agreed to visit "every time the almond trees flowered". Honorat, thinking the trees bloomed once a year, must have been dumbfounded when, purportedly after his sister's constant prayers, the almonds began blossoming once a month. He learned, long before John Donne expressed a similar observation, that no future saint is an island.

I always wonder how long the little tribe of monks can keep the place going but each time I come back not much has changed. Today about 35 monks live on the island, half of them bearded, a dozen of them also priests, and all of them sporting sandals year-round. Besides devoting their lives to reading, prayer and work, they also busy themselves tending bees and cultivating lavender, oranges, grapes and honey.

Because of their white unbleached cotton habits, they're frequently called the White Monks. But I often refer to them as Green Monks because they are environmentally correct. There are reforestation programs throughout the island, they save kitchen scraps for compost and they've even put *Respecter les Plantations* signs next to plants, flowers and cacti in the garden near the entrance.

Like I said, they're my kinda guys.

When we dock, I walk ten minutes across the island and get a kick out of thinking that the Med is now "flowing" around me rather than me walking around it. I reach the abbey with its red-tiled roofs, stone-hewn buildings, cloisters with pointed arches, stained glass windows, a square courtyard, well-tended gardens, sprawling palm trees, a small oratory for meditation, and a room with Gothic arches called The Holy of the Holies because of its religious relics. The interior of the church, except for a wooden cross and some simple stone statues of the Virgin Mary, is unadorned. There's no sound system but the acoustics, especially when the monks are chanting, are heavenly. Still, it's not all ancient and holy. There's a computer and fax in the office and solar panels in the garden. The place even has its own website.

As I enter the vestibule, I see Jean-Marie, pale beneath his white robe and his head covered with a cowl, behind his wooden desk. He looks up as I tap on the open door.

"I heard you might be coming for a room," he says.

"How?" I ask. "I just decided an hour ago."

"I'm joking," he smiles, laughing at the baffled expression on my face.

"May Zeus, all highest, and all the gods give you your heart's desire for taking me in so kindly, friend," I reply, translating Odysseus' words to his swineherd Eumaios when he returned to Ithaca.

I first met Brother Jean-Marie, who joined the order at twenty, after he'd already been here for 13 years. We spent an hour discussing Aristotle, Saint Augustine, the human condition, contentment, the obviously disturbing fact that I wasn't baptised, my time in Buddhist lamaseries, the pivotal role of monasteries centuries ago when they welcomed every brand of pilgrim and voyager, his attitude towards the homeless, the value of an occasional retreat, and the house 'rules'.

The latter were clear: Do not talk to monks, go into the monks' living quarters, or chat with other 'guests' inside the abbey grounds. And for God's sake don't forget the code to enter the side gates after dark. Otherwise, *pax vobiscum*. Or peace be with you.

Brother Jean-Marie is not only allowed to talk but also usually greets guests— women are permitted, men are permitted, couples are permitted, kids and dogs are not—with some existential banter. Maybe it's just part of the shtick. Tonight I mention my conversation with Delphyne concerning technology and sex on the Riviera. That segues into a chat about how monks can reside on an island where, in the summer, women sunbathe topless just a few body lengths away from the abbey walls.

"We cannot ignore the reality of the world and sex but we realise that flesh is but flesh," admits the tall, bespectacled brother who, with his hood, looks like a monastic version of Merlin. "And we are monks. Prayer, work, silence and simplicity rule us and, we hope, rule people like you on a retreat. Nothing is forbidden, but this is a place of balance. I came because I was called by God and, know it or not, you're here for the same reason right now. Everyone needs a spiritual retreat and a spiritual guide."

He shows me to my room. One of 37 in the 'hotel', it's separate from the monks' cells and is clean and simple. A small wooden cross above the pine writing desk, a parquet floor, a washbasin, a closet covered with a curtain, a small bed, a reading light and a Bible. There are showers and toilets at the end of the corridor, a spacious reading room on the ground floor and stone benches in the garden. Guests are given keys, but I've never locked my door. And I don't tonight when I head down to dinner.

I try to be a pilgrim rather than a tourist once I enter the monastery walls. But even tourists here maintain silence, especially during meals included in the modest 32 euro price, when pleasant classical music is played between opening and closing prayers. Tonight the other guests are a varied bunch—relatives of monks, Catholic teenagers on a retreat, older couples, younger Christians wearing big crosses, a priest or two. Dinner is sliced carrots, rice salad, lasagna and applesauce with a simple table wine or tap water. No honey-hearted wine, godly nectars or heavenly ambrosia here.

After a couple of hours at the abbey, I always become more monkish than the monks. Tonight I initially refuse to pass the mustard when a fellow guest dares to use his voice to request it. I put a finger over my lips, point to the condiment and then hand it to him.

Most visits to the abbey are limited to a one-week stay and everyone is encouraged to help with the dishes and do some chores, though a visitor can also just choose to sleep, meditate, walk, read or enjoy the contemplative island. But be prepared for surprises in paradise. On one stay I left my tennis shoes at home to illustrate my elevated spiritual state. That same visit, I was bemused by the sight of two nuns abandoning their habits and jogging late each afternoon. I've also caught the abbot and some of the other monks going for an early morning swim. The first time I did the leisurely 75-minute swim around the entire island, I made the mistake of diving in near the pipeline that empties some of the waste from the monastery into the sea. My two days of prayer and meditation, which had led to a semblance of sanity and serenity, were immediately flushed into the Med.

When I spent the last day of 1999 and the first few days of 2000 with the monks, I spent hours helping them clear pine trees felled by a tempest that struck all of France.

"It teaches us humility," said one monk about the wreckage, which included the destruction of the church-top cross. "We consecrate certain hours to manual work and others to divine reading and prayer. But it's said that we will only be truly monks when we live from the work of our own hands."

It was amusing to watch the monks gently argue amongst themselves to determine various job functions during the clean up. The abbot unquestionably orchestrated the overall operation while one monk tried to appoint himself chief chainsaw operator and another insisted he knew the best way to pile the wood. I silently cleared away fallen debris, amused that this was not much different from the jousting among men anywhere when a clean-up project gets underway. But I didn't try to get any of them to join me on a naked plunge in the Med at the end of the afternoon on December 31 to end the day/week/year/decade/century/millennium in swimming fashion.

The monks are usually in bed by 9pm. But after the last service I decide to sit for a while on a butt-polished wood pew within the thick walls of the sturdy Romanesque church that, though it was rebuilt in 1869, makes me feel like I'm back in the 11th century. I want to savour the permanent scent of lavender incense and gems of saintly wisdom that have soaked into the arches, pillars and walls after millions of prayer and chants. And I want to let my mind settle and think a bit about the pros and cons of constant companionship on the MedTrek – and in my life.

Brother Jean-Marie approaches me and silently suggests that I follow him. We slowly walk through the monastery gate and, despite the cold night, sit on a stone bench in the garden under the sparkling stars. He offers some counsel.

"The interesting thing about your walk is that it could teach you to keep calm and quiet amidst the to-ing and fro-ing of life," he says. "If you do get ruffled, simply retreat into the silence of communion with God wherever you are to recover your composure. If you have trouble doing that, remember how peaceful you are when you're here. You can carry that sentiment with you, whether you're alone or with others. In the end, being calm will be more productive than an active day of walking. Speak to the world by your silence."

"*Merci, mon frère*," I reply, clasping his hands. "Rest assured that I'm really not looking for stress or trouble. In fact, the only thing I'm trying to figure out tonight is whether I should walk in solitude or with Delphyne."

"Perhaps it's more profound than that. I think your real question is '*Quo vadis?*' because you haven't quite figured out the true purpose of your journey," Jean-Marie concludes as we rise to return to the monastery and our respective cells. "There will be times when you should walk with other people, who are each capable of teaching you a valuable lesson, and times when you'll need to walk alone. Start off by getting a good night's sleep and the answers will begin to arrive."

One thing I'm not worried about is sleeping in tomorrow morning.

The 'balanced' life at the monastery begins long before "the young Dawn with finger tips of rose" (one irritating constant in *The Odyssey* is that Homer mentions "finger tips of rose" at almost every damn daybreak) at 4am, when bells ring to announce the Vigils. These are the first of eight daily communal prayer, meditation, mass and/or choir services consisting of psalms, hymns, Bible readings, and delightfully melodic and tranquil chanting. These morning bells are followed by the 'silence' of roosters, birds and breakfast—which for me is coffee and bread with monk-made honey – before Lauds at 7:45am. But it's the bells that perpetually set the pace at the monastery. Every quarter of an hour, every time there's a prayer session, I hear bells.

Before I head back to Cannes on the first ferry back at 8:30, I bid adieu to Brother Jean-Marie and make a donation to the monastery when I pay my bill. Then, ready to "speak to the world by my silence" and continue the MedTrek in a more meditative frame of mind, I board the ferry.

After a night with the monks, I really do feel pretty serene and definitely much more monk-like than when I arrived. I don't speak unless spoken to. I try to be humble. I seek refuge in God. Then, shortly after I debark near the Croisette, I step in some warm ripe aromatic dog shit. "*Merde!*" I shout. So much for speaking softly.

I can hear Odysseus laughing his head off.

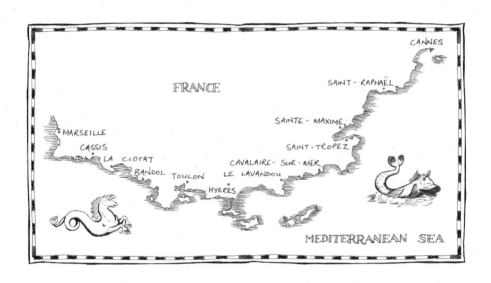

FRANCE

MEDITERRANEAN SEA

CANNES
SAINT - RAPHAËL
SAINTE - MAXIME
MARSEILLE
CASSIS
SAINT - TROPEZ
LA CIOTAT
CAVALAIRE - SUR - MER
BANDOL TOULON LE LAVANDOU
HYÈRES

Part Two

Marching to Marseille: Staying on the Path

5. What's Forrest Gump Doing in the Esterel?

"This is the moment of embarking. All auspicious signs are in place. Though we may be intent on the magnificent journey ahead, all things are contained in this first moment: our optimism, our faith, our resolution, our innocence." – Deng Ming-Dao, 365 Tao Daily Meditations

I don't let the dog *merde*, Odysseus's laughter or Liza Minelli's 'bunker' hold me up. After all, this is only day two of the MedTrek and I'm bubbling with enthusiasm and excitement.

I scamper up the hill to Le Suquet to visit La Castre museum before heading out of Cannes. Its intriguing archaeological and ethnographic collection includes an inspiring 17th century statue of a Buddhist god with forty arms that makes me feel like I can juggle anything thrown in my path. Duly motivated, I climb to the top of the 12th century Mount Chevalier Tower and gawk at the coastal route that Delphyne, Bogart and I trekked yesterday. So that's what 20 kilometres on the seaside looks like when it involves a walk around a jutting cape and along a ribbon line of coast.

A downhill stroll on a nearly vertical and very narrow cobblestone street takes me to the Marché Forville, a bustling outdoor food market that sells vegetables, herbs and spices from almost every Mediterranean country. After buying tomatoes from Spain, dates from Tunisia, tangerines from Morocco and Brie cheese from France, I'm ready to move westward. The seaside sidewalk and sandy beaches continue along the Golfe de La Napoule, which dominates the bay between Cannes and La Napoule, into the reddish Esterel Mountains.

Starting off just after daybreak and walking until dusk is my intended day-to-day rhythm and this morning's flat beachside walk should be a comparative breeze. The church bells toll nine times and I quietly hum "Ahhh ommm", my morning mantra.

There's no real hurry. Although my odyssey is a serious pursuit, I'm not worried about completing the circumnavigation of the Med within a particular timeframe. Most of my French friends living on the Riviera are influenced by a Mediterranean disdain of time and a macho mentality dating back to the first Greek invasion. They have absolutely no sense of punctuality, refuse to bow to a clock and get very upset if anyone suggests that they introduce some stress into their lackadaisical lives. They'll often talk about something that happened decades ago as though it occurred yesterday, and I'm trying to bring their nonchalant mindset to the MedTrek.

I give Delphyne a call but don't intend to make any dramatic declarations about walking with her or without her on the telephone. That's a sensible tact because she's already made the decision for me.

"I'm too tired to walk today and so's Bogart!" she says pleasantly enough. "We'll take the day off and meet you tomorrow. But Robert wants to walk with you. Call him at the Sofitel."

I'd chatted with Robert, a filmmaker visiting from London, about my project on Christmas Day and it piqued his interest. He's working on a documentary about how the French have historically related to the English and wants my opinion concerning certain national characteristics and foibles. Although he isn't joining me on the MedTrek for the long haul, he wanted to come along and interview me.

"It might be smarter, or certainly more profitable, to write documentary scripts about the sea rather than hike around it," the more-academic-than-active Cambridge grad with a degree in literature suggested when we met a week ago. "But I'll walk with you just for fun for a few hours to see what it's all about."

Wearing loafers and slacks suited for tea at the Savoy, Robert is standing in Napoleoonic pose on the steps of the Sofitel Hotel just beyond the port. I suggest that he might wear something more comfortable, but he says this is his usual walking attire.

"I don't even own a pair of jeans or hiking boots," he boasts.

"Well, I don't own any loafers," I reply. "So I guess we're even."

Fortunately today's walk, at least until we reach the Esterel, won't require too much effort. Our morning stroll to La Napoule parallels the beach and passes an aging satellite manufacturing facility that occupies a prime piece of seaside real estate. The one-time Aerospatiale Cannes plant manufactured key bits and pieces for French and pan-European spacecraft/aircraft programs for decades. It now goes by the fanciful sounding high-tech moniker of Thales Alenia Space. My favourite feature of the place is the Space Camp Patrick Baudry where I went into orbit without leaving earth shortly after it opened in 1989.

Then we amble alongside the Cannes-Mandelieu golf course with its scores of unique umbrella pine trees topped with rounded, flat parasol-shaped crowns thick enough to snag golf balls.

"That's a sport that always frustrated me!" I tell Robert, mentioning that I've shot dozens of balls into these treetops. "Even with practice and lessons I never got any better at that game. I've got no tiger in my woods and can't keep my head down and my mouth shut. But my worst moment was when a pro in California asked me if I'd had polio as a kid after he watched me swing. One reason I'm walking the Med is to avoid playing golf."

"And to write about the journey, correct?" he asked.

"Actually, I've vowed not to write a word until I walk at least 500 kilometres," I reply. "I want to get a sense of the mission and the rhythm first. And start seriously considering some of the questions that will kick-off some significant self-examination. But I'll keep notes and maybe my journal will blend *The Odyssey* with *On The Road, Zen and the Art of Motorcycle Maintenance* and *The Razor's Edge*. Without the dope or the chopper. Been there, done that."

"Well, why don't you start today by telling me what you personally know about the French after so much time here," says Robert, holding a small tape recorder in one hand. "How much different are they from you and me? Have you become French and developed that sense of '*je ne sais quoi*' or '*je ne sais trop*' that everyone keeps telling me about?"

I hate to disappoint him but I really haven't become very French since I've lived here, unlike many American expats who fastidiously perfect their grammar and endure the Kafkaesque bureaucratic process to become upstanding French citizens

"Actually I love being a foreigner and, no matter how I try, I'll never become French nor completely understand them," I tell Robert. "But I've learned to appreciate their general arrogance, sense of historical importance and Cartesian way of thinking – that handy '*thèse, antithèse, synthèse*' dialectic and 'I think therefore I am' approach to life.

"And I believe, as King John of Bohemia said back in the Middle Ages, that France offers 'the most civilised sojourn in the world'."

King John was not the only Francophile among our predecessors. More recently, Thomas Jefferson said that "every civilised man has two countries, his own and France". And Oscar Wilde, my favourite-ever pundit, inspired me when he said that "when good Americans die they go to Paris". I just came a bit before my death to check things out.

But, I continue, I'll never call a French person if I plan to commit suicide because the classic reaction will almost certainly be a dismissive '*je m'en fous*' ('I could care less') or '*c'est la vie*'. I recount how I initially came to France to meet a girlfriend, whose father made her fly back to Seattle the day I arrived in Paris in March 1970. Then I mention my audition with a nude dance troupe in a Pigalle revue when I fell on the first pirouette; my year as a waiter at the Joe Allen restaurant in Les Halles where I was fired for hitting a customer; my stint writing a guidebook to Paris for Pan American Airways; my abrupt abandonment of France to drive through Africa to establish myself as a freelance journalist based in Cape Town in 1973; and my return to Paris as a correspondent for an American publishing outfit in 1976.

"Since I've been here, I've bet at most the country's horse racing tracks, tasted wine at thousands of bars, hiked in every *département* and covered the Cannes Film Festival for decades," I continue. "And now I'm walking their Mediterranean coast. But my actions, reactions, thought processes and emotions still aren't French. I'm just a naïve American alien with a passionate project."

"How long will the walk take?" Robert asks as we near the Royal Hôtel Casino, where I'd promised him a mid-morning tea. "And what do you think it'll do to you?"

"It's probably over 900 kilometres by foot to the Spanish border and I hope to average about 30 kilometres a day. But I really have no idea how long it will take to walk around the Med because I try to avoid any serious projections or expectations about my little mission," I reply truthfully. "I already learned yesterday, as soon as I hit the trail, that my initial calculations did not take topographical variations into account, which makes me look a little stupid. And although the obstacle is often the path, I have no clue how often cliffs will block me and wide rivers will force me to head inland to find a crossing. It's certainly possible that, like the time my anticipated two-week drive from Paris to Cape Town became a year-long excursion, it will take longer than I expect.

"But my main intent is to walk every inch of the coast. Or at least give it my very best shot. Maybe it'll take a decade, maybe a bit more. And it's a certainty that the person you see before you today won't be the same one you'll see a year or ten down the road. Not knowing what's going to happen, or what's truly at stake, is part of the thrill. Watch this space!"

"Aren't you worried that you'll get robbed or run into trouble?" Robert asks. "Maybe, like Ulysses, you'll meet man-eating Laestrygones or have to build your own Trojan horse." Then, as if to show off his academic credentials, Roberts adds: "And remember the line in *The Odyssey* that counsels: 'Don't stay too long away from home, leaving your treasure there, and brazen suitors near; they'll squander all you have or take it from you, and then how will your journey serve?'"

Robert, like many, prefers to call Odysseus Ulysses, the Roman equivalent of his Greek name. Instead of speculating about potential problems, or mentioning that a brazen suitor has already run off with my wife, I abruptly change the subject and tell him that I prefer the Greek nomenclature.

The Greeks predated the Romans so for me Odysseus is Odysseus and not Ulysses. Zeus is Zeus and not the Roman Jupiter, Hera is not the Latin Juno, Athena is not Minerva, Dionysos is not Bacchus, Aphrodite is not Venus, Ares is not Mars, Hermes is not Mercury and Poseidon is not Neptune.

But despite his preference for Latin over Greek names, Robert is very familiar with *The Odyssey* and its fabled realm of gods and nymphs that commanded the world. His classical British education had brought him up to speed about the blind bard Homer's oral narratives that passed from generation to generation and were, if you can believe contemporary philologists like Gregory Nagy at Harvard and Richard Martin at Stanford, gradually put into writing as *The Iliad* and *The Odyssey* around the sixth century BC. At that time the tales were so popular that colourful depictions of the exploits appeared on stone statues and sarcophagi.

"I guess something could short-circuit my journey," I remark after describing my affection for the Greeks. "It's probably guaranteed that I'll discover my own Achilles heel or encounter some unforeseen personal limitations. I already know from *The Odyssey* that 'Of mortal creatures, all that breathe and move, earth bears none frailer than mankind.' And that would include me."

I tell Robert that I've had trials and tribulations on much shorter walks than this, like the time I ran into Irish-born-but-French-in-spirit playwright/author Samuel Beckett on a street corner near the Odéon Theater in Paris during the summer of 1970. I'd just been to a wedding reception at La Mediterranée restaurant and found the renowned writer waiting for a few seconds after the light turned green on Boulevard Saint Germain.

"*Vous attendez Godot?*" I asked, with a smile.

The tall literary genius responded with a silent scowl. Maybe he didn't get the joke. Maybe he just didn't find it funny. Or maybe I reminded him of the pimp who once stabbed him in the chest during a Paris street fight. But the look of arrogance, contempt and confusion on Beckett's face after I uttered those three words was unmistakable. It wasn't the last time I'd see that expression in France.

It's just after 10am when we reach the Hôtel Royal and enter the casino to make our first New Year gamble. I wish Delphyne, who says she inherited her psychic prowess from her paternal grandmother in Indiana, were here to tell me how auspicious things look when I win a few hands of video poker. Omen or not, I feel especially content about the MedTrek while we relax at the Blue Wave Piano Bar listening to a piano player and singer rehearse for that afternoon's *thé dansant*, a revived pastime that evokes the bygone era of ballroom dancing.

"Pretty impressive, isn't it?" I say to Robert as I stare, transfixed, at the sea.

"And it's much more than just a geographical and historical entity. The Med's a state of mind and a delight to be near. The coffee's strong, the lunches long, the evening stroll obligatory, the dinners late, the past omnipresent, the weather warm and the people laid back.

"I love repeating the poetic names of melodious Mediterranean destinations, like Carthage, Lou Lavandou, Larnaca, Djerba and Taoramina. Or recalling the exploits of the seafaring Babylonians, Phoenicians, Arameans, Etruscans, Ligurians, Minoans and Myceneans who've lived around a sea that's seen it all."

As we walk into La Napoule, the clouds eerily obscure the sun and the local chateau resembles a 14th century version of the Addams Family house. This is largely due to the creative "restoration" undertaken by American sculptor Henry Clews and his architect wife early in the 1900s. The result blends Romanesque, Gothic and Oriental influences with Clews' fantasy sculptures.

We hike uphill past the castle when Robert decides to wrap up his MedTrek after eight kilometres. He takes a picture of me standing in front of a sign that says, in English, "Watch Out for Car Breaking!" This apparently does not mean that there's a braking car screeching around the bend but, rather, encourages tourists to be on the lookout for people breaking into their cars.

"Another good reason to be on foot," I tell him.

"It was a splendid outing and I'll be back for more," he replies. "And next time I might even dress for the occasion."

I wait with Robert until he catches a bus back to Cannes, then turn a corner and enter the colourful Esterel mountain chain that runs from La Napoule to Saint-Raphaël. Alone on the massif that gets its fiery red tint from a base of volcanic rock, I'm bombarded with a kaleidoscope of poetic late winter morning sights, sounds and smells. The cooing of cuckoos and quail; fishermen returning to the port with their catch; wet-suited windsurfers and divers arriving to explore the top and bottom of the opaque sea; the invigorating scent of sea air and pine trees; and the physical beauty of a sparsely inhabited coast just a few minutes away from dancing teas and slot machines.

I reflect on the three hours spent with Robert and wonder how many random people, both known and unknown, are destined to take a few steps with me during my Mediterranean excursion. Whatever the number, whoever they may be, each companion will undoubtedly have a personal perspective that will enrich or challenge my appreciation of the project, the path and my fellow trekkers.

The highest point in the mass of multicoloured Esterel peaks, which contrast so dramatically with today's dark grey sea, is called Mount Vinegar. The hues of its rock covering range from red to blue, green, yellow, purple and grey and a yin-and-yang effect is created when the jagged mountain edge meets the turbulent sea.

A *boulanger* in Théoule-sur-Mer tells me that there's a cobblestone path along the sea that will eventually cut up to the main road. When I sit on a rock to make and eat a sandwich with my baguette, brie and tomatoes, I have a view of last night's monastery from the sandy beach and, nearer to shore, another fish farm owned by Cannes Aquaculture. No wonder Denis could spare a fish. Then, back on the path, I run into an impassable cliff and hike straight uphill on a sculpted trail.

Most of the afternoon's hike is going to be along the Corniche d'Or, a two-lane blacktop road built by the Touring Club de France between 1901 and 1903. I'll have to stick to it because the steep hillsides preclude the creation of a seaside path, except those heading down to the occasional cove or beach.

The Corniche d'Or was not the first road through this area. The Romans get that honor with the Via Aurelia, or the Aurelian Way, which was the primary land route between France and Italy. That remarkable road, named after Roman emperor and writer Marcus Aurelius, stretches from the Porta San Pancrazio in Rome through Civitavecchia, Pisa, Genoa and San Remo in Italy to Arles in western Provence.

Originally built of large flat basalt stone, the Via Aurelia wasn't as smooth 2000 years ago as it is today but even then, with a foundation that went down four feet, it provided stability for the Roman legion. Though it was a highwayman's paradise, the stone distance indicators methodically placed after each Roman mile gave us the concept of a milestone. Presumably so voyagers could report precisely where they'd been robbed.

My walk is not much different than it would have been for the first travelers on the Via Aurelia. I pass creeks, narrow bays, small beaches, underwater reefs, remarkable rock formations, islands, inlets, coves, rocky beaches, small ports, cliffs, rocks for diving and shimmering water reflections. About the only structures that would have surprised my Greek and Roman predecessors are isolated chapels built on the seaside rocks and the railroad tracks that stretch alongside the coast. And, on the other side of the Corniche d'Or, a few blazed trails and fire roads leading into the hills.

Not surprisingly, I'm one of the few walkers out on the second day of January. But after an hour I run into a character who resembles Forrest Gump after he'd jogged around the United States. Everything about this bedraggled chap – his beard, his socks, his hair, his legs, his expression, his clothes, his backpack – is scruffy and scrawny. Is he just finishing a decade-long clockwise hike around the Mediterranean, I ask myself? Thinking I'll resemble him after a few months, I'm not particularly encouraged. But I manage a bemused smile as he approaches, his head down and his eyes hypnotically glued to the tarmac.

"Forrest?" I ask aloud. *"Tu veux une bôite de chocolats?"*

Forrest raises his head just long enough to give me that memorable Samuel Beckett glare. But it's such a wry, askew glance that it gets me thinking: maybe this raggedy man is a god in disguise. As we pass each other I hear an echo from Homer: "How many bitter seas men cross for hunger!"

Of course, I can't be sure he's a god.

Even Odysseus, who was favoured by the gods and frequently ran into them in various human forms, had trouble telling whether he'd met a god, a goddess or just a regular mortal. He sometimes even had difficulty recognising Athena, his spear-carrying patron goddess who was considered one of the most beautiful of the Greek gods, in some of her disguises. The problem is that the gods – once you discount their superhuman powers and immortality – often weren't much different in appearance from you, me and Forrest Gump.

Odysseus was always on the lookout for gods because they frequently helped him out of tight spots. Ino produced a magical veil that prevented him from drowning when Poseidon struck his ship with lightning. When Circe turned his men into swine, Hermes slipped him a magical herb that protected Odysseus from her spells. And Aeolus, the King of the Winds, gave Odysseus a safe sail home from the Strait of Messina. When he finally made it back to Ithaca, Athena turned him into a beggar, who very much resembled this Forrest Gump-looking guy, in order for him to gain access to his palace.

So, yes, Forrest Gump might be a god. I'm glad I didn't insult him, or anyone else that I've met on the road so far. It pleases me that today, and this wasn't always the case, I practice the simple dictum that I'm no better than the next person.

Let me assure you that this has not always been my *modus operandi*. Arrogance, anger, anxiety and aggression frequently dictated my actions and reactions back in my drinking days and I undoubtedly would have had a packet of insults to unleash on an unsuspecting Forrest.

"Have you escaped from the cuckoo's nest or are you just too poor to drive?" I would have heckled him with a remark that, at the time, I thought overflowed with humour. I had absolutely no reverence for gods when I was younger.

Odysseus, like most Greeks of his generation, treated the gods with respect. He prayed to them and offered them sacrifices because, Homer wrote, "It was important to give something to the gods to get something back in return."

In practicing this you-scratch-my-back-and-I'll-scratch-yours philosophy, Odysseus usually gave the gods more than a box of chocolates. When he visited Hades, and met the dead in the Underworld, he sacrificed a ram and a ewe. He made a similar gesture after he blinded Polyphemus the Cyclops and again when he slaughtered the arrogant and pesky suitors competing to seduce his wife. Once he made "burnt offerings to Poseidon of the Waters: a ram, a bull, a great buck boar".

More significantly, Odysseus was certain that he would not prevail without help from the gods. "When those hard deeds were done by Lord Odysseus the immortal gods were not far off," Homer said about Odysseus' encounter with the men who'd invaded his home to win his wife's hand. "I saw with my own eyes someone divine who fought beside him, in the shape and dress of Mentor. It was a god who shone before Odysseus, a god who swept the suitors down the hall dying in droves."

The fact that the gods played a leading role in that massacre indicates that they weren't just onlookers, amused by the foibles and romance of mortals. They actively participated in the human board game. Homer claimed "some god has killed the suitors, a god, sick of their arrogance and brutal malice–for they honoured no one living, good or bad, who ever came their way."

No wonder the Greeks thought twice before committing grievous sins or making presumptions about a guy who looked like Forrest Gump.

That was then, of course. While respecting all gods and everyone's personal higher power, I endorse a more contemporary version expressed by Buddhists and Taoists. Lao Tsu postulates that "gods are not our parents or protectors. They are there only to inspire us to be better people." And Deng Ming-Dao says that "in your meditations, you will meet gods … your inner gods will grant gifts of knowledge and power … you can trust your gods. They will never betray you, for you cannot betray yourself."

I've quit thinking about the gods, the Greeks and Gump by the time I arrive at four modern apartment complexes, with pretentious names like Prince des Iles and Azurine, that each claim to have "the best view of the Côte d'Azur". These are among an outrageous number of garish real estate developments along this part of the Esterel. Honeycombed Flintstone-like places – including one pockmarked mushroom-shaped villa with dozens of oval-shaped rooms built by couturier Pierre Cardin – dot the Port-La Galère marina. And the gigantic Cap Esterel development near Agay looks bigger, and much more pretentious, than the prince's palace in Monaco.

The sea seems oblivious to these coastal blemishes. And although some Italian vacationers parade in campers much too large for the narrow *corniche*, today's crowd is nothing compared to the masses and mess here in the summer. There's even a refreshing winter ceasefire conveyed by the '*Fermeture Annuelle* – Open in Spring' signs on most restaurants and hotels.

The lack of commerce and tourists, as well as the many shuttered villas, make this a pleasurable stroll, despite the road walk. Not that I'm completely out of the way of potential disaster. One sign says 'Prudence' and features an illustration of rocks falling onto the road. A score of bicyclists, who stubbornly hug the side of the *corniche* as they whiz by, almost wipe me out while some blind corners put me in the path of drivers in no mood for car braking. There are enough trains rolling by to discourage any thought of walking along the tracks as I cross the boundary between the Alpes-Maritimes, the French *département* or province that starts at the Italian border, and the Var.

Away from the coast the Var is, compared to the Alpes-Maritimes, wild and rustic with a hilly countryside punctuated by olive groves, fields of aromatic herbs, perched villages like Cotignac and Tourtour, cork oak forests and plane trees on many main streets, and welcoming religious monuments like the Abbey du Thoronet. Even most towns along the seaside seem less pretentious, or certainly less affluent, than their eastern counterparts. I'm tempted to take one of the many trails back into the Esterel and lose myself in the hills amidst the sea pines and bright yellow mimosa. Although frequent summer fires consume and destroy the pine and cork forests, one particularly inviting hillside is thick with heath and lavender. But I stick to the sea and keep as close to the rim of the Mediterranean as possible.

I breeze along for twenty kilometres, at a pace of five kilometres an hour, before reaching a stone bench overlooking Agay harbor, historically one of the best anchor points in the Esterel. Two thousand years ago a Roman ship sank here and left loads of amphorae, but today a large catamaran is the sole boat anchored in the bay and it's theoretically illegal to dive for antiquities.

I approach the hilltop lighthouse in La Dramont and then descend to a tiny port inhabited by dozens of cats. A few hundred metres off the coast is the magical Ile d'Or, an island adorned by a simple stone damsel-in-distress tower. The Sirens, who had the heads of women and bodies of birds, would definitely have preferred this Golden Island to the three little rocky outcrops they inhabited when they unsuccessfully tried to derail Odysseus.

Nearby is a memorial to the US Army's 36th division that debarked here on August 15, 1944, to "achieve the complete destruction of the German Army and Nazi regime". A hull of one of the landing craft, now a favourite for local skateboarders, has '*Sieg Heil*' written on it.

To the west are two craggy rock formations called the Lion of the Sea and the Lion of the Land that denote the entrance to the Gulf of Fréjus. Rock configurations always crop up in Greek legends and myths. Jason and his Argonauts had to sail between two rocky cliffs known as the Symplegades that clashed together when anything passed between them. The sailors overcame the predicament by releasing a dove that flew between the Clashing Islands, causing them to rush together. Then, as the islands parted, the crew rapidly rowed the Argo through the channel. The sailors made it, the dove lived and the islands never clashed again.

Odysseus had an even tougher encounter in the turbulent Strait of Messina that separates Italy from Sicily. He had to sail past both Scylla, a six-headed monster living on a cliff, and Charybdis, a whirlpool that "swallows the sea". His efforts were less successful than Jason's. Scylla ate six of his men in one sweep and Odysseus's dilemma led to the Latin expression *Incidis in Scyllam, cupiens vitare Charybdim*, or "You fall prey to Scylla in trying to avoid Charybdis".

In contemporary lingo, my hero was caught between a rock and a hard place. We all know the feeling.

6. If This Is Tuesday, Is It Time to Walk to Paris?

"Zeus does not bring all men's plans to fulfillment." — *The Iliad*

The next morning Delphyne and Bogart arrive in Saint-Raphaël, where I'd spent the night, and the three of us have a casual café-and-croissants breakfast near the dawn-bustling market. Despite my reflective monastery stopover and last evening's equally mellow wallow in a jacuzzi at the Hôtel San Pedro near the Esterel golf course, I still haven't come to an absolute conclusion about hiking with Delphyne. Just as well since she once again makes the choice for me.

"I really think you should bond with Bogart until I get in better shape for this kind of long-distance walking," Delphyne casually announces, as I pick out freshly baked bread, Gouda cheese with cumin, bananas and dried figs for lunch at various market stands. "I'll meet you in Saint-Tropez. But don't give up on me. I definitely want to hike the *calanques* and the Camargue. And see Libya too."

Libya? That's thousands of kilometers from here!

But it's Delphyne's decision not to walk today that makes me feel like I'm a lousy guide and should have better prepared her for the rigours of the journey. At the same time, I have to admit that I'm happy to be heading out alone, accompanied only by Bogart. After all, he's much better prepared for the trip. We've been hiking on a regular basis for the past two months to get in shape and reduce the inevitable aches, pains and physical challenges of the first days on the trail. Bogart also watched attentively while I practiced arranging my pack to reduce the weight and came along when I studied walking meditation with Thich Nhat Hanh.

"Walking meditation is like eating," the monk told us before daybreak one morning during our stay. "With each step, we nourish our body and our spirit. When we walk with anxiety and sorrow, it's a kind of junk food. The food of walking meditation should be of a higher quality. Walk slowly and enjoy a banquet of peace."

Get that, Bogart?

Our mental, physical and spiritual preparation was smart. Too many enthusiastic hikers burn out when they attempt longer-than-usual walking stints without being in the right frame of mind and body. Though my legs are slightly stiff after two days on the road, I'm certainly eager to keep moving. On the other hand, I don't want to fall prey to an obsessive-compulsive hiking disorder. Some long-distance trekkers, including a British woman who walked the entire length of Africa, insist on maintaining a speedy pace that leaves their fellow trekkers in the dust. I resolve to take the MedTrek a step at a time and move no faster than my slowest companion.

I'm also sure Delphyne's momentary defection is not the only change of plans that will occur. Consequently I don't bother to think too far ahead or worry that, like Odysseus after he lost his crew, I may be without human companionship during much of my odyssey.

"Trying to predict the future is like going fishing in a dry river bed," a Tibetan lama used to tell me. "Don't worry about where you've come from or where you're going. Rejoice where you are."

Got it!

This isn't the first time that Bogart and I have hiked out of Saint-Raphaël. We launched our walking trip to Paris on the seashore here. That jaunt took us through Provence, up the Rhône River to Lyon, across the Loire River and finally to La Tour d'Argent, the renowned restaurant overlooking Nôtre Dame owned and run by my friend Claude Terrail. We chose the Tour because we both like pressed duck and it's near the exact spot used to calculate distances from central Paris to cities throughout France.

I can be completely existential, addictively precise or somewhere in between when I plan these longer outings. I was more diligent about plotting the Paris walk than the MedTrek because basically all I have to do now is keep the sea on my left.

The week before we left for Paris, my dining room table was covered with maps, guidebooks, photographs, lists, a dog dish and other paraphernalia. In the end, the forty-day walk was relatively easy to accomplish by sticking to marked hiking trails called *grandes randonnées*, or simply GRs by the cognoscenti and their hounds. GRs criss-cross France and are easily recognisable by their white-over-red horizontal trail markings. Unfortunately there's not a GR around the entire rim of the Mediterranean, though there are some blazed segments and GRs can be found in places like Monaco, Nice and Saint-Tropez.

To get to Paris Bogart and I walked 20-40 kilometres, or between six to eight hours each day during one May and June. After a few days, I came to prefer him to more loquacious companions. He never complained about the direction I chose, quietly tolerated his sore paws, and kept our conversation limited to subjects that interested me.

There were incidents, of course. At a fountain in La Louvesc, Bogart plunged into the holy water and was screamed at by a socialist mayor who obviously considered this transgression one of the most important political affronts since he was elected to the largely ceremonial office in a town with less than 500 inhabitants.

"I could fine you for parading a dog through town without a leash and encouraging him to jump into our sacred fountain," the mayor threatened me with a voice that carried across the main *place* to resonate among the employees in the *mairie*, or city hall. "But because I'm a socialist, because I'm tolerant and because I support disadvantaged animals and mentally challenged human beings I'll let you off the hook."

Whew.

The most sublime, or surreal, moment of our hike occurred around 7am one morning in the Ardèche gorge when a lone alto saxophonist played soaring sounds that reverberated off the canyon walls. The improv of blue notes was a contemporary siren song that immediately got me thinking about the important role that jazz plays throughout France, from festivals in places like Juan-les-Pins to jam sessions in dozens of hole-in-the-wall clubs in the centre of Paris.

And our best meal, if you don't count all the cherries we picked and ate on the run, was a three o'clock *plat du jour* at a little auberge near Auxerre that served us when they realised '*le pauvre chien*' had been walking for eight hours.

"You don't deserve to be fed after treating your dog like that," the owner scowled as she served Bogart. And then, reluctantly, me.

I didn't tell her that during our walk the fresh food I bought at *boucheries* and *charcuteries*, or the *magret de canard* and other choice morsels that restaurant kitchens sometimes served Bogart on their best china certainly beat the cans at home.

An invigorating mistral wind has cleared every blemish from the awe-inspiring blue sky by the time Delphyne departs after our visit to the dog-friendly Saint-Raphaël archeological museum, where we examine amphorae and an original milestone from the Aurelian Way. But the most striking aspect of contemporary Saint-Raphaël, a port made famous by Napoleon in 1799 when he returned from Egypt, is the expanding and sprawling marina in the Bay of Fréjus where thousands of pleasure craft are moored. To get there we stroll by a casino that two millennia ago was, according to a brochure I pick up at the local tourism office, "a terraced Gallo-Roman holiday resort with thermal baths".

The Michelin guide contends that the Roman ruins here are "unspectacular" but I'm pleasantly surprised by the well-preserved ramparts, aqueduct and towers. Perhaps they're in such good shape, I tell Bogart, because the monks on Lérins ran this place in the tenth century and hired the Templar knights to maintain their defenses.

Saint-Raphaël also features picturesque cobblestone pedestrian-only streets, which have been the downtown renovation rage in many French cities since the 1970s. Things were not always this clean and proper. Marsh fever in the 18th century led to inhabitants here being known as 'pale faces'. That reputation began to change when journalist Alphonse Karr arrived in 1855. He beckoned his friends and readers to "Leave Paris! Come and plant your walking stick in my garden; the next day, when you wake you will find that it has sprouted roses."

The wind and waves combined to cleanse the sandy Saint-Raphaël beaches during the night and we begin the day's walk on sand blemished only by the imprints of seagulls, which fly off as we approach and take advantage of the cool morning breeze to effortlessly soar above us. Not wanting to become a pale face or have roses sprout on my non-existent walking stick, I lead Bogart across the arched steel bridge to Fréjus on the other side of the Garonne River.

Founded by Julius Caesar in 49 BC, Fréjus became a booming metropolis ten years later when Octavian, the future Emperor Augustus, turned it into a Roman Empire naval base with 40,000 inhabitants. Today, it's kept remarkably neat and tidy by motorised lawnmower-like vehicles that constantly patrol, wash and clean the sidewalks and gutters. I'm so intrigued by these machines that I make a deal with a maintenance man to purchase one when the city wants to replace them with newer models. If enough readers are interested we could probably get a substantial discount. Let me know.

I get extremely excited when I spot a poster with the word 'Odyssey' and think there might be some Greek culture in town. But a closer look reveals that it's a nightclub 'for women only'. Next door to it is a spa offering thalassotherapy treatments. *Thalassa* is Greek for sea and the baths utilise mineral-rich ingredients for prevention, healing and relaxation through marine hydrotherapy.

"We haven't walked far enough yet to justify a massage," I tell Bogart.

"Well, let me know when we have," his look seems to say.

Fréjus, like many modestly-sized towns on the Mediterranean, has some questionable looking seven-story high-rises near the beach. But one advantage of being a popular tourist destination on the French Riviera, which officially runs from the Italian border to Saint-Tropez, is that these complexes, as well as the port infrastructure and the water treatment facilities, are constantly being monitored, upgraded and improved. Not that the corresponding refurbishment and resulting improvements are a long-term plus.

"Even though there is a direct economic benefit from tourism, the overall impact is negative because all tourism pollutes," explains Kevin Walsh, a British environmental archaeologist whom I'd arranged to meet for coffee at a café on the port. "There's little natural seaside left in France and a moratorium on building would be welcomed. As filmmaker Werner Herzog, who once walked from Germany to Paris to visit an ailing friend, says 'Tourism is a sin, travelling by foot a virtue'."

I tell Kevin that the seawater doesn't look too dirty from my perspective.

I added that "It seems pretty clean when you consider that the submerged Gibraltar Ridge restricts the inflow of cool and oxygenated water from the Atlantic into the Med," showing off my little bit of knowledge about the sea. Then I mention measures adopted by France that specifically concern environmental protection of the coast and punishment of ship captains who deliberately dump oil, garbage and other pollutants.

"Actually the confined Mediterranean basin, which has more salinity and more varied water temperatures than the Atlantic, is an environmental laboratory that exaggerates the impact of every natural and man-made event, from fires and storms to pollution," Walsh replies. "Today we're in a period of damage limitation. French and European environmental controls, while not perfect, are rigorous and they make considerable investments to improve things. But they must strengthen policing to become more effective. A serious accident at sea is the major threat, but so far the Med has an incredible capacity to deal with all the crap we throw into it."

Most permanent Riviera residents constantly bemoan the incessant urban sprawl, haphazard housing developments and seasonal influx of tourists that clutter the coast. The resulting security, pollution, congestion and environmental problems have prompted many residents, French and foreign, to consider abandoning the south of France.

Bogart and I are no exception. But when we feel down about the Riviera, we usually head, on foot, up to one of many small perched, fortified hillside villages located on mounts, peaks, mesas, domes, buttes, hills, pinnacles, crowns and summits in the *arrière-pays*, or back country. The definition of what is perched and what is merely a town on a hillside is, in the end, subjective. But an authentic perched village is surrounded by ramparts and was built primarily for protection, often quite distant from both farmland and water supplies. This precaution was a necessity for survival during the era of Germanic invaders, Muslim pirates and Middle Age mercenaries.

When we reach an aerie like Gourdon and look down on the majestic sea, we quickly realise how lucky we are to be living and walking here, despite the increase in people, places, cars, garbage and other offensive stuff.

Fortunately, the MedTrek enables us to avoid a lot of urban pollution because we stick close to the water and almost always look out on the sea. This morning we miss the hideous Casino shopping market (do not, like some foreign visitors, confuse this chain of supermarkets with gambling casinos!), sleazy commercial outlets and rows of billboards located just a block back from the sea. We're also some distance from the busy national road, a congested hell-on-wheels that is pretentiously called the Corniche Côte d'Azur and is the main thoroughfare to Saint-Tropez.

We head out of town on the pristine sandy beaches and inadvertently enter what a sign calls a 'decommissioned military zone'. But it turns out that it's not completely decommissioned. There are 20 soldiers hobnobbing around a large and impressive villa and I get the first minor cuts and scrapes of the MedTrek when I scamper under a fence to avoid detection. Then I lurch along on slippery boulders as Bogart, smartly, swims in the sea to the mouth of the Argens River. As he paddles nonchalantly upstream, I edge my way along the rocky riverbank until we reach a paved bike path that parallels the national road.

We then run into a *sentier littoral*, a seaside path blazed with slashes of yellow paint, in Saint-Aygulf, which is named after the founder of the Benedictine religious order. This delightful *sentier* meanders through resorts like Val d'Esquières, San

Peire, Les Calanques, Les Issambres (the name comes from 'Sinus Sambracitanus', which is what the Romans called Saint-Tropez Bay) and La Nartelle, another landing site for Allied troops in 1944.

The *sentier* occasionally wanders through groves of pine, cork and oak trees or diverts us to a sidewalk through a village. At one point it traverses flamingo-filled marshes where the mid-morning sun accentuates the birds' pink hue as they stand remarkably straight legged, absolutely unfazed by the wind. But most of the time it abuts the seashore and just before lunch takes us past the fascinating remains of a *vivarium*, in which the Romans used to keep their captive fish alive, fashioned from gigantic rocks.

As we approach Cap Sardinaux, the wind dies down and I spend 20 minutes helping a seventy-something Tunisian man remove sand piled up around the doors of his boss's beachside restaurant. A bit later, just outside of Sainte-Maxime, I sit under a sprawling pine tree and gaze across the comparatively placid bay to Saint-Tropez, the Riviera's most famous jet-set resort and home of actress-turned-activist Brigitte Bardot.

We reach Sainte-Maxime, which was also founded by those industrious Lérins monks and has an odd museum dedicated to Mechanical Musical Instruments and Recording Machines. But when I try to buy an entry ticket they won't let Bogart inside. Instead I take him to a sporting goods store, which he seems to find just as interesting, and purchase a new pedometer. To ensure that it works, I clip it to my pants and walk up the hill towards the local lighthouse to get a look at the coastline and the Massif des Maures mountain range.

Bogart, who seems to think we're taking a detour to Paris when he sees the steep hills, looks a bit distraught. He's visibly relieved when I tell him that we're going to return to Saint-Maxime where there's a swell surf-and-turf restaurant and a warm hotel room. The mention of food and a room had the same calming effect on Odysseus, especially when he was hungry, soaked and tired.

Nausikaa, the daughter of King Alkínoös and Queen Arete of the Phaeacians who ruled what is now Corfu, once found our Greek wanderer in a completely miserable state on the Skheria Island beach. Odysseus and "his hungry belly" had just washed up "swollen from head to foot" after 20 days in the sea. "Seawater gushed from his mouth and nostrils", there was a "coat of brine" on his back and shoulders and a "clot of sea-spume" in his foamed hair. He was not a happy camper.

"What more can this hulk suffer?" Odysseus asked.

Nausikaa immediately told her maids to "take care of him", an order that included food, drink and a bath. Then she took him to stay in her father's house where he was given a place of honour at their table. Odysseus's mood changed almost immediately.

"The wine urges me on, the bewitching wine, which sets even a wise man to singing and to laughing gently," he said as dinner progressed. "And rouse him up to dance and bring forth words which were better unspoken."

That wasn't the only time that Odysseus apologised for drinking and talking a bit too much. "The wine's behind it, vaporing wine, that makes a serious man break down and sing, kick up his heels and clown, or tell some story that were best untold," Odysseus blurted out during another lengthy meal. And of course he used liquor to subdue Polyphemus the Cyclops in Sicily when he said, so innocently, "Cyclops, try some wine." He then blinded the one-eyed beast, an act that might have created the expression 'blind drunk'.

Again, the gods may have had something to do with the outcome because Polyphemus, one embodiment of arrogance and evil in *The Odyssey*, always refused to pay them homage.

"We Cyclops care not a whistle for your thundering Zeus or all the gods in bliss," Polyphemus told Odysseus. "We have more force by far."

Uh, not for long!

That night, when I share my steak-and-sole meal with my dog, the waiter says "Bogart, try some wine."

Obviously smarter than Odysseus and the Cyclops, Bogart refuses. Then he looks at me as though I should take the glass of rosé from the locally renowned Domaines Ott vineyards.

"Trust me, Bogart," I said to him as I thanked the waiter and declined his offer. "The world's a much better place since I quit drinking."

7. Will I Take a Job or Run Into Brigitte Bardot?

"A small rock holds back a great wave." – *The Odyssey*

We set out from Sainte-Maxime towards Saint-Tropez the next morning and Bogart completely ignores me while I calculate the number of centimetres (75) in each step and the number of steps (1333) in each kilometre. I'm fastidiously regulating my new pedometer when, after just 746 metres, I'm hailed by a scruffy North African wearing a black cloth cap who is sitting in a distinctly dented once-white van parked alongside the road.

"Are you looking for work?" he shouts at me in French.

"What do you need?" I reply as I approach the van, wondering how this man, no matter where he might be from, could mistake a middle-aged white guy like me for an itinerant worker.

"Are you a mason?" he asks, obviously not alluding to the fraternity of Freemasons.

"Actually, I've done some masonry work in California and this is the best guard dog in France," I answer confidently, slightly exaggerating our résumés. "How much are you paying?"

"A hundred euros a day," he responds, perhaps impressed by the California aspect of my experience. Or maybe Bogart.

I think about it for a few seconds. The idea of working to support the MedTrek as I make my way along the sea is tempting and I recall that Odysseus occasionally boasted that he could cut grass with a scythe, drive a pair of oxen and plow a clean furrow. But I refuse the job offer.

"I'm afraid that I've just started walking around the Mediterranean and have to stick with the program or I won't make it very far," I say, also well aware that my relative inexperience as a mason would be embarrassingly obvious in less than five minutes.

This isn't the first time that I inflated my home improvement capabilities. I sent an incredible resumé in response to an ad in the *International Herald Tribune* in 1971 and got a job converting a barge in Rotterdam. Like all but one of the other five purported 'carpenters' on the team, I was fired within a week.

"Why would you walk around the Mediterranean?" he asks.

"Just for fun, just to do it, just for exercise, just to think about some personal stuff."

"Well, be careful in Algeria," he cautions, as though he meets MedTrekkers and would-be masons a few times a day. "That religious war takes no hostages."

He's got a young boy, presumably his son, with him and I invite them both to walk with me. The father looks at me like I've just asked him to lend me his kid to carry my backpack.

"Do you think I'm looking for a mason so I'll have time to walk?" he asks. "I'm looking for a mason to finish a garden wall today."

Then, he adds prophetically, "Don't go into Algeria."

The Med, its colour and tone dramatically influenced and tinted by the dark gray sky, looks and sounds exceptionally angry this morning. There's not a soupçon of sun and the wind has whipped up the waves, creating a furious ocean spray that forcefully and repeatedly crashes over the seawall. Although the Med's wide basin produces little variation in tides, the sirocco, Levanter and mistral winds can transform it from a placid to hostile environment within minutes.

That's what's happening this morning and it makes me think of Lao Tsu's perceptive thought about the yin-and-yang properties of water. "Under heaven nothing is more soft and yielding than water," he said. "Yet for attacking the solid and strong, nothing is better. It has no equal."

Maybe today's weather is influenced by Zeus, the lord of cloud. Homer recounts that Zeus "roused a storm against the ships, and driving veils of squall moved down like night on land and sea". Then "the bows went plunging at the gust, sails cracked…and we saw death in that fury". Whether weather changes like the one today are caused by nature or Zeus, some friends of mine drowned in the early 1980s while sailing from Nice to Corsica, learning fatally that this calm sea can get very angry very quickly.

The Greeks knew that too.

"A man could well despair of getting home at all, if the winds blew him over the Great South Sea—that weary waste, even the wintering birds delay one more winter before the northward crossing," Lord Nestor of Gerênia told Telémakhos.

There aren't many people out today. It looks like a neutron bomb has hit the seasonally animated resort of Port Grimaud, a miniaturised labyrinthine replica of Venice with a cornucopia of canals and hundreds of Lilliputian houses, each with a yacht or motorboat parked at the back porch. Although we get lost in this peopleless maze, the officers on security detail surprisingly don't seem to mind us walking around a development that is strictly off limits to non-residents in the summer.

I mention to one guard, whose German shepherd sidekick completely ignores Bogart, that the place is depressingly desolate and dilapidated at this time of year.

"When I was here a few years ago trying to find actress Joan Collins I thought this was the lap of luxury," I tell the guard. "Now, with debris everywhere, it looks beaten down and defeated by winter and weather. What happened?"

"L'été c'est l'été, l'hiver c'est l'hiver," he replies commonsensically. "Come back in May and it'll be as chic as it was the last time you were here."

The even less upmarket development of Port Cogolin a little further down the coast features an unattractive fenced-in facility run by the French Ministry of Defence. With typical military panache, the imposing cement monstrosity completely blocks the seaway and forces us to hike on the road. But the diversion leads us to a street-side baker selling a scrumptious piece of pine nut cake, though my enthusiastic appreciation could be due to the ten kilometres that, according to the pedometer, we've just trekked.

In an illustration of the constantly cyclical nature of a MedTrek, we're soon walking on another *sentier littoral* that parallels the coast into the fashionable resort of Saint-Tropez. We stick to the beach, sidestepping the many jellyfish washed up on shore, and return to the main road only once. That's when I show Bogart the L'Oasis Clinic where Brigitte Bardot has been hospitalised during her frequent *dépressions nerveuse* and occasional suicide attempts.

Bardot, whom the French refer to as B.B., once called her hometown of Saint-Tropez "*le trou du cul du monde*", or "the asshole of the world". She also says her right-wing husband has "a strong personality and, like me, the character of a pig". Still the French continue to adore B.B. Even in her 70s, she's considered one of the country's most notorious sex symbols, a devoted defender of animal rights and the most infamous woman in Provence. Ironically, she helped make *le trou du cul du monde* famous when she starred in *And God Created Woman*, which was shot here in 1955.

Saint-Tropez, which despite B.B.'s pronouncement is still the most celebrated jet set playground on the Riviera, has all the 'right' ingredients required to attract celebrities. The stars bivouac at the luxurious, multi-terraced, sand-coloured Le Byblos hotel; play boule on the red earth in the Place des Lices; hit the midnight party scene at clubs like Regine's; and in the summer lounge on beaches with seductive names like Bouillabaisse, Pampelonne and Tahiti.

If you're rich and/or famous, or even if you're not, it doesn't take too much effort to fit in.

"Nudity and topless sunbathing are *de rigueur* down here," former model and successful lingerie entrepreneur Elle Macpherson told me a few years ago when I interviewed her around the pool at the Byblos.

The Australian once known as 'The Body' won't get much argument around these parts. And no one can guess the extent or lack of your fortune when you're not wearing any clothes.

I avoid the Mediterranean in general, and Saint-Tropez in particular, in the summer because I loathe the crowds, the traffic jams, the inflated prices and the too warm seawater. But it's a pure delight now, in early January, when a coffee costs what a coffee should cost and the water temperature is a chilling 11 degrees Centigrade.

An art gallery owner on the port tells me that the forty-kilometre walk from Saint-Tropez around the Rabiou Point to Cavalaire-sur-Mer is feasible despite the winter wind and severe sea spray. Maguy, who's from Rio de Janeiro, then compliments my accent and I applaud the authentic ochre paint job being completed on her boutique.

"The colours, ah the colours and the light, that's why I love the Mediterranean," she says, in grammatically perfect French with a bouncy Brazilian lilt. "Not just the sharp cobalt sea, the crisp azure sky and the soothing rainbow-coloured landscape, but the shades of building façades with a cast of earthly tones created from natural mineral pigments like ochre, sienna and umber. For me, this symbolises the romantic history, lore and character of the Mediterranean."

She's right, of course. This luminous resonance is found everywhere from Paleolithic cave art to the colour of cities, from ancient Pompeii to Saint-Tropez, Nice and Genoa. Even Odysseus, not to mention painters like Picasso and Van Gogh, was influenced by the light. Homer, thought to be from the Greek island of Chios, said that "the light on the sea rim gladdened Odysseus".

Saint-Tropez, topped by a 16th century citadel, has not always been colourful and celebrity congested. Founded by a Christian centurion named Torpes, the main reason a number of Genoese families settled here in 1470 was because the town had no taxes. And the place was still a backwater a century ago. Then de Maupassant wrote about it; painters like Signac, whose work is on display at the local Annonciade Museum, painted it; and Colette, Jean Cocteau and B.B. inhabited it.

Nonetheless it's still an enchanting four-star hike from the Saint-Tropez cemetery to Rabiou Point and the renowned Pampelonne beaches. Bogart and I stop near B.B.'s place in the bamboo-and-cane-filled Cannebiers Bay, which is rimmed with villas of the very rich and impermanently famous, and share a light lunch of Boursin cheese and rice crackers.

I recall first meeting B.B. in Paris in 1976, when she led a campaign to save baby seals, and fantasise about what I'll say if she walks out of her home to discuss my MedTrek.

Probably something like "I'm in the midst of existential self-examination that, following a divorce and general weariness after thirty years as a working journalist, has me wondering where I'm going and why. Although I've been sober for a while, I haven't felt at loose ends like this since I dropped acid to watch *Easy Rider* in the 60s. I'm hoping the walk will clarify things a bit."

Not that I'm likely to get much sympathy from the cantankerous woman who hasn't made a film since 1973 and, though she thoroughly disdains her one-time profession, remains the country's most enduring female symbol since Joan of Arc. After all, B.B. launched flowered bikinis, ponytails, the teased chignon, ballet slippers and wide skirts, and was considered a female James Dean, so successful a rebel against the conformist Fifties that she was even denounced by the Vatican. Her career led to a break with traditional French values and B.B. became as much a mark of the era as beatniks, existentialism, the hullabaloo around Saint-Germain-des-Prés and the Club Med.

She was the incarnation of sexuality, egocentricity, pleasure, beauty, youth and sex. "She's not just sexy," postulated one magazine back in the day. "She is

Le Sexe." "The impossible dream of married men," added another publication. "Bardot is a myth and one does not replace a myth," said Coco Chanel.

The mythic B.B. now lives among, more or less, dozens of cats, ten dogs, her fourth husband and numerous other beasts in the ten-room villa La Madrague that she bought in 1958. There's a cemetery in the garden studded with crosses bearing the names of deceased pets – like Nini, Cadichon and Prosper – and inside there are cat baskets and dog rugs everywhere. La Garrigue, another home a few kilometres away, has a quaint outdoor chapel for the animals where Bogart long ago indicated he wished to be buried by lifting his leg and peeing on the wall.

But this afternoon, as the sky clears, *Le Mythe* and *Le Sexe* is presumably not at home. Perhaps we'll return in the morning because she not only might have some advice for me but she's also the one Frenchwoman that I'm sure Odysseus would consider of goddess potential.

Not that the gods liked the idea of mortals shacking up with goddesses.

"Oh you vile gods, in jealousy supernal!" Kalypso said to Hermes when he carried the message that she must permit Odysseus to leave her bed and return to his odyssey. "You hate it when we choose to lie with men—immortal flesh by some dear mortal side."

Jealousy wasn't limited to the gods, of course. Homer made it clear that "All of us on this earth are plagued by jealousy."

Beyond the luxurious villas, on a rocky point between the Salins and Tahiti beaches, I stumble upon a dilapidated shack. The ramshackle lean-to is built primarily from driftwood and occupied by three impoverished-looking nomads who have managed to gather and stack enough firewood to make it through the night.

"Isn't this the best day of your life!" one of them, a bottle of wine in his hand as he raises both arms to the dark heavens, yells at me over the wind. "This is why we're alive. To have days like this. Come and get a drink!"

"This *is* the best day of my life!" I shout back. "Unfortunately I've got to keep on the move but please take a drink on my behalf."

He toasts me with the bottle, takes a big gulp and screams "*A ta santé!*"

Seeing the rich and poor coexisting on the same stretch of sea reminds me that the Med is economically diverse and that the wealth apparent in B.B.'s hood is certainly not the norm. Although intrigued by my walk through France and Spain, I look forward to checking in on current and former fighting states (Algeria and Israel), one-time outlaw states (Libya), problematic states (Greece and Turkey), former Communist basket-case states (Albania) and newly independent states in the former Yugoslavia.

I continue to Tahiti Beach, where cafés and everything else are closed and shuttered, and decide to hoof it back to Saint-Tropez, a distance much shorter by road than by the seaside, to find a place to spend the night. As Bogart and I tranquilly trudge towards town, an Algerian on a motor scooter stops and, much to my amazement, offers me a ride. I sit on the back of his teeny moped and it occurs to me that the way to hitchhike is not to hitchhike, especially with a dog.

Bogart lopes alongside us until we get to the Clemenceau bar in the Place des Lices and I buy my chauffeur a beer. He tells me that he's unemployed, I tell him about his compatriot looking for a mason. Then I describe my MedTrek and within a few minutes everyone in the bar is laughing about an American foolish enough to consider walking around the entire sea. Apparently an outing of this nature is, in this particular bar anyway, a difficult concept to grasp. From now on I'll simply mention that I'm on a day hike with my dog.

Still, I enthusiastically invite my bar mates to join me for coffee and a stroll back to Tahiti Beach the next morning.

"Walk with me for a bit," I say. "You'll enjoy it."

There are no immediate takers but everyone wishes me a rousing *"bon voyage"* when I leave to check into the nearby Hôtel La Maison Blanche. Like most French hotels, this one warmly welcomes Bogart. He's never had to utter, as Odysseus once did, "Is he not sacred, even to the gods, the wandering man who comes, as I have come, in weariness before your knees, your waters? Here is your servant; lord, have mercy on me." No, no poetry is required from Bogart. Hoteliers seem to love him.

During a long, hot bath I certainly feel like I just walked the 29 kilometres and 38,657 steps indicated on my pedometer. The bottom of the bathtub displays the detritus, including sand and twigs, of the day's trek. I realise I can determine the degree of difficulty of a day's walk by the state of the tub. Bogart seems ecstatic that he doesn't have to participate in this little experiment.

That night, fresh smelling if not cleanly clothed, I take Bogart to a nearby meeting with some fellow alcoholics and he sleeps on the floor while we discuss our experience with booze, the bottle and sobriety. I describe how my arrogance, anger and anxiety have gradually been supplanted by a semblance of honesty, humility and a more honorable way of life.

"And I expect to learn a lot more about these traits by walking around a sea when so much, from the weather to the terrain and the people I meet, is beyond my control," I said. "When I'm incapable of staying calm and doing the next right thing, I'll admit that I'm powerless and turn it over to Mother Med."

The next morning we decide to keep the room at the welcoming White House and I head back to the beach carrying only a small daypack containing water, a parka and the makings of lunch that I bought at the market in the Place des Lices. Today we'll be away from the road and cars on a seaside nature walk to Cavalaire-sur-Mer. Then we'll return here at nightfall to meet Delphyne, who plans to arrive late this afternoon and hike with us tomorrow. Once she joins us, I may make another attempt to find B.B.

Our first brush with nature disturbs me. The entire 4.5-kilometre long Pamplonne beach is covered by almost everything known to man. There's not only driftwood, sea grass and moss, which collects in huge piles to create a natural levy, but also the discarded remnants of every receptacle, container, article and invention found in industrial society. The paraphernalia ranges from used needles and condoms to discarded bottles, barrels, boats and deflated footballs. I'm not sure this will be the filthiest beach I'll find on the Med—after all, there's no oil slick and no visible human waste—but I like to think it'll be in the top ten. Otherwise, the sea's got a real problem.

I survey the grubby scene from a lifeguard stand and, rather than harboring a justifiable grudge against plastics manufacturers and my fellow human beings, decide that the beached garbage is an essential part of the sea's winter cleansing cycle. I know that, here anyway, the Med's seasonal vomit will be cleaned up by large tractors and trucks by early spring due to the importance of tourism. And my trash-collecting penchant is reborn when I realise that I'll certainly be able to collect an eclectic bag of litter today. I also express relief that I have not yet gotten a whiff of human sewage.

Then my mind meanders onto weightier topics. A sea's parts, I theorise, cannot be divided. "From the point of view of the water, there is no beginning, no end, no up, no down, no birth and no death," Thich Nhat Hanh wrote in *The Long Road Turns To Joy*, his guide to walking meditation. Maybe. But I wonder about the sea path taken by each bit of refuse. Where did all these rubber balls and buoys start out? How long do two fins, lost together, flip-flop as a pair in the water? Who used all these condoms? Have this morning's waves already lapped the shores of Turkey and Tunisia?

This mental pinball game runs its course and concludes with the not-too-startling realisation that I am—that all of this is—just a tiny speck on the perimeter of a vast sea. Yet apparently this is the right place to be.

"The narrow ribbon between land and ocean is a perfect place to understand the mind of wisdom," a Taoist once told me. "Just as there is a dynamic balance between sand and water, so too is there a dynamic equilibrium between the quiescent and active sides of our minds. Just as the sand is constantly being washed, so too should we keep our minds."

It's not quite 8am and I decide to wash my mind on the isolated lifeguard stand on the deserted, if much littered, beach. Meditating on the seaside each morning will be one pleasant and serene aspect of the MedTrek and I recall an inspiring line from *Chronicles of Tao*: "His master had told him that water was a special element for him, advising him to gaze at its surface to bring calmness and introspection."

I'd begun meditating, or thinking I was meditating ('they' say that if you think you're meditating you're not meditating), in the 1960s at a Buddhist monastery atop Mount Kōya in Japan. Since then, following numerous spiritual retreats and treks to monasteries in the Himalayas, Ethiopia and Europe, I try to spend 30 minutes early each morning letting my mind settle. I've had instruction, but my simple personal practice is neither exotic nor complicated. One of my masters says that meditation is like letting the mud in a stirred glass of water settle to the bottom. Another says meditation has an honored place in people's lives because it can "span a continuum from better bowel movements to spiritual bliss" which, face it, is pretty spectacular. And a third teacher claims it's like watching turbulent waves on the sea subside as the surface gradually calms.

That's what I'm doing this morning. Letting the waves subside and settling my muddied and muddled mind. Putting aside expectations and projection, I draw energy from the sea, the sun, the earth and a moment of meditation that, believe it or not, gives me a sense of calm, strength, confidence, goodness and purpose.

It's not always easy because, as Lao Tsu said, "Who can wait quietly while the mud settles?" Indeed, thoughts come and go, waves rise and fall. I'm a long way from nirvana. But probably just as far away from complete chaos, though that word meant primal emptiness, rather than disorder, to the ancient Greeks.

As I descend from my seat of non-judgment and not-too-profound musing, a German shepherd playfully runs towards Bogart. The dogs are sniffing each other when I make a serious mistake. I pick up a stick and throw it.

The visiting shepherd is the kind of mutt that becomes a mate for life due to one toss of a stick. He races to the inanimate quarry and wrestles with Bogart to take command of the gnarled piece of wood. Then he follows us to the end of the beach and continues to tag along on a *sentier littoral* that takes us on craggy rocks past sweet-smelling shrubs and under parasol pines. As we continue, the water and sky gradually turn the same shade of tranquil turquoise blue and I visually voyage to the bottom of the sea and into the infinity of space.

The 37-kilometre hike from Saint-Tropez to Cavalaire-sur-Mer is my longest uninterrupted contact yet with the sea. It's easy to understand why people, both locals and tourists, flock to these expansive beaches, silent coves, majestic capes, solitary lighthouses, jutting rocks, crashing waves and vegetation that includes eucalyptus, cork oak, pines, chestnuts and full-flowering mimosa.

The rhythmical names of the capes – Camarat, Cartaya, Taillat and Lardier – complement the physical beauty. At the tip of each cape I sit for a few minutes just to gaze at, into and beyond the expansive sea. At Camarat I even imagine that I can see the Rubis, a 66-metre long submarine that's been lying in the sand at a depth of forty metres a mile to the southwest since it was sunk over thirty years ago.

The rocky and indented seaside is due to the Maures mountain range. The name is derived either from the Provençal word *maouro*, which was used to describe the area's dark rock and impenetrable forests, or from Spanish Moorish pirates who controlled the coast in the 8th century. Whatever the origins, the craggy terrain makes for occasionally dicey footing and there's one place where I have to perfectly time my steps to avoid being swept away by waves. I figure the dogs will almost certainly take an unintentional dip, but the three of us deftly negotiate the problematic passages without a serious misstep.

This entire area is now a nature reserve and ardent efforts have been implemented to reduce erosion and protect the environment. I'm extremely impressed when both dogs seem deferential to a silent hawk majestically sitting at the tip of one rock.

Maybe that's because they, as animals, appreciate what the hawk symbolises. Deng Ming-Dao wrote that "Hawk doesn't think during the hunt. It does not care for theory or ethics. All that it does is natural. Animals live simple lives close to Tao. They do not need to think or reason: they never doubt themselves. When they are hungry, they eat. When they are tired, they sleep."

No doubt Bogart and this other dog know this already.

According to the shepherd's collar its name is Kimba, which seems an odd handle for a male, and he lives at La Plage des Jumeaux, one of the Pamplonne beaches. Kimba and Bogart tend to stick close to my heels and we lunch together – on Tomme de Savoie cheese, crabmeat, *pain complet*, tangerines and a banana – at Cap Cartaya. A bit later another solitary male hiker near the Bay of Blue Rocks throws a stick for the dogs. But Kimba apparently prefers my throwing, or my crabmeat, and continues following us on the oft-forested path past Cap Lardier to Gigaro Beach.

After dumping the trash I've collected into a large municipal garbage bin, I call each of the four numbers on Kimba's collar. I leave four similar messages and decide that, rather than trying to ditch him, getting Kimba home will be my late afternoon mission. The three of us move back from the beach, walking through a decapitated vineyard that recently provided grapes for Côtes de Provence wines, to La Croix-Valmer. This is where, in 312, Constantine had his vision to convert to Christianity and create the Roman Empire. The dogs, obviously not impressed, leave their mark on a stone cross erected in 1893 to commemorate the miracle.

A bus heading to Saint-Tropez stops when I wave and signal, but the driver wants nothing to do with Kimba and Bogart. As she pulls away I get a call and learn that Kimba's owner is a dentist in the middle of implant surgery. He can't come to fetch his dog.

"He got Kimba from the pound a month ago to guard a restaurant he owns on the beach," the dentist's secretary tells me. "There's a guardian there who will be happy to see him returned."

"I'll find a way to get him back," I reply.

Since hitchhiking with Bogart and Kimba is not an option unless my Algerian friend happens to drive by on his motor scooter, I contact Delphyne who's en route to Saint-Tropez from Antibes and let her know about Kimba and where she can find us. Then the three of us spread out on a grassy patch near the road and I read the dogs excerpts from the Kazantzakis book for an hour. Though they're a wet-and-sandy mess, Delphyne doesn't mind letting the dogs into her black BMW once we cover the leather backseat with a blanket and towels.

"Thanks so much for fetching us and letting the dogs in your car!" I tell Delphyne. "It was a great day, a superb walk, but after 37 kilometres we really don't have the strength to make it back to Saint-Tropez by foot. You're our salvation!"

She smiled so broadly that I knew she'd love my next revelation.

"Incidentally I had a vision today, just like you do," I announce, in an effort to further explain my slightly Zenned-out state after the long day. "I was Odysseus' dog, Argus, in an earlier life. And one of my tasks in this lifetime is to be nice to all dogs."

"That doesn't surprise me," Delphyne says seriously. "I knew you had some kind of profound connection to the ancient Greeks."

"And we also may have an appointment to visit dog lover Brigitte Bardot in the morning," I add. "She can probably give me some guidance about this whole project."

We get lost on the back roads but finally find Kimba's home, meet the guardian, bid the dog adieu and head back to the White House.

It's pouring at dawn the next day and I decide, with regret, to put the MedTrek on hold until the ferocious rain lets up. I walk through the ongoing downpour to the port with Delphyne and Bogart just after noon and marvel at how yesterday's clear azure water has become a turbulent brown sea. The Med's in such turmoil that I wonder if the Eurasian and African tectonic plates, which come together on the geologically active seabed, have clashed. I tell Delphyne that we'll have to give B.B. a rain check.

"You don't want to walk because there's a little bad weather?" Delphyne, now sounding like a Greek chorus with this particular refrain, asks. "I'll bet you one hundred euros that you don't make it around the whole sea. Do you think Odysseus would let a little rain deter him? You're not made of the same stuff as he was."

But who is? Odysseus was a special kind of guy. Everybody said so.

"In my life I have met, in many countries, foresight and wit in many first rate men, but never have I seen one like Odysseus for steadiness and a stout heart," said Menelaos, the King of Sparta.

Athena – the goddess of wisdom, warfare, arts and crafts who frequently had an owl as her companion – told Odysseus that he was "coolheaded, quick, well-spoken" and "of all men now alive you are the best in plots and storytelling".

"Whoever gets around you must be sharp and guileful as a snake," she told him. "Even a god might bow to you in ways of dissimulation. You! You chameleon!"

And this comes from a goddess who admitted that her "own fame is for wisdom among the gods–deceptions, too".

Odysseus must have been unique because even Zeus had kind words for him. The chief god contended "There is no mortal half so wise; no mortal gave so much to the lords of open sky."

Did that swell the mortal's head? Odysseus admitted himself that "men hold me formidable for guile in peace and war" and "this fame has gone abroad to the sky's rim".

Okay, modest Odysseus I'm not. But I plan to keep walking and tell Delphyne that I accept her 100-euro wager.

8. A Promise to the Med Gods

"The miracle is not to walk on water. The miracle is to walk on the green earth, dwelling deeply in the present moment and feeling truly alive." – Thich Nhat Hanh

The incessant rain shows no sign of letting up and I somewhat reluctantly head back to Antibes with Delphyne and Bogart for my first break from the MedTrek. When I return to Saint-Tropez a few days later, the weather's improved but I'm alone. Delphyne, promising to accompany me further down the road, has returned to her high-salaried day job and my conniving kids somehow convinced me that Bogart's no longer capable of long-distance walking.

"His hips don't look so good," said my son Luke, who plans to join me during his upcoming school break. "Are you sure he's up for this? He's 12 years old now, about ten times your age in human years. Could you do this if you were 500?"

"I can't believe you made Bogart walk on that rocky coast and let him run next to a motorcycle," criticised my daughter Sonia, who said "let me get back to you on that one" when I asked her to join me on my hike. "Leave him home from now on. You can kill yourself but not our dogs. They don't have any existential questions that need answering."

I took Bogart for a short stroll along the Brague River in Sophia Antipolis to break the news to him about the conclusion of his MedTrek just before I returned to Saint-Tropez. He was a bit forlorn until I told him the story of Odysseus and his dog Argus, swift and strong when his master left on his odyssey but frail and near death upon his return. Bogart perked up when I explained how, after a two-decade absence, Argus "knew he heard Odysseus' voice nearby" and "did his best to wag his tail, nose down, with flattened ears, having no strength to move nearer his master".

Then Bogart barked, which I presume indicated that he'll make a similar effort if he's still around when I complete the MedTrek.

And what happens when I return to the exact spot on the beach in Cavalaire-sur-Mer where I'd ended the seaside hike with Bogart and Kimba? I immediately meet yet another dog, a handsome collie that's aggressively barking at three French Navy frigates anchored off shore. There's got to be a god, I figure, in one of these dogs.

I immediately begin to silently hum, then softly sing, then wildly scream a verse from "K9 Love" by the Bacon Brothers that I'd recently heard Kevin and Michael sing at a music festival in Cannes:

"You might think I'm a bit sick
Or maybe I'm a heretic
Maybe I'm just dyslexic but you see
That d-o-g is like a g-o-d to me."

You had to be there!

As the collie quickly wanders off, I stare at the sea and have a peculiar sensation that the Mediterranean is my mother and, whether dog gods or no gods accompany me, she'll be the one to nourish me. The glorious sunrise and the soft lapping waves reinforce an awe-inspiring sentiment that I should stay as close as possible to the Mother Med.

"*La Mer est ma mère*," I say to myself, recalling that Lao Tsu once wrote that he was "nourished by the great mother", though he wasn't exactly alluding to the Med. "I've got nothing to worry about."

As I consider the implications of sticking close to my watery mother womb, the sea seems to shrink to the size of my childhood security blanket. I have an equally comforting "Ah, they're doing it right!" sensation when I see that Cavalaire-sur-Mer, unlike most other small municipalities on the coast, has separate recycling containers for paper, cans, plastics and used clothes. That's something the Greeks, and everyone who came after them, would appreciate once they made the mental time leap from their comparative austerity into our wasteful consumer society.

Once beyond Cavalaire-sur-Mer I climb up, down, over and around countless obstacles. Not only parts of the Massif des Maures, which is sometimes translated in English as the 'solid mass of the Moors', but also the parasol pines, maritime pines, cork oak, chestnuts and unidentifiable bramble that cover the solid mass. A volunteer worker at the tourism office in La Croix-Valmer tells me that the Maures is one of the oldest forests in France, the largest forest in the Var and home to two species of endangered tortoises. He also thinks that there might be a seaside path running parallel to it along the coast.

When I return to the sea, the turquoise-tinted water is so translucent that I feel like I'm in the Seychelles. But I can't find the path and don't see any turtles. In fact, every time I take a few steps along the seaside I'm confronted by a vertical sea cliff that forces me to backtrack and head uphill through thick underbrush. After an hour of meaningless meandering, I stumble upon a forest service fire road that beelines through a 'protected nature zone' where the only house has a 'Bird Protection Zone' sign in the front yard. And a big contented cat sitting right next to it.

Sweaty and tired, I stagger into the Relais des Maures in Rayol-Canadel-sur-Mer, which has a garden rich with herbs and plants imported from Chile, China, California, South Africa and Tasmania. In order to prevent my muscles from stiffening, I usually stop for no more than 15 minutes when I'm hiking and get by with a light picnic lunch. But today, wiped out, I casually sit on the restaurant terrace, take off my shoes, savor each bite of my *chou farcie* and relaxingly read the local paper, including an article about a no-nonsense female customs agent in Lou Lavandou. The only disruption is a travelling salesman at the next table talking to his secretary about the intimacy and privacy of email. Little does he know.

Lou Lavandou is only ten kilometres away, according to the owner of the relais. "The hillside is terraced like a Roman amphitheater and there are fine views back to Cap Lardier and forward to Cap Bénat," he says. "Just follow the red dirt road."

Yearning to be closer to the sea, I unwisely ignore his suggestion and head downhill to again attempt a walk on the rocks at the water's edge, below steep cliffs that have been eroded by wind, rain and time. Bogart would definitely have been smart enough to boycott this stretch but I give it a shot.

Half an hour later I'm stuck yet again. I can't go on. I can't face going back. Changing hiking boots for tennis shoes and donning gloves, I decide to go up. Straight up.

Tackling a cliff alone in this isolated terrain isn't particularly smart, especially without any rope or rock-climbing equipment. In less than 15 minutes I'm silently invoking the names of all of the immortal Greek gods on Mount Olympus, promising each of them that I'll never again stray from the path if they'll just get me off this crumbling rock face in one piece. Homer says in *The Odyssey* that "He too must pray to the gods on whom all men depend." He, in this case, is definitely me.

Although perhaps not truly staring imminent death directly in the face, my prayers aren't inappropriate. After all, Odysseus frequently prayed to the gods. Once, when a storm showed no signs of abating, he "withdrew to the interior to pray to the gods in solitude, for hope that one might show me some way of salvation." And his prayers generally worked. "Never have I seen the gods help any man as openly as Athena did your father," Lord Nestor told Telémakhos.

I'm hoping for a similar response, though I've been taught not to pray solely, if at all, for myself. "When you pray only for good weather for your own picnic and not for the farmers who need rain, you are doing the opposite of what Jesus taught," I'd heard Thich Nhat Hanh say.

Selfish or not, someone or something somewhere hears my plea. I'm gradually able to pull myself up to the top of the cliff and, arms aching, shimmy onto a manmade walkway. Much to my surprise, a cliff-hanging path features ornately carved stone benches, wide terraces and statues of sculpted mermaids amidst trimmed greenery.

"Is this a celestial dreamland or a paradise on earth?" I ask myself. "If so, will I be welcomed by 72 virgins, four pro hookers or a chorus of angelic harpists?"

"To be ready to enter the Pure Land, you simply have to learn to make peaceful, anxiety-free steps," Thich Nhat Hanh also told me. "In fact, if you can learn to take peaceful, anxiety-free steps on the Earth, you won't need to go to the Pure Land. When you are peaceful and free, the Earth itself becomes a Pure Land, and there is no need to go anywhere else."

Unfortunately, I haven't stumbled upon an earthly or heavenly Pure Land.

"I've been watching you for an hour," screeches a beefy uniformed guard who jumps out from behind a bush, points a handgun at me and almost pushes me off the side of the cliff. "You're trespassing. On a supermodel's property."

"There are no *Propriété Privée* signs," I reply.

"Of course, there are no signs the way you came. Our video cameras caught you sneaking up that steep cliff. Do you think you're a Green Beret or something? I could shoot you, you know."

"I didn't have a clue this was private property," I say, not too apologetically. "But there are 50 hikers following me so you better shoot me and dump my body before you're invaded and overwhelmed by all of my followers."

This bantering, bickering and braggadocio continues until the guard finally allows me to head through the luscious estate to the main gate. As I walk toward Le Layet, I visualise the headline in tomorrow's paper: "Supermodel Has Man Arrested for Walking Around The Mediterranean".

Actually, if I were intercepted in 2008, the commotion and the threat of arrest would have made some sense. The place belongs to Carla Bruni who married the president of France.

I speculate about the lively content of the newspaper article for only a few minutes before I meet a day hiker with a rainbow-coloured backpack.

"Ah, you're American," he says disdainfully when I tell him I've walked here from Antibes and just outfoxed a supermodel's security force. "That explains it."

Philippe introduces himself, tells me he's a high school professor and immediately challenges my contention that the Lérins monks once had connections in this community.

"That's simply incorrect unless, of course, you are more educated and cultivated than I am," he sniffs, as he points to a sign declaring this an "*espace naturel sensible*" or nudist beach. "You may not know your history but I'll bet you're in the mood to sunbathe with me."

Apparently, though uneducated and uncultivated, I'm fair game. He's wrong about the monks, but that's not the only reason I decline his offer and continue to walk alone on bikini-shaped beaches in Aiguebelle and Saint-Clair. Again and again, though, I'm trapped by surging waves and protruding rock formations that make it difficult to make much headway. I finally sprint up through the grounds of the closed Les Roches Relais et Château hotel to a small road that runs into Lou Lavandou, which gets its name from the lavender on the banks of the Batailler river.

There are dozens of boats in the port, many advertising tuna fishing excursions, and I chance upon the female customs agent whose picture was in the newspaper. I tell her I liked the article and describe my altercation with the Tyrannical Security Guard of Cap Negre.

"You have to go to the gendarmerie for that kind of problem," she says. "And they won't do anything unless you were physically assaulted. After all, you were trespassing."

The terrace on my fourth floor room in the Espadon Hôtel faces the Hyères

Islands, which include Port-Cros, Porquerolles and Levant. During a pleasant solitary dinner of fish soup and small tasty *rougets* at the Krill restaurant, I decide to MedTrek for another day and then ferry out to Port-Cros, a well-known sanctuary for flora and fauna that was Europe's first national marine park when it was created in 1963.

The next morning, looking out over the water where fish can be seen sporting, I rise and meditate to the tuna of the sunrise. The islands, also known as the Iles d'Or, begin glimmering as the sun edges over the horizon. Their golden glow is apparently due to the reflection of mica shale rock. Or is it more than that? "Dawn is a shimmering of the horizon," Lao Tsu explained. "Dusk is a settling of the sky. … This represents the cycle of existence."

I take off at a pleasant clip, strutting away from Lou Lavandou on a narrow wooden walkway constructed above the sandy beach. My mind suddenly bubbles with a few of the words that describe the various gaits of the Medtrek: ambulate, perambulate, somnambulate, stride, canter, pace, patter, promenade, prance, wend, tread, trip, traipse, stroll, swagger, limp, sweep, parade, hobble, shamble, shuffle, slog, stagger, traverse, reel, stumble, waddle, mince, roam, ramble, strut, march, hike and tiptoe. At some point today I'll probably realise each of these moveable states.

There certainly aren't that many words used to describe walking in *The Odyssey* but Homer does list names of numerous Phoenicians—including Tiderace, Sparwood, Hullman, Sternman, Beacher, Pullerman, Bluewater, Shearwater, Runningwake, Boardless and Seabelt—that appropriately reflect a man's relationship with the sea and seamanship.

As I head out of town, the bright sun at my back, there's no place to get, or even buy, fresh water before the boardwalk turns into a well-marked *sentier littoral*. Real smart, I grimace, resolving never to start off without filling my water bottles. I'm walking around one of the world's largest bodies of water and my own faucet is empty. *Vive le paradoxe.*

Volunteer members of local hiking associations frequently clean the trails and regularly repaint the markings on the seaside sentiers, GRs and other hiking paths. But this morning there's a gigantic crane and a dozen workmen replacing a washed away portion of the footpath to Cap Bénat.

"Superb walkway!" I yell over the din of their machinery. "Thanks for doing the work."

"We're making it even better," one man bellows in a your-tax-euros-are-at-work tone. "And it looks like you've got it all to yourself today!"

After trudging over more of the Massif des Maures, my shirt is soaked from constant to-ing and fro-ing by the time I reach Cap Bénat. I'd love to find a shortcut but instead obey the *Privée* sign when I pass a large villa, decorated with a half dozen Matisse-like sculptures, that extends down to the sea. Then I walk next to a two metre-high wire fence with signs that threaten 'Arrest for Trespassing'.

I certainly want to avoid another Cap Negre scene but it's impossible to completely disregard the finely blazed trail on the wrong side of the fence. Especially now that I'm muttering "No more hills". When I approach Cape Bregancon, which is topped with a fairytale-like Rapunzel tower, I'll be the first to admit that I'm on the wrong side of the fence. But I'm still surprised when my one-step-at-a-time cadence is abruptly shattered by the scourge of all Mediterranean hikers.

"You're trespassing, you're screwing everything up," a security guard yells at me. "You're an asshole!"

"I made a mistake and got on the wrong side of the fence," I reply. "It's my fault and I'm sorry."

"You're still an asshole."

"Is that so?" I say, ending the civil part of our conversation.

Words do not quite come to push or shove, indeed they rarely do in France, and I move on, a little irritated by the sanctimonious attitude of all these defenders of private property.

I should prepare myself with better retorts for occasions like this. Odysseus probably would have called the guard "a thick-skinned menace to all courtesy" and Deng Ming-Dao almost certainly would have reminded him that "ownership of property is only an artificial construct". I translate the lines into French and practice them in preparation for my next confrontation with a security official who believes that he's man's answer to Zeus.

The unpleasant incident fades into memory the second I walk onto an expansive sandy beach at the edge of a gorgeous bay. It's winter and the water is cold, but my shoes come off, I wade in up to my knees and then plop down on the sand to catch a few winks.

Still desperately seeking fresh water when I awaken, I traipse through an empty campsite, where the tap has been disconnected for the winter, and arrive on a Route des Vins. I tiptoe through the vineyards, which are cut back and naked at this time of year, until I arrive at the entrance to the Domain de l'Eoube and follow the 'wine tasting' arrows leading to a well-lit barrel-filled *cave*.

"You're the first person to ever come here asking for water," says the young hostess when I enter and almost too impatiently ask for a *verre d'eau*. "Take as much as you'd like. Then try our wine. Without the water."

"Actually the Greeks, who considered Dionysos the god of wine, used to mix their wine with water," I tell her. "Back then wine was too strong to drink unless it was diluted. So now I just drink water straight."

She looks befuddled. And why shouldn't she be. Anyone who drinks 'normally', or someone like this young woman who perhaps has never been drunk, doesn't have a clue that a self-confessed alcoholic like myself can't risk taking a sip of alcohol, diluted or undiluted. One drink could kick off a downward boozing spiral that would land me right back in the proverbial gutter.

"Just one drink?" you might ask.

I'm afraid so because, for me anyway, one is too many and one thousand is not enough. Anyway I've seen too many friends with years of sobriety try to drink moderately and, in most cases, come to the very painful realisation that it not only doesn't work but also gets worse.

After another eight kilometres on the Route des Vins, about twice the distance that I would have walked next to the sea, I arrive in Port Miramar where there's a public toilet facility with, thank you gods, running water.

That's about all that's running here. The government's defence facility is shut down and in shambles. There are no ferries to Port-Cros until May, there are no shops, all of the restaurants are closed and the much-touted Resort des Bahamas looks like it's been hit by Katrina. After walking 34.79 kilometres today, and reaching the 201-kilometre mark, I have to hike another three kilometres to get to the main road and find a bus back to my base camp in Lou Lavandou.

For the record, I never add any kilometres that I walk off the MedTrek to my running total. The extra walking to the bus stop, or anywhere away from the seaside, doesn't count. And if I take a bus, train or hitch a ride after a day's hike to find lodging, I make a point of going back to the exact spot I left off to resume the MedTrek.

The next morning, the Ile d'Or XV ferry heading to Port-Cros Island out of Lou Lavandou traverses a sea that is rough and wavy, or "*très agitée*" as the captain calls it. It takes just a few minutes, as my body disagreeably reacts to the stomach-churning movement, for me to rejoice that I'm walking and not sailing around the Med.

Odysseus was also seasick from time to time and, like any of us, was always grateful when the ordeal passed. "May I invoke you as I would a goddess, princess, to whom I owe my life," he said to Nausikaa when she helped him survive one bout of nausea.

Nausikaa, as Greek women generally did back then, took the compliment in her stride.

"You know Zeus metes out fortune to good and bad men as it pleases him. Hardship he sent to you, and you must bear it," she told Odysseus. "But now that you have taken refuge here, you shall not lack for clothing, or any other comfort due to a poor man in distress."

"Will I ever run into that kind of goddess?" I wonder aloud as the boat docks.

Port-Cros, four kilometres long by less than three wide, is just the right size for a half-day getaway. The Michelin guide describes the national park specifically designed to protect Mediterranean flora and fauna as a Garden of Eden. There are numerous botanical nature paths criss-crossing the island inhabited by the Lérins monks in the fifth century after it had previously been controlled by the Greeks, Ligurians and Romans. According to a plaque at the port, Richelieu built the Estissac Fort here in 1635 and the Canadians landed in 1944 to take out some German batteries.

To keep Port-Cros pristine, there's a strict no-smoking policy, dogs aren't allowed and it's forbidden to pick up seashells, step off marked trails, fish or even moor a boat in certain places. The goal is to protect the sea fans, black coral, white grouper, sharp-snout sea bream and the *Pinna nobilis*, or pen shells, Europe's largest shellfish, living in the water. And also avoid damaging the intriguing mélange of vegetation—blooming yellow mimosas next to statuesque palms next to gnarled cork oaks next to spreading parasol pines—flourishing on the island.

After walking through the Valley of Solitude, I head to the top of Port-Cros' highest mountain before strolling along the high cliffs. I'm so lost in reverie admiring the dizzying 200-metre drop to the sea that I almost miss the last ferry back to the mainland.

The first thing I see when I return to the MedTrek just outside Port Miramar are two green lawn chairs lapped by crashing waves under an umbrella-shaped pine tree. I imagine Napoleon and Horatio Nelson sitting there, chatting loudly enough about military strategy to be heard above the sea's delightful concert, and visualise David Hockney painting the surreal verbal battle scene.

It's early on a Sunday morning but I'm not the only one out. Mountain bikers and weekend walkers are already on the path to Ayguade, a headquarters for the Crusaders in the 13th century. Beyond that is Hyères, one of the oldest outposts on the coast that features a tantalising *vieille ville*, or old town, on the sloping Castéou hill.

Hyères declined under Louis XIII in the 1600s, when Toulon became the regional capital, but today it's a popular tourist destination and a renowned producer of wine, strawberries and peaches. I visit the Collegiate Church of Saint-Paul, which dates to the twelfth century, and enjoy a stunning view back to Cap Negre and ahead to Toulon.

The most enticing aspect of Hyères, for a hiker anyway, is the Presqu'île de Giens, a peninsula linked to the mainland by two sandbars separated by the Pesquiers salt marsh and a huge lake. There's a *sentier littoral* around the entire peninsula but the morning mist, which makes it difficult to distinguish the nearby Porquerolles Island, gives the entire bay a sinister appearance. I remind myself about seasonal cleansing cycles as I walk by shuttered bars, restaurants and hotels with fanciful names like Eden and Altitude Zero.

The circumnavigation of the peninsula itself, a little over 20 kilometres, rivals the spectacular hike from Saint-Tropez to Cavalaire. It doesn't take a geological genius to surmise that the peninsula is a chip off the old Maures block. Negotiating the rocky seaside requires agility and concentration on an up-and-down-the-hill path that detours around one of the world's largest hospitals. After that, the cliff-top views, dazzling panoramas and clear, jaggedly indented bays are a refreshing contrast to the garbage-covered beaches on the mainland.

I lunch at the top of Escampobariou Point and play with six sea gulls that sweep down to catch pieces of tuna that I toss over the towering cliff. Underneath the water below I can make out the *Posidonia oceanica*, a protected flowering plant that is endemic to the Med with leaves said to produce twice the amount of oxygen per square metre as a forest. Nearby, though, is *Caulerpa taxifolia*, a tropical algae that is rapidly spreading and threatening not only the *Posidonia* but also the entire ecosystem.

The walk back towards the mainland is on the Route de Sel, or Salt Road, which is closed to automobiles and speckled with pink flamingos whose colour is accentuated by their steady diet of brine shrimp. By the end of the day I've walked my farthest daily distance – 38.47 kilometres – and am humming "Hyères Today, Gone Tomorrow".

Having packed cheese and rolls from the hotel breakfast buffet for my lunch, I march in driving rain towards Almanarre, where the Greeks had a trading station called Olbia that the Romans later renamed Pomponiana. Dressed like an Abominable Medman with baseball cap, gloves and umbrella, I'm so disappointed at the lack of any significant ruins in Almanarre that, despite the weather, I feel the need to stay near the Mother Sea.

This is, and I know Odysseus would agree, one rocky stretch of seaside. Negotiating it tests my brain-eye-foot coordination and forces me to dodge waves as I leap from rock to rock. I spend a slow three kilometres avoiding contact with the sea by climbing over villa walls, grabbing onto tree trunks and rock climbing. But by the time I get to Carqueiranne, after only an hour, my shoes, socks and gloves are soaked.

The little Carqueiranne port has a plaque detailing its history since 1458 and I learn more than I want to know about contemporary horticultural activities. A fisherman insists that, because the sea is so high at this time of year and I'm not wearing waders, it will be impossible for me to make it around the Cap de Carqueiranne. I continue for a few kilometres on the seaside and learn that he's right. The water lapping the rocks has taken a non-negotiable position against MedTrekkers. I've got to retrace my steps.

I pass the same fisherman and he gives me a friendly "I told you so" grin. I nod back a bemused "You were right!" smirk before moving inland through a new housing development and over the hill to Le Pradet on a road with Arabic-only signs advertising the sale of live sheep and chickens. I figure they're left over from Ramadan. I eat my hotel-swiped lunch on a public dock in the tastily named village of Les Oursinières. A seaside seat provides a panorama of the Bay of Toulon, traditionally considered one of the safest and most beautiful harbours on the Mediterranean.

On the Var Corniche road I see a sign in English that reads 'Dark Side of the Moule', *moule* being French for mussel. I immediately begin musing about its meaning, or lack of meaning, until I somehow remember that it's the title of a pop album by the Belgian group Sttellla. Beats me what it's doing here.

After a number of false starts and thwarted access to the seaside, I stumble upon a *sentier littoral*, though another fisherman in San Peyre tells me that this rocky coast is inaccessible and dangerous.

"Walk on the road for a while," he says. "Or you'll regret it."

I take his advice and, though I didn't think this was possible so close to the Med, I get lost and head into a *tabac*, a combination tobacco shop and bar, to get directions. I ask the owner, who has a prize Roman nose and sunken eyes formed from the apparent consumption of the half-empty bottles in the bar, how to get back to the sea.

"*Où est ma mer?*" I ask.

"How would I know where your mother is?" says the man behind the bar.

"No, not my mother," I reply. "*La mer*, the sea!"

"The sea?" he asks, as he slowly towel-dries an unwashed glass. "I haven't been there in at least a decade."

He acts like he lives in the middle of France and sneers as though I've just posed the stupidest question he's ever heard.

"Do you have an idea where it might be?" I ask, lowering my voice to avoid further upsetting him.

"You might find the path if you follow the little trail across the road and turn right," he says dismissively, his lips pursed. "Years ago, with a little wave dodging and rock jumping, someone I know actually made the walk all the way to Toulon on the seaside. But I'm not dumb enough to try it myself."

After 15 minutes near the water, I sit down under a sign that says 'Risk of Falling Trees' and think about the humbling strength of the Mediterranean.

I recall a story in my book of myths about a powerful king, Canute the Wise, who, to show his courtiers what little power he really possessed, had his throne taken to the seaside. He took his seat, raised his arm and commanded the waves to stop. But they rolled farther and farther up the shore until they splashed over his feet and wet his royal garments.

"'Look, ye vain and foolish men!' he cried. 'How weak and powerless we are. My kingdom and my power are as nothing before the great King, the King of Kings, who rules the world. It is He you should praise and glorify, not any mortal man!'"

Lao Tsu not only agreed with Canute but also gave another definition of a sea's royal stature. "Why is the sea king of a hundred streams?" he asked. "Because it lies below them."

If he were alive today, the ancient Chinese philosopher would probably say something like "You can't stop the waves but you can still learn to surf."

I pass another sign – "Nudism Forbidden – See the Tourist Office for Details" – and wonder what King Canute, Lao Tsu and Sttellla would think of that advice.

After a few kilometres I arrive at the Fort du Cap Brun, one of the many former security lookouts on the coast and now the official residence of the Maritime Préfet, a position equivalent to local governor. A little further along is a 17th century fort and, near the entrance to the expansive Toulon harbor, the Royal Tower built by Louis XII in the early 16th century to defend the place. Its seven-metre thick walls are one of the reasons it was later used as a prison.

Toulon is by far the largest harbour and city I've come across and the overwhelming naval and military presence here will almost certainly block my access to the sea. The arsenal covers some 240 hectares to house and maintain the French Navy's fleet of frigates, submarines, aircraft carriers and mine sweepers.

To get through Toulon, a town renowned for some of the most dilapidated and disgusting architecture on the coast, requires a trudge through low-cost housing developments and rundown industrial plants. The smell of poverty rivals the odour of spilled oil and the walk illustrates the yin-and-yang of MedTrekking. Without a less-than-glorious Toulon, it's difficult to appreciate its many sublime opposites. As Lao Tsu said, "Under heaven all can see beauty as beauty only because there is ugliness." Maybe, but I'm definitely not at the spiritual hiking level suggested by Thich Nhat Hanh: "Whether the Earth is beautiful, fresh, and green, or arid and parched depends on our way of walking."

No matter how I walk, this place is definitely not the Pure Land.

Despite its bleak appearance, Toulon has a colourful history. Purple, in fact. During Roman times imperial purple dye – which has signified wealth, class and royal lineage since the Minoan civilisation in Crete in 1900 BC – was obtained from the glands of the pointed conches found along the coast. Legend credits its discovery to Heracles, or rather to his dog, whose mouth was stained a mauve colour from chewing on snails along the Levantine coast. King Phoenix received a purple-dyed robe from Heracles, whom the Romans called Hercules, and immediately decreed that the rulers of Phoenicia should wear the lavender-like colour as a royal symbol.

Because I refuse to bypass even the worst parts of the Med, it takes two longer-than-usual hours to reach the other side of this floating garbage dump that had to look much better when it was first constructed in 1589. Finally, admittedly a little dispirited, I almost collapse when I reach the colourful, red boule courts in La-Seyne-sur-Mer that is 285 walking kilometres from Antibes.

Near the centre of La Seyne, which was founded in 1856 to build merchant ships, I jump on board the Sirene IV ferry heading back to the Toulon port. The trip through the harbour enables me to appreciate the size of the ships and extent of military installations.

Just being on the water wipes out some of my negative thoughts, but I'm going to take a few days off before tackling the next stage of the MedTrek. That will take me beyond Toulon towards Fort Balaguier, Tamaris, the Lazaret Bay and Les Sablettes beach to the Saint-Mandrier peninsula. There, I'm told by a passenger on the Sirene IV, "no matter who you are or what you're doing, you'll be gunned down by the French Army if you try to trespass. Don't say you weren't warned."

9. MedTrekking With a Teenager and La Femme Mystérieuse

"May men say, 'He is far greater than his father', when he returns from battle." – The Iliad

Luke accompanies me on the MedTrek for the first three days of his school vacation. I'm mentally prepared to slow the pace, reduce the daily distance and patiently tolerate any misgivings my 13-year-old son might have about my Mediterranean mission. Just beyond La Seyne, with the industry-tainted and military-mighty Toulon harbour on our left, he provides the first glimpse of a teenager's viewpoint of MedTrekking when we pass some abandoned buildings and sunken boats.

"This would be a great place for a gang of kids to hang out," Luke says with enthusiasm as we walk amid tons of decaying cranes and rusty machinery. "They could turn this into a gigantic skateboarding park. Get someone to do that and your walk will truly benefit mankind."

Actually Luke's come a long way since I first described my intentions a few weeks ago.

"So now when people ask what my dad does for a living, I'm supposed to say 'He's walking around the Mediterranean because he's 50 and thinks he's Odysseus?'," he had said. "Uh, I don't think so."

My sensible son, who recently studied the Mediterranean basin in his geography class at the international school in Sophia Antipolis, also pointed out that a trip of this nature was full of danger in places like Algeria, Libya and Lebanon.

"You'll probably get killed," he added matter-of-factly.

This morning he's a bit more sanguine.

"If you don't make it all the way around the Mediterranean, I might just finish the trek for you," he told me during breakfast. "A son should probably follow in his father's footsteps to some degree."

"That's what Telémakhos, Odysseus's son, felt when he left to look for his missing father," I reply. "It's a very noble sentiment, especially at your age. But if you ever do follow in my footsteps, know that it's you, not me, who makes the decision. Everyone's got to follow his own path during this short stint on earth. There's not enough time to do much else."

This isn't the first occasion that Luke, who's passionately competed in judo and devoutly studied acting since he was five, has displayed an assured awareness of self. Blonde and cursed with good looks, he frequently behaves with a sense of balance, certainty, consideration, direction and dedication that never fails to amaze me. Capable of becoming anxious simply as a result of my own oft-imagined projections and expectations, I frequently turn snails into dinosaurs. Luke usually manages to turn dinosaurs into snails.

Although he sometimes accuses me of being stressed when I ask him at seven what he wants for dinner at eight, I'm overjoyed that we're walking together. Not just to create and enjoy more shared father/son experiences and memories, but also because my relationship with my kids is one of the most vital aspects of my life.

I'd understand, though, if Luke were reluctant to hit the road with me. His mother Chloé and I took both kids trekking in the Himalayas when they were five and seven. It was a disaster. Luke had a virus and a temperature when we arrived in New Delhi but, thinking it was something benign, we continued by road to the Kulu Valley. My daughter Sonia and I went out on the trek with some friends from California while Luke remained in Manali with his mother, who planned to bring him along and join us when he was fully recovered. Three days later a porter hiked into our distant camp at dusk with a note that read, "Come back immediately. Pneumonia!" Naturally I imagined the worst.

By the time we returned, Luke had lost about a quarter of his body weight but had stabilised and appeared to be out of danger. When he gradually regained his strength, I put him on a donkey and we toured Manali to pay our respects and give our thanks to gods, spirits and other saintly presences at a Hindu shrine, a Buddhist temple, a mosque and a Catholic church. The spiritually satisfying two-hour expedition was, both at the time and in retrospect, a momentous and memorable moment for both of us. We've since taken numerous father/son journeys, including an amusing one to discuss the birds and the bees in the Seychelles and on the island of Réunion in the Indian Ocean, but the voyage to India was the most heartrending. And now we're MedTrekking.

Just beyond the skateboarding park-to-be is Marepolis, an industrial development that features fenced lots, paved sidewalks, potted palms, planted pine trees, berths for boats, mailboxes, everything really that a seaside business campus might require. Except buildings and people. The French government, the European Union and local municipalities have all backed numerous costly and extensive schemes to renovate and rename some of the outmoded ports on the Med. This one isn't quite afloat.

"The people behind this project will either be local heroes or run out of town," I tell Luke, adding that it costs a fortune to get rid of the old bits and pieces and bring in the new. "But, don't worry, we're almost out of the Toulon harbour and back on the open sea. Look, there's Fort Eguillette built in 1672 to protect local ships from pirates."

We also pass Fort Balaguier, which was constructed in the 17th century to protect the harbour entrance during the reigns of Louis XII, Francois I and Henri IV. Now a naval museum, there's a special exhibition about Napoleon's 1798 Egyptian campaign. We marvel at the gigantic anchor outside the front door, are astounded by the building's four-metre thick walls and admire model ships made by convicts in Toulon prisons. A boat berthed next to the fort has an amusing name: *Laborieux*, or 'Laborious'. A joke, we both hope.

There's a seaside sign in Tamaris, the resort where George Sand wrote some of her novels, that says *Vente à la Ferme*. This usually refers to chicken or cheese that can be purchased directly from a French farmer. But on the Med, this is an invitation to ring a bell that heralds a mussel farmer to board his boat and take us out to his 'farm'. Like dozens of other fish farms in the Lazaret Bay, this one's constructed on stilts and resembles a floating village in Thailand. The 'farmer' simply shrugs when we explain that we've just started hiking and can't carry much of his perishable crop. He smiles wryly when I buy a dozen mussels for, I explain, *la beauté du geste*, or the 'beauty of the gesture'.

Another odd sight in Tamaris is numerous pashas' palaces with minarets and other Arabic influences. These were built, we learn at the Office du Tourisme where I give away the mussels to some touring Danes, by Blaise Marius Michel, the creator of Tamaris at the end of the 19th century. Why? Apparently he was also known as Michel Pacha after a career designing lighthouses in the Ottoman Empire. Who knew?

Beyond Les Sablettes, obviously named after its expansive sandy beach, we tackle the Presqu'île de Saint-Mandrier, the theoretically off-limits peninsula with a *Base Aeronavale* military facility. Luke is bowled over by the scores of trucks and tanks driven by uniformed personnel, a half-submerged submarine heading out to sea, a large docked battleship and the razor-sharp wire atop the fence surrounding the military installation.

Although I'd been forewarned, we ignore the *Propriété Privée* signs and attempt to find a break in the wall to sneak onto the base. But within five minutes two armed military guards appear and insist that we move away from the perimeter.

"*Maintenant!*" Now!

We obey without any hesitation or argument and, after a brief descent to the fishing port of Saint-Mandrier, head back to Les Sablettes. A laidback Tunisian nonchalantly assures us that we can easily ("*Pas de problème!*" he asserts with a smug smile) walk alongside the Med for hours, but within ten minutes we find ourselves on a very stony, mossy and rock-obstructed bit of shore. I should obviously be a little more sceptical about taking directions I get from locals.

I slip and take my second minor MedTrek fall that, yet again, knocks my pedometer towards the sea. As I head down a narrow path of loose rock to retrieve it, there's an old woman, knee-deep in water some 20 feet away, gathering sea urchins. She's filled a burlap bag and, perhaps impressed by my catapult, offers me one.

"Are you in love or drunk?" she asks in a barely comprehensible Provençal accent, her twisted smile revealing two gold teeth just before she scampers like a goat up the trail that laid me out flat.

Luke sits next to me as I cut the prickly sea pear in half and offer him his first taste of the little orange tongues of edible ovaries.

"That tastes like a gummy bear gone sour," he says as he spits out one of the most delightful delicacies to come out of the sea.

"It's an acquired taste," I tell him. "In a few years you'll change your mind."

Then, in complete defiance of my recent promise to the Med gods, we spend 45 minutes climbing a cliff face until, three-quarters of the way up, I realise we can't make it to the top. We carefully retreat.

"We should have heeded the sign we saw when we started this rock walk. It said 'Do not take this path!'" Luke says when we're forced, after an hour's concentrated walking and climbing, to retrace our steps. "I know you think you should walk as close to the sea as possible but this is ridiculous. Let's call it a day."

We run into a Parisian couple waiting at a bus stop and listen to them bitch that the bus is a few minutes late. "We're in the Midi and nothing runs on time," the man complains to his wife. Their penchant for punctuality reflects the uptight North versus relaxed South divide prevalent in many Mediterranean countries, especially France and Italy.

"Well, at least we don't have to worry about bus schedules," I tell Luke as we board the bus back towards our hotel. "And tomorrow we'll be next to the open sea for the whole day."

Not wanting to start our second day together on the wrong feet (sic), I decide to trust the hostess at the Office du Tourisme in Les Sablettes when she insists that "you can walk a long way on this coast in the summer when the water's low, but only a fool would try to go too far at this time of year when the water's up. Take the high road.

"But at any time of year there are remarkable views during the up-and-down stroll next to the Mediterranean and you should try to visit two islands off Le Brusc," she continues. "One is the Ile des Embiez where the Ricard Oceanographic museum, created by Paul Ricard of *pastis* fame, features museums and aquariums."

We follow her advice and walk around the Cap Sicié Peninsula, starting off on a well-marked *sentier littoral* that is quickly transformed into a steep, energetic climb through the conifer-filled Janas forest. As we climb, we're serenaded by rounds of ammunition being shot from ships at sea and artillery on the military base in Saint Mandrier.

The cliff-side walk passes a rock formation known as the Two Brothers and, after a 358-metre climb, we arrive at Nôtre-Dame-du-Mai, a chapel dedicated to Our Lady of the May Tree. There's an annual religious pilgrimage here every September 14 and the church is still littered with various offerings left by visiting pilgrims. But the panoramic view back past Hyères and forward to Marseille outshines the spiritual icons. Everything visible on this sunny winter morning is crisp and well defined, from the one bather on Le Jonquet nudist beach to the warships in the Toulon harbor. After lunch on a patch of grass near the church, we survey the lay of the land and sea by consulting a mosaic orientation map that takes in everything from Tunis and Rome to the Toulon port.

During a steep descent I pepper Luke with some walkabout trail wisdom. I tell him how I always keep the sea on my left and learned from Bogart to urinate and stretch as frequently as possible. I joke that I was so inspired by Jason and the Golden Fleece that I almost named him "Fleece" and point out the "*Dur, Dur*" ("Difficult, Difficult") someone has etched into a rock as we negotiate our way downhill. I show him how I bow to the waves as a form of respect for the sea and insist that this rugged, jagged, rocky, wavy Brittany-like coast is the most dazzling I've yet encountered. "The sunshine on the sea turns the water the colour of Champagne," he says.

"Speaking of alcohol, I read in the local paper this morning that the area's wine producers have just launched a marketing campaign proclaiming that the local rosé produces '*La vie en rose*'."

"Not for you, though," Luke smiled.

Although I have no clue (yet) whether my son might be genetically disposed to the disease of alcoholism, I'm very pleased that he's never seen me drunk, babbling and bewildered. At the end of my drinking days, I was not only a bloated mess but also a potentially lethal weapon that could have verbally or physically gone off around my kids. I like to think that one of the best things I've demonstrated to Luke and Sonia is that life is not over should they have inherited my inability to tolerate alcohol. They've seen that it was possible for me not only to quit drinking but also transform a potentially fatal problem into a foundation for sobriety, sanity, spirituality and serenity. Once that occurs, and it's not quite as simple as I make it sound, alcoholism is like a spring rain compared to almost every other serious illness.

The fishing village of Le Brusc is much further away than it looked from the heights of Nôtre-Dame-du-Mai. To get there, we're mutilated by briar patches during our descent on a badly chosen non-existent trail.

"Why did you lead us into this mess?" I chastise Luke.

"Me? How can you blame me?" he innocently asks. "You chose the way."

"That's because I'm always the one to blame when I'm by myself," I smile. "It's nice to blame someone else for a change."

We don't return to the seaside until the middle of the afternoon, too late to take the ferry to the islands and check out the museum. But there's a relatively straight and smooth seaside walk, punctuated by sandstone rocks pitted by weather and erosion, to Six-Fours-les-Plages.

Our seven-hour, 27-kilometre (16.77 miles) hike breaks Luke's personal record of fourteen miles (22.53 kilometres) for a one-day outing. And the steep and energetic hike dispels any thoughts he might have had about the MedTrek being a mere sandy stroll.

"That's amazing," Luke exclaims, as he looks up and back at Nôtre-Dame-du-Mai. "I can't believe we walked that far."

A teenage kid who charges up and down hills blazing paths through briars for twenty-seven kilometres one day is not too enthused about walking the next.

"Dad, I'm stiff, I can't go on," Luke says as we set out from Six-Fours-les-Plages. "I've never, ever, been this sore. My legs won't move. I'm crippled for life."

I can't interest him in anything. Not the idea of stretching. Not the surfing shops. Not the pebbles being strewn over the beaches by a gigantic piece of earth-moving equipment. Nothing. He displays absolutely no interest in the weekly Wednesday morning market in Sanary-sur-Mer, a town named after Saint Nazaire and whose buildings are coloured various shades of pink and white. Instead, he sits on a bench while I buy some wild boar ham.

Although we're at sea level, Luke just can't get going. Even when we get past the frequently stiff first kilometre of a third day's walk, his pace doesn't pick up. When we wend our way around the Cride point, and pass one comfortable looking-out-to-sea house that advises us to 'Beware of the Chien Lunatique', a long-retired couple stroll by us without taking a breath. I tell Luke that we're hiking less than three kilometres an hour and are going slower than people five times his age. But he's unmoved. And doesn't move.

My objective, at dawn, was to head through Bandol, another picturesque resort on a sheltered bay, towards La Ciotat. But it's obvious that even getting to Bandol will be a challenge. Luke doesn't want to listen when I describe the delights of walking meditation, though I toss out a quote to try to keep him going.

"Thich Nhat Hanh says that 'when we practice walking meditation beautifully, we massage the earth with our feet and plant seeds of joy and happiness with each step.'"

"Dad, that's nonsense," Luke says as he sits down on a park bench facing away from the sea. "The only thing each step gets me is more tired. I'll bet Thich Nhat Hanh never walked 27 kilometres in one day."

As we finally limp into Bandol, past three sandy beaches and groves of flowering yellow mimosas, a gray-haired woman sitting on a seaside bench beckons us.

"Weren't you at the market this morning?" she asks.

She too has walked here from Sanary and, she tells us, frequently hikes with a local club. We chat about the Med ("It's so nice on a sunny day like today when it's still not too warm," she adds), Luke ("You're lucky to get a teenager to walk at all," she says. "In fact, you're lucky to have a teenager.") and the passages beyond Bandol on the *chemin des douaniers*, the generic name given to many coastal trails in France. These seaside tracks, created along the French coasts in the 1790s, were initially patrolled by custom's agents looking for contraband and smugglers and are now part of the country's seaside hiking network.

"I know all the trails around here," she tells me as we near the centre of town. "Maybe I could walk with you for a while."

This is the first knowledgeable hiker I've spoken to on the MedTrek. After chatting for just a few minutes we make plans, without even exchanging names or telephone numbers, to meet at the Bandol bus stop in six days at 9:20am and walk together.

Once she leaves I suggest a side-trip to the little Bendor Island, which has a Provençal village selling arts and crafts, to Luke.

"A coffee and a visit to the Universal Wines and Spirits Exhibition would be the right way to end the three-day hike," I tell him. "You'll appreciate a museum that traces the production of wine and liqueurs in 45 different countries and has a display of some 7000 bottles, decanters and glasses."

But no. It's all over. Luke simply wants me to take him home. The experience reminds me that, when I'm walking with anyone for the first time, I should always encourage them to take the second or third day off.

Luke was a little more reflective about our outing two days later.

"I don't quite understand all of the spiritual implications of your journey, but I'm glad I tightened my laces and showed some support," he told me. "It's a cool way of bonding away from all of the family drama."

I return to the Bandol bus stop six days later and wonder, first, if the mysterious woman will be there and, second, if she's there, whether she's mentally ill. After all, not many women suggest hiking with a man they just met. Luke's so curious that he wants me to call in a report.

When I get to the bus stop, it's pouring and there's no one there. This is easily the worst downpour since I started the hike and it's definitely not walking weather. But then, at 9:23, she appears and, because of the unremitting rainfall, I suggest we take the ferry to Bendor Island for a coffee and a look at the museum.

Once there we pretend to ignore the rain and walk around one of the smallest inhabited islands on the Mediterranean. It can't be more than a kilometre in circumference but both the Provençal shops and wine museum are closed. It's just us, a tiny café and six divers in wetsuits. Everyone has an opinion about the short-term weather forecast. It'll rain through the weekend says one diver. No, there'll be sun in an hour, predicts the barman.

He turns out to be right. The rain stops and the skies start to clear around eleven. We take the return ferry and start hiking on the *chemin des douaniers* towards La Ciotat.

During the morning, the mysterious woman tells me that she first saw Luke and me buying fruit at the Sanary market an hour before she set off on her own walk. Then, quite quickly for a Frenchwoman, she gets personal. Her name's Marie, she's 45, was born in Alsace, moved to Bandol in 1985, and has a physical handicap that keeps her from working. She gets by on a small government pension and, though once a well-paid computer specialist, lives in a small studio with very little money and a limited social life. She doesn't have a phone of any sort, hasn't been in the local casino since 1986 and loves to walk.

"My problem is a combination of rheumatism, lumbago and migraines," she explains as we start out. "I visit a lot of doctors, walk a few times a week, and sometimes just sit on a bench overlooking the beach and watch the water. I think I'd go crazy if I didn't hike."

Marie's a whiz when it comes to local lore. She rattles off and defines the many spots we'll see today, like the Pointe des Trois Fours that got its name from three stone bread ovens. And Fauconniere, named after the local falcons, and Ile Rousse, called that because of its striking red colour. She knows her trails and has even brought enough lunch for two. Obviously either a goddess or a very kind mortal.

I notice almost immediately that we walk slightly slower together than I do by myself, perhaps because Marie stops frequently to point out sights and sites, take photos, remark on the dark green colour of the Med and describe the effect of erosion on the shape of the rocks. She discusses wave action, gets me to look into caves, recites the names of just-blooming flowers, and points out a variety of other natural phenomena, like the strange "sand rug" that runs through a pine forest on a nearby mountain slope. I have to agree that much of what she shows me really is, as she enthuses, "*Beau*", "*Extra*" and/or "*Super*!" How much of this would I have seen by myself, I wonder, as she points to Submarine Roc just off the coast? Would I have noticed that the colour of the rocks has gradually changed from Esterel red to limestone white? She's opened my eyes.

Then Marie tells me about some of her local hiking partners. One woman in her weekly hiking group, she says, fell off a cliff to her death near here a year ago. Another friend slid from the trail on his mountain bike and also died.

"One man, about your age, had a heart attack and succumbed during our walk," she continues, without displaying any emotion. "And my own doctor died when he cut his leg and it became infected. Apparently an animal had urinated on the branch."

This many hiking fatalities are rare on Mount Everest and I wonder if Marie has anything to do with the unsettling statistics. I mention that her intimate knowledge of hiking deaths makes me realise that I'm lucky to be alive at all.

We continue past the Plage Barry, where a plaque commemorates Jacques Cousteau for making a scuba dive here in 1943, into the Athena complex that has an innovative network of bridges and paths to enable hikers to pass without stepping on any private property. Marie tells me the project was jointly "conceived and inaugurated" by property owners and walkers a few years ago. And that this entire area is now a protected zone, though today there's no sign of any hikers, joggers, mountain bikers, or anyone else – dead or alive.

The sun, which Homer said "sees all things and hears all things", comes out as we reach the peak with the three old kilns and look across the bay to La Ciotat, a port distinguished by the Bec de l'Aigle, a rock formation that resembles an eagle's beak. To get there we walk through La Madrague, which features a three-story high vertical boat storage facility, a unique outdoor aquarium and the Tauroentum Museum built on the foundations of a Roman villa.

A massive project to renovate the seafront is definitely running behind schedule, but there are two newsworthy tidbits here. A young boy about eight years old lands a fish, which, though I've seen many fishermen, is the first time on the MedTrek that I actually see anyone catch anything. Then outside Les Lesques a dozen surfers are coasting on some actual whitecaps.

"Well, I guess these are big waves for the Med," sniffs an Australian woman who's watching her French boyfriend surf.

As we edge toward La Ciotat, along a tranquil road that parallels the sea, we cross the official boundary from the Alpes-Maritimes and the Var into Provence and the Bouches de Rhône.

La Ciotat, wilted by an economic downturn that began when the shipbuilding industry took a hit decades ago, lacks any decent hotels and we bus back to Bandol. The driver, when we tell him we'd just walked here, doesn't charge us the fare, and Marie and I agree to meet the next morning and walk again. Then I get a room at the unremarkable Hôtel Ile Rousse in Bandol where I have an extraordinary room service dinner. Butternut squash soup with nut oil, a fresh fish stew and nut-flavored crème brulé. It's too cold to eat on the terrace but I position myself so the light from the full moon, which is reflected on the sea below, spills onto my table.

I figure it's going to be a trouble-free day when the same bus driver takes us back to La Ciotat and again refuses to let us pay for the tickets. Then I unwittingly create some trouble.

"You know, I'm a journalist and accepting freebies is against my code of ethics," I tell the driver. "Please let me pay for the tickets."

"There are no tickets, this is a free bus," the driver quickly replies quite gruffly. "You either ride for free or you have to walk."

"How about letting me give you some money to buy a beer?" I quip.

"Do you really want to walk?" he asks.

As we take a seat Marie asks me what that was all about.

"Why not take things for free if they're offered to you?" she asks. "Are you an idiot?"

"I'm very old school and when I first started out as a journalist it was against my employers' policy to accept anything that could be interpreted as a bribe," I told her. "I once did take a free night in a luxury hotel near the Champs-Elysées in the early 1980s in order to write a review. It was equipped with bullet-proof windows, a fancy Jacuzzi and other amenities. But nothing worked and the breakfast cart was too wide to fit through the door.

"After writing a scathing appraisal for *Business Traveller* that really infuriated the PR and advertising types at both the magazine and the hotel, I came to the personal conclusion that it's better just to spend corporate or personal bucks and write whatever I want, though I'm probably never going to write about accepting a free bus ride."

"Well, I certainly won't tell anyone," said Marie. "No one will ever know that you violated your ethical code on the MedTrek."

The next optimistic sign is a large pile of new clothes that's been dumped just off the road near what remains of the shipbuilding works. There are probably a few thousand dollars worth of abandoned cowboy hats, firemen's garb, T-shirts, pants, uniforms and other goodies. We take a couple of camouflage-coloured T-shirts (so much for my long-standing ethical stance about not accepting free gifts) and are amazed that no one has yet plundered this textile treasure chest. As we turn towards the sea we tell a man with a little truck about our find and presume he'll start a department store because of the tip.

La Ciotat has been an important port since it was called Citharista by the Romans in the fifth century BC and its harbour has been known as the Golfe d'Amour, or the Gulf of Love, since French poet Alphonse de Lamartine bequeathed the name in the 1800s. The former shipbuilding yard, with its gargantuan cranes, is almost as impressive as the Bec de l'Aigle rock formation. The town is also renowned as the location where, in September 1895, the Lumière brothers had the premier of the world's first motion picture. And for the many paintings by Georges Braque when he was here in the 1900s. Although there's a slightly sinister feel to the place, La Ciotat is much more pleasant than most towns in decay.

We head towards the Cap de l'Aigle, walk through the Parc du Mugel, admire the nearby Ile Verte and spend two excruciating hours climbing a mountain of lava covered with a shower of pebbles. The unofficial name of this stuff, a reddish conglomerate of small rocks and sand, is pudding stone. Avoid walking on it if you can because we covered only 4.5 kilometres in two hours.

When we finally reach a decent path beyond the unpretentious and pinkish Nôtre-Dame-de-la-Garde chapel, which was built on a cliff in 1610 and is decorated with *ex-votos* left by sailors and fishermen thanking the Virgin of the Garde for her protection, we're still technically within La Ciotat city limits. We head uphill, steeply uphill, across the limestone range of towering white cliffs called the Canaille (the word comes from the Latin *Canalis Mons*, or mountain of water) until we reach a century-old semaphore with a vertiginous view stretching back to Nôtre-Dame-de-Mai and ahead to the Château d'If, one of the islands off Marseille.

There we encounter a couple who have just walked, and camped out, on the *calanques*, the seaside limestone rocks and coves between Cassis and Marseille formed by rivers during the ice age. They underestimated the effort required to hike through the rough terrain, battle a constant mistral wind and sleep in the cold.

"Take warm clothes, good sleeping bags and a lot of water," they tell us.

Their account makes me happy that, at this time of year, I find a cheap room after each daily hiking segment. It also makes me resolve to get a map of the *calanques* with detailed descriptions of the coastline that one Greek academic refers to with the lovely word *periplooi*.

We walk towards the tip of the Cap Canaille. At 416 metres, this is touted by the local tourism office as the highest seaside cliff in Europe. While enjoying the outstanding view we stumble upon one of those pleasantly eerie hiking scenes that becomes an indelible MedTrek memory.

A couple, oblivious to everything and everyone, is dancing cheek to cheek to music playing from their car radio near the edge of one of the cliffs. Only a few steps further there is a plaque on a cross that reads "*L'amour de nôtre fils Eric le 25 avril 1993.*" Eric, dancing or not, presumably tumbled off the top of the Canaille towards the sea.

"All roads lead to love or death," I tell Marie.

10. Prancing Along the Calanques and Making the Marseille Connection

"Hiking strengthens the legs, increases stamina, invigorates the blood, and soothes the mind. Away from the madness of society, one is freed to observe nature's lessons."
– Chronicles of Tao

Marie and I reach the bustling port of Cassis, the seaside village that gained fame after Frédéric Mistral wrote a poem entitled *Calendal* about it in 1867, on the GR 98-51 hiking trail. This is my first time on the well-known network of blazed national walking paths for any distance since I left Antibes and the much-trod track into town parallels well-tended terraced vineyards that have been yielding grapes since the 12th century.

A young and enthusiastic Irish intern at the Office du Tourisme plies us with brochures about Cassis, reminds us that Mistral also wrote that "Who says he has seen Paris but not Cassis should say he had seen nothing", and gives us detailed maps of the cliffy Massif des Calanques that we'll tackle tomorrow. "You'll be smart to study the map before you set out," she tells us. "People are always getting lost out there and they never take enough water."

One pamphlet about the area's history claims Cassis has existed since 500 BC, when it was settled by the Ligurians, and is now reputed for its wines, walking paths and the Museum of Art and Popular Traditions. There's a footnote indicating that foreign writers who've come to town for inspiration or vacation include Virginia Woolf, who committed suicide, and Henry Miller, who attempted to kill himself.

I began reading Miller in college (it was the 1960s, after all) and now, the second I see his name, I recall the foiled suicide attempt he describes in *Nexus*. He wrote that he took Conason's white pills as he lay naked in his apartment "while the icy winter winds blow in from an open window". A bit later he's surprised to awaken, obviously alive, but admits that "something feels dead within himself, leaving him only with the mind-machine".

Ah, that internal mind-machine that occasionally torments each of us.

The Irish lass amicably suggests that I head to Le Jardin d'Emilie hotel and book into Room 6. "There are only eight rooms and that one has a view on both the sea and the Cap Canaille, as well as a glassed-in bathing area," she says in a convincing I-know-my-way-around-here voice. "You deserve the best room in town after all your walking."

Who could resist?

Marie busses back to Bandol for the night and, after a lingering bath with a view that completely obliterates any suicidal thoughts, I meticulously plot the next day's ramble along the limestone *calanques* – with names like Port-Pin, En-Vau, Morgiou, Sormiou, and Sugiton – that stretch towards Marseille for twenty kilometres as the cormorants fly. Delphyne will be joining us for the day and I want to be well prepared.

The *calanques* are renowned for their white, weathered pinnacles and numerous deep inlets that marry sea, rock and sky. The area, which has its own peculiar microclimate and ecosystem, would definitely remind Odysseus of the "peaked sea-mark" of Ithaca, which Homer describes as "a rocky isle, but good for a boy's training". The climate here, arid and hot even in winter, is just right for vegetation like the few green oaks and wild olive trees standing amid dense clumps of sea lavender, rosemary, sage and juniper bushes. And it suits a population that includes one of Europe's largest lizards; the Montpellier grass snake, which is Europe's longest snake; a few rare Bonelli eagles; and lots of *sangliers*, or wild boar. A favourite for rock climbers and underwater divers, the *calanques* are frequently explored by boat and many Marseillais walk miles into the area to reach their preferred flat rock or pebbled beach.

When the three of us set off the next morning after brief introductions and a quick coffee in the main place in Cassis, we almost immediately run into a mustachioed man attired in a bright blue uniform that looks like it was nicked from the abandoned booty tossed off the truck in La Ciotat. I get the same surreal impression as we watch three-dozen army recruits dramatically rappel down one sheer rock wall into a Zodiac boat. They too, I tell Marie and Delphyne, are definitely wearing purloined uniforms.

"None of these people are whom they appear to be," I insist. "The austere *calanques* with their ferocious winds are known to attract crazies or drive people crazy. Lots of people commit suicide around here and occasionally murderers are judged innocent because they were apparently driven to kill by the wind, an extenuating circumstance that enables them to plead temporary insanity. In fact, a law prohibits access to the massif when the wind speed exceeds 40 kilometres an hour."

The first *calanque* we reach, the boat-jammed Port Miou about 1.5 kilometres from Cassis, is crowded because it's accessible by both boat and car. From there the GR 98b, blazed in 1973, takes us to the Trou Souffleur de Port Pin, or the Blower's Hole of Pine Port which gets part of its name from the Alepo pine trees balancing on the rocks. The Blower's Hole designation is due to waves cascading into an underground cavern that expels air through a vertical passage and creates an array of different sounds depending on the condition of the sea.

"Today the Trou Souffleur de Port Pin sounds like a farting frog," Delphyne says as she imitates the gaseous noise.

"Actually I think it resembles a grunting *sanglier*," Marie counters.

I'm pretty sure that neither of these comparisons would have occurred to me had I been walking alone. Thank Zeus and Athena for providing me with such perceptive companions.

The GR is so well trodden that the rock path both glistens, as though polished with wax and buffed to a blinding sheen, and is extremely slippery. Once the sparkling trail comes to an end, a much more difficult and slippery portion of the GR descends to the Calanque d'En Vau, where an unembellished pinnacle, known as the Finger of God, dominates the indented rocky beach. En Vau, a favourite for rock climbers and swimmers, would have been the ideal hideaway for the Hole in the Wall Gang if Butch Cassidy and the Sundance Kid were outlaws in the south of France. While we enjoy a brunch of *pains aux raisins* on a large rock overlooking the emerald coloured water, a large boat of tourists enters the inlet and the passengers gawk at us as though we're an outlaw gang and the most prominent and interesting feature of their tour.

As we hike up the crevice through irises and violets, I know that Marie finds this terrain, which is often closed to visitors during the summer to reduce the risk of manmade fires, more striking than our hike from Bandol to Cassis. She replaces *"Beau"*, *"Extra"* and *"Super"* with *"Magnifique!"* Equally impressed, Delphyne matches that with an *"Extraordinaire!"*

Except for their use of superlatives, there are few discernible commonalities between cosmopolitan Delphyne and reclusive Marie. But much to my amazement and delight, they seem to hit it off and increasingly bond with each step they take during the daylong stroll. I've frequently seen this type of quick and intimate friendship occur when strangers get together for a hike. Away from the hustle and bustle in their daily lives, or perhaps because they know they may never see each other again, they intimately discuss an array of topics. I can't help but overhear disjointed bits of their conversation.

"Every man I meet wants to destroy a simple friendship by insisting on sex," Marie said.

"One man I went out with wanted me to change my name to Nancy," Delphyne replied.

"I think it's perfectly natural for him to walk around the Mediterranean," Marie said.

"It's a little weird but that's one reason I like him," Delphyne replied.

I'm enchanted with the landscape and frequently walk too far ahead to listen in on their chat. But I overhear snippets of their discussion about the beauty of the *calanques*, the wonders of nature on the sea, the French government's enlightened social policy, their experience with French bureaucracy and their feelings about Mediterranean men. Both women are moderately excited when I announce, with a loud whoop, that I've just reached the 400-kilometre mark on the MedTrek.

"Super!" smiles Marie.

"Extraordinaire!" adds Delphyne. "You really are beginning to make some progress."

The various paths in the *calanques* are designated with different names and colours. We traverse trails called, according to signposts, the American Promontory and Cliff of the Roofs and look onto rock formations designated, obviously because of their shapes, as Camel or Torpedo Boat. Frequently hiking in the shadow of Mont Puget on rocky terrain that resembles a barren lunar landscape, we continually venture down to the water to investigate the different *calanques* and then climb back up to enjoy spectacular belvederes, or vistas, on cliff tops that overlook the expansive Mediterranean. Some crosses mark spots where earlier hikers, including Jerome who was only 19, fell to their death either accidentally or suicidally.

At tea time we take a four-kilometre detour into the Luminy research and educational complex, a science university conceived in 1961 that is spread over seven acres and consists of public research laboratories, 7000 students and 1500 researchers interested mainly in biotech R&D. Delphyne, promising she'll return to join me on the other side of Marseille to explore the Camargue, has to head back to Antibes after we stuff ourselves with *palmiers*, a crisp caramelised pastry sometimes called an 'elephant ear' in English.

"I thought I'd be jealous if you met someone else and hiked with her," Delphyne told me while we sought a taxi back to Cassis. "But Marie is so genuine, friendly and harmless that I'm actually comforted knowing that she's with you."

Marie and I set out from Port Morgiou just after sunrise the next morning and start the day with a strenuous uphill hike.

I study the map and am surprised that there's no sign indicating the location of the submerged Grotto Cosquer, an underwater cave discovered near Cap Morgiou in 1991 that contains a wealth of paintings dating back to the Upper Paleolithic era over 20,000 years ago when the sea level was much lower than it is now. Remarkably, not even a plaque indicates its whereabouts some 37 metres beneath sea level where it can be entered through a 175-metre long tunnel. There is a scent, though, of pollution entering the sea that might originate at the nearby Baumettes prison. And they're refitting the cabanas at the Sormiou *calanque*, which the Michelin says is "considered by the local Marseille population to be the best of all the *calanques*".

The rock paths in Callelonque once again have a polished twinkle and signal a return to civilisation that is further demonstrated by a seaside restaurant with tablecloths and silverware. We picnic near the end of the GR in Port Madrague, pass a gay nudist beach, watch kids jumping off rocks into the crashing sea, and stop to enjoy a view of the Château d'If of *The Count of Monte Cristo* fame. Then we near Marseille, a city given a rare three-star rating by the Michelin green guide.

I realise that I've been walking with other people – good people, but people nonetheless – during the past seven days. Right now I'd rather be clambering over the rocks, gazing into the glimmering water, investigating the Ile de Riou and entering the mythical city of Marseille by myself.

I mention to Marie, who'd planned to return home at the end of the day, that I look forward to hiking alone.

"There's something I like about the liberating feeling of being by myself with nobody to slow me down if I'm in the mood to walk and nobody to prod me on if I feel like stopping," I told her. "And I'm always surprised by the ideas and fantasies that brew in my mind. I have the craziest thoughts, which is one of the reasons I never listen to music when I hike. The other day I was absolutely certain that I would save someone from drowning and was even a little disappointed when, at dusk, I still hadn't saved anyone."

"But isn't it lonely and depressing?" she asks. "I prefer going out in groups, which often number as many as 40. The more the merrier."

"I like hiking with other people in short stretches, but when I'm with a bunch of people, in places like the Himalayas, I always tend to get up early and leave before the other hikers," I reply. "I find it enjoyable and enlightening to walk alone, like a Sufi marching the length of India. I might go crazy but I rarely feel lonely, desolate, panicked, depressed or in mortal danger when I'm by myself. But I'm sure that, like Odysseus, I won't always enjoy being by myself on the MedTrek."

I turn to a page in *The Odyssey* and translate a line into French: "I find relief sometimes from loss and sorrow; but when night comes and all the world's abed I lie in mine alone, my heart thudding, while bitter thoughts and fears crowd on my grief."

"That's likely to be me at some point during my little walk," I tell Marie. "Everybody encounters fear and depression at one time or another."

"That's one reason I walk," she replies. "To leave my depression at home and overcome my fears."

Marie, who still hasn't given me her last name or address, catches a bus back to Bandol when we reach the edge of town.

"Thanks so much for accompanying me," I say as I kiss her three times on each cheek and immediately, a bit to my surprise, feel a tinge of regret about our imminent separation. "You made the whole hike a lot more fun and I'm really going to miss you. If you ever do get a telephone please send me the number."

She quickly turns away hiding, I fear, a tear.

We never do meet up again. And, though right now I look forward to strolling solo, I find myself frequently reminiscing about the totally random manner in which Marie hooked up with me. The way that she unabashedly invited herself along was impressive, especially for someone who communicated so little that she didn't even have a telephone in her small apartment. In addition, her illuminating knowledge of trails and various sites vastly increased my appreciation of the area. She was also walking proof that even if a woman is considered physically disabled by the French government, she can still meander around the Med.

It would be a delight to find a Marie in every locality who would volunteer to hike with me for a day or two while vividly describing her neighbourhood.

Marseille, the city the Michelin guide calls "the oldest of the great French cities", looks particularly inviting and, well, m*agnifique* if not *extraordinaire*! As

I walk past Pointe Rouge and La Plage, I have the odd feeling that I'm in San Francisco. The low houses with bay windows, some stately 19th century villas, the rolling hills, the turbulent surf crashing over the ramparts, the cold wind, the Alcatraz-like islands in the bay, some wood sculptures and even the fishing boats and shops selling tackle seem very Californian. I'm almost convinced I'm in the US as I walk on the President J.F. Kennedy Corniche.

Wherever I might be, the approach to town is soothing, not shocking and severe like the walk into Toulon. There are green parks, sandy beaches, roller bladers, surfers, kayakers and lovely little inlets. There's even a mobile aquarium featuring a 'Dangerous Live Sharks' exhibit at the Prado Plage near a garish reproduction of Michelangelo's *David*. I pass the Marseille swimming complex, where I've swum in competitions, and walk by restaurants like Peron and Fonfon in the Vallon des Auffes, where I've feasted on lobster or bouillabaisse after meets. This time, though, I ignore the mouth-watering menus.

The calm beachfront appearance is certainly contrary to the malicious reputation that Marseille has had for much of its 2600-years existence, from its days as Massalia to its post-*French Connection* cinematic fame. Although amused when I pass a bus stop called "Counterfeit", the world of museums, theatre and music in Marseille is so prevalent that the city should be regarded as a cultural centre rather than a crime capital.

The gilded statue of the Virgin at Nôtre-Dame-de-la-Garde, the basilica that towers over the city on a limestone hilltop perch, keeps me in her site as I wander through town. But the Historical Museum at the Centre Bourse, which traces the city's Greek past, is closed "for an indeterminate amount of time" because of a fire. It's too windy to take a ferry to the Château d'If so I amuse myself by checking out the fish being sold on the Quai des Belges. After walking through the Garden of Vestiges that has traces of the perimeter of the ancient Greek port, I join some academics for a lunch of lamb sandwiches.

I'd set up the meeting to get an overview of the Mediterranean from the perspective of various scholarly specialists. It's fitting to undertake this appraisal in a multi-ethnic city that, with a population representing every country bordering the Med, is a microcosm of the human spirit around the sea.

"For someone like myself to be in Marseille and recall that my forefathers were here in 600 BC is very moving," says art historian Constantine Christofides, a Greek born in Alexandria, Egypt. "We Greeks are a country of Odysseuses, always pushing out on ships to pursue our own Homeric myths."

Christofides, who has spent over three decades photographing various European and Middle Eastern pilgrimage routes, says "This is where it all started and there's a confederation of knowledge, culture and disciplines everywhere around the sea. Every human being, before dying, should see Marseille as well as the citadel in ancient Mycenae, the Knossos palace in Crete, Saint Sophia in Istanbul, the Pyramids in Egypt, Carthage in Tunisia and Fez in Morocco.

Obviously Odysseus didn't have this opportunity in his day, long before tourism and UNESCO heritage sites got off the ground. But everyone in the Middle Ages was walking and spreading their art and culture in visual forms and, like them, you'll have a lovely walk."

The professors all teach at a university in nearby Aix-en-Provence, a town founded in 122 BC that is now known as a 'city of water and art'. A political and judicial centre under the reign of Louis II in the 1400s, Aix has almost forty major monuments that date from the Roman era and 40,000 university students who give it a youthful air. It's long been associated with impressionist artist Paul Cezanne, who was born there in 1839 and produced 50 different paintings of nearby Mont Sainte-Victoire. His atelier is the most visited tourist site in the city and there's even a marked path around the city streets that follows in Cezanne's footsteps.

The academic consensus is that the South of France was the right place to launch the MedTrek.

"France is the most important European player in the Mediterranean basin today," says David Wilsford, an American political scientist and former president of the Institute for American Universities. "The French 'look south' much more than other European countries and have tried to preserve their cultural and military links by putting money everywhere around the Mediterranean."

Still there's always a shortage of funds, especially when it comes to promoting culture and the environment.

"The problem of cultural resource management is a serious one in France because budgets always restrict the development of sites," explains Padraig Fournier, an Irish-Canadian specialist in Roman heritage. "In addition, there's so much archaeological wealth on the Mediterranean that much of it gets shunted aside."

Fournier doubts that I'll discover the Holy Grail during my walk.

"Most archaeological sites are well preserved and, with 400 archaeologists in Provence alone, you're not likely to stumble upon anything new on the surface," adds Fournier. "But you may still find pieces of ancient amphorae washed onto the beaches."

Preserving culture isn't the only challenge on the Med.

Robert Mantran, a specialist and professor of Islam who spent ten years in Egypt, nine in Turkey and six in Tunisia, puts a contemporary spin on political events.

"Some countries, like Tunisia, have always been in contact with the Occident and are theoretically now too westernised to be thrown into religious turmoil," he says. "Others, like Algeria, have been badly managed since independence and extreme Islamist attitudes have been fuelled by politics, religious fervour and poverty. There's a continual backlash against Western culture, education and dominance. Many Arabs still invoke the Golden Age in the 9th to the 10th centuries when they dominated the Mediterranean and many would like to see a resurgence of that epoch."

No one expects the situation in Algeria to be resolved by the time I get there.

"One of the biggest question marks is whether there will ultimately be a fundamentalist takeover in Algeria," agrees Wilsford. "No one in Paris has a clue what to do about it because the regime is strong enough to hold on and the opposition is strong enough to keep killing. I wouldn't suggest you walk there."

It takes me two and a half hours to get around and through the old port, still one key hub of life in contemporary Marseille. And the same amount of time to walk along the long stretch of harbour and warehouses that dominate the western half of the city.

Docks of one form or another have always been here despite changes of governments, revolutions, wars and a decline in shipping. But it's hard to tell if some parts of the port are dying, dormant or just being converted. Old warehouses built from stone, brick and cast iron to reduce the risk of fire are being torn down and replaced by contemporary structures like 'Les Docks' and 'Acropolis' with lots of tinted glass. A tall silo owned by Panzoni Pasta has sparkling silver vats to store wine and vegetable oil and a billboard informs me that I'm in the Marseille Europort.

Undisturbed by security guards, I sit on a bench to witness the frenzy associated with shipping on the Med, which links the Atlantic Ocean with the Suez Canal and, beyond that, the Orient. Who can conceivably keep track of all of the cargo ships, like the *Linda Rosa* from Bari and the *Triposa* from Algiers, cranes, trucks and other paraphernalia in the port today? How, I wonder, will containers owned by Yang Ming and Tiphook ever get back to their owners? How odd to see one truck filled with the crushed-into-boxes remains of old automobiles next to another stacked with sparkling new Renault cars. And I'm amazed to learn that one million passengers, and 300,000 vehicles, travel on boats out of Marseille heading mainly to North Africa and Corsica each year.

A few kilometres beyond the Europort is l'Estaque, a town that Cezanne described to Camille Pissaro in 1876 as "like a playing card—red roofs on a blue sea". Pleased to make it from one end of Marseille to the other, I celebrate with a fish burger sold at a takeout stand near a modern fishery with its own private port.

Odysseus never had it this easy finding fast food.

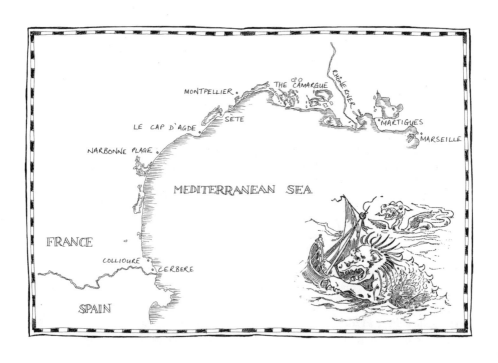

Part Three

Finishing France:
Nudists, Buddhists
and a Fish Called Joel

11. Walking On Forbidden Tracks and Love-Making in the Woods

"You know how Zeus gives all of us in turn good luck and bad luck, being all powerful."
– The Odyssey

I'd been warned that Fos-sur-Mer and the Etang de Berre, both renowned as intimidating hubs of industrial and shipping activity for the French oil and chemical industries, pollute and scar the entire coast immediately after Marseille. Many Cassandra-like doomsayers urged me to prepare for the worst.

"The area west of Marseille is shocking, a real disgrace, a festering pimple on the face of the earth," insisted Michael Boweren, an environmental business consultant in Marseille. "You'll need a gas mask to walk through it."

Fortunately I didn't spring for a gas mask because, in contrast to this gloomy admonition, a surprisingly splendid seaside called 'The Blue Coast' commences just beyond l'Estaque. Granted things perhaps aren't quite as pristine as they were in the early 1900s when Renoir, Braque, Dufy and other artists came here to paint. But when I conduct a scouting mission by train to gauge whether a gas mask or other precautions are actually required, I discover that the initial section of the coast is a comparatively benign blemish as far as earth pimples go.

The railway passes through numerous tunnels as it picturesquely curves along the Med for 15 kilometres from l'Estaque to Carry-le-Rouet and the environment seems to be in decent health. But train riding is not walking, and my seated view proves to be a bit deceptive. Once I return and get going on foot, I quickly ascertain there's no path paralleling the sea and wind up scrambling on a difficult-to-negotiate rock-and-limestone hillside. The surface is so loose that to avoid careening down the steep escarpment I not only walk on the railroad ties but also sprint through a 150-metre tunnel.

On the other side of the tunnel I meet the first dead seagull of the MedTrek. In fact, it's the first seagull that I've ever seen that has obviously been hit by a train. Birds, especially eagles, are omens in *The Odyssey* and this one is almost certainly an ill prophecy. A bit later a sign, which the seagull obviously missed, says '*Train: Danger de Mort!*'. As I confront another situation that Odysseus didn't have to face, I vow not to walk through any more railway tunnels. And next to, not on, the tracks.

Forget being seduced by luxurious villas here. There are some ramshackle bivouacs built on one slope strewn with tons of garbage tossed by the inhabitants towards the sea. Here the crumbling rock surface is also covered with cans, plastic and sewage. Although I don't need a gas mask, I do plan to write a letter about this lamentable state of affairs to the European Union in Brussels to simultaneously encourage them to develop a pan-Mediterranean sanitation program and allocate funds to blaze a path next to the cliff-hanging train track. I might even ask them to create a GR around the entire sea and plan to end my letter with a quote from Thich Nhat Hanh: "The path is your dear friend. She will transmit to you her solidity, and her peace." Yeah, they'll love that. That'll get 'em.

The remains of bushes and trees burnt during a forest fire last summer gradually blacken my Levi's, which are also ripped by a jagged piece of steel that attacks me while I investigate gun mounts atop a camouflaged World War II bunker. There's a faded 'Do Not Walk On The Tracks' sign just before I finally hook up with the more agreeable *chemin des douaniers*.

A dozen people in wetsuits at the Niolin *calanque* are braving a ferocious wind and raging sea to learn how to scuba dive. I leave them to quiche (the verb "quiche" replaces "lunch" when that's what I'm eating) near Mejane almost directly on top of a thunderously loud seaside cauldron. No farting frog noise emitting from this hole. It sounds like a freight train is rolling directly underneath the rock, though the thunderous blast is actually an echo created by smashing subterranean waves.

The Michelin guide describes the port of Carry-le-Rouet, as well as many other little villages on the Blue Coast, as "a fishing village that is now a seaside resort", presumably an indication that the fisherman have disappeared and the tourists have arrived. By the time I get there what was 15 kilometres by train has become, without those distance-cutting tunnels, 26 kilometres on foot.

Ignoring the universal admonition to never eat in a place called 'Mum's' or stay in a hotel called 'Modern', I check into the nondescript Modern Hôtel run by a bland woman that everyone calls *La Mère*. Breakfast after coffee the next morning is a large *pain sportif*, a rounded bread roll filled with nuts and raisins sold in an increasing number of French *boulangeries*, that I buy as I return to the seaside. I compliment the baker and ask how long she figures it will take me to walk to Martigues. Before she has a chance to answer, a Senegalese customer interjects that he knows a *mec*, or guy, from Mali who will take me to Martigues in his *taxi arabe*, a private car that constantly picks up and drops off riders en route, for ten euros.

"It's 20 kilometres from here to there and his fare's a lot less than a metered taxi," he says.

I tell him that I'm walking along the *chemin des douaniers*, like French customs officials of yore, and mention that I'm actually a CIA agent on the lookout for illegal immigrants and terrorists. He may be in France illegally, he may even be a terrorist, but he doesn't seem too worried about my claim to be an American spook. Nobody seems to take US spies seriously anymore.

"You want to go by foot all the way to Martigues? Nobody in the CIA could be that stupid," he laughs. "Why do you think the railway and taxis were invented?"

That's too rhetorical a question for me to answer. So I don't.

Another customer, a fisherman buying a baguette, tells me that I can walk near the sea, which is an unsettled brown colour after a night's rain, through Sausset-les-Pins to Martigues.

"But watch out," he warns. "The industrial developments start there and you'll wish you had a gas mask."

When I reach the 500 kilometre mark on the MedTrek, I'm looking back towards Marseille and beyond Sausset-les-Pins to the alleged land of the gas masks. The map and a GR signpost indicate that I've got about 20 kilometres of somewhat virginal seaside before I encounter the reality or myth of smoke, stacks and smells.

To avoid the possibility of sleeping with a gas mask next to a pollution-spewing factory, I book a room at the Hôtel Paradou in Sausset-les-Pins and leave my backpack at the front desk. Planning to catch a train back here at the end of the day, I continue along the rocky coast to the divine Chapel Sainte-Croix at the end of Cap Couronne. I stop to watch some surfers and wind surfers playing in the waves and begin stretching, elongating, cracking and creaking my back and legs on a large rounded rock. I undertake this type of callisthenic limbering, as well as some push-ups and sit-ups, a few times a day to soothe sore muscles, prevent cramping and get some upper body exercise. When Odysseus was travelling, there obviously weren't any churches on the Med and I'm not sure that push-ups had been invented. Though he was in very good shape, he certainly never mentions working out.

Cap Couronne has a long, sandy and manicured beach and it's here that I encounter the first bare-breasted female sunbather during my mid-winter hike. I'm wearing a heavy red flannel shirt, which both keeps me warm and will be easily spotable by helicopter if I'm injured, and topless bathing seems out of the question, or at least out of season. But there she is.

Stacks of fishnets are drying along the port in Carro, which is 20 kilometres into the day's walk and signals the abrupt end of picturesque ports, topless sunbathing and the Blue Coast. The industrial scene, the one that prompted all those references to gas masks, actually does begin just after there in Lavera, which features a gigantic thermal power station, oil refineries and imposing docks with supertankers pumping their cargo directly into onshore installations. I traipse through an industrial development called Ecopolis, which means "city of habitation", to the Martigues train station.

Despite having to backtrack by train, getting the room at the comparatively paradisiacal Paradou was smarter, or more relaxing anyway, than staying in built-up Martigues. As I board the punctual 17:12 train, I ask the conductor about the quickest way to get across the Canal de Caronte, which connects the Mediterranean to the Etang de Berre, a gigantic lagoon that serves as an oil pipeline terminal and a port for shallow-draught oil tankers.

He tells me to take the train. I tell him I'm walking. He says that it's definitely forbidden to cross the railway bridge by foot. He asks if I have a car. I tell him I'm walking. He says it's also forbidden to walk on the *autoroute* viaduct. That imposing bridge, located a bit further inland than the train trestle, was built in 1972 and has a 300-metre span about 50 metres above the water.

"The only way to walk is to go into Martigues and cross over the drawbridge that lets tankers into and out of the Etang de Berre," he says. "After the bridge, walk across l'Ile Brescon, turn left and you'll return to the sea. It's quite a distance."

That's tomorrow's problem and I'm not particularly concerned with it when, around 7pm, I reach my room and upon entering it am greeted by an extraordinary rainbow, which the Greeks considered to be the bridge between heaven and earth, settling over the sea. The multihued arc of light above the town's sailboat-filled port is so close that I can touch it, so well defined that I can't see 'through' it. A favorable omen after a day that began with a *taxi arabe* and ended with a French train.

The next morning I return by train to the Martigues station, walk to the end of the platform and imagine myself deftly sprinting on the tracks across the bridge to the other side of the canal. But, now carrying my heavy pack, that's pure hiker fantasy. I'd probably be arrested and put in a straightjacket.

The only alternative is, as the conductor suggested, to walk into Martigues, cross the canal drawbridge and hike back to a spot that's less than half a kilometre away from me as the train rolls. This option, which will take me about two hours, is an apt definition of 'not as the bird flies'.

It would be worse if I had to trek around the entire Etang de Berre. The 60-square mile body of water is surrounded by limestone hills, fed by the Arc and Touloubre rivers, and polluted by the refineries and petrochemical complexes that treat all of the crude oil brought in by tankers, river barges and pipeline. That trip actually might necessitate a gas mask.

"Some of the things that man has done around the Mediterranean, like terracing hillsides to improve agriculture, are actually beneficial," British archaeologist Kevin Walsh told me the other day. "Others, like putting out forest fires, are questionable. But many, like insufficiently planned industrial development, are real black marks. The Etang de Berre, for example, is now void of plant and fish life due to pollution. It's a disaster."

Walsh added that towns beyond Martigues – like Ros, Port-de-Bouc, and Port-Saint-Louis-du-Rhône – "are a conglomeration of storage tanks, chimneys, warehouses, and power lines". The industrial facilities take up such a large space on my map that the Sollac, Atochem, Air Liquide and Esso factories appear to be five times the size of the fishing villages. And things are going to get worse. The local paper has an interview with the head of Shell who says his company is going to invest 20 million euros and encourage more diversified businesses to 'Invest in Provence'. It's probably just luck that, with a quarter of global oil traffic going through the Med, there hasn't yet been a truly calamitous environmental catastrophe. But Walsh cites one study that claims 225 million gallons of oil or fuel are dumped in the sea each year by ships flushing their tanks.

Before I leave the railway station, perhaps encouraged by last night's inspirational rainbow, I ask permission to walk over the bridge. Remarkably, and in bureaucratic France this actually is remarkable, the stationmaster contacts the national railway's communication official in Marseille. Once he learns I'm a journalist on a long 'nature walk' and his colleague verifies my press card and carte de séjour, he surprisingly approves my request. At exactly 10:25am, I calmly stroll across the railway trestle.

Odysseus would have felt that this favour demands some kind of gesture. Once on the other side I followed the Greek's example and "kissed the earth, and lifted up my hands prayed to the nymphs". I didn't look back to see what the stationmaster, who I could feel watching as I took each step, made of my histrionic gesture.

The canal I follow towards the sea goes through Port-de-Bouc, where new apartment buildings are presumably the pay off from the economic renewal prompted by the industrial activity. There's also a nifty conversion of a 12th century tower, part of a fort erected by Vauban in 1664, into a lighthouse.

A record number of flies are buzzing around a record number of mutilated mussels on the seaside, where another canal leads to the much-maligned town of Fos-sur-Mer. Though a cement plant is producing an unhealthy amount of dust, I'm surprised to see tranquil fisherman and tourist barges on the inland waterway.

One fishermen tells me I can, if I traipse through the marshes, get to Port Louis on the Rhône River in 20 kilometres instead of the 25 it takes by road.

Fos, in conjunction with Marseille, is the largest port in France with docks capable of handling oil and liquefied gas, commercial traffic and containers at the Fos Distriport. Perhaps this was the intended destiny of the *fos*, which means pit or hole, which was first excavated by Marius' legions in 102 BC. But it's not a pretty sight and I probably won't bring any MedTourists here. "Once a philosopher, twice a pervert," I say to myself, stealing a phrase generally attributed to Voltaire.

But I do have a memorable encounter. When I get beyond the town I stumble, literally stumble, upon a couple making love on a very small blanket in the marsh. The woman, who's on top, gives me a sly, bemused, and inviting Mona Lisa smile as I stroll by, immediately picking up my pace. She says nothing and the guy underneath is completely oblivious to my presence. Ah, only the French.

As I leave them in the dust, I recall that my wife and I were making love during a hike near Paris 25 years ago when we were similarly interrupted. We both looked up with an "uh oh, you caught us" expression.

"Don't worry, I'm a doctor," said our coitus interrupter. "I've seen it all before."

I'm amused by the confluence of lovers, marshes, pheasants, ducklings and a variety of long-legged birds amidst all of the industrial activity. But it takes me hours to make any progress. The factories are so oversized that distances are difficult to calculate and the kilometres keep mounting on my pedometer.

When I reach one gate at the sprawling Sollac steel plant, the guards offer to have a truck driver take me to Port-Saint-Louis-du-Rhône. I explain I'm walking ("You *want* to go that far by foot?" three guards ask me in unison, making me glad that I didn't mention that I'm walking around the entire sea) and one points to a short cut that traverses the marshes. Direct access to the seaside is restricted by the industrial facilities and docks and my final stretch of the day is along a high-speed road that abuts the Air Liquide, Ascometal and Atochem plants.

I'm a bit less Zennish about all of the local truck traffic and economic prowess by the time I finally reach Port-Saint-Louis, a town at the mouth of the Grand Rhône River. There's a sign indicating that, by road, it's 40 kilometres back to Martigues. Lost in the marsh maze though I was, I clocked only 29 kilometres by foot and am glad to learn, with the Rhône at my feet, that walking isn't always the longest route.

Besides, whether I have to walk double or half the real distance, it was worth discovering that, even in an industrial armpit, "*l'amour, l'amour fait tourner le monde*", or "love, love makes the world go round."

12. Counting Flamingoes in the "Most Romantic" Part of France

"Ornate birds here rested their stretched wings—horned owls, falcons, cormorants—long-tongued beachcombing birds and followers of the sea." — The Odyssey

One of the problems with walking around the Med, or almost any sea, is the rivers, cliffs, lagoons, ports, swamps and canals that frequently force detours either inland or, worse, into the water. Beyond Port Louis are flamingo-filled marshes, a nature reserve called the Domaine de Mazet and a sandy beach at the tip of a *they*, which is the French word for a delta created by siltation.

They, for me anyway, also means dead end. Not only because the mouth of the Rhône River is too broad and deep to ford. But also because it's a 15-kilometre hike upriver before I reach a ferry that crosses the Rhône to the Camargue, a 328-square mile protected botanical and zoological nature reserve and national park on the western bank of the river.

The Camargue is considered, according to the Michelin guide (and who would want to argue with them?), "the most original and romantic region of Provence and possibly of France". One particularly fascinating feature of this alluvial plain is a landscape that constantly changes as Rhône-deposited silt gradually widens the distance between the Camargue and the sea. Just look at the fortified city of Aigues-Mortes, or Dead Water, a one-time maritime centre that was on the Med during its heyday under Louis IX in the 13th century. Today it's five kilometres away from the sea.

The ferry, called the Bac de Barcarin, takes me across the Rhône for free because I'm a pedestrian, though it costs five euros for a car. Yet another advantage of MedTrekking over driving. Floating across the broad brown river, I recall Siddhartha's days as a ferryman and Huck Finn's escapades on the Mississippi. And how the Greeks, when marching on Troy where Odysseus fooled King Priam with the well-known Trojan horse ruse, had to cross the Scamander River without a ferry. According to Homer "much ox-hide armor and helmets were tumbled in the river mud". A short walk and a free ferry ride make this seem like a piece of *gâteau*.

I've purchased detailed maps to get me through the Camargue's maze of marshes, sand banks, dikes, canals, lagoons, salt flats and sea inlets to the town Saintes-Marie-de-la-Mer, which is Europe's Gypsy and nomad capital. Each May 24th over 10,000 Roma arrive here to pay homage to Black Sarah, the black Madonna that is their patron saint. But getting there might take longer than I think.

"Trudging through the Camargue on the seaside will be impossible," the French equivalent of a forest ranger tells me at the ferry dock. "A storm put a big hole in the dike near the Etang de Beauduc in December. There's serious flooding."

I resolve to walk as far as possible. No projection, no expectations.

Six white Camargue horses renowned for their stamina and intelligence, as well as the fact that they're born brown but change colour around the age of five, are feeding in a field near Salin-de-Giraud. Nearby are black Camargue bulls destined to appear in Provençal *corridas* held in bullrings throughout the region. Unaware of their bleak future, the formidable beasts graze amidst an intriguing array of over 300 species of migratory and settled birds, including teals, herons, egrets, gulls, cormorants, larks, flamingoes and tits.

A dike leading along the river to the mouth of the Rhône passes a gigantic mountain of salt at the Salins de Midi. The popular Camargue salt is 'manufactured' when seawater, pumped into the pans to the depth of about a foot, evaporates on the flats between March and October. But this must be the off-season. The only ship docked to pick up and transport salt is the Venus from Kingston, Jamaica.

I drop into the Domaine de la Palissade, a conservation office where I get the lowdown on bird spotting, traversable paths and walking conditions. A ranger tells me that I won't get lost in the vast marshland if I use the Faraman and Beauduc lighthouses as reference points. He also confirms that the unplugged dike will prevent me from making it along the sea.

"You'll wind up walking in circles once you cut inland," he predicts. "The Camargue is a veritable labyrinth."

Due to today's rough sea and cloudy skies, a dozen campers from The Netherlands who've set up tents at the Piemanson beach might feel that they should instead have gone to the blustery North Sea for their winter vacation. The beach is the end of the road for cars and a robust, gusty wind pushes me towards the Faraman lighthouse along a dike that separates the Med from the salt flats. Except for three wet-suited men "fishing" with two-handed rake-like contraptions with wire mesh scoopers that catch shellfish when pulled through the sand, I encounter nothing more than flocks of flying pink flamingos, scurrying rabbits and a few recent horse tracks.

The large-rocked breakwaters are taking a severe beating from the waves today and everything in the Camargue, including the majestic and tall lighthouses, is deserted. There's definitely a breach on the dike that permits a steady flow of water into the Etang de Beauduc and ends my stroll along the seafront.

Delphyne joins me the next day at a flamingo observatory where we learn that, though no one is sure who did the counting, 14,000 adult flamingo pairs thrive in the Camargue. After admiring thirty of the 28,000 flamingos through a telescope, a ranger explains that seagulls are the flamingos' most feared predators and that the cannon blasts in the distance are intended to keep all birds out of the rice paddies.

As we walk down a dusty road to the sea, we're attacked by a vicious band of super gnats. We're not their only prey. It's a three-day weekend in France and the wide, sandy beach is filled with families setting up elaborate campsites that seem to include day care centres for hoards of tiny tots. Little do they know that the gnats have them in their sights.

As we move along the sea, our eyes start playing games. Depth and distance perception, due to the mirror-flat sand and angle of the mid-morning sun, become problematic and it's difficult to tell what's a mirage and what's real. In addition, we walk and walk but seem to get nowhere. There are some landmarks, including another lighthouse and a distant dike, but nothing seems to get any closer. Then, in one of those surreal hiking moments, a sixty-something man with a top hat on marches by us completely naked.

"I think I need to lay down for a while," says Delphyne, now carrying a light pack and wearing low-cut hiking shoes. "I'm seeing things. This can't be happening."

We take a break before continuing on a wide dike crowded with bicyclists, hikers and bird watchers. I'm able, for the first time on the MedTrek, to put my first aid kit to use when a small boy falls off his bike and badly scrapes his knee.

"*Merci beaucoup!*" says his mother to the two of us after we fastidiously clean and carefully bandage her son's wound.

With the marsh to the right and sea to the left, we continue to Saintes-Marie-de-la-Mer and pay homage to the black wooden statue of Saint Sarah in a crypt beneath the local church.

"The Gypsies, thousands of them, parade this statue in the Med each May to give her a ritual cleansing," I tell Delphyne as we light votive candles. "They've been coming here for years but the locals still don't like them much. The Gypsies are always blamed for everything that goes wrong."

Our rooms in the Estelle Hôtel on the other side of town have picture windows looking onto the calm, quiet swamps. As we quietly eat chunks of grilled local bull for dinner, flocks of flamingos fly against the backdrop of the full moon just above our terrace table.

"Homer said that land birds flying from starboard are a lucky augury," Delphyne smiled. "This is a very good sign!"

There's no bridge across the next obstacle, the Petit Rhône River, but it's only a five-kilometre hike upstream to the Bac du Sauvage, or Savage Ferry. During the short crossing, which is free for both hikers and cars, I meet some bicycling Americans. They actually smile with a sense of appreciation and understanding when I mention that my MedTrek may take a decade or more.

The adventurers tell me that their 'BikeAbout the Mediterranean' project, which consists of a team of four riders undertaking a circumnavigation of the sea, has been underway almost a year. They've biked some 8500 kilometres next to the Med and travelled about the same distance on boats, trains and planes.

"Our objective is to bike around the Mediterranean and interactively communicate with kids in the US about the unique aspects of our journey through a website and chat sessions," explains leader Ethan Gelber, who spent two-and-a-half years organising the trip. "We've also given talks to dozens of schools in half a dozen countries. Little kids never ask 'Hey, why are you doing this?' They just get into it. But adults often don't get it."

"Yeah, I can't believe the reactions I get when I mention the MedTrek to people my age," I tell the twenty-something Gelber, who's kept count of their broken spokes (32), flat tires (34) and olives consumed (2200). "Some are fascinated but most look at me as though I've lost it – or am about to."

Gelber smiles in agreement.

"After all of this cycling," I ask, "is there anything you would have done differently?"

"If I did it again I'd tackle one or two countries at a time, or bicycle a month and take a month off, rather than undertake one continuous trip," Gelber tells me. "Fortunately, unlike your step-by-step trek, we didn't have any desire to spin our wheels on every inch of the seaside."

Although the BikeAbouters avoided Libya and Algeria, their trip went smoothly except for a minor road accident in Cyprus, illness in North Africa and an encounter with a pack of dogs in Italy. The group averaged 80-90 kilometres a day, went 160 kilometres one day and didn't bike at all during twelve days of R&R in Cairo. They took over 2000 photographs and recorded 200 sound files for their information-filled web site.

"What was the most unexpected surprise?" I ask as the ferry approaches the riverbank.

"The way people deal differently with time and space in Mediterranean countries is what impresses me most," replies Gelber, who insists that the shape of the Med resembles a flying duck and that every country has at least one seductive attribute that would encourage him to return. "And I guess I was surprised that we didn't have any serious problems with thieves, perhaps because our clothes smelled too bad to steal and no one guessed that we were carrying thousands of dollars in electronic equipment."

There are probably profound psychological reasons why Gelber and myself choose this type of travel rather than remain content with more traditional tourism.

I'm convinced that some of us are hard-wired to slowly journey over wide distances and almost obsessively seek the unexpected. Maybe mankind's collective genome has evolved to ensure that there are always some adventurous travellers around to explore the planet. Or maybe we've become this way because of some childhood experience. Who knows? But Gelber and I, not to mention more serious explorers who head to the bowels of Africa or the tip of the world's highest mountains, seem to enjoy tempting fate and meeting the unknown. Perhaps we're practicing the Buddhist doctrine of aimlessness. Or maybe we're incapable of holding down traditional jobs and surviving with only a few weeks off each year.

I certainly don't begrudge the vast number of travellers who, content with a recuperative holiday, solely seek pleasure and a safe vacation. There's absolutely nothing abnormal about a catered stay at an expensive resort, quarantined entirely from the local population and environment, where the toughest decision is whether to order a Mai Tai or a Margarita while lounging on the beach with *The Odyssey* or, more likely, *The Da Vinci Code*.

And it's commendable for anyone to attempt to visit the globe's most interesting natural and manmade sites, even if the main purpose is to tick them off the list. I admire people who embark on a package tour with a 100-sights-you-must-see-before-you-die sort of goal. It's a worthwhile form of relaxation and escape, a melange of convenience and experience.

But can it possibly be totally satisfying to be among the hordes of tourists programmed to be bussed around and swarm over popular destinations like invading army ants? I recall that the Aborigines at Ayer's Rock – that giant monolith in the middle of the Australian outback that is sacred to the local people – refer to tourists who walk all over their natural cathedral as *minga* or ants. And from the air the visitors certainly look like long lines of ants following each other on sugar-coated trails. Because there are more original and enjoyable ways to check things out, I encourage everyone to explore some variations, especially going it alone for a while or volunteering to work on projects that help indigenous communities.

Perhaps hard-core travellers like Gelber and I have a little quiet masochism at the bottom of our souls. Maybe we have a willingness to suffer or unconsciously hope the unknown will cajole, challenge, outwit or even potentially destroy us. Maybe we're simply slightly more audacious *minga*.

As Delphyne and I head downriver through one of the large private Camargue *manades*, or ranches, a crop duster whizzes just a metre or two above our heads. A few minutes later a large truck passes with what looks like enough hay to feed every bull, calf, cow and horse in the park. The 6.5-kilometre walk through rice paddies and marshes is gnat-free and we maintain a take-it-easy gait because a cowboy tells us that it's only a three-and-a-half hour hike to Port Camargue, although it looks like 30 kilometres on the map.

The flat cobalt sea changes to deep gray as the clouds thicken. The wind is also picking up, and the smell of salt blends with the fragrant odour of cow dung to create, and you've got to trust me here, a not wholly unpleasant aroma. Egrets, flamingos and a buzzard soar above us, at least one of them presumably waiting to gorge on the remains of a cow carcass on the side of the road. Delphyne keeps seeing mirages, including the head of the Loch Ness monster that turns out to be a piece of sculpted driftwood emerging from the sand. She says she feels "transcendent" and claims the two of us resemble Adam and Eve.

"I wonder whether Odysseus was ever mistaken for the first man on earth?" I ask her. "I know I won't be."

We wade across the Rhône Vif, another minor tributary winding through the Camargue, and immediately stumble onto scores of sunbathers, all of them naked despite the clouds and most of them same-sex couples. We realise that the mood is exceptionally relaxed when an ice cream man offers us two free Eskimo bars when he doesn't have change for my 20-euro note.

There's a gigantic parking lot paralleling the beach, but the Espiguette Lighthouse in Port Camargue still looks miles away and it's getting late. Delphyne has to return to Antibes and we head to the parking lot to hitch a ride back to Saintes-Marie. Miraculously, the first car that comes our way picks us up. Delphyne says it's due to Zeus and I tell her that it's also probably due to Delphyne.

"Who could resist stopping to pick up Eve?" I ask.

"I don't know when I'll be free to walk again," Delphyne says as the sun sets over the Camargue and she prepares to head home. "But don't forget that I've promised to join you in Libya."

Neither of us realised it that afternoon, but this is a promise that won't be kept. Delphyne has been dating a Frenchman who doesn't quite comprehend her desire to frequently join a male friend, an American at that, on a long hike. He's told her to make a choice between "your wandering Yankee minstrel", which is how he referred to me, and himself, "an established and mature businessman".

Delphyne, apparently as practical as she is spiritual, chose the latter. That's perfectly understandable and I take her rational choice in stride. When it's apparent that my first MedTrek goddess has bitten the dust, I send Delphyne an email thanking her for the time she spent with me and, in retrospect, the wisdom she conveyed.

"Although it grated on me at the time, you really taught me a lesson when you kept repeating that Odysseus wouldn't let a broken pedometer, a forgotten pizza or the rain bother him," I wrote. "You were totally right! It took a while for me to get comfortable with the path and reach a more calm walking state.

"And do you remember that you didn't like me greeting the *clochard* or the French women we ran into on the first day? That taught me that whenever I invite someone to walk with me, I must more consciously take their temperaments into account instead of imposing my own habits, instincts and impressions. Great lessons and I hope the two of you might consider joining me for a stint when I become a Mediterranean tour guide in a couple of decades."

The weather the next morning scares almost everyone else away from the beach, including the gay and lesbian sunbathers, and I walk alone, accompanied only by seagulls and those omnipresent shell fishermen, across wavy whitish brown sand dunes to Port Camargue.

This small town is separated from the Camargue by a too-deep-to-wade-across canal and I have to hike a few kilometres inland to find a bridge. Walking,

I now grudgingly admit, is not only one of the slowest ways to get around the Mediterranean. It's also one of the longest. Delphyne told me the other day that it's three hundred kilometres from Antibes to the Camargue by car, but the same journey has been twice the distance by foot.

Port Camargue is another up-market residential development where every home has its own sailboat or yacht. Even the nearby campgrounds, which are full of trailers with German licence plates, are a notch above the usual. Nearby Le Grau-du-Roi has a recently paved promenade, new seaside hotels and tourist attractions that include an aquarium and a sturdy old lighthouse.

La Grand-Motte has more tourism developments per square whatever than anywhere I've been on the Med but it looks like the town was designed and built by the losers of an architectural contest. The hodgepodge of forms, colours and styles offends my usually tolerant sensibilities. Or maybe I'm bothered by the urban overflow because it contrasts so dramatically with the animal-filled and people-scarce Camargue. Perhaps it's that instructive yin-and-yang effect again. In any event, this is the type of place that leads to the mistaken characterisation that the entire Med coast is lined with cement. And ugly cement at that.

A delivery man, who says he'd seen me hiking earlier in the day, stops to offer me a lift. He's amazed to hear that I've been walking since Antibes, amazed to hear that I think the Camargue and the *calanques* are niftier than many parts of the US, and amazed to hear I think that, at least when I'm walking, France seems as spacious as America.

He says he'll tell his grandkids about my exploit and that they'll tell theirs.

"Everyone will know about the American who thinks France is the biggest country in the world and walked around the Mediterranean to prove it," he laughs.

13. A Revealing Visit to the World's Largest Nudist Colony

"The man was born for trouble." — *The Odyssey*

It's pouring in Grand Travers just beyond La Grand-Motte. Make that deluging. I spend three hours clumsily walking with an umbrella but everything still gets wet—drenched jeans, soaked socks, soggy money, waterlogged pack—and the heavens show no sign of letting up.

There are some immediate benefits to the rain. There's absolutely no one on the beach, the compacted sand makes walking a breeze and there are menacing sounds as the Mother Med crashes against stone breakwaters in Carnon and Palavas, pleasant working class seaside towns near Montpellier without any hideous high rises.

A narrow isthmus between the sea and a string of marshes—known as *etangs*, with enticing names like Etang de Mauguio, Etang de Inghi and, in deference to Odysseus, Etang du Grec—leads into Sète. The flamingo-posing, fish-jumping, egret-squawking swampy atmosphere on my right contrasts dramatically with the bullying, noisy and turbulent sea to my left. The 'marsh and mer' effect is accentuated by barges floating along the Canal du Midi, an innovation dating from the 17th century when Louis XIV attempted to link the Atlantic with the Mediterranean. From my sea level perspective, the boats appear to be floating on land.

It's unclear in Palavas whether it's possible to reach Sète on the seaside. No one in the Maison du Tourisme, where I stop primarily to get out of the rain, seems to be sure. Though one lady, and there's always one, insists *"C'est impossible!"* Not too eager to return to the rainy path, I patiently wait until her colleague makes a telephone call and ascertains that, yes, it's possible to walk on the seaside into Sète.

"On sand too!" enthusiastically and approvingly exclaims the woman who insisted it was *impossible* just a few minutes earlier.

I smile at her and to myself. I'm again amazed that the chances of any French functionary admitting that maybe, just maybe, he or she doesn't know everything about everything are about as slim as me getting a job in this tourism office.

A brochure provides a glowing description of the 11th century Maguelone Cathedral, about five kilometres out of town on the Etang de l'Arnel. The abbey is currently a residence for the working adult handicapped and, after more marsh and mer marching, I arrive in time for a lunch of *salade Niçoise* and a *croque monsieur* to the tune of taped choir music. I spend a relaxing hour enjoying the peaceful place, even taking my shoes and socks off inside the cathedral in an attempt to dry off as the physically challenged tenaciously tackle their chores.

The rain has stopped and back on the sea it's warm enough to remove my still-saturated hiking boots and walk barefoot. An old Frisbee is in my path and I throw it ahead of me, then walk to it, reach down and throw it again. This goes on for two kilometres until Mas des Dunes, where an apartment complex illustrates the frequent lack of originality on the Med when it comes to naming buildings. There's the usual Tahiti, Miami and Sun City.

Frontignan-Plage, of Muscat wine fame and about 700 walking kilometres from Antibes, provides my first view of the 180-metre high Mont Saint-Clair hill that dominates Sète. But the final slog into town is extremely disagreeable. The only way to avoid walking on the fast-paced, truck-filled national road is to jump from gigantic boulder to gigantic boulder on a retaining wall that separates the road from the sea. I avoid looking down to count the bodies of MedTrekkers that may have slipped between the cracks.

Sète, a town with wide canals and a port featuring ferries departing to Tangier and other North African destinations, is known as the *Ile Singulière*, or 'Singular Island', after either a song by Georges Brassens or a poem by Paul Valéry. No one I speak to seems quite sure. My pastel-coloured room at the Grand Hôtel on the Quai de Tassigny looks onto the Canal Royal where some late evening rowers are preparing for an annual competition that involves jousting while standing up on their colourful boats.

Even Odysseus, who was challenged to an athletic contest or two in *The Odyssey*, might not have fared too well in a game that requires such a peculiar mix of balance and skill to avoid a dunking.

In honor of the 700 kilometre mark, I mentally change the spelling of the name of the town from Sète to Sept (seven). I'm not the first person to spell it differently. It was called Mont Setius, then Cette, before it finally became Sète in 1928.

The canal-filled city, an island until siltation linked it to the mainland a few centuries ago, has fourteen bridges and is the entry point to the French Med's best sandy beaches. A sandbar to the west separates the sea from the gigantic Bassin de Thau, where 400 species of sea bass, gray mullet and other fish spawn each summer and return to the sea in the autumn.

The next morning I casually meander along the canals, walk slowly through the fish market, breeze past a bus stop called *Le Chant des Vagues* (The Song of the Waves), and reach Corniche Beach that is, as poeticised in a song by Georges Brassens, gloriously sandy and relatively uncrowded.

During the 12-kilometre sand stroll, I visit Listel where a famous 'sand wine' is produced from grapes cultivated between the sea and the Bassin de Thau. I consider walking around the huge lagoon to Marseillan, home of the Noilly Prat vermouth cellars; Meze, a ground breaker in techniques for protecting the marine environment; and Bouzigues, the region's oyster capital. But I don't want to put on my shoes – the sand underfoot is too invigorating.

Two kilometres after Marseillan-Plage is Le Cap d'Agde's 'nudism obligatory' beach. Although unsure what to do with my pedometer, I find myself walking completely naked with a full backpack and try to stand as erect as possible despite the weight. I decide to spend a night in the gargantuan nudist resort that, like the monastery in Cannes, has its own simple guidelines and, excuse the expression, a unique hang-loose lifestyle.

"It is quite natural and easy to live naked in the sun at the Cap d'Agde naturist centre if you follow the naturist way of life and a few simple rules," explained a brochure. It extols the "carefree shopping in spectacular supermarkets *au naturel*" and "boutiques where you can use the changing room, or try it on where you stand!"

What would Odysseus make of this?

Personally I don't think he would have noticed the nudity the way we do today. And, despite my monastic and meditative nature, I've got to admit that I *do* notice the nudity.

There are dozens of naturist beaches on the Mediterranean (Europeans prefer the word naturism to nudism because this is a back-to-nature activity); sometimes they're called clothing optional communities. But Le Cap d'Agde, the nudist community reputed to have something for everyone (and I mean everyone), is the largest and best known.

It doesn't take me much time to master doing most things without wearing any clothes. As the brochure suggests, I "practice complete nudity in harmony with the other nudists ... behave in an acceptable manner ... maintain law and order and avoid shocking or bothering other people."

Everyone visiting the Naturist Quarter at the sprawling seaside community, where the undressed population soars to 40,000 naked souls in July and August and one of the mottos is "See And Be Seen", is similarly exposed. And there's certainly no shortage of conveniences.

Although clothing boutiques in a nudist colony might seem contradictory, it's easy to shop in the raw. I nakedly and nonchalantly visit X'Style – which sells leather, chains, piercing material and very elevated shoes – and the Green Bazaar, where I buy some nudist-oriented postcards. There are over 50 bars, including one place that bills its piña coladas as "provocatively sensual", and restaurants, ranging from La Loco and Le Yanka to the Waikiki Beach and L'Horizon.

In addition, there are ATM machines, bakeries that sell erotically shaped bread, banks, delicatessens, doctors' offices, a gas station, a pharmacy, a police station and a post office with one entry for the clothed and another for the naked. Want more? There are saunas, supermarkets, a beauty salon called Adam and Eve, and the Ladybel massage parlor where "we speak F-GB-D-NL-I-SP" (French-English-German-Dutch- Italian-Spanish).

There's no shortage of international naturists, each with his own reason for choosing Cap d'Agde. "I've been coming for decades because there is more finesse, a bit more *je ne sais quoi*, to French naturism," a well-tanned Austrian explains while we watch the sunrise during breakfast on the rooftop terrace at the Hôtel Eve and he prepares for another day of overexposure and full disclosure.

"There's nothing like this in the world – it's unique, it's big and there's a lot to do," enthuses Claudine Tartanella, a travel agent from Florida. "Americans like the complete freedom, the lack of regulations, and the fact that everything is open 24 hours a day."

"Naturism is a part of my lifestyle and I haven't been to a beach with a swimming suit on in over thirty years," adds Christian Bezes, who works at the local tourism office. "Nudity brings everyone to the same social level."

I don't have much trouble with utopian concepts like naked freedom and nudist egalitarianism. I agree with William Congreve's remark that "to go naked is the best disguise" but must tell you that the unclothed at Le Cap d'Agde are blessed with good, bad, ugly and very ugly bodies. The place might remind some of the naked and the dead, but I'm pleased to see frequent access ramps for physically disabled people to the 1.6 miles of nude beaches and admire an octogenarian with the balls, and that has to be the right expression, to meander everywhere with his walker.

Everything's geared to nudity – young, old or middle aged. Beach volleyball, bicycling, boating, fishing, jogging, miniature golfing, petanque, ping-pong, roller blading, tennis and yoga are all done nude. People dine with nothing on (it's *de rigueur*, while eating the proverbial naked lunch, to put a towel over your chair) and my room looks onto the pool where a couple is, *bien sûr*, sunbathing nude.

"The whole resort is focused on living completely in the nude," an Irishman named Bruce, who has been coming here for years, tells me during afternoon tea at Le Galion restaurant and beach club. "The experience is much more sensual than sexual."

"No sex?" I ask a visiting thirty-something German woman.

"I think you've been misinformed," she replies as we walk into Cleopatre, a gay and lesbian nightclub "Reserved for Anti Conformists". "What do you think happens when 40,000 naturists get together? Absolutely everything goes on here – and not much of it behind closed doors."

"There's certainly a risqué and unorthodox element at Cap d'Agde, which is part of its image and attraction, but it's probably less than ten percent of the overall population," Bezes tries to convince me during a clothed conversation at his office in town. "Most people come for the natural elements – the constant sun, the clean sea, the groomed sand, the lack of constraints."

There's a pleasantly laid-back atmosphere to life in the nude lane. The employees at the various shops and restaurants, clothed while they work, seem especially relaxed. The woman running the local naturist club says "there is a certain tendency towards naturism in this part of France and we promote naturism ethics", whatever they may be. Oddly, she offers a free T-shirt with membership.

Everyone else endorses the concept.

"I'm working here because naturists are more cool and less stressed than people in the textile world," says Ségolene, the hotel receptionist who wears a tight-fitting, black mini-skirt that seems more provocative than anyone else's total nudity.

Although there are billboards urging visitors to 'Protect Our Naturist Village – It is Unique and a Privilege', most naturists don't boast about the virtues of a nude environment. Everyone here already accepts that premise. Still, there's a sense of anonymous camaraderie and no one complains that it is 'illegal' to wear a swimsuit or use a camera.

As I walk around the resort, I notice that few people close their curtains and that some of the apartments – in complexes called Heliopolis, Port Nature and Port Venus – and commercial outlets are showing their age. At the same time a luxurious 30-villa project has just been completed and the rental agent at Genevieve Naturisme, which claims to be 'The No 1 Naturist Real Estate Agency', suggests reserving a year in advance.

Not that visitors to Le Cap d'Agde just rent villas and apartments. There are also 10,000 campers in tents, trailers, bungalows and chalets – with names like Zeus, Apollo, Neptune and Olympus – at a tree-lined campground. All tasks, from raking the leaves to cleaning the trailer, are performed in the nude and no one seems to mind that there are no curtains on the showers.

Nudism has, of course, been around since the Garden of Eden. The word comes from the Latin *nudus*, while naked is derived from the Old English word *nacod*. References can be found from the Bible ("And they were both naked, the man and his wife, and were not ashamed") to Chaucer ("Nakid as a worm was she") and John Donne ("Full nakedness! All joys are due to thee!").

Greek athletes, who celebrated the gods and goddesses at athletic games, frequently competed nude in wrestling, boxing, footraces and the pentathlon after being rubbed down with olive oil. The winners were often paid with amphorae of olive oil – which back then, often scented with herbs or flowers, was also used as food, soap, fuel and a cure for many illnesses – and frequently asked to pose naked for sculptors. When a statue was completed, the stone effigy was frequently rubbed with sacred olive oil to make it resemble a gleaming god.

Although the visitors, facilities and boutiques in Le Cap d'Agde are more plentiful than ever before, the launch of naturism here began humbly in the 1950s when the campground began attracting Northern Europeans who wanted to strip down in the summer sun. The real growth at Le Cap d'Agde, in both the textiled and non-textiled worlds, began almost forty years ago when the French government made a decision to diversify the local economy due to a decline in the fishing and wine-making industries.

"The inland town of Agde was founded by the Greeks over 2500 years ago, but there's no record whether there were any nudists around at the time," recalls Bezes from the Tourism office. "There was almost nothing on Cap d'Agde in

1970 and the naturist quarter was part of the plan when it was earmarked for development simply because the campground already existed. Now this is the world's largest naturist centre and naturism is a key aspect of the economy."

Naturists visiting the clothed portion of Cap d'Agde will find one of the most animated, Disneylandish man-made ports on the Mediterranean. The winter population of 5000 expands to 160,000 scantily clothed tourists in the summer when crowds flock to the large harbour, bullfight ring, museums, amusement park, golf course and enough boutiques to clothe a small country. There are 17 hotels, 21 resident hotels, 34 rental agencies and almost two hundred different apartment buildings called Bali, Beverley Hills, Jules Verne and Sun Set.

I venture onto the textiled Richelieu beach to determine why not everyone here is a naturist. I approach a topless twenty-something woman who is attired, if that is the correct word, in perhaps the most microscopic string on earth. Why, I ask her, isn't she over in the nudist colony to see and be seen?

"Mon Dieu, not me!" she smiles. "I'm much too self-conscious for that."

At the Plage de Rochelongue I decide, perhaps in reaction to all of this flesh, to leave the sea and head to Lerab Ling, a lamasery in the mountains north of Montpellier that's run by Sogyal Rinpoche, who wrote *The Tibetan Book of Living and Dying*. I've been on retreats here before, including a five-day teaching session by the Dalai Lama, and have always appreciated that Rinpoche, who calls the spiritual journey "the long hard road to the soft red pillow", frequently invites his students to "Walk with me".

When we stroll through the hilltop grounds, I tell Rinpoche that I'm still practising *apranihita* or aimlessness, learning that "the goal is the path, the path is the goal" and mastering the concept that "my worst enemy is my best teacher".

"On my hike I'm practising that sacred Buddhist principle you taught me: good in the beginning, good in the middle, good at the end," I say, repeating phrases that I'd stolen from his lectures. "When I eat, I eat; when I sleep, I sleep; when I walk, I walk. And I'm about to write magazine stories about the monastery and the nudist colony."

"Maybe you'll become so enlightened during your walk that you won't even want to write about the exploit," giggles Rinpoche, who snickers just like the Dalai Lama when he thinks he's told a joke. "Maybe you won't even have to walk as far as you plan to! Maybe you are the path and the goal!"

"Who knows?" I reply. "But the walk is already beginning to increase my sense of inner peace, clarity and serenity. I've had a chance to walk with my son, as well as some strangers, and I'm rereading every word ever created by Homer, his peers, his imitators and his many admirers, including Shakespeare, Tennyson and James Joyce."

Rinpoche looks at me with the bemused smile that many all-knowing masters have perfected when they encounter a well-meaning novice.

"Like any project, your MedTrek will go well with the right motivation, the attitude of non-grasping and dedication," he says. "The most important thing on any path is patience, endurance and compassion. Be disciplined, be confident, be generous. Leave your garbage behind. And don't forget to meditate. Every day you meditate is a day that generally goes much smoother than one when you don't."

"Anything else?" I ask.

"You may not understand the sun but it shines on you," he says, massaging his round Buddha belly. "Tomorrow will not be like today."

"And I should probably consider that gem of wisdom from Lao Tsu!" I say as I prepare to head back down to the sea the next day. "The real sage, and that would be you Rinpoche, knows without travelling."

"Om sweet om," replies the master.

"Home sweet home," I laughingly respond.

14. "Very Dangerous Path—Entry Strictly Prohibited to the Public"

"We who have two legs can easily practice walking meditation." — Thich Nhat Hanh, The *Long Road Turns To Joy*

Logistics promise to be a challenge after I cross from Grau d'Agde to the other side of the Herault River on a small passenger-only motorboat known as a *passeur*. Paul, the ferryman, charges me one euro for the trip. A remarkable deal!

"There are many more rivers but not a lot of *passeurs* working at this time of year," Paul warns me. "You may have to get wet."

Storm clouds, a drizzle and a rousing wind make the recent walk under the nudist camp sun seem like more than a few kilometres, and a few days, ago. Are they still naked back there, I wonder? Do nudists bother carrying umbrellas in the rain? I have absolutely no desire to return and find out. You'll have to do that yourself.

Shortly after the river crossing, there's a gigantic swamp and nobody / nothing resembling a *passeur*. I take my shoes off, change into shorts, put my pack on my head and audaciously step into the water near the spot where the quagmire is fed by sea. If Paul's right, it's better to get wet right away than postpone the inevitable. Submerged up to my chest, I slowly wade across.

On the other side I tramp past campgrounds that, despite ridiculous names like California Plage and Daffy's Cafe, look quite spacious and comfortable. Especially to someone as wet as I. The *corrida* season is approaching and anti-bullfight posters are plastered on every available wall. Other notices proclaim "SOS Dunes" and provide instructions about saving the sand dunes and protecting the environment.

At Portiragnes-Plage, the turbulent waves give the sea a sinister Atlantic Ocean-like appearance. I scramble behind a dune to escape the wind and spray before continuing barefoot to the wide Orb River. There I find a berth for a *passeur* called *Lily's* but, after waiting a Zenlike 15 minutes, it becomes clear that *Lily* isn't around to take me or anyone else across to Valras-Plage.

As the Buddha said, "If someone is standing on one shore and wants to go to the other shore, he has to either use a boat or swim across. He cannot just wish, 'Oh, other shore, please come over here for me to step across!'" So I hitch a ride with a trolling fishing boat to avoid walking six kilometres upriver to the nearest bridge – and another six back down to the sea – and gladly hand over a few euros *"pour une bière"*.

Valras has a wide paved promenade and lodging options for visitors in every economic bracket. But even in winter it's too crowded for my tastes. I speed walk to another river, the Aude, and trudge two kilometres up the riverbank to a bridge, where dozens of cars are parked while their owners try to snag fish. After reaching Grau de Vendres, I meander through the Etang de Pissevaches, which

I translate as the Marsh of the Pissing Cows, and follow a route de vin through a swampy Camargue-like bog with horses, bulls, frogs, wind-blown cane and towering bamboo.

There are few cars but every driver seems to be staring directly at me. Walking nude through Cap d'Agde, I attributed similar stares to the white mark left by my swimming suit. Today I surmise that people think it odd to see someone strolling in the middle of nowhere with storm clouds circling above and the sky darkening.

After negotiating the Marsh of the Pissing Cows, I reach Saint Pierre-sur-Mer and follow a long promenade into Narbonne-Plage. There are no open hotels, no buses running and I attempt to hitch a ride in the rainy dark. Remarkably, a car driven by a single woman picks me up.

"Why'd you stop for me?" I ask as we traverse the Clape mountain range to Narbonne.

"I'm a hiker and I can tell another hiker when I see one, even in the dark," she says. "You would have done the same thing for me. How far did you walk today?"

"Actually, I set a one-day MedTrekking record of 41.5 kilometres and have had a daily average of 38.66 kilometres for the past three hiking days," I reply, knowing that another hiker would appreciate such detail. "I'm on a fairly long walk and am going longer distances each day because I'm in shape, the coast is flat and the days are getting a little longer. It should take me four or five more days to reach the Spanish border."

It's so dark on the rural road that during our 20-minute drive I don't get a very good look at my saviour. I do learn, as we chat and I tell her about the MedTrek, that she's left her five kids at the coast and is picking up her husband, who's been working in Toulouse, at the Narbonne train station. She tells me that they've recently hiked *en famille* throughout southwestern France and loved the walks in the Pyrenees around Pau and Tarbes. She asks me to go into all kinds of detail about what I've got in my pack, how heavy it is and how I plan each day's outing.

"Your walk sounds absolutely delicious and, quite frankly, if I didn't have a husband and five kids, I'd invite myself along for a few days," she says when she drops me off at the train station under a streetlamp.

I finally get a good look at her and she resembles, though maybe it's just the lips and the dark hair, Angelina Jolie. And Angelina Jolie, I immediately think, looks like one of those angelic Greek maidens wearing a long loose-fitting tunic, or *peplos*, as she hovers near the banquet table to pour wine for Odysseus.

"Don't forget to have fun!" she smiles as I shut the car door.

"Ah, what a day for me, dear gods!" I say to myself, quoting Homer, the next morning as I set out on a well-defined walking lane painted on the tarmac promenade in Narbonne Plage. The skies are cloudy and gray and it looks, feels and sounds, as frogs croak madly and birds chirp excessively, like rain. But after six kilometres the sun is out.

In Gruissan Plage I get the usual array of conflicting advice about the state of the coast when I stop for coffee before buying some bread, sardines and bananas for lunch. The coffee maker says that a few kilometres from here there's a shallow sandbar in the sea that will enable me to wade across to Grau de la Vieille Nouvelle. The sardine seller insists that this passageway was 'desanded' during the December storm, the same one that took out the dike in the Camargue, and tells me that I'll have to walk around a gigantic lagoon, adding about ten kilometres to the day's walk. I'll know who's right in a couple of hours.

When I enter a vegetable store to get some fruit, I'm in line behind a teenage boy who picks up a not-quite-ripe peach, squeezes it and sniffs it.

"*Ne touchez pas!* Don't touch the merchandise!" the shopkeeper screams as she abruptly snatches the peach and puts it on the scale. "If you touch it, you buy it."

The poor kid, who can't speak French and turns out to be Dutch, looks so bewildered and embarrassed that I feel compelled to intercede.

"*Traitez pas vos clients comme des cochons,*" I tell the screeching femme as I hand over a few coins to pay for the kid's peach. "*Votre futur dépend d'eux.*"

"I'm sorry about that," I say to the young man as I hand him the apparently damaged piece of fruit. "French *commerçantes* can occasionally be a little overdramatic."

"What did you say to her?" he asks me in English.

"Don't treat your clients like pigs because the future of your business depends on them," I reply as I leave the store without buying anything for myself.

I pass piles of harvested salt on the way to l'Ayrolle where, now 800 kilometres from Antibes, I celebrate by practising what Thich Nhat Hanh suggests: walk like you're giving the earth a massage, always stroll with a smile on your lips, be conscious of your breathing and enjoy walking with no particular aim or destination.

"Walking meditation helps us regain our sovereignty, our liberty as a human being," the monk had explained to Bogart and me. "We walk with grace and dignity, like an emperor, like a lion. Each step is life."

At one point I keep my eyes closed and let the soles of my feet concentrate on the consistency of the undulating sand. When I open my eyes after about ninety seconds, I spot a light bulb on the beach.

"Another washed up idea," I say to myself.

Rather than take the long trek around the lagoon, I wrap my pack in a discarded plastic sack and rotting inner tube, change into a swimming suit and hike into the sea. Inching across the sandbar, I imagine that the crews of dozens of tankers moored offshore, waiting to load or discharge cargo in Port-La-Nouvelle, all have their binoculars on me during the crossing to ensure a quick rescue should I hit a deep spot. But the coffee maker was right and the water never gets above my waist.

Port-La-Nouvelle is a miniature version of Fos-sur-Mer and it's a few kilometres walk up the channel and around some gasoline storage tanks to the closest bridge. Then I climb over Cap Leucate, the first hill-like mound I've seen since Sète, and reach Leucate Plage. The German campers here have parked their RVs in a circle, just like the wagon trains in the old West, and seem prepared for an attack, or perhaps are buffering themselves from the constant wind. I wave to the 'sentry' before continuing down the coast where I encounter another nudist colony.

This naturist resort consists of buildings named after Eden and Aphrodite, the Greek goddess of love and sexuality. The nudists aren't deterred by the cool morning, though there are some "No Photos" signs depicted by a camera with a red diagonal line through it.

A municipal employee I meet at a café in deserted Port Leucate says the population here reaches 60,000 in July and August.

"We get a lot of money from all the infrastructure that's been created for those two months," he said, pointing out the new Peugeot he's driving. "But we destroyed nature to do it. Don't miss the Lydia, a beached cruise ship that's in the water, before you get to Port-Bacares."

Does it make sense to devastate nature to create a tourist-based economy for two months of the year? Personally, I could do without it. After all, wealth has always been overrated. Odysseus knew its limitations and certainly valued life, home and friendship more than money or possessions.

"How gladly I should live one-third as rich to have my friends back safe at home!" said Lord Menelaos.

Throughout *The Odyssey*, gods and mortals consider it normal to spread the wealth rather than hoard it. When Alkinoös invites Odysseus to remain in his kingdom he promises "A home, lands, riches you should have from me if you could be content here." And Zeus says "Let these men take him to their hearts in honour and berth him in a ship, and send him home, with gifts of garments, gold and bronze."

But Odysseus certainly knew that money wasn't the answer.

"Where shall a man find sweetness to surpass his own home and his parents?" he asks. "In far lands he shall not, though he find a house of gold."

At the same time, he wasn't stupid enough to refuse the many offers of wealth. "Better by far that I return with some largesse of wealth about me," he admitted. "I shall be thought more worthy of love and courtesy by every man who greets me home in Ithaka."

Saint-Marie Plage inaugurates a region that, if not quite Spain, has signs in Spanish with easily recognisable words like *bodega*, *tapas*, *sangria*, *cervesas*, *mar y sol*, and *playa*. This is the Pyrénées-Orientales department, also known as French Catalonia because it was part of Spain until 1659. The steep Pyrenees and rugged Spanish coast will be a striking change of pace after walking on sand for over 360 kilometres.

I see two old men (and old, to me at my age, is someone over 90) driving a blue Cadillac with American flags on the hood in Canet-Plage and feel like I could be someplace in south Florida.

There's a reconstruction of traditional thatched fishermen's cabanas on the Etang de Canet that, a very animated woman tells me, "is an attempt to create a fishermen's village as an example of the Catalan Maritime culture". The ten huts contain equipment still used to fish the marsh to catch eels, carp, crab and a fish called joel that is only 6-8 centimetres in length. There are also 1375 species of fauna, including 300 types of birds, and 742 species of flora.

Nudist camps, Buddhist retreats and a tiny fish named after me, or before me. Did Odysseus encounter these things during his adventure?

Just beyond Saint-Cyprien-Plage, another built-for-tourism town with 2.5 kilometres of seafront promenade, I decide not to try my sandbar wading technique when I get to Le Tech river. Instead I walk through the swamps of the Mas Larrieu nature reserve on a cane-shaded path to the accompaniment of a splendid suite orchestrated by a variety of birds.

After picking some peaches, I climb up to a bridge and figure that I've just gone from low Tech to high Tech. As usual, I've accumulated some plastic and garbage to dispose of. Sometimes, when I think about the reasons for the MedTrek, I recall the opening line to Edward Albee's *The Zoo* and simply want to cry out "I've been picking up garbage on the Med, I've been picking up garbage on the Med." But whenever I try out the line people look stupefied.

Argeles-Plage, which features another long promenade with numerous beach huts offering swimming lessons, is the closest thing to a party town since Saint-Tropez. I realise that I'm entering another world, or another part of this world, when I have a Moroccan salad and sweet tea at La Casablanca restaurant.

Beyond Argeles is an orientation table that illustrates the GR that cuts from Banyuls-sur-Mer across the Pyrenees. This was the path taken by many Europeans—including Hannah Arendt, Marc Chagall and Thomas Mann—to escape the Gestapo and Hitler during World War II.

As I continue on a rocky path, a seagull poops on my head, a MedTrek first after almost 900 kilometres, before I make my last mistake in France when I completely ignore a sign dated April 1997 that says 'Very Dangerous Path – Entry Strictly Prohibited to the Public'. Fifteen minutes later, a bridge is out and I swim across the channel, one hand holding my pack on my head as the other strokes vigorously. I'm slightly comforted, as I struggle to pull myself up the rocks, that my passport, money and credit cards are carefully packed in plastic bags. But it's not just the lack of a bridge that makes entry prohibited. This is military property and the training terrain includes a James Bond-like cable course that soldiers use to cascade down into the sea. Braced for an attack, I'm relieved when I scamper over the rocks and arrive in Collioure unscathed.

My last hotel room in France looks onto the Pyrenees, specifically Fort Saint

Elne at the top of a peak. The receptionist at the Office du Tourisme doesn't think it's possible to walk on the seaside to the Spanish border but, in true MedTrek fashion, I ignore her.

Wisteria-filled Collioure, one of the coziest towns on the French Mediterranean coast, gets up early and at daybreak there are swimmers in the water and boats with divers heading out to the crystal clear-watered coves in its two bays. The cypress trees, brightly painted fishing boats, dominant castle and colourful houses in the Catalan village haven't changed too much since they attracted Matisse, Picasso, Dufy, Derain and other artists in the early 20th century.

As I set off, I practice chanting in Spanish. There's a single house on a cliff, with some lovely saxophone music being played by a naked man on his terrace, just before the well-worn sea paths reach Port-Vendres pass. As I enter the fish-smelling port a workman says to me "Good day, I'm scraping off old paint!" I reply "Good day, I'm walking to Spain."

"C'est bien ça," he says. "Vaya con Dios."

From the lighthouse at the tip of Bear Cape is an extraordinary view back towards Cape Leucate and ahead to Cape Cerbère. Green vineyards and flowering yellow cacti gradually replace the marshes and sand.

Although I'm still in France, the area from Canet to the border is considered the northern flank of Catalonia and there are inviting isolated coves along the Abeille, Rederis, Peyrefite, Canadell and Cerbère capes. A trio of European, French and Catalonian flags flying above the city hall in Banyuls-sur-Mer illustrate the confluence of nations and cultures.

A national road takes me into the last French Mediterranean outpost of Cerbère. I head into a cafe for a celebratory Perrier and suggest to the bartender that the town's name is derived from Cerberus, the dog that is the guardian to Hell in Greek mythology. He looks at me like I'm from outer space.

The border post, located at an altitude of 600 metres at the top of the Col des Balitres, looks like an easy climb and, since I'd like to take a few Spanish steps, I march directly up the hill and look into the next country on my itinerary.

At the crest of the Franco-Spanish border I compose my first 'press release' to email to my online friends and followers:

MedTrek MileStone #1 – Col des Balitres, Spain

MedTrek, my ongoing on-foot circumnavigation of the Mediterranean Sea, crossed the border from France into Spain today. This is 923 kilometres, or 11,125,842 steps and 31 walking days, from my starting point in Antibes. Don't think I actually counted each step just because I heard Thich Nhat Hanh remark that "while walking, practice conscious breathing by counting steps. Notice each breath and the number of steps you take as you breathe in and breathe out." No, I let the pedometer do that for me.

As I left France, I asked the one remaining customs official at the half-shuttered, 600-metre elevation frontier post if there is, in this age of European union, still a border between France and Spain.

"There isn't, but there is," the Lao Tsu-like government employee replied, as he offered me a glass of water and wished me well with my Spanish steps.

I told him, border or no border, not to worry.

"The goal is still the path and the path is still the goal," I said, somewhat exuberant after so much walking meditation.

He smiled. Kind of.

Part Four

Starting The Spanish Steps

15. Dedicating The MedTrek And Walking Into A Cow

"And we see across a weary land a straggling road in Spain, up which a lean and foolish knight forever rides in vain." – G.K. Chesterton on Don Quixote

I dedicate the hike along Spain's seaside to Ed Mervosh, a journalist friend who has just died while riding on the subway in New York to his office at *The Economist*. And to the indefatigable Don Quixote. Not that mine is a quixotic quest. But Quixote and his sidekick Sancho Panza, driven by the seductive vision of Dulcinea, certainly embarked on an intriguing odyssey. And Ed, who recently gave me a number of books written by Deng Ming-Dao, was an early enthusiast about, and ardent supporter of, my journey.

"This is what life is all about," he told me before I set out. "Taking time off, finding a mission, walking and indulging in self-examination and self-cultivation. You'll learn how to do nothing and be ready to die at any moment."

This wasn't the first bit of instruction that Ed had given me.

We met in late 1971 at Elaine's, the celebrity-filled bar and restaurant on New York's Upper East Side that's still run by Elaine Kaufman, its hefty founder. I went there almost every night for four months to, get this, 'research' my Columbia School of Journalism master's thesis that profiled the literary salon. Somehow I'd gotten my advisor to accept the concept of a treatise investigating whether 'new journalists' – as Norman Mailer, George Plimpton, Gay Talese, Tom Wolfe, David Halberstam and others were tagged back then – were especially creative just because they frequented Elaine's.

Mervosh was an executive at a multinational bank at the time and we immediately discovered that we both liked to drink to excess, sniff similar amounts of cocaine, incessantly bullshit about life and project about the possibility of careers as new journalists. We continued cavorting in Europe five years later when we both worked as foreign correspondents, though he was based in Brussels and I was in Paris.

I went to his home in Belgium to celebrate Thanksgiving every year and we embarked on numerous inebriated capers during the heyday of *The Paris Metro*. When the magazine went down the tubes, I fled to Ed's place to get away from the French legal heat and we spent a meditative day in Bruges discussing the pitfalls of our profession as new journalists.

"Well, you've still got your health if not your wealth!" he reflected as we took a boat trip on the canals. "And you still know how to write. You're a survivor, you'll be fine."

Today, as I walk in his honour, I recall a hike we once took with our wives and friends in Burgundy. The corkscrewless Mervosh, and another equally enthusiastic reprobate named John Keeney, tried to open a bottle of wine, though I'll never quite understand how or why, by smashing it against a toilet in a family-run hotel near Beaune. I can still hear Ed's cracked hearty laughter when the toilet bowl broke, the room flooded and the owner of the place went utterly berserk.

Since then the two of us trudged the road of sobriety together and met frequently in New York, Paris and the south of France to retell war stories and marvel at our present and future opportunities. There's something especially cosy about having a friend who, over the decades, has shared the journey from extreme drunkenness and debauchery to a semblance of sanity and normal living. And I treasure my memories of our time together.

A student of Lao Tsu, Ed had contemplated the complex but simple phrase "Understanding and being open to all things, you are able to do nothing." Although influenced by Saint Francis of Assisi, I'm not yet capable of doing nothing for very long and I have mixed feelings about death. But if I were to learn that I'll die later today, I'm pretty sure that I'll keep MedTrekking until it's time to go. Unless, by then, I actually am capable of doing nothing.

Incidentally, this wouldn't be the first time I'd been dead, or been thought to be dead. I was doing a story for *Business Week* in Liberia in 1975 about Stephen Tolbert, the country's powerful Minister of Finance who also happened to be President William Tolbert's brother. Stephen Tolbert was killed in a plane crash the day I arrived in Monrovia and, as news of his death gradually leaked abroad, some colleagues at the Associated Press office in Johannesburg mistakenly but understandably got the idea that I was onboard.

Due to a national communications blackout, which was common in an African country in those days when something dramatic occurred, I couldn't be contacted or send a message by telephone or telex. A day or two later, after informing my girlfriend in Cape Town about my presumed demise, my AP buddies tagged a brief notice of my death onto Tolbert's more colourful obituary. It was so short, so incomplete and so poorly written that I immediately composed, and have frequently updated, my own obituary complete with funeral instructions. I'm carrying a copy in my backpack now.

And, for the record, President Tolbert didn't fare too well himself. He was executed following a military coup in 1980 and died after being stabbed 15 times. Ed, in comparison, passed quite peacefully. There's always that.

The Costa Brava, the savage and wild coastline of Spain's Gerona province that gets its name from the steep cliffs and impressive escarpments, will be a physical challenge. Especially after so much flat sand during my first 923 kilometres.

The Pyrenees foothills and Catalan sierras dramatically plunge into the Mediterranean at the border and continue to influence the coastal topography to the south for 250 kilometres. Spain's renowned stretches of sandy beaches, the ones that attract all of the tourists, don't begin until the Tordera River, which officially separates the Costa Brava from the Costa Dorada. There, it's said, the savage coast becomes the gold coast.

Steep steps and bittersweet sweat kick off a countryside march that poetically embodies the Mediterranean. Twisted rocks and a rainbow of intense colours; hillsides covered with cork oak and olive trees; thick clumps of strongly scented rosemary and thyme; sunsets as crimson as the country's wine; sailboats flying and skimming over the sea; weathered windmills; and a history that has included everything from Islamic invaders to fascist dictator Generalissimo Francisco Franco. Not to mention the haphazard construction of some of the worst monuments by contemporary man, if that's what you can call some of Spain's seaside apartment buildings.

Spryly descending from the mountain pass, I follow a cacti-congested seaside path to the bay of Port Bou. Lights in the port, and the outline of a soon-to-be-glowing full moon on the horizon, herald nightfall. I'm not thinking about Mervosh, the Tolberts, my own death or where I'll be tomorrow. I just walk peacefully and contentedly.

A very welcoming receptionist at the Masia hotel treats me like I'm her only client (which I am) and, after introducing herself as Señora Lopez, enthusiastically tells me there's a free parking lot nearby.

"I don't have a car," I said. "I've walked here from France and I'm going to keep walking to Barcelona."

"Why in the world would you want to do that?" she asks as she carefully investigates my American passport. "Are you trying to hide from the authorities? Lose your driving license? Have an argument with your wife? Trying to kill yourself?"

She says all this in a tone of voice that indicates that I'm not the first person with something to hide that has taken refuge in her border town boarding house.

"None of the above," I calmly answer. "I just enjoy wandering aimlessly along the seaside."

"It's not normal to just walk and walk and walk," she says. "I think, especially because you're alone, that a lot of people in Spain might consider you the village idiot. At least they won't try to rob you. They'll be too scared."

Her attitude changes when she learns how far I've come and, after a dinner of fresh squid that she personally prepares for me, she lets me use her private telephone line to check email.

"You're the first American client I've ever let do that," she claims.

I awake at 7am and meditate until the unhurried morning sun gradually moves over France and casts the first rays of light on Spain. Señora Lopez gives me a cup of coffee that's strong enough to put hair on my feet and says the apricot jam that she encourages me to spread on finely browned toast comes from her brother's farm back in the hills.

Beyond Port Bou, sticking close to the sea, I'm thwarted by protruding rocks that I can't get around, under or over. I climb, climb and climb some more up a steep hillside to the winding road which hairpins down Spain's zigzagging northeastern coast. Despite the frigid winter dawn I'm sweating like I've just run a mile across the Sahara at high noon.

The brush-and-cacti-covered mountainside continues until the downhill march through fields of silver-gray olive trees, naked vines and spiky heather to Colera. Ignoring train tracks that enter the town through a tunnel, I arrive in the sleepy village after tumbling down the loose gravel on a steep hillside.

On the other side of town is the Camines de Ronda de l'Alt Emporda or, as a sign abbreviates it, the Cami de Ronda. This superb *camino* through the Alt Emporda, the name given to the area north of the Fluvia and Ter Rivers, was designed and financed by the European Union and the Generalitat of Catalonia, the governing body of this autonomous region of Spain. It's the equivalent of a hiker's yellow brick road and, along with the GR 92 that also parallels the coast, is the best-marked path I've encountered. The well-tended up-and-down seaside route traverses fallow brown fields and passes through the whitewashed villages of Puerto de Llançà and Gerbat.

I stop to shop in Llançà, a pueblo that is so white-on-white that it could be renamed Blanca. In this town, my haphazard Spanish doesn't seem to unnerve anyone. At least not the way my French upset that Gypsy near Cannes. Probably because the Spanish often think, when they hear me speak, that I'm Italian. And Italians are convinced that I'm Spanish. I learned both languages at the same time in the early 1980s and tend to combine them when I speak. It's not always a soothing sound.

But unlike the French, most Spaniards still make a sincere effort to understand me without, so far, criticising my accent or inventive vocabulary. The pastry bakers, cheese sellers, hoteliers and coffee brewers actually seem pleased to see a sweaty T-shirted foreign hiker, no matter how or what he speaks, at this time of year. Their humble and welcoming attitude says, to me anyway, a lot about the mindset of a nation so seemingly relaxed that it makes the French appear even more arrogant and supercilious in comparison.

"Puedo tomar una bottiglia di jugo di arancia, esta formaggio aquí, questo bella jamón y une poco di pane," I say rapidly with a feigned sense of I-know-I'm-saying-it-wrong-but-please-pretend-I'm-saying-it-right attitude.

I got exactly what I asked for, or thought I'd asked for. There wasn't the oh-my-god-who-is-this-imbecile-and-why-should-I-bother-to-help-make-his-life-any-easier look that I often got in France.

The houses in El Port de la Selva are painted with a deep-white lime and explode with sparkles when struck by the sun. A barman tells me that in early June the entire bay will also 'explode with tourists'. He's so exacting about the tourism deluge that I assume he knows what he's talking about when he tells me to follow the GR for three hours to reach the much larger town of Cadaques.

The lighthouse where I lunch on bread, *jamón* and *queso* from a local Catalan farm features an astounding vista back along the rugged coastline and majestic mountains towards France and forward along the equally craggy coastline towards Barcelona. Over my right shoulder are the snow-covered Pyrenees and below is the winter-raging Med.

I'm glad not to be on the water on a day like this because many boats will be wrecked, battered and sunk by Poseidon, the lord of the earth-surrounding sea. He's the one god who really had it in for Odysseus after the wandering warrior blinded his son Polyphemus the Cyclops on the slopes of Mount Etna. Not that Poseidon actually wanted to put an end to Odysseus. "He (Poseidon) does not kill the man; he only buffets him away from home," Zeus explained.

As I munch on my sandwich I recall that Generalissimo Franco, in one of his many inane despotic decrees, created large government-run dairy cooperatives that made small cheese makers and dairy farmers illegal and forced them to go underground, if not completely out of business. But today Spanish cheeses, like the goat *queso* I'm enjoying, are on a par with their French counterparts.

"Another chink in the armour of the French," I say to myself.

The mountain path moves through meadows full of calmly grazing sheep near the inland ruins of the Monastery of Sant Pere de Rhodes, built by the Benedictines between 979 and 1022 on the side of Mount Verdera. It passes the

10th century Ermita de San Baldiri de Taballera, a romantic ruin near a mountain stream and bathing pool surrounded by blossoming flowers and large oaks.

As John Muir, the American naturalist and one of the world's first true environmentalists, wrote in *A Thousand-Mile Walk to the Gulf* in 1867, "every tree, every flower, every ripple and eddy of this lovely stream seemed solemnly to feel the presence of the great Creator". As he did during his floral pilgrimage, I "lingered in this sanctuary a long time thanking the Lord with all my heart for his goodness in allowing me to enter and enjoy it."

The sea laps dozens of bays and coves like El Culo de Moro ('The Black Ass') and Serena ('Serenity'). I take a refreshing dip in Taballera, washing away the now-constant odor of not-so-sweet sweat, and discover that the large cove creates a remarkably distinct and long-reverberating echo. The sound of my "Ahhh ommm" bounces back as I repeat the mantra.

The GR repeatedly dips down to the sea and back up into the hills, but by late afternoon there's still no sign of Cadaques. New hiking shoes are painfully pinching both my little toes and I stupidly forgot, for the first time, to put a worn pair of tennis shoes in my pack. Two lessons learned: (1) even in Spain do not presume that locals are intimately familiar with distances and (2) always carry a second pair of shoes. Having completely forgotten John Muir and the great Creator, I'm feeling very inadequate when I finally spot some white seaside buildings and pass the Club Med resort and the Mas Duran horse-riding centre on Cape Creus.

I arrive, exhausted, in the enchanting port of Cadaques at dusk. What's exhausted? While shopping I step into some freshly poured cement in an area of the market that is clearly cordoned off to the public by bright yellow plastic tape.

"Are you blind?" one of the workmen asks me sympathetically as he smoothes over my indentations with his trowel. "Have you had a stroke? Do you need help?"

"No, don't worry," I reply, remembering what the fisherwoman in France said to me when I fell. "I'm just drunk and in love."

I'm also worried about the smell of my clothes when I walk into the foyer at the somewhat chic Rocamar hotel. But the reception by the young English-speaking manager is one of the warmest I've had. Once he hears about the MedTrek, he cuts the rate for the room and gives me the best seaside view table in the restaurant.

The next morning, as Homer wrote, "the sun rose on the flawless brimming sea into a sky all brazen–all one brightening for gods immortal and for mortal men on plow lands kind with grain."

With that kind of sunrise, it's easy to understand why Cadaques has been a magnet for artists like Salvador Dalí, the versatile surrealist painter whose birthplace and semi-circular museum and tomb are in nearby Figueras.

Converted from a theatre by the artist in the early 1970s and crowned with egg-shaped sculptures, the museum is a magical mystery tour through holograms, oozing watches and other typical Dalí motifs. The crypt holding the eccentric's remains, inscribed simply 'Salvador Dalí' and '1904-1989', is adorned with his cane, a hat and other personal effects.

Many considered Dalí a commercial genius but an artistic hoax because of his eccentric appearance, indefatigable self-promotion and habit of producing multiple reproductions of his 1500 paintings. But whatever the worth of his prodigious output, Dalí deserves credit for creating a personal trade name and brand long before the thought occurred to many other artists and fashion designers. I'll also always remember that he proudly claimed to be a descendant of the Moors who were responsible for "my love for everything that is gilded and excessive, my passion for luxury".

My buddy Nall, an Alabama-born artist who's lived abroad as long as I have and is one of my pals in the South of France, studied with Dalí for seven years and constantly recalls that the best advice he received from his moustachioed mentor was "Draw from life, draw again and again!"

Dalí's influence is sometimes so evident in Nall's surrealist images, materials (we're talking lots of bones) and picture frames (even more bones) that I've suggested he change his name to Nalí. Watch this space …

"Dalí surprised us every day he was alive and the works here will continue to surprise people long after we're all dead," curator Antonio Pitxot, an artist and director of the Dalí Museum where everything from Dalí T-shirts to Dalí perfume is on sale, told me when I visited. "He deplored any limitations that might be put on individuals."

There aren't many limitations put on me, either by the gods or by myself. Yet I try not to have many unrealistic expectations or projections. I've always bought Lao Tsu's argument that "if you try to cut wood like a master carpenter, you will only hurt your hand." And don't even ask me what happens when I make the mistake of tackling a domestic plumbing problem. Maybe my reluctance, or inability, to engage in the home improvements game is, like golf, another reason I'm on this walk.

My first step of the day is a killer. My constantly squeezed little toes are now squashed bright red blisters that resemble plump about-to-burst cherry tomatoes. I cushion them with toilet paper and resolve to make it a relatively short day. That resolution hardens with every step until I buy some foam rubber 'toe condoms' at a pharmacy. These cushioning protectors fit over my scrunched little digits and reduce the pressure from my shoes and steps. Tip: current state-of-the-art silicon toe protectors, which can be found in most pharmacies, definitely beat wadded toilet paper. I now carry them, as well as similar patches for blisters, on every hike.

The steep hike out of Cadaques continues along the GR with extraordinary hilltop vistas of the Med. When I look back on the seaside town it's 'picture postcard perfect'. I've hated that expression since Richard Nixon once used it to describe the Great Wall of China, but that's what I see. Picture Postcard Perfect Cadaques.

I once, very enjoyably I might add, got back at Richard Nixon for that remark, and some of his other idiocies, when we were both in Yamoussoukro, the administrative capital of the Ivory Coast, in the early 1980s.

Côte d'Ivoire President Félix Houphouët-Boigny was promoting his birthplace and the country's new capital, with avenues wider than those in Paris and a moat around the pretentious presidential palace, with a pro golf tournament to which he invited a few dethroned heads of state. I first spoke to Nixon on the golf course and, as we watched Gary Player take the lead, we amicably discussed how remarkable it was that Houphouët-Boigny had been president since 1960 (he lasted until 1993).

"Some countries know how to keep the right man in office," Nixon snickered after saying hello to Billy Casper, Calvin Peete and Bernhard Langer.

That night we greeted each other at a gala dinner and dance. Quickly bored with watching Nixon stiffly waltz with Madame Houphouët-Boigny, I left the party and told the former president's Ivorian chauffeur that Nixon said I could use his car (you could still get away with a lot in Africa back then if you were white). I had the driver drop me at my hotel and gave him a nice tip before adding, "Take the rest of the night off."

Just for the record, don't blame this on booze because I wasn't drinking at the time. I simply didn't like Richard Nixon.

That's not all that I remember about Yamoussoukro. At dusk each day huge crowds gathered to watch the Nile crocodiles in the presidential moat slowly and methodically pursue, catch and eat live chickens, which didn't have much chance because their feet were bound with string. There was also a lot of buzz about the upcoming construction of a Roman Catholic Church that was, a few years later, christened as the Basilica of Our Lady of Peace of Yamoussoukro. Consecrated by Pope John Paul II in 1990, it's still reputed to be the largest church in the world. And why not? Yamoussoukro was Houphouët-Boigny's birthplace and he didn't want anyone to forget it.

This stretch of the Costa Brava rivals the Great Wall more than it does the Côte d'Ivoire and I try to ignore my toes as I march, daydreaming and fantasising, through the countryside. Then I turn a corner and walk straight into a cow. She's in the middle of the path and bears an uncanny resemblance to Buttercup, the calf my parents gave me as a graduation present from the eighth grade. Proof of reincarnation, I wonder?

Buttercup, or whatever her name is in this lifetime, doesn't seem at all intrigued by our little run in. But she gives me an excuse to stop for a few minutes and wonder if Odysseus, who wore a helmet with "the shining teeth of a white-tusked boar" when he was fighting in Troy, ever encountered a cow. Or what he would do with this one? Eat it? Pet it? Offer it to the gods? Or maybe just concoct a moral tale like *The Lion and the Mouse* or *The Fox and the Grapes*. My own parable, called 'The Cow and the MedTrekker', goes something like this.

A man decides to walk around the Mediterranean Sea. He doesn't want to go fast and he doesn't want to go slow. He just wants to stay close to the water, appreciate nature and go with the flow. He wants to let his mind settle, meditate and take it easy. A day at a time. A step at a time. Smelling the roses, living in the now. He keeps walking and is gradually able to avoid anger, arrogance, anxiety, aggression and other potentially destructive emotions.

But one day he starts thinking too much. About his life, the meaning of success, the limits of wealth, his painful little toes and immortality. All of a sudden, in the middle of a forest next to the sea, he's created his own stress, become distracted and made things very complicated. Without realising it, he forgets he's walking and his head is in a cloudy haze.

He's so distracted that he doesn't even notice a cow in the middle of the path until he runs right into it.

Moral: Look too far ahead and you'll miss what's at your feet.

16. The First 1000 Kilometres and Layers of Life in Ampurias

"Where shall a man find sweetness to surpass his own home and his parents? In far lands he shall not, though he find a house of gold." – The Odyssey

The GR dips into another luscious bay before rejoining the Cami de Ronda to Rosas, which the Greeks called Rhode when they settled here in 600 BC. This part of the coast has seen it all—the Phoenicians, the Carthaginians in 300 BC, then the Romans, the Arabs, Charlemagne and the Catalonians. Rosas is now particularly renowned because of El Bulli, which has three Michelin stars and is frequently touted as one of the world's best restaurants. But I'm in no mood for a lingering meal, however good it might be.

My curt and dismissive attitude towards El Bulli obviously says something about me. Twenty years ago I made a point of eating in every three-star restaurant in France, even if it meant a long drive, an overnight trip and wasn't covered by my expense account. I was such a knowledgeable (read arrogant) gourmand and so learned (read obnoxious) an oenophile that I continually talked to excess (read boasted) about my gastronomic exploits. I remember giving a detailed description of one lavish culinary experience (I didn't use the word food, or even cooking, to describe a meal because it was always a culinary experience) to my father and, rather than applauding the extent of my appreciation of the cuisine, he said simply "That's obscene." Offended at the time, I now find myself in partial agreement with him.

That doesn't mean it wouldn't be well worth it for you to drop into Ferran Adrià's restaurant overlooking the Cala Manjoi bay. It was first opened by a German couple in 1961 that chose the name El Bulli because they owned two bulldogs. Now at least one food critic considers it the "most imaginative generator of haute cuisine on the planet" (yes, not just the Mediterranean but the planet) and it would, no doubt, be an extraordinary culinary experience. But dropping in for a bite is not as easy as it sounds. The place is only open from April to September and tables are booked well in advance. Not only is it the wrong season but this type of restaurant also isn't quite the right pace for my *décontracté* MedTrek eating mode.

I have friends, of course, who would simply die to eat here and meet the brilliantly eccentric chef who's created a philosophy, recipes and *menu de dégustation* that propelled haute cuisine into the 21st century.

"Adrià is the Dalí of gastronomy and if you had any sense you'd pitch your tent outside his restaurant and beg him to let you carry out his garbage," one persistent fan insisted, noting that more than 2500 articles have touted the chef's genius and imagination. "He not only invented light froths to replace sauces but has a grasp of molecular gastronomy and has created 20-course meals consisting of mini-sized portions that are a gateway to heaven."

I'll bet he's also pissed off the French.

I remove my shoes to let my swollen toes, now begging for amputation, wallow in the soft sand and soothing seawater. It's remarkable how important, when constant pain impedes walking, two toes become. These irritating tiny snails, which I've mentally converted into cancerous dinosaurs, are no longer my only physical ailment. The soon-to-be-gangrenous digits have altered my stride and created fire-hot hamstrings, sore calves and pulsating cramped muscles.

This won't do. I sit on the beach and try to ignore my tortured toes and hammering hamstrings. I concentrate on releasing the pain by pushing it down my legs, through the throbbing toes and into the wild blue sea. The dinosaurs become snails again and I absorb the moral that one must become aware of one's little toes in order to become more stable. I've overdone it and should stop walking for a few days.

Initially impressed with the quality of the generally upmarket apartment buildings in Rosas, I gradually notice a number of haphazard and unplanned architectural monstrosities that sometimes characterise the Mediterranean coast in Spain. My toes remind me that I shouldn't be too concerned about architectural horrors. They beg me to sit down at an outdoor café and soak them in warm saltwater. That's what I do.

Staring south across the Bay of Rosas the next morning, I briefly contemplate a break but figure the stroll along the fertile low-lying and soil-rich Emporda plain should be tolerable. After three kilometres on the promenade and sandy seaside in Rosas, I hit a canal, cut inland and jump, leapfrog and backtrack through the marshy and wet Aiguamolls Natural Park. A never-ending number of rivers and creeks, from tiny trickles and gurgling streams to flat expanses of rippling greenish water and motionless quags, crisscross the plain.

At the 1000-kilometre MedTrek mark, a potentially momentous milestone, I find myself in a German bakery near a fake Mississippi riverboat parked on a canal in Santa Margarita. And we walked 1000-kilometres for this, my toes ask in unison?

Multilingual signs and international business logos hint at the large number of foreigners living in the high-rise apartments in a hell-on-the-Med development called Empuriabrava. This chaotic mix of yacht-filled canals and indecently cheap housing claims to be the biggest development of its kind on the sea. It's certainly the ugliest suburban blight I've encountered and reinforces the Spanish coast's reputation as a string of overbuilt cement barracks.

I climb a fence to get out of Empuriabrava and am loudly chastised by a beefy German housewife.

"*Was ist los con usted*?" she screams, waving a broomstick at me. "*Hier alles ist privado.*"

"*Das weiß yo, pero ich soy aquí weil yo kann nicht leben ohne usted,*" I said, trying to imitate her mélange of German and Spanish. "*Ich liebe dich.*"

She screamed and ran into the house.

Dark clouds accumulate overhead and I maintain a five-kilometre-per-hour pace on the flat seaside until I arrive at the mouth of the full-flowing Fluvia River. The depth is so difficult to gauge due to the wind, waves and turbulent water that I head inland through duck-filled marshes on a nifty GR that passes canes, cottontails, domestically planted fruit trees and flocks of wild, quacking mallards. I cross the Fluvia on the bridge in Sant Pere Pescador, trespass on an expansive private *finca* or rural estate and return to the sea near the Big Whale campground.

The mad Med is swirling with white caps, the wind freezes my entire body and there's sand in every pore as I approach Ampurias, which the Phoenicians founded as Palaiapolis in the 6th century BC. Later called Emporion, the namesake of the Emporda plain features distinctly layered slices of history. That's because the Greeks also built here, as did Caesar in 49 BC when he created a colony for war veterans. Then the Moors took over the town in the 8th century. Although not nearly as majestic as ruins in Carthage or Crete, frequently invaded Ampurias is an archeologist's delight.

"The strata of civilisation illustrate what happens when there are different tenants during 2500 years," a local guide tells me. "There are the temples that once were filled with altars and statues of the gods, a shrine built to honour Zeus, remains of the agora and a museum filled with archeological finds that bring the past to life."

As I investigate the ruins, I feel like Odysseus must have as he stumbled upon different tribes and settlements during his journey. I'm ready to create my own Trojan horse to befuddle imaginary Trojans and rescue "lovely-haired Helen", the queen of Sparta whose abduction led Agamemnon to launch a thousand ships and cross the Aegean Sea to Troy. Or be tested as Odysseus was on his return to reclaim his wife Penélopê by firing arrows from his old bow through 12 iron axe-helve sockets to prove his identity. Bring 'em on.

Beyond the tourist-chic village of Sant Marti d'Ampurias is L'Escala where I find a truck stop that, for $25, provides me with a suite-sized room and a warm bath. My entire body is stiff as a stick the next morning and, reluctant to get going, I waste time. I buy the *International Herald Tribune* because it contains a 5000-word section I wrote following a visit to Rwanda a few weeks ago. I critically reread every word about the land-locked country's attempted economic, social, political and judicial comeback since the civil war, genocide and economic collapse in 1994.

My articles made it clear that it will take the nation of under 10 million people much more than a single decade to rebound from the cataclysmic and criminal nightmare that resulted in almost one million deaths, displaced about half of the population, led to a collapse of government institutions, and destroyed most banks, schools, hospitals, factories and utilities. I noted that there are still constant indications, from begging amputees on the streets of Kigali to refugee resettlements in the hills, that one of the world's poorest countries will long be haunted by the deathly shadow of ethnic hatred.

But nothing I wrote could adequately convey a horror that may require a few generations to digest. I've been to Rwanda three times since the genocide but am still regularly haunted by a repulsive apparition during my first visit to the Nyamata/Ntarama genocide memorial site, where many corpses were left untouched in a church that had been transformed into a human slaughterhouse.

One naked long-dead woman, her legs spread-eagled after being raped before being whacked to death with a machete, still had a broomstick stuck up her skeletal cunt (there's no reason to be delicate here) and a look of frozen terror on her shrunken, desiccated face. The image will disturb and torment me forever.

I complete *The New York Times* crossword puzzle before limping along the promenade to a Burger King for another coffee. I spend 15 minutes admiring a nifty sculpture of a child sitting on an old Roman wall and drop into a restaurant for a mid-morning plate of *tapas*. Then I stop at the vista point at the Calo Montgo on the rocky promontory that officially separates the Alt Emporda from the Bas Emporda. Why hurry?

The GR wanders away from the sea and I can no longer see the water from the mountaintop and forests. When I finally traverse a long plateau, I ask an elderly woman tending her garden for directions. She points to Torroella de Montgri, a village dominated by a hilltop fortress built by James II in 1294 when the town was a large port at the opening of an estuary.

"You're two kilometres from the coast," she says as she directs me to a hillside path to L'Estartit. "That's the end of the northern rocky coastline and the beginning of the long beach to Barcelona."

There's something about her, more than just her appearance, which reminds me of my grandmother. It's a long way from North Dakota, where Gramma lived, to the Costa Brava. But I like to think that she's still keeping an eye on me. Even though she's been dead for over a decade.

Gramma never came to Europe. Never wanted to, really. But sitting in Grand Forks on the back porch of her plantation-style three-storey white house overlooking the Red River, she kept closely attuned to my life progression, encouraged every adventure and rarely criticised my steps and missteps.

Not a peep when I marched in protests, resisted the draft and obstinately opposed the Vietnam War. Nor when, after graduating from Stanford and the Columbia School of Journalism, I promptly ran off, jobless, to Paris where I didn't know a soul. No aspersions when, sick of the dreary winter weather in northern France, I spent a year chugging in a red Simca with no air conditioning through the African wilderness with an adventurous girlfriend to Cape Town.

Not a raised eyebrow when I invested, and lost, almost every cent I had in *The Paris Metro*, a free-thinking alternative English-language magazine (think *Village Voice* with an accent) in the late 70s. Nor when, deluged in bankruptcy debt, I up and married a stylish blonde Franco-American, had two kids and decided that the best place in the world (yes, the whole world) to raise a family was in the south of France. A long way from North Dakota.

Gramma, who eagerly read my first front page newspaper story about the Woodstock Music & Art Fair in 1969, kept abreast of my movements through my magazine and newspaper articles with exotic datelines from Africa, Europe and Asia. She carefully filed the stories, and my rambling single-spaced typewritten letters that she once likened to incomprehensible poems in *The New Yorker*, in an antique roll-top desk in her library that was wall-to-wall books.

As I became a contributor to various international magazines and newspapers, Gramma read my interviews with French hookers, French politicians, French cooks, French crooks, even French poodles, to gain insight into the country and its quirky customs. Her unquestioning support gave me, I think, the emotional grounding and backbone to take risks and rebound from inevitable setbacks.

At one point Gramma became part of my journalistic evolution. To repay one *Metro* debt, I wrote a column for *Le Matin* newspaper in Paris for two years in the early 80s. I'd frequently conclude an item by asking "And what would my grandmother in North Dakota think of that?" Then I would proceed to put words, a lot of quaint *Fargo*-like words, in her mouth. She was a real witty philosopher. Or I turned her into one.

But she was also the real deal. In one column I described the time I visited Gramma in the hospital after a routine cataract operation. I found her stretched out like a corpse on the bed, her blue eyes shut, her face serene and peaceful. She held a bouquet of wilted flowers in her bony hands, clasped prayer-like on her chest. Her hair spilled over the pillow and her choppers were drowning in a glass of water on the bedside table.

As I burst into tears and rushed to her side, the corpse broke out laughing. When she finally stopped, she explained, "I just wanted to scare that young doctor."

Gramma's devotion to me actually began the day I was born. She was an alcoholic and, from the tales I've heard, a typically messy one. My mother was afraid to bring friends home from high school because she never knew if Gramma would be soused. And it's certainly common knowledge that Gramma was blitzed the day she fell down the basement stairs and broke her wrist. In those days, the only 12 steps she knew were the ones down to the basement.

Before I was born, my mother told Gramma "You'll never hold my baby in your arms because you're a drunk." Gramma never took another drink, although Grandpa, the publisher of the *Grand Forks Herald* morning daily newspaper, made up for it. And so did I. But helping Gramma get sober was my first, and perhaps most notable accomplishment, in this lifetime. It certainly rivals my own effort to stop drinking when I realised that booze had me beat.

A few years ago Gramma gently and quietly passed away just before her 96th birthday. I went back to Grand Forks, picked up the urn containing my grandparents' ashes and held them on my lap on a flight to San Francisco. Then I drove up the California coast and pow-wowed with my family about a fitting memorial service – and Gramma's desire to have her ashes spread over the Pacific Ocean.

My three brothers and I put our grandparents' remains in a brown paper bag and, on an exceptionally windy afternoon, reverently carried them to the edge of a cliff overlooking the Pacific Ocean. My brother Lars, a professional pilot, claimed to have performed funeral services for others from his plane several times. On his instruction, we put a fist-sized stone in the sack with the ashes, attached a cord to it, said some prayers, threw it off the cliff, and jerked.

Instead of bursting, the bag flew back towards us, hit the cliff and most of the ashes blew right back into our astonished faces and open mouths. Even though we all looked like chimney sweeps, I'm sure some of the ashes floated into the ocean. And I figure that some of them have made it to the Mediterranean by now.

That's why I'm wondering, after meeting a woman that reminds me of Gramma, what she'd think of the MedTrek. Would she understand why I wanted to leave my home on the Riviera to, basically, take a hike? Would she comprehend what inspired such a Herculean quest? Or would she think that this was nothing but an idiot's odyssey?

Looking at the steep cliffs from l'Estartit, it's easy to see why I wound up so far inland. The coastline has some odd angles and each hilltop resembles another. This is my first unintentional deviation from the seaside path but, because there isn't a trail any closer to the water, there's not much I can do about it.

I get a $30 room at the Medes II hotel, run by a young couple whose four-year-old daughter serves my $5 dinner. My dining companions are 45 Spaniards in their late 70s and 80s who, if the volume of their guffaws during dinner is any gauge, are having the time of their lives.

I sit by one man who's got the look of a weather-beaten fisherman. He doesn't mind my remedial Spanish and seems sincerely interested in the details of my walk. I spend an hour spinning tales about my trek in Spanish and feel like Odysseus describing his voyage to Alkínoös. He tells me that he always intended to motor along the Spanish coast from Port Bou to Tarifa in his fishing boat. But never did.

"You'll be very happy you've done this when you get to be my age," he says, adding that he too enjoys seaside towns like this in the off-season when apartments are abandoned, campgrounds closed, villas shut and shops shuttered.

I head to bed around ten but can't sleep because the octogenarians keep dancing until well after midnight. I could complain but don't want to put a damper on the fun. I stuff toilet paper, which seems to be the panacea for any MedTrek ailment, in my ears and gradually pass out.

The Medes Islands, renowned as the longtime-lair of pirates who ravaged the coast, are on my left as I cross the Ter River. At a broader tributary, the Daro River, I hike upstream and pass a kilometre-long fenced-off area containing scores of communication towers, a seaside golf course and the closed Green Dolphin campsite.

A stone path leads to the Fishing and Biodiversity Marine Reserve in Ses Negres and beyond that to the delightful whitewashed villages of Sa Riera, Aiguafreda, Sa Tuna, Fornells de Mar, Aigua Blava, Tamariu, Llafranc and Calella de Palagrugell. Everywhere – and this is a Spanish trait during winter – there are workers repairing, maintaining or building something.

Cliffs frequently make it impossible to stay on the water and near Sa Tuna I spend an hour thrashing through overgrowth. Sweaty and dirty, with leaves in my hair and cuts on my forearms, I arrive at the top of a hill and lunch near the burnt-out hull of a house. On the walls inside, close to randomly scattered and stained mattresses, lovers have chalked their names ('Martina and Antonio') and dates ('Julio and Gloria '87') of their trysts.

The GR 92 is a splendid seaside stroll along the rocky coast and through Fornells de Mar, Aigua Blava and Llafranc to a hotel on the Cabo de Sant Sebastia. It's dusk when I arrive and I splurge on a $70 room. I consider this a bargain after I take a bubble bath in the Jacuzzi tub and dine on my terrace on sole wrapped in Jabugo ham, complemented by grilled vegetables with olive oil. The receptionist asks if I want to buy a CD-ROM that will enable me to take 'A Virtual Reality Tour of the Costa Brava'. I tell him that I'll let reality do.

The Cape Roig Botanical Gardens, says the description in the Michelin guide, feature "Mediterranean shrubs and rare plants in a garden of shaded paths and terraces built out of living rock, sheer above the sea." A large pine trunk blocks the GR 92 exactly 1100 kilometres from Antibes – a sign that I should cut down to the coast. I scamper along the sea on slippery rocks, sliding rocks, cracking rocks and unstable rocks. After 45 minutes, I'm exhausted and cut up a cliff, picking up thorn punctures through my gloves that are no match for the cacti-covered mountainside.

Typically, and this often happens after an arduous uphill climb, I arrive at the top to find a manicured segment of the Cami de Ronda. Why, I wonder, bother coping with challenging rocks and cliffs where there's a hiker's highway on the crest of the hill? Once again, I vow to avoid off-path hiking.

The four-kilometre seaside strip in Palamos is abutted by high rises. Individually each building is not especially unattractive but together they're a disastrous disfigurement. After Saint Antoni de Colange, the GR continues on past half a dozen secluded beaches until another high-rise pueblo called Playa d'Oro. The unremarkable buildings on this two-kilometre golden sand beach have a hidden talent that I find enchanting. They create a meditative echo of the sea and I'm in Zen mode when I check into a $33 room at the Eden Roc Hotel on the rocky coast in Sant Feliu de Guixols. No echoes or virtual reality required here.

17. Walking Around 365 Curves to Reach the Gold Coast

"Here were no coves or harborage or shelters, only steep headlands, rock fallen reefs and crags." – The Odyssey

My room at the Eden Roc is perched, somewhat precariously, directly above constantly crashing waves on the rocks below. Inspired by the cymbal-like sea sound and the presence of a Benedictine monastery located here since the tenth century, I'm eager to walk on the seaside to Tossa de Mar, a well-known resort 23 kilometres away that gets a three-star rating from Michelin.

But after passing a "Traditional Chinese Medicine" spa run by Dr. Chun-Bai and dead ending on three different paths, I reluctantly agree with five people who've insisted that it's impossible to walk near the water. The steep escarpments oblige me to take the GI 682, a stretch of two-lane blacktop road that's so picturesque it's been declared a "European Monument" by the European Union.

This is the first time I've hit the tarmac for any length of time since the Esterel on my second day out and I immediately remember what Thich Nhat Hanh told me: "The way is not an asphalt road." But the GI 682, abutted by forests on the right and the sea on the left, is a paved delight. Though traffic is bumper-to-bumper in the summer, only three cars drive by during my first hour out and I have one of the most beautiful roads in the world, and the 365 curves it makes between Sant Feliu and Tossa de Mar, almost completely to myself. I wish I could tell you that I counted each curve as I walked but a bus driver who makes the round trip six times a day conveyed the number to me. He should know.

The two-lane blacktop occasionally plunges to beaches, coves, campsites and resorts, like Rosemar and Cala de Salions. But it's best up high where frequent panoramas merit all sorts of superlatives. I fleetingly wish that Marie were with me because this is the place for a *"Super"* or *"Magnifique"*.

Workmen have been repainting the central dividing line but, because the road is so narrow, many of the Day-Glo orange witch-hat shaped cones have been knocked over. I keep picking them up and putting them back in place until I arrive in Tossa de Mar, a winter-sedated resort. Here it must be a local rule that all fishing boats are equipped with either old school gaslights or newer electric versions. Known as *lamparas*, the lights were initially put on the bows of the boats to attract anchovies into the fishing nets.

I run into some American and Australian tourists, a rarity at this time of year, exploring the 12th century walls in the old town where graffiti touts an "Anti Tourism Terror Organisation". The threat obviously didn't deter today's visitors.

Further along is Lloret de Mar which, like La Platja d'Aro, is so popular with the party crowd that discos and bars seem to dominate the local economy. The area near La Carpa commercial complex, a down-market mall, is full of garish hotels like Acapulco and Miami. In Playa Canyelles, I'm 243 kilometres from the border and Spain is finally becoming flat.

A waiter tells me that it's not just the topography that's changing.

"South of here people consider themselves to be part of Barcelona rather than the remote Costa Brava," he explains. "It's a completely different mindset. Much more business than relaxed."

A dozen older people from a tour bus look at me with amazement when I take a vertical cliff route outside Lloret to reconnect with the GR. Flying over a tower on a hilltop is the Catalonian flag, with four red stripes on a yellow background. The design, according to locals, dates from the ninth century when Wilfred the Hairy had his blood wiped on his yellow shield by Louis the Pious, Charlemagne's son, as he lay dying.

The coast from the Playa de Fanais to Blanes consists of one sandy beach after another. In Blanes, I'm on a sparkling three-kilometre promenade, part of an ongoing Plan de Costa renovation program in this part of Catalonia. I take a detour to the Marimurtra Botanical Gardens where there are over 3000 types of Mediterranean plants.

The Tordera River officially marks the end of the rugged Costa Brava and the onset of the smooth and ostensibly flat Costa Dorada. Spain's famous Golden Coast justifiably gets its name from the band of fine and shiny gold-tinted sand that stretches well over 250 kilometres south beyond Tarragona. Its seemingly endless beaches are a big draw for tourists, which perhaps explains why the railroad track now begins to run parallel with the sea.

Between Playa de Sabanell and Malgrat de Mar I encounter, step-per-step, more used condoms than I've ever seen, anywhere. Ever. Even when I worked at a pharmacy in high school and had a collection of different brands and sizes. And to the right, two foul-smelling German chemical plants, one of them owned by the German company Henkel, appear to be operating in violation of European environmental regulations.

The surreally disgusting scene is oddly complemented by a blend of orchestral muzak, including *Summertime* and *Oh, What A Beautiful Morning*, on a two-kilometre stretch of Plan de Costa promenade in Malgrat de Mar. There are speakers on every lamppost and I wonder whether, somehow, the government is financing the project as a kind of subversive or subliminal propaganda. Then I hear some Germans on a bench complaining about a Spanish dog, which they call a 'Schweinhund', and wonder if it isn't German propaganda. Or maybe it's just the Plan de Costa trying to be cosmopolitan.

There are German, Dutch and French bars, pubs and restaurants on both sides of the tracks in Malgrat. I head south past the eight-storey Tahiti Hotel, just down from the Hotel Royal Sun, across from the Hotel Riviera and not far from the Florida Hotel, the Hotel Caprici and the Hotel Indalo Park. It takes Los Pinos

Hotel on the edge of town to remind me that I'm in Spain.

Dozens of campers, trailers, vans and cars with German plates, and lots of Germans, are gathered in a campground near Pineda de Mar. Even the officers at the nearby Guardia Civil post look German. I remember my first encounter with Spain's once severe Gestapo-like paramilitary police in 1969, during the Franco dictatorship, when they busted me in Seville for kissing my girlfriend. Maybe it's my age, democratic Spain or the latest generation of guards, but they now seem as carefree as the German tourists.

My room on the fifth floor of the aptly named Promenade Hotel in Pineda de Mar looks onto the promenade, the railway tracks and the coast. I'm the only guest on their own amidst a bunch of French teenagers on a school outing and a few very organised German tour groups. The waiters speak German to me because they apparently don't see any Americans in Pineda in the winter.

I decide to make this my base for the week because the train station is just across the street and Monica and Peggy, the Dutch receptionists, convince me that everything is much more expensive closer to Barcelona. They also insist, correctly, that the rubber tires on the trains create a swoosh rather than clank sound and won't keep me awake.

"What have you learned about walking the Med so far?" one of the French kids asks me at breakfast.

"To stay as close as possible to the water and not get frustrated when a seaside cliff forces me to backtrack," I reply, adding that it's always nice to find a $35 room that includes a sea view, breakfast and dinner.

"And is your walk like *The Odyssey*?"

"Well, I'm beginning to think it will take me about as long to get home as it took Odysseus," I say. "It will be a while before I, like Odysseus, utter 'I am ashore in my own land'."

Seriously destabilised by a German woman who crashes the coffee line at breakfast, my day doesn't get off to a great start.

You don't understand the meaning of destabilised? Don't worry, it's my fault. Like many Americans who live abroad, I occasionally speckle my conversation, writing and thoughts with an Anglicised bit of French that sometimes requires an explanation to convey its intended meaning.

It's easy, for example, for you to grasp phrases like "I really like French *femmes* (women) and French cuisine (food)" or even "*La vie* (life) with French *femmes* is a real *cauchemar* (nightmare)." But only a few people on earth, and my hiking/swimming companion René is one of them, know precisely what "destabilised" means. To me anyway.

Did I mention that I used to swim in open sea competitions off Cannes and that a particular city official, who was in charge of the municipal sports programs and organised this specific race, would regularly cheat by having a boat drop him near the finish line? He pretended, of course, to have swum the entire race but he was such a lousy cheater that everyone would boo him when he had the temerity to stick out his chest, saunter to the podium and pick up a trophy. But, hey, he was a city official and every year he'd do the same thing and get away with it.

After three years of this nonsense, I decided that something had to be done about this sporting scandal. I sent a number of faxes to the town's mayor, who would shortly be tried and imprisoned for even more serious wrongdoings, to get the ball rolling. Then René and I began to call the director of sports and badger him about his illicit and immature behaviour. Apparently, this drove him to the brink of tears and, he claimed, really tormented him.

"*Vous me déstabilisez!*" he shouted at René during one call. "You're destroying me and my career as a public servant."

Well, on a much lesser scale, that's what this German did to me. She destablised the start of my day. Get it?

Fortunately she didn't prevent me from heading south toward Calella and Arenys de Mar, two towns that initially prospered due to the hosiery trade. Do they sell hiking socks, I wondered the night before as I washed mine in the sink?

The walk to Calella, which means small cove, features a wealth of athletic options for summer tourists. There are facilities for beach volleyball, beach soccer, beach go-karting, beach watersliding, beach windsurfing, beach trampoline, beach minigolf, beach tennis, and beach everything else.

Tourists aren't the only active people. Throughout the day I see dozens of sixty-something women out walking. They begin early in the morning, end around 10am and get going again in the late afternoon. Spanish women walk more than French, the sociologist in me notes, but are not quite as sleek and fashionable.

Sant Pol de Mar and Canet de Mar have campgrounds with typically Spanish names, like El Globo Rojo and Playa Sol. A statue of Poseidon on the paved promenade in Canet successfully inspired local fishermen and the day's bountiful catch is being sold at the port in Arenys de Mar. Just out of town I run into the first signposted nudist beach in Spain across from a McDonald's, the latest Mediterranean invader. Rather than hiking naked, I change into shorts and continue along the sand to Caldes d'Estrac and Sant Vincenc de Montalt.

The elegant homes on the beach in Sant Vincenc prompt me to start a list of seaside towns that have best maintained the local architecture and resisted the construction of shoddy hotels and high-rise apartments. Perhaps I'll even award a prize to the best example when I complete the MedTrek. If so, Sant Vincenc is definitely in the running.

Before continuing to Port del Balis and Sant Andreu de Llavernas, I lie down on a bench and read from *The Odyssey*.

"Do you need any help with directions?" asks a waiter in Mataro as I study my map at a seaside café. A few kilometres later I leave my "USA" baseball cap on a rock and a teenager chases after me to return it. After that, on the train back to Pineda, half a dozen women simultaneously come to my assistance when my empty water bottle falls out of my pack.

Spaniards, or Catalonians anyway, are distinctly more polite and down to earth than most Frenchmen. There's no Gallic arrogance, no moaning and groaning but, rather, pleasant smiles from people who run to return baseball caps and help out misdirected MedTrekkers. If the French are caviar and Champagne, the Spaniards are eggs and beer.

The path on the other side of Mataro, a town reputed for its carnations, doesn't have anything floral about it. The GR has cut into the mountains and left the coast while a large rock breakwater and a littered path just beside the train tracks replace the beach. Chemical plants take the place of commercial, business and residential buildings, though things improve slightly in Cabrera de Mar and Villassar de Mar, where train stations are being renovated with European Union funds.

There's been a garbage brigade in the area and trash-filled plastic sacks are neatly stacked every 50 metres. It's so warm and the beach is so clean that I strip and run into the chilly sea. Recharged, I walk barefoot through Premia de Mar to Ocata, the first of a string of beaches leading into Barcelona.

I buy a round-trip train ticket back to Pineda in El Masnou, which is only about 17 kilometres away from Barcelona. I'm quietly admiring the view over the water from my carriage seat until, on the platform at the stop in Mataro, I notice a veritable hippie who makes the scrawny Forrest Gump in the Esterel look like a corporate executive. Dirty, disheveled, matted hair, torn pants, dirty hands, dirty pack, the real thing. Naturally, though there are a number of other vacant seats, he and his slightly cleaner girlfriend choose to sit by me which, I might add, doesn't destabilise me a bit.

"Do you know which way the train line goes after Blanes?" he asks as the train starts to roll.

The couple are thrilled when I share my detailed map and travel expertise with them. I point out that the railroad heads inland and joins the coast again just south of Port Bou.

It turns out that he's English and, after living in a caravan in England for five years, has been on the road in Europe trying to make a living busking with his guitar. She's from Montreal and has been collecting donations for him in Málaga for the past four months. With no money and no train tickets, they're hoping they don't get kicked off the train because hitchhiking has been a drag.

"Well, it's not like you have a tight schedule," I say, remarking that one of the delights of being on the road is not having any schedule, tight or otherwise.

"No, but we want to get to Amsterdam because we can crash for free and make some money busking," he says.

"But a few days won't make much difference," I reply.

"Actually we have a flight to Canada next week," the woman interjects. "Hitching and trying to travel for free isn't as easy as it used to be in your day."

My day?

The woman, who can't be much over twenty, tells me she's taking the boyfriend home to meet her parents.

"Good luck," I tell her. "Don't let them give you any guff about his hair or profession. That happened when I met a girlfriend's parents and poisoned the whole relationship. They called me scruffy."

During the half hour ride we swap stories about hippiedom and I make 1969 sound like nirvana. I wonder how someone in Homer's time would have reacted to the unkempt couple.

"Have you some business here?" Lord Nestor, the prince of charioteers, would have asked. "Or are you, now, reckless wanderers of the sea, like those corsairs who risk their lives to prey on other men?"

Reckless wanderers! What a compliment. I like to think I'm one myself.

18. Goodbye Mañana, Hello Tomorrow

"You cannot talk about apple juice to someone who has not tasted it." – Thich Naht Hanh

I calmly watch the splendid sunrise spread over the Med from my terrace. I'm excited, suffering from MedTrekidation even, about reaching Barcelona, the first notable urban milestone since Marseille. The tune emanating from the hidden seaside speakers a few days ago has inspired me to sing *Oh, What A Beautiful Morning*. Then I out-Spanish the friendly Spanish by wishing everyone I see a hearty and sincere *"buenos dias"*.

I apply sunscreen, put on my "USA" cap and take off from Ocata with my full pack at a brisk pace, expecting to make it to Barcelona's Gothic quarter for a lunch that, in Spain, continues into the late afternoon. Oddly, hallucinating almost, I pass a number of people who look at me like I should know them. One is a Prince Albert of Monaco lookalike, the other bears an odd resemblance to Toothless John from New Zealand, and a third is the spitting image of Ringo Starr.

A North African palace complete with minarets in El Masnou explains the Arabic name of the town, though many Catalans like to pretend the Moorish occupation that began in the 8th century and continued for the next 300 years is just a minor footnote to their history.

A road sign indicates that Barcelona is only 15 kilometres down the road. When I arrive in Montgat on a paved sidewalk between the railroad tracks and still-narrow beach, workers are intently bagging both weeds and garbage. This is noteworthy because many gardeners, at least those on the Med, resolutely refuse to pick up litter when they weed.

"You guys are doing a great job," I tell them. "This place is almost as clean as Monaco. The prince would be proud of you."

A considerable industrial conversion program is underway in the town of Badalona north of Barcelona. But despite a main drag with palms and tolerable architecture, the place is punctuated by out-of-use factories and an unappealing mix of oil storage tanks, garbage treatment plants, and chemical and electricity facilities. Why do Opel and Akzo put their logos on their buildings? I'd want to keep my association with this place a secret.

There's a narrow dirt road between the beach and tall brick wall running along the perimeter of the factories. Pipes extending into the sea, water running into the sea and smells coming from the sea all justify frequent signs indicating that it's dangerous to bathe.

Don Quixote knew he'd arrived in Barcelona when he came to an orchard where executed bandits were hanging from the trees. I keep my eyes open and, though there are no hanging bandits, my spirits soar when I see the large MAPFRE insurance building and, beyond it, the 17th century fortress atop Montjuic mountain.

Everything comes to life near Spain's second largest city and biggest port. Hundreds of Barcelonans are walking, jogging, sunbathing and playing on the Platja Nova Mar Bella, the beach near the former Olympic Village built for the 1992 Games in Poblé Nou. The nearby Platja Icaria has dozens of restaurants and exemplifies how Barcelona, once renowned for turning its back on the sea, now eagerly beckons the Mother Mediterranean. This part of town has been so completely transformed since I was first here in 1970 that I can only imagine the surprised expression it would evoke on the faces of the Romans who first broke ground on the port in 201 BC. Despite the Roman connection, the city gets its name from the Carthaginian Hamilcar Barca, father of Hannibal, and legendary founder of the town.

Within the maze of shipbuilding facilities in La Barceloneta, a *teleférico* flies over the water to the top of Montjuïc and it's possible to see the top of the famous statue of Christopher Columbus, which is almost 50 metres high and was erected during the Universal Exposition in 1888. The historic explorer is still pointing to the Americas – albeit in the wrong direction – from his perch in Plaza Portal de la Pau.

Although I'm breezing through town today, I spent a lot of time here just before the country joined the European Union in 1992. A nine-part special section I wrote for *Time*, which appeared in the magazine between 1988 and late 1991, was aptly called *Spain: Western Europe's Last Frontier*. The first part, *Goodbye Mañana, Hello Tomorrow*, explored the electrifying sea change in the country's overall mindset as it set a breakneck pace to replace outmoded Spanish myths with contemporary European reality. The chapter on Barcelona, which described the city's Herculean efforts to prepare for the summer Games, was unoriginally entitled *An Olympic Champion* and the series culminated with *1992 – The Year of Spain*, which also happened to be the 500th anniversary of the discovery of America.

1992 might seem like a long time ago but that particular epoch, between the end of the repressive and isolationist Franco regime in 1975 and the advent of the flourishing country I'm walking through today, was the setting of an impressive national renaissance. There was action everywhere. Seville hosted a Universal Exhibition, Madrid was the European Capital of Culture and Barcelona prepared to greet the world's speediest athletes.

The astonishing growth spurt and exhilarating transition to national adulthood fuelled everyone, from the concierges and chicas of the streets to corporate chairman and chic boutiques on Barcelona's Paseo de Gracia and Rambla de Cataluna. To repeat what Columbus said 500 years earlier, "Spain, which was reckoned poor, has become the richest of countries."

The pre-1992 buzz in Barcelona, which was a thriving city long before inland Madrid became a metropolis, accelerated advances that might otherwise have taken decades. Richard Meier designed a new Museum of Contemporary

Art and architect Ricardo Bofil doubled the size of the airport. The Montjuïc museum, with its Gothic and Romanesque collection and breathtaking views over the city, was completely renovated, as were the Liceo opera house and scores of churches and libraries. Robert Hughes even chose that year to publish *Barcelona*, a comprehensive tome that evokes the city's evolution during a period "of monks and ruthless knights, mystics and hard-fisted merchants, anarchists and monarchists, tricksters and artists".

"Modern Spain is like the table of contents of a good novel," book publisher Mario Muchnik told me in early 1991 during a breakfast at the Palace Hotel. "The outline is exciting but most of the chapters are still being written."

The dynamic goings on put an end to the jokes that Spain's northern neighbours traditionally told about the country.

"The French used to think that Africa started with the Pyrenees and that Spaniards were lazy," a vice president at the SEAT car manufacturer, which has sold cars with names like Málaga and Marbella, explained to me during a visit to his office in the late 1980s. "We were once, perhaps, humble but now we're hungry."

I'm hungry too and I rush into the colourful Gothic Quarter, a part of town that has been thriving since the 13th century, and head for *tapas* at a hole-in-the-wall restaurant that I used to frequent. Despite all the renovation and hullabaloo during the last decade of the 20th century, the Gothic Quarter really hasn't changed much. Its inner physical density and narrow lanes, often dark with age and grime, evoke a profound sense of the medieval that contrasts with the open airiness of a city like Madrid.

Take just a few steps back from the sea and you'll immediately discover the essence of a city with an intriguing heritage that includes Greek, Roman, Phoenician, Visigoth, Muslim, Jewish and Christian influences and Gothic, Baroque and Modernist architecture. There's a mysterious intensity to the deep-rooted centre and, like one of the many gargoyles staring down on me, I imagine myself the latest witness to the thousands of dramas, murders, pleasures, passions, invasions and improvements that have occurred over the centuries.

I choose a mussel salad, a prawn tortilla and a tuna and stewed cabbage concoction from twenty different *tapa* options on the bar before taking a seat next to a teenage American couple who look like they've already had enough sangria for the three of us. Chris and Barbara, both 16, introduce themselves and immediately begin chatting in that inimitably friendly (and often irritating) American manner. They readily admit that they don't know much about Spain, which enables me to rattle off a few factual observations and personal impressions.

"Spaniards still watch more television and gamble more often than any other Europeans," I point out, not mentioning the reason I'm carrying a backpack.

"But what still baffles me after all the time I've spent here is when they find time to sleep. They usually don't eat dinner until ten or eleven, the nightlife doesn't really get underway until 2am and most of them are in their offices by ten. If you can discover how the Spanish get enough shut eye you'll both become respected sociologists."

They seem so interested in my random patter that I offer to give them a quick walking tour of some Gothic Quarter highlights.

"Barcelona, though isolated in many senses from the rest of the country, is especially important because it's been Spain's link with Europe for over 2000 years," I tell them as we head into the labyrinth of narrow cobblestone streets. "And this region gave the world Pablo Picasso, Salvador Dalí, Joan Miró, Luis Buñuel and Antoni Gaudí."

"Luis who?" asks Barbara.

I lead them first into the inner courtyard of the Palace of the Generalitat, or government, of Catalonia and point out the elegant staircase and a flamboyant Gothic façade. Years ago I used to come here frequently to interview Jordi Pujol, the fiercely nationalistic and popular president who led Catalonia, which is considered an autonomous community by the national government in Madrid, from 1980 until 2003. As we now examine one of the fountains in the courtyard, I explain to the couple how podgy Pujol riveted me with his account of Spain's transition from Francisco Franco's 39-year dictatorship to its then-upcoming membership in the European Union.

"Pujol told me that the dictatorship and era of repression paradoxically ripened Spain for an exciting evolution following Franco's death," I said, adding that Barcelona was an active revolutionary centre during the country's civil war in the 1930s and that Catalonia is considered, by Catalans anyway, as a *naçio*, or nation, of seven million people with its own culture and language. "The pugnacious (yeah, I dropped the word pugnacious into the conversation) president convinced me that every aspect of Spain – the arts, culture, society, even cuisine – would explode in 1992 and that the entire country was ready to make a major contribution to the construction of contemporary Europe. He was right."

I describe how Pujol insisted that the Spanish concept of *mañana*, the symbol of easygoing procrastination, had been replaced by an upbeat morale that verged on national euphoria. Compared to backward Spain during the fascistic Franco regime, Pujol also correctly predicted that Western Europe's second largest (after France) and second highest (after Switzerland) country would continue to break fresh ground long after 1992.

"The president and I were taking a walk not far from here and he urged me to stop and savour the seductive scent of a soup emanating from a tiny, family-run restaurant," I continue. "After I closed my eyes and took in the incredible aroma, Pujol said 'that fish stew contains a piece of every type of fish that's ever swum in the Mediterranean'."

"And how many kinds of fish are there in the sea?" asks Chris.

"As many as there are in that soup, I guess," I reply.

As we continue our walk, I briefly stop at the Cathedral that is a reconstruction of a Romanesque church constructed between 1300 and 1450.

"Start digging and, even if you're not trained archaeologists, you'll learn what was here long before this church was built," I explain. "This specific piece of ground was initially the Temple of Augustus, then a fourth century basilica and later a Visigoth palace."

I take them by the Frederic Mares Museum in the Royal Palace, which has a riveting collection of crucifixes, before we walk through the Placa San Jaume and back down to the sea on the Via Laietana.

"What would you do with your life if you were our age again?" Chris randomly asks.

"Yeah, any pearls of wisdom for us?" wonders Barbara.

I think for a moment before I attempt to pass on a bit of my own experience, strength and hope.

"I learned very early on that I needed to create my own adventures and carve out my own niche without worrying too much about what people thought or where it might ultimately lead," I say. "I'd do it all over again in a second but the adventures, and maybe even the outcome, might be completely different. After all, a few decades ago I seriously considered joining a monastery in Ethiopia, becoming a game warden in the Serengeti or leading a revolution in the Seychelles."

"Do you still have that sense of adventure today?" Chris asks.

"Well, actually, now that you mention it, I'm on a hike around ..."

A guard near the World Trade Centre politely informs me that I'm not allowed to walk through Barcelona's sprawling port with its gargantuan free trade zone. That direct route towards the airport would enable me to immediately cut down the Llobregat River to the sea. Instead I have to backtrack a kilometre and head up Montjuïc where I find a trail that looks like a shortcut around the face of the mountain.

I'm so confident about my chosen path that I discard the advice of a family living in a lean-to on the hillside. They insist that there's no way around the front of the mountain but perhaps because locals often mislead me, I don't believe them. They also apologise for their three barking dogs that try to break their chains and take a chunk out of me. They call them *perros locos*.

I negotiate rocks and cacti to slowly traverse the mountainside and, after forty-five minutes, stop to catch my breath and look towards the sea. The size of Barcelona's port and Zona Franca, which could have more shipping containers than any single place on earth, are stupefying. Then, even more stupefied that

I'm at a dead end, I retrace my steps.

"*Yo soy muy stupido,*" I say to the couple, who nod in agreement.

Chastened by my frustrating detour, I follow the road to the top of the mountain and spend a few minutes admiring a Montjuic panorama that takes in the city, the Joan Miro Foundation, a Spanish Village with replicas of the different styles of Spanish architecture and the Olympic stadium. After the descent to L'Hospitalet, where the Gran Via leads to the airport and the resumption of the Costa Dorada, I drop into a cyber café to compose and email my second MedTrek press release.

MedTrek MileStone #2 – Barcelona, Spain

There are easier ways to get here from Antibes, France, than by spending 41 days walking 1255 kilometres, and taking 15,127,770 steps on the Mediterranean seaside. In fact, it's a less-than-two-hour flight, not even a six-hour drive, and an overnight train ride.

I was inspired to continue MedTrekking beyond Barcelona when I had coffee near the city's well-known statue of Christopher Columbus, his stretched right arm pointing towards the sea. A barman on La Rambla called me a contemporary Don Quixote and bid me "*Vaya con Dios*" as he pointed towards Cartagena, the Costa Blanca and Gibraltar.

I have no idea what's ahead but, as Kalypso told Odysseus, "If you could see it all, before you go – all the adversity you face at sea – you would stay here, and guard this house, and be immortal."

Since there's no Kalypso and no one's yet offering me a shot at immortality, I'll keep moving on. There are easier ways to make this trip. But what kind of tale would we have had if Odysseus came straight home from Troy?

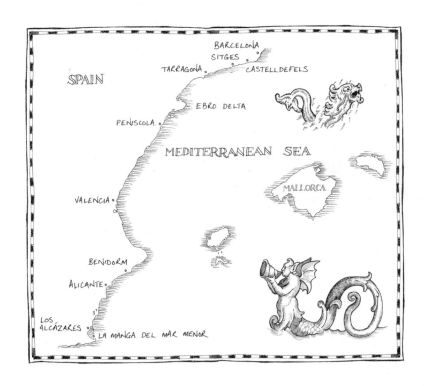

Part Five

Coasting Through Spain and Sharing the Path

19. Gay Paths, Dead Birds and a Nuclear Plant

"No matter how extreme a situation is, it will change. It cannot continue forever. Thus, a great forest fire is always destined to burn itself out; a turbulent sea will become calmer." – Deng Ming-Dao

Getting out of Barcelona is a breeze. Sure, there's some urban blight, including mountains of rusty orange shipping containers in the port and the whine of planes taking off and landing at the city's seaside airport, El Prat de Llobregat Aeropuerto. But once I cross the Llobregat River and walk four kilometres down to the Mediterranean, I'm in the swampy and deserted Llobregat Delta Nature Reserve.

Two days of incessant rain have turned the water a sick coffee colour and transformed all of the paths into muddy corridors, though the grazing sheep and flocks of wild birds seem perfectly content. I mount an observation tower and try to assess the impact of the airborne activity and noise on the flora, fauna and environment. It's got to drive some of the animals and plants batty.

A large sign says 'Don't Swim Here For Reasons of Sanitation'. The candour is impressive but the problem must be very serious because Mediterranean municipalities usually exaggerate the cleanliness of the beaches and purity of the water to attract tourists.

I pass a golf course, a fenced-in military barracks and two-dozen cranes - the construction, not flying, kind. There's an 'our beach is longer than yours' competition between Llobregat, Gava and Castelldefels with each town featuring billboards indicating the specific number of kilometres of beachfront it possesses. I walk into Castelldefels at sunset under glaring lights positioned along the paved maritime promenade until I reach the Hotel Bel Air, where my $50 room is less than 100 metres from the sea.

Just before sunrise, I step onto the terrace and look south. A few kilometres away is a sloping hill topped with an oil storage tank. Hills on the flat and sandy Costa Dorada? Undeterred, I start off on the beach and quickly learn that the terrain, including numerous hills that start at Port Ginesta, resembles a mini Costa Brava. The cliffs soon force me away from the seaside and I find myself walking on an obviously dangerous road that is much narrower than those in the Esterel or on the Costa Brava.

It's idiotic and precarious to walk here and I feel like I'm cheating death with each step. There are lots of big trucks, no shoulders, no sidewalks and every driver is probably thinking, as Homer wrote, "He has a peg loose, that one." I imagine that my obituary will be titled 'Killed By Coca-Cola Truck Near Barcelona'.

Despite the danger, the views of the opal green sea are stunning and I frequently dip down to the water to look for a passable path. I finally find a walkway along the lip of a cliff about 15 metres above the sea. My faith in nature is immediately restored. Positive things appear the moment I compose my obituary.

Sitges, the Michelin forewarns, is a "favourite resort with wealthy Catalan families who have built elegant houses along the Paseo Maritime". The guide waxes eloquently about the rose-coloured façade of the parish church, the streets lined with white-walled houses and "carpets of flowers".

The description is remarkably accurate and Sitges is a delight, especially after my roadside death march. I linger while lunching on gazpacho and a shrimp omelette at the Costa Dorada restaurant and it's apparent that the town's tourist population is overwhelmingly gay. The Ruta de las Cales, the hilly hiking trail to Vilanova y la Geltru that passes by numerous gay nudist beaches, is the best-beaten path I've seen. I run into more hikers here than anywhere else on the MedTrek and do my best to ignore the naked men that frequently pop out of the bushes with straightforward propositions.

Cunit, an industrial-zone-to-be, is another unrealised field of dreams on the Med. Once again, there are streets, lampposts and designated lots but no commercial activity. The only action is at the power station, which has a towering smoke stack and gigantic pipes disgorging steamy water into the sea. A sign strongly discourages swimming and fishing but the beaches are dotted with fishermen, pétanque players and campers, including a German from Stuttgart whose tent is topped with a high-tech wind speed indicator and a sophisticated satellite dish. I wouldn't be surprised if he's also monitoring the water quality.

German tourists are presumably responsible for keeping the McDonald's, a Swisspic Bar, a Monaco Bar, a Hollywood Beach bar and the crowded beach restaurants in business in Calafell. Why, I wonder, do I walk while all of these people are content to lay in the sun and tan? Is it because I generally dislike sand and saltwater? Or is it, like bridge and maybe even golf, another activity that I'm reserving for later in life? Whatever the reason, I have no desire to plop on the sand and slowly toast myself for more than a few minutes at a time.

I stop at the Ancora restaurant for a cappuccino at exactly noon and try to decipher a conversation in Dutch at the next table. On the seaside, a piece of compact earth-moving equipment is grooming the beach, a passionate 24/7 activity on the Costa Dorada.

There's a local battle underway concerning a port extension in Roc de San Cayetano and a number of *No Al Puerto* banners are hanging from terraces. I have so much trouble figuring out how to spell 'Cayetano' that I ask a woman to write it in my notebook. Her expression seems to convey something that Odysseus once heard: "Stranger, you must come from the other end of nowhere, else you are a great booby, having to ask what place this is." But she patiently writes it down and pleasantly corrects my pronunciation.

I leave town on a pine-smelling hill trail near Roca de Bara, where the Bank of Spain has a luxurious private retreat, and continue to Creixell, where an elderly Spanish woman is vigorously tapping castanets as she walks alone on the hard-sanded beach. I'm obviously not the only booby with a peg loose.

The townspeople are out for their weekly Sunday morning stroll in Torredembarra, 1345 walking kilometres and 44 days from Antibes, and some kids are singing "Hola, Hola, Pepsi Cola". Within an hour, I (1) walk on a rocky seaside path equipped with lights and electrical outlets, (2) see the first lighthouse under construction since I started the MedTrek, (3) witness a diver pull a gigantic octopus out of the water, (4) drop into a superb seaside *"castillo"* where a cacophony of chefs, preparing an immense buffet, offer me breakfast and (5) stumble on a bouquet of fresh roses being lapped by waves on the Medside.

I can only imagine what prompted someone to leave the roses: a drowning death, a distraught lover, a couple's squabble, a fall off a nearby ship?

I opt for the distraught lover scenario.

After all, Latin lovers are part of both myth and reality in France, Spain and Italy. Their starry-eyed and theatrical actions and reactions in the face of challenged, thwarted or unrequited love put us staid and unimaginative Americans, Australians and British to shame. There is, usually, no practical mental thought process or scheming hidden agenda behind their melodramatic, daring and gallant deeds in the romantic arena. It's pure emotion. When confronted with a conundrum involving passion and ardour they, almost without fail, simultaneously act straight from the heart, gut and soul.

I visualise a dashing Spanish suitor, his face closely shaven and his shiny black hair greased back to create a fusion of a classical Don Juan (the original Don Juan was created in a Spanish play by Tirso de Molina around 1630) and a contemporary Antonio Banderas, being rebuffed by his lover, or maybe his lover and her mother. Instead of docilely admitting defeat and leaving the roses, which his grandmother had urged him to buy and present as a token of affection, he stoically and silently turns his back, walks 300 paces to the sea, strides into the surf and, as he's about to submerge and drown, valiantly lets the flowers float to the surface and drift to the shore, a final romantic exploit that is testimony to his dying love. The locals will be talking about him for years.

That's not how I, a practical and scheming Anglo-Saxon to the core, would have handled it. I would have either (1) gotten some rope and hung the flowers from a high branch in the pine tree in the front yard as though they, and my one-time consort, had been sentenced to death, (2) screamed, shouted and wailed as the cops were called to the house and I was taken into custody after I threw the roses at the former object of my affection and punctured her eye with a thorn, (3), and this is the alcoholic in me, left without a word and spent a brooding night in my car keeping an eye on the house and confronting my paramour the next morning with a dishevelled look, sunken eyes and wilted roses in my hands, (4) never spoken to her again and given the roses to the first *chica* I ran into or (5) sold the roses to the Latin lover down the street. Mine would have been an act, cowardly and heartless perhaps, of thought, cunning, revenge and personal profit. In any event, you get the picture; I wouldn't have thrown the roses into the Mediterranean. Only a distraught Latin lover would do that.

The 18-kilometre walk to Tarragona is along rocky coasts, through pine forests and on sandy beaches that have been declared 'Clean' by a European Union directive. Altafull and La Mora, quaint little towns with gingerbread-like houses on wide promenades, have a pleasant scarcity of large hotels.

The Miracle Beach in Tarragona is being completely revamped and the bulldozing and earthmoving hullabaloo has created a real mess. I head uphill to explore the old city, visit the Cathedral erected on top of the Roman Temple of Jupiter and look for remnants of the Romans who were in control here in 218 BC. Before I leave the 12th century Romanesque/Gothic church, I light a candle for a friend's recently deceased father amidst the vaults, tapestries, praying nuns and morning bells. The maritime museum on the seaside has an exhibition of the boats, known as *llauts*, which once ran up and down the Ebro River. Nearby a dozen women painstakingly repair purple-coloured fishing nets while their husbands try to sell the day's catch.

Then I hike through one of the least attractive industrial zones and port complexes since Toulon. There are chemical manufacturing multinationals like BASF, Dow and Repsol; companies such as Citroen, Renault and SEAT shipping cars; and cranes and ships waiting to transport these commodities throughout the world. The fenced-in duty-free trade zone prevents me from walking close to the sea and a security officer politely curtails my shortcut through the mammoth SEAT lot. When I ask the guard what would happen if I ignore him and keep walking, I'm shown, with a smile, his handcuffs. The only somewhat bright light in this muddle is the Tarragona Educational Complex where students are taking classes in buildings erected under the omnipresent umbrella pines.

It takes two hours to get beyond the unpleasant sights, smells and sounds. I eat lunch near an odd sculpture that resembles vertical exhaust pipes topped with a gigantic mushroom. Things improve near Cape Salou when I see a fisherman land a sea bass and find myself on a slow-going rocky sea walk that, at one point, passes through a quarry. Dozens of people, like ELISA, have spelled out their first names in gigantic letters using stones and bricks.

The garbage cans in Cap Salou are yellow and blue, colours that remind me of the Swedish flag and indicate wide scale recycling. The pine-covered cape has one of the widest palm-and-flower-planted promenades on the Med and the Spanish women come out for their speed strolls as I approach Cambrils. I'm flabbergasted, and I don't use that word much, when two women, one of them wearing a leather dress and semi-high heels, zip past me as though I'm standing still.

I awake at the Hotel Rovira in Cambrils after a rare nine-hour sleep and, slightly less inspired than usual due to too much slumber, head to a nearby seaside café for a few cups of undiluted espresso. The local paper has a front page story about 50 birds found dead on a beach near Tarragona yesterday afternoon at 5:30pm. It's illustrated by a photo of one dead bird. Why, as I recall my trudge through that gloomy industrial disaster zone, am I not surprised? There are some fishing boats trawling the waters and I recall the adage that "If you want to learn to pray, learn to sail". I'll bet that shipwrecked Odysseus would agree.

The Michelin guide colours the road south of here in brilliant green, perhaps because this part of the coast is not littered with any high-rise buildings. One-storey white villas and spacious campgrounds seem to embody sensible housing and environmental balance. The beaches, including the aptly named Torn nudist beach (the name makes me think of unaware newcomers having their clothes torn off them by old-fashioned nudists enforcing their you-must-be-naked-to-sunbathe-with-us philosophy), stretch on and on until the GR turns rocky and cliffy. Then, in mid-afternoon, I hit a large nuclear plant called Vandellos II. It is – with double fences, barbed wire and surveillance cameras – the most secure and protected installation I've seen on the Med. The sight of it, coupled with the story about the dead birds, gets me thinking about nuclear power closer to home and my own efforts to improve the environment.

France, a country fuelled primarily by nuclear power, has avoided, as long as I've been living there, a major calamity due to a blow-up or technical catastrophe at a generating plant. Every Frenchman is aware of the Three Mile Island accident in 1979 and the numerous cases of cancer and birth defects attributed to the radioactive fallout from the Chernobyl reactor meltdown, or whatever it was, in 1986. But there's been no public outcry against nuclear power and, on the contrary, it continues to have widespread support.

However, I want to let you in on one of my ongoing adulthood character abnormalities that began in Paris when I first learned that my toaster was operating on nuclear input. Every, and I mean every, time the electricity is cut at my villa, or even when a light bulb blows, I'm convinced that there's been an explosion at the local nuclear plant and that I've got ten seconds to live. I relax a bit after I flip the fuse or replace the bulb, but only after I've survived an imaginary, and agonising, death caused by a nuclear power malfunction. Can you imagine an entire country living with this type of death-will-come-at-any-minute type of stress? No wonder they're often a bit short-tempered.

I attribute my own inflated and perhaps irrational reaction to nuclear energy to initial suspicions that were ignited when I became a tree-hugging environmentalist a few years before I participated in the first Earth Day event in April 1970. I've got solar panels on my roof, I'm all for wind and wave-generated electricity, and I'm a constant practitioner of the "if it's yellow let it mellow, if it's brown flush it down" precept.

After living with nuclear power for decades, I have cultivated a love/hate relationship with it that is often thought to be an unseemly environmental contradiction by some of my eco friends. On the love side it's much cleaner and, in the long run, cheaper than coal or oil-fired power. On the hate side I'm well aware of the holocaust that might result from a catastrophic accident. The result: I'm upset that I'm in favour of nuclear power. Explain that, would you.

In fact, most of us, no matter how ardent our support of the environment and how fervent and well-intended our convictions that we must each take personal steps to avoid annihilation due to climate change, have encountered similar contradictions and conflicts in our well-meaning efforts to be clean and conscientious citizens.

Take paper recycling. Back in the 1980s, at my home in France, I meticulously piled every newspaper, magazine and scrap of paper in the garage for two or three months. I'd planned to take it all, eventually, to a recycling plant, a drive that would, of course, necessitate using gas and producing exhaust. I obviously didn't want to undertake the task until I could completely fill the car. My father-in-law was staying with us and came into the living room one afternoon beaming like a kid who'd just cleaned his room without being told.

"I've done you a great favour," he said in his heavily French-accented English. "I cleaned out those immense piles of paper, which were a real fire hazard, and took them all to the garbage bins today. It took me hours and I hope you appreciate it."

I just killed 250 trees.

Then there were my encounters with Michel Rolant, the Socialist mayor of my village, and the town's generally innocuous municipal police officers.

To celebrate the 20th anniversary of Earth Day in 1990, I used my daily radio commentary on Riviera Radio to mobilise scores of like-minded folk to clean up the debris along the Brague River in Valbonne Sophia-Antipolis, which is what my community has been called since it was clear that the high-tech park was a financial success and not a white elephant. Armed with shovels, gloves and waders we spent the entire day collecting refuse, packing it up to a large parking lot and building a gigantic garbage sculpture not far from city hall. At the end of the day, the mayor, who hadn't picked up a single piece of paper, proudly came and posed in front of our miniature Eiffel Tower and took all the credit for it in an article on the front page of *Nice-Matin*, the local daily paper.

I just promoted the faux environmental credentials of a politician.

A year later, on Earth Day #21, I cleaned the roadside forest near my home and constructed another sculpture between the sloping woods and the two-lane blacktop. Two policemen came by and threatened to arrest me because I didn't have a construction permit, was endangering traffic and was a public nuisance.

"You're arresting me for making my hometown cleaner?" I asked with astonishment. "You should arrest all the people who throw this crap here."

The cops admitted that there was some rationale to my argument, that even they noticed a slight contradiction, and let me go after taking me to the police station where they encouraged me to sign an admission that I'd knowingly and wilfully broken the law, which I guess, if there actually was such a law, is true. After my signature, I wrote 'Ecosculpturist', though I wasn't sure if that was the word for a garbage-collecting street artist/environmentalist.

I just became a threat to society.

Even my kids thought I was a little weird when I insisted on getting a small, potted Christmas tree that would mature and gain a little height each year. My living Tannenbaum was less than three feet high but unfortunately, and I'm sure you've all had this experience, it withered and died by April 1.

The kids thought my attitude about picking olives and taking them to the local mill in exchange for oil was even odder.

In the early 1990s, around the time of the first Gulf War, I decided to quit travelling, cut my workload in half, do without half my freelance income and spend more time with myself and my family. One thing I did, each morning at sunrise, was walk down to the olive trees in my garden and fastidiously pick up fallen olives one at a time. No nets or wastage at my place. During the next few weeks, in the interest of helping humanity and getting a free stockpile of good local olive oil to grease my Mediterranean diet, I collected a couple of cardboard boxes of olives. After a month I quite proudly packed the kids in the car and we headed to the mill in Opio.

It turned out that because I neglected to take the olives to the mill on a regular basis, three-quarters of my crop had rotted and I only got a few litres of oil. The kids thought that was pretty amusing. I didn't.

I just realised that I'm not an organic farmer.

Today, comforted by the fact that almost everyone is aware that we have seriously damaged our Earth Mother and face possible extinction due to climate change, I simply try to keep my side of the street clean by picking up litter, being environmentally aware and gently encouraging others to do the same. And I'm basically convinced that, largely due to the taxes generated by tourism, the Med is probably getting cleaner as most of its inhabitants try to make things better before it overflows and floods due to global warming. But not everyone is on the right side.

I saw a guy take his ashtray out of his car this morning in Cambrils and ceremoniously dump his cigarette butts in the middle of the street. Maybe it was this incident rather than the nuclear plant or dead birds that inspired these environmental ruminations, but as a hiker I can tell you that discarded cigarette packs and cigarette butts are a major component of litter throughout the world (well, wait, don't get me started about the variety of debris in India and China) and it infuriates me to see anyone add to the mess.

"Don't do that," I screamed, really screamed, at him in Spanish. "You're screwing up the whole balance of the Mediterranean's fragile ecosystem."

"Shut up!" he said with his voice and fist. "We pay street sweepers to pick up after us."

"Well I hope that nuclear plant down the road explodes and kills you before the cigarettes do," I yelled back, making an up and down butt-fucking gesture with my arm. "If you're not part of the solution you are the problem. *Idiota* asshole!"

I spend an hour, constantly hissed at by nuclear-generated high-power electricity cables, cutting inland to encircle the plant and don't return to the sea until Calafat. As I edge out of town, a young Spanish woman is poetically describing the beauty of the universe and the bliss of Mediterranean to three twentyish American men who don't seem to appreciate the expressive nature of her poetic description.

"Isn't it amazing with all the manmade problems, the shabby apartment buildings and the sewage we create, that this sea is still so majestic and clean," she seriously concluded as she approached a shallow tide pool in the rocks and pointed to some breed of living organism. "It's still a source of life."

One of the guys, and this is an American mind you, is drinking a beer and smoking a fag. I am absolutely flabbergasted (again already!) when, after just getting a lesson about creation and the universe in lyrical Spanish (which, granted, he didn't appear to understand), he flicks his cigarette butt into the water.

I'm disgusted but, and this is rare for me, decide to keep my mouth shut and hope that the dark-haired chica displays her fangs and teaches the guy a lesson.

And she does.

"Jesus Christ, you dumb fuck [my translation], I live here and I don't want some stupid American screwing up my sea," she said. "Go home!"

I end the day in L'Ametila de Mar in a bar that, the owner proudly informs me, "is both three minutes from the train station and three minutes from the beach".

"You've found the most practical place to stop on the entire Costa Dorada," the barman says.

When I investigate l'Ametila de Mar in daylight, it's clear that I'm buffered from reality by sticking so close to the sea. The many seaside high rises are even more unattractive from the rear than they are from the coast. The further away from the seafront, the worse things get.

I approach the edge of the Ebro River Delta, a natural park that extends into the sea like a dog's head with its tongue stuck out, along an almost unbroken range of cliffs adorned with villas and a New Mexico-like pueblo village nestled amidst aging trees in a terraced olive grove. These terraced gardens, which are found in every country surrounding the Mediterranean, were first instituted centuries ago to cope with steep hillsides, thin soil and high winds. They're still so important to farmers and agriculture that it's rare to see the stone walls that form and separate the terraces in disrepair. I craft a wreath out of a leafy olive branch and, like a victorious Greek athlete, put it on my head.

After the Paseo Maritime de Santa Lluciam, I get my first glimpse of the low-lying Ebro Delta from Cape Roig and take a break in L'Ampolla at 3:30 for a long, lazy lunch at the Can Pinana on the port. I bask in the sun, dine on *paella* and octopi, and just relax.

I stop at the medieval Reial Monestir de Santa Maria de Poblét on the 830-kilometre trip back to Valbonne. This Cistercian monastery, whose name is derived from the Latin *populetum* (grove of white poplars), was founded 'to give thanks to God' after Catalonia had been recaptured from the Moors. The ground was broken around 1150 by twelve Cistercian monks who left the Fontfroide Abbey in Narbonne, France, and Poblét became a frequent stop and retreat for royals and pilgrims travelling between Barcelona and Saragossa.

As I peacefully walk through the calm monastery grounds and restored buildings that house only a few monks, it strikes me that I've been hiking alone since Marseille. The solo MedTrek has certainly had a beneficial and calming impact on my mind, body, spirit and behaviour.

I'm reminded that some of my best travel experiences – and I think this applies to many people – derive from solitary adventures and the unique interpretation of them by my own mad mind. The flexibility of being a solo voyager makes it easier for me to meet people, explore offbeat phenomena, proceed at my own pace, eat what and when I want to, and even find a place to stay without too much hassle. Although some people are wary of a backpacker out by himself, overall I'm also more approachable when I'm on my own. Alone, in the eyes of others, I'm fair game … for anything. In fact, by being alone I'm always un-alone, as if some law of physics attracts others to a solo traveller or attracts the traveller to people and situations.

I can understand why most people prefer to travel with someone else for reasons of safety, sharing experiences, avoiding loneliness and maybe even saving money. But a duo or group is often seen as a self-enclosed unit, its members content amongst themselves and less willing to be disturbed. Being part of a group, even a group of two, can isolate travellers from exposure to local people and to themselves. And, quite frankly, when I run into busloads of Americans visiting well-known European cities I often want to point out what they're missing. My advice to almost anyone, and certainly any youngster, is to try going it alone at some point in life. You don't have to go into the wild, but let the world open up in fuller, more unexpected ways.

Despite all this reflection about the virtues of being by myself, it's time to invite people to walk with me. Dozens of friends have asked if they could come along and I'm about to extend some invitations.

Who shall be the first, I wonder?

20. Crossing the Ebro and Reaching Valencia

"We will enjoy our walk without thinking of arriving anywhere." — Thich Nhat Hanh

A week later, during our drive from the French Riviera to the Ebro Delta, Bill Anderson and I take a detour to the cliff-hanging Sierra de Montserrat monastery in the hills above Barcelona. We pay homage to a wooden virgin in the mountaintop monastery founded by Benedictines in the ninth century. Although destroyed by the French in 1812, Montserrat was elaborately reconstructed and its 12th century Black Madonna is venerated as the matron saint of Catalonia.

We climb the staircase to her niche above the altar and, after paying our respects, descend to a weathered wooden pew where we sit in absolute silence for fifteen minutes. We light two candles to burn among hundreds of others when we leave the sanctuary located on a massif that Wagner used as the setting for *Parsifal*.

"What a mellow way to start a trip," says Bill, whom I'd met a few years ago in Aix-en-Provence and later profiled in a piece I wrote for *Time* about contemporary American expatriates. The story described how Bill and his partner Lorie Strait had abandoned their prosperous careers with American multinational companies to move to a small village in the south of France. Two of the subtitles I submitted with the piece were *We've Got Mayle* and *Aix Marks the Spot*.

In fact, Bill and Lorie hadn't read Peter Mayle's many books before they bought a home in Provence in 1996. But the adventures in their stone house situated amidst fields of lavender and groves of oak could easily provide yet another sequel to *A Year In Provence*.

Their three-acre spread was a ten-minute walk from the tiny and little-known hilltop village of Viens, which was founded in 990 A.D. and has a population of 462. The property included a garden with the requisite massive stone picnic table, a fountain waiting for a plumber, and a driveway that required a four-wheel drive vehicle to negotiate. Paolo, the couple's young Brittany Spaniel, had humorous run-ins with the neighbour's mule while Lorie, a former media company lawyer who created an atelier in the house for her figurative sculpting, told amusing stories about her seemingly innumerable contacts with local models and artisans.

"The initial appeal of this area was due to all of the trite stuff you hear about … the light, the food and the countryside," Lorie told me while waiting for a mason to arrive to install a new fireplace. "But I had a 'feeling' the second I saw this solid, sturdy house that I could live here for a long time without any headaches."

Her partner, meanwhile, often found daily life both comical and frustrating due to his not-yet-quite-fluent French.

"We loved this part of France and wanted to get a new place together while we both made the transition from full-time work to something completely different," added Bill, who had been based in Florida during his 25 year career with two international booze companies. "We wanted a location with a unique rural culture amidst virginal countryside with very few distractions."

"We conducted almost no academic research before we started looking for a place in Provence," he continued. "But we did spend a total of two to three months investigating the area around Aix-en-Provence over a period of three years. It then took us two weeks of constantly visiting different homes before we found the one we wanted. I think that actually 'being' in the area for a while before buying is the most important aspect of moving here. Trying to buy without getting to know the location and culture could be a big mistake."

The couple, who often walk up the hill each morning to retrieve their snail mail from the village post office and swap stories with the local electrician at the hole-in-the-wall café, kept in constant touch with the outside world using the Internet.

"It's very easy now, compared to two decades ago, because of email and inexpensive telephone connections," said Bill, who started a little computer and networking business on the side. "I sometimes feel a bit isolated because I lack the structure of my job and miss some friends. But I return to the US three times every year and these frequent visits keep me in touch."

Bill and Lorie also take early morning jogs on local roads and frequently hike on dozens of marked trails that meander through tiny villages. Bill, who's about my 5'9" height and maybe weighs a bit less than my 180 pounds, is in great shape for someone our age. At one point he lends me a butt-tightening DVD that, he says, is one key to staying trim. I watch it once.

The newly retired baby boomers don't entirely ignore the bright lights of the city. They have a *pied-a-terre* in Paris, a three-hour train ride away, and frequently visit Aix, where Bill has taken French lessons at the Scandinavian Institute.

"We're only 25 miles from Aix as the crow flies but the trip takes an hour because of the Luberon mountains, the small roads and the fact that we're usually not in a hurry," said Bill as we inspected his property. "Aix has the colours, smell, sights and ambience that I find very inspiring."

But it's not just Aix and the countryside that Bill's gotten to know.

"The greatest pleasure I've had since leaving the US is a sense of discovery of my own identity. I had too much tradition, too much baggage and too many habits to really learn about myself when I was living among 300 million Americans who shared many of my experiences," he reflected. "Here people really don't care where I come from but what I am, and how I act, on a daily basis. I find I am a little unique here as a foreigner and that accentuates who I am as a person. I'm Bill, not American Bill, just Bill."

We once took a trip together into Aix, which was a political and judicial centre under the reign of Louis II in the 1400s, to check out some monuments dating from the Roman era, as well as nine museums and dozens of magical fountains. The renowned tree-lined 17th century Cours Mirabeau, the city's main street named after the infamous Count Mirabeau, is a delightful tunnel of greenery with sprawling plane trees and elegant mansions with colourful façades.

"Aix vibrates throughout the year, unlike many places in Provence which only come to life during the summer tourist season," explained Lorie, who attends the International Festival of Lyrical Art held in Aix each July. "The city has a movement and lifestyle that is a great counterpoint to our somewhat isolated home."

One hot spot that Bill and I visited was the Thermes Sextius, the thermal baths named after the Roman general who founded the spa of Aquae Sextiae in 1 BC. Built above the original excavated foundations where the Romans once bathed in the natural hot springs, the modern spa offers an array of massages and thalassotherapy treatments. Our favourite: a 'Zen massage' that included a fine spray of spring water with specially chosen essential oils.

If you happen to be in the area, Bill and Lorie can frequently be found at Les Deux Garçons, the café and restaurant on Cours Mirabeau that is a watering hole for artists and writers, or at one of the many restaurants that serve Provençal cuisine replete with local herbs. They often walk the maze of back streets in Aix that wind through markets, historical monuments, artisan boutiques, art galleries and art supply stores.

"Living for substantial periods of time outside the United States without the structure of a job has forced me to recreate myself in an alien environment," Bill said as we drove back to Viens. "This has been a lot of fun, as well as a mental and emotional challenge, and I might be getting ready to write a book entitled *An American Retirement In Provence.*"

Bill once spent a week with me at the Abbaye de Lérins near Cannes and I knew he would love the sense of peace and serenity in a holy place like Montserrat. I asked him along on the MedTrek not only because he's a close friend and has been an invaluable sounding board as I work my way through the gut-twisting of my divorce, but also because he'd practiced walking meditation during a retreat with Thich Nhat Hanh at Plum Village in France.

As we walk beyond the monastery grounds to a towering rock pinnacle with a remarkable view of the Mediterranean, I describe the spiritual aspects of hiking.

"The Taoists had a thorough rationale for every activity, and hiking was no exception," I say, paraphrasing Deng Ming-Dao. "The physical benefit was undeniable, but there were also religious overtones. In the swift walking, one was allowed to trample neither plants nor insects. By walking in perfect silence, the students were expected to contemplate the beauty and meaning of the landscape they travelled through. A student who could sharpen his perception and understand the subtle inner workings of nature could also enhance his awareness of the Tao."

During the drive from Montserrat to L'Ampolla, I tell Bill about Delphyne's experience with a too-heavy pack, Luke's refusal to walk on our third day out, and my own sore toes due to cramped shoes. I encourage him to not try to hike too far at first and mention that my intended decade-long trek could expand into a two decade-long project.

"With that kind of timetable, there's no reason to get impatient about taking a day or two off," I said. "The Med and the path aren't going anywhere."

"Well, I've got a new pair of Mephisto hiking boots that the salesman claims won't produce any blisters," Bill said. "And I've got enough stuff in my pack for four days."

This is the first time I've hiked with anyone since Delphyne and I cantered through the Camargue. That was over 800 kilometres ago. Coincidentally the Ebro Delta, like the Camargue, collects tremendous quantities of alluvium carried down the Ebro River from the Cantabrian and Pyrenees mountains. The silting process is so intense that it adds ten metres a year to the rich-earthed depository that, since the 19th century, has been planted with rice and other crops.

We begin our trek near a fish factory where we're completely ignored by the employees in the whitewashed building as they clean and package everything from shellfish to eels. Once in the delta, we pass information points with signs that feature questions and answers concerning the Ebro National Park. We learn that it's home to mallards, red-crested pochards, grebes, ducks, coots, herons, warblers, gulls and flamingos. And that the abundant plant life includes sea daffodils, sea holly, sea spurge and sea medrick. Rice paddies have been recently harvested and there are fields of oranges, tomatoes, artichokes and cabbage waiting to be picked. We also discover that the delta has more than its fair share of bugs and mosquitoes. In 200 metres we both ingest more insects than I've met on the entire MedTrek.

"You know these things are really good for us," says Bill, who started the hike with a new pair of Columbia sportswear cotton hiking pants, a weathered Ralph Lauren brown shirt and a Boston Red Sox baseball cap. "They're full of protein, carbohydrates, calcium and iron. Eat as many as you want."

"Quit bugging me!" I joke.

As we circle Fanger Bay on a peninsula heading to the mouth of the Ebro, numerous small houses share two characteristics. They're all built on cement platforms, presumably to protect the rice-harvesting inhabitants from humidity and flooding. And they each have at least one barking dog tied by a frayed rope to the front gate. Presumably to alert the owner should a MedTrekker think about stealing fresh fruit or strutting chickens.

A comatose dog tied to one gate appears to be almost at the end of his earthly tether due to an apparent lack of water and food. Bill takes a canteen out of his pack and fills one empty bowl. Then he gets some granola, mixes it with water and puts the concoction in another bowl. He hand spoons some water into the dog's mouth and gradually gets the pooch to lick at some of the mush. We debate about untying the dog and taking him with us but instead explain the situation to the closest neighbour about a half-mile down the road.

"I hope that's the worst thing I see out here," says Bill, who's obviously reminded of his own dog. "I can't stand it when people mistreat helpless animals."

"Well, you did the right thing," I reply. "One beneficial aspect of MedTrekking is helping out strangers. You've gained merit by this action. Maybe you'll come back as a dog in your next lifetime! Or maybe even a god."

"A dog will do," Bill smiled. "As you know, I'd hate to consider myself the centre of the universe like some of those damn gods."

The 'real' Mediterranean is at our feet after a 14-kilometre walk on the bay. It's another nine kilometres, which we tackle barefoot, to the bank of the Ebro, easily the largest river since the Rhône. The width and lack of boat traffic force us to walk upriver. I tell Bill not to worry about our detour.

"Once we find a way to get across we'll have to walk just as far back down to the sea," I say. "It comes with the territory."

"Hey, I don't mind," he says as we start upriver. "It's so neat that we're doing this, just two guys going off on a hiking caper, that I'm ready for anything."

"I hope you feel that optimistic at the end of the day," I tell him. "But you're right, and it's something I remind myself every day. This is a unique little exploit and a lot of people would love to have this opportunity."

"Actually, I think this adventure is going to turn out to be your biggest payoff from staying sober and hitting 50," says Bill. "You know what you're about, know what you want to do and now you're doing it. That's pretty satisfying."

"You don't think there's partially an escape element to it all?" I ask. "Chloé thinks it's part of a mid-life crisis, just like it was part of a mid-life crisis when I went from being an alcoholic to a workaholic after I was sober for a few years."

"There's an escape element to everything we do," Bill replies. "But this is a lot better than some things. Just think that you could be back in Zambia where, I recall from a story you told me once, you got drunk, hijacked a bus and took twenty hookers from a nightclub back to your suite. This is a religious experience compared to that kind of mad behaviour."

"And I'm a monk compared to the wild man I was then," I smile.

There are few cars on the narrow road but we attempt to hitchhike whenever one comes by. It's clear that the only pursuit more dubious than one fifty-something-year-old guy hitching with a backpack is two fifty-something-year-old guys hitching with two backpacks. We meet a French couple that tell us they hike 15 kilometres around the delta every day during their vacation here. They reassure us that the road, which parallels the inaccessible riverbank, will take us to La Cava where there's a ferry to the other side of the Ebro.

It's past 6 pm when we arrive and the ferry has just stopped running for the day. Not that it matters. The ferryman explains that there are no hotels or restaurants on the other side of the river. "You'd have to sleep in the marsh over there," he says as he ties up his boat for the night. "You've got everything you need here."

We walk through La Cava until we find a room at the Delta Hotel on one of the many canals just outside town. Though we can't see much in the dark, this apparently is not just any hotel on any canal.

"The hotel is located in the middle of a micro system in front of a typical Delta pond with its islands and autochronous vegetation," according to a pamphlet in my room. It features a construction that 'imitates typical Delta huts' and a menu that has 'more than 70 courses which represent the traditional Delta cuisine and are elaborated in our grandmother's genuine style'. Who could resist? We eat five or six of the local dishes, including black rice and a strange type of carpy catfish.

"I feel like I'm a combination of Tom Sawyer and Huck Finn," Bill says as we plough into a sweet *crème brûlée* for dessert. "And I'm going to sleep like a baby after all that walking."

We arrive at the ferry at 7am after walking two kilometres from the hotel. Bill knows that I don't count this little walk as MedTrekking kilometres but questions whether I shouldn't start tallying the extra walking.

"I think you're cheating yourself by not counting every step you take," Bill says as we cross the Ebro. "It's obvious that you need to take every step. You're probably adding another twenty percent to the MedTrek."

"You might be right," I reply, "but I can't change my accounting methodology in midstream."

The path back to the sea leads us into the maze of rice paddies segmented by canals, dikes and waterways. The manmade water network may be an ingenious form of irrigation but it's difficult to make progress and we're completely disoriented. As we attempt to cross one ditch, we both slip into the omnipresent combination of grime, muck, bog, manure and mud that, says Bill, smells bad because it's rich in nitrogen, phosphorous, potassium, calcium, sulphur and magnesium.

"Jesus, whatever it is, this place smells worst than a Kinshasa whorehouse on a humid and hot Sunday afternoon," I say, when I realise that the stench is being absorbed by my skin and clinging to my clothes. "Phew! Easily the worst I've smelled so far."

"Try to look at it like the yin-and-yang," Bill reminds me as he touts the virtues of natural fertiliser. "The world would be a bore if everything smelled like roses."

The labyrinthine characteristics make for an adventurous walk that, says first-timer Bill, is "simultaneously rich and stark, a combination of Louisiana, Iowa and North Carolina." And this just a few minutes after his remark about nitrogen. Like Marie, Bill spits out allusions, references and information that offer a refreshing perspective to the hike. In fact, these perceptive comments often make me feel a bit stupid.

"I wish I could find comparisons like that when I hike," I tell Bill. "Instead, sometimes my brain gets so vacant as I march on that I'm unable to make those types of mental associations and colourful contrasts."

"I think it's great that you don't try to make comparative references," Bill replies. "Your mind is just taking things in without evaluating them. People would pay a lot to get to that stage."

The canals, marshes, swamps and waterways on the Trabucador Peninsula continue to interrupt our seaside walk after Els Muntells and we take the road to Poblé Nou, which gets its name from the 'old' Poblé del Delta. On the outskirts of Sant Carles de la Rapita are aquaculture and fish-raising ventures that include inland ponds covered with nets that prevent birds from swooping down to snag fish.

That night I know we've accomplished something momentous because there's a bubbly effect created by the nitrogen when I submerge myself in the bathtub.

Bill dutifully takes the next day off and I set out from Sant Carles, named after King Charles III who wanted to establish a model port here in the 1700s. The town has a remarkably uniform grid-like street plan and its palm-lined seaside promenade marks the end of the Ebro Delta, the Costa Dorada and Catalonia. I'm in the Levant region of Spain that continues through Valencia via Cartagena to Andalucía.

An eerie swamp-like mist obscures my look back at the Ebro Delta from a very pebbly Miami Beach that, a billboard proudly proclaims, 'has existed since 1959'.

As I take in the sight I feel like I've entered the Isle of Mists that Odysseus allegedly encountered during his journey home. You didn't read about that incident in *The Odyssey*? Some pundits in sci-fi circles claim the tale is missing from Homer's account because it was apparently too horrible for him to relate.

Why? Because our hero and a half dozen of his remaining men encounter winged creatures trying to destroy the human race at the behest of Persephone, the goddess of the underworld.

Five kilometres further is the Cementos de Valencia, a monstrous and rusting cement factory that has significantly scarred the nearby hills. I give its owners some credit for creativity because they named the beach near their private port the 'Platja del Ciment', or Cement Beach. I'm chuckling about the ludicrous name as I pass a shuttered Hostal Monte-Carlo and a closed Hotel Biarritz.

After Las Cases d'Alcanar, as I traverse cliffs and artichoke fields about twenty metres above the pebbled beach, I see an obviously confused and frightened flock of geese. They're hooting and honking their displeasure and fright as they alter their perfect Vee flight pattern to avoid a Goodyear blimp in their path. The Czechs, Lithuanians and other Eastern Europeans inhabiting the modest bungalows in Els Ametllers are all transfixed, heads bent back, looking up at the geese as I walk through town.

The situation reminds me of a time I was with my stepfather and a half-dozen colleagues from work in the mid-70s at Le Crazy Horse dance revue in Paris. A magician, who performed after Lova Moor and the nearly nude chorus girls sang *Hey, Big Spender*, made a duck disappear. My dad, who was an avid hunter (as was I as a kid), imitated a duck call so well that the disappeared bird came back on stage and wrecked the act. Today, though I'm not nearly as proficient at imitating a quack as my old man, I screech my version of a goose's mating call. The geese are so scared of the floating goose egg that they completely ignore me but everyone in town breaks out in applause.

That wasn't the first time I got some mileage out of my ability to imitate the intonations of honking squeaky squawking geese.

I covered Haitian dictator Jean-Claude 'Baby Doc' Duvalier's asylum-seeking exile in France beginning in 1986 and managed to trick the geese guarding one of the first of many villas he had on the French Riviera into thinking I was one of them and letting me onto the property. I called my article about that little invasion *The Grasse Isn't Greener on the Other Side*.

I had other ruses to get to Baby Doc who was not, as you probably already know, the smartest dictator to ever inherit power from his father.

I got my kids to play slaves and terrorists, which was a politically correct version of cowboys and Indians, with his children one day when we were all at a local tennis club and they managed to pick up a few titbits about the family. And I used to book my hairdressing appointments at the Jean-Louis David salon in Cannes when I knew Michele, Baby Doc's wife, was getting her hair done. In fact, that's why I wound up having my hair streaked for a few years. I needed to have something done to my do to justify sitting next to Michele for over an hour as she spun tales about the couple's $3 million wedding in 1980 and their life on the lam. Needless to say (and she thought only her hairdresser knew!), I wasn't surprised when they divorced in 1993. When I did my last articles on Baby Doc, after photographer David Koppel and I once caught him leaving his house in Vallauris and trailed him during a tryst with a female acquaintance in Cannes, I had access to one of his employees and got all sorts of gossip for the price of a few meals. With the coiffeur and the restaurants being paid for by *People*, the former president didn't have a chance.

A while later I have a coffee near the local bullring in Vinaros before continuing through more cliffside artichoke fields to Cala Punta, where a community of Germans has built numerous Hansel and Gretel-like bungalows. Serious work is underway on the promenade between Vinaros and Benicarlo, which has a decent-looking parador, one of the Spanish government-owned hotels found in scenic and historic locations throughout the country.

I arrive in Peniscola (it's pronounced Pen-is-co-la, not Penis Cola) where the seafront is also being refurbished as part of a multi-million euro European Union program. Bill's booked us into the Hostaria del Mar and there's a busload of Taiwanese tourists entering the hotel when I arrive. They, like us, have heard that the hotel's vegetarian paella is among the most remarkable dishes in the country. And, although I don't want this to sound like an effusive adjective-filled guidebook, I urge every reader to visit this place just to sample that scrumptious mouth-watering dish.

Peniscola's stone castle is built on a rocky outcrop just off the shore, and is connected to the mainland by a narrow spit. Built by the Knights Templar above the remains of Arab fortifications between 1297-1317, it was partially restored in 1960 when it was used for the Charlton Heston film *El Cid*. It's 64 metres above sea level and Bill and I climb it to start the next day's hike. We walk through the Renaissance entrance that was the 'obliged passage' from 1578-1754; visit the Gothic room, chapel and towers; discover that the walls are so steep that it's impossible to walk on the seaside below; and learn that the fortress was the refuge of Pope Benedict XIII and Clement VII during the Holy Schism in the 1400s.

A dirt *camino* stretches south along an undeveloped sea front with no road, no homes and almost no people. We see only one shepherd with a scattered flock during a twenty-kilometre hike along inviting rocky inlets and scenic cliffs next to a mirror smooth sea. Homer's line that "bad shepherds ruin flocks" comes to mind.

The pleasant diversion from humanity and urbanity lasts until Les Fonts, which consists of two completely vacated apartment complexes in the middle of nowhere. There are some nude sunbathers (Germans, *natürlich*) in the white-washed resort town of Alcosebbre, which has a boutique called Beautiful People, but the most significant phenomenon in Cap i Corp is a building dating from 1724 that's been converted into the Tunel discotheque.

"Kids could make as much noise as they wanted to out here and nobody would hear a thing," Bill remarks.

"It's a great place for a party but the problem with discos like this is that invariably some kid gets into a fatal accident while driving back to civilisation," I reply.

We find a hotel at the northern edge of Torrenostra and I leave half the sand of the Costa del Azahar, or the Orange-blossom Coast, on the bottom of the tub.

Bill heads back to France the next day and misses an interesting local innovation when I start the trek wearing a clean, blue 'Niagara Falls, Canada' T-shirt and a 'USA' baseball cap. The strip of the coast, separated from the *autopista* by marshes and swamps, features play areas on the sand with games intended only for kids of specified ages – 3-8 years old, 8-12 and 9-15. There's a guard at work to ensure that kids go to the appropriate part of the playground.

I have a MedTrek mirage moment when I see three swimmers in the distance. As I approach, I realise that the image is created by three large slanting logs with seagulls, their wings flapping, atop each of them. I recall that Odysseus saw such apparitions on a regular basis, though in his case it was usually that pesky Athena or one of the other gods in some kind of disguise.

There's a second MedTrek vision, though this one is real, in Oropesa del Mar. That's the Hotel Marina d'Or, which is fifteen storeys high and located right in the middle of the proverbial nowhere. Apparently, it's the forerunner of a to-be-built 'vacation city' that will include a nightclub featuring 'tropical dancing'. At the time of my visit, the building is empty and forlorn, though other high rise buildings, called Marina d'Or 2, 3 and 4, are planned to surround it.

I hit the 1600-kilometre mark on the MedTrek and am now, in theory, about ten percent of the way around the sea. This is an appropriate place for the ten percent mark. There's a recently renovated promenade with attractive benches, lots of high rises, a typically named Hotel Playa and a bar called La Sevillana serving *tapas* and *bocadillos*, which is the catchall Spanish word for any type of smallish sandwich or snack. *Torres*, or towers, decorate the cliffs and hilltops above the rocky and craggy beach path to Oropesa.

I leave my 'USA' cap at the $20-a-night Hotel Canada and can't find a replacement amidst the debris on the Estoril, though I do see a used condom, a used toilet and a used refrigerator. It's not yet summer but I'm severely sunburned by the time I get to the Pinar Beach in Castelló de la Plana, where the only cap I can buy is embroidered with 'Happy Sailor'.

I walk past a planetarium, golf course and the restaurant-filled Palacio de la Mar getting to El Grau de Castelló. *Grau* means landing place and there are dozens of these on the Azahar coast, usually linked in name with a town a few kilometres inland, like El Grau de Castelló or El Grau de Valencia. This one exports oranges, ceramics, textiles, shoes and other local products.

Across Platja Ben Aphelia and the Rambla de la Viuda River, a dry riverbed boulevard with crops growing in the rich soil, is Burriana. This is a working class part of the Med with large rock dikes, shacky houses and no hotels. In Nules, they've even shuttered up the ATM for the winter season that lasts until May. What would Odysseus have thought if he'd stumbled upon an ATM that, after all his trials and tribulations, wouldn't let him use his card?

This is a much more complicated question than you might think. Would Odysseus simply, as you might imagine, use his renowned strength to tear the machine out of the wall, take the money and run? Or maybe, like me, just shrug and walk on, knowing that there'd be another ATM in the next large city? Because he existed long before so many things that we all take for granted were available, like paper money and credit cards with smart chips embedded in them, it's hard to know what he'd do. My bet is that if he had instantly time travelled forward to see inventions like an ATM, an airplane, air conditioning, a necktie, YouPorn.com, a nuclear power plant, portable toilets and Miranda Kerr he'd either have a heart attack right on the spot or go absolutely insane. Who could blame him?

The dike and pebbly beach continue to Moncofa, which I presume is pronounced with a soft 'c', and my mind starts word gaming. "Moncofa I've come, man so far I've got to go," I chatter aloud as I continue along a seaside promenade with a pharmacy but no hotels, shops or restaurants.

"Does Moncofa have a centre?" I ask a woman on a bicycle.

"*Aquí no hay nada*," she replies. "And we pronounce it Monkofa."

There are some dikes being built between Moncofa and Xilxes and there's a lovely MedTrek moment when a carefree German sunbathing nude near his van is shocked to see me and, in scripted slapstick, jumps up and hides behind a towel when I approach.

"It's pronounced Chillclass," I'm told when I arrive in the next town.

Xilxes does have class. There's a plaza named after the Spanish Armada, new dikes, fresh sand on the beach and, remarkably, no high rises, ugly urban developments or hotels. But the beach becomes lower class just outside Xilxes. The shacks are so dilapidated on the edge of Casa Blanca and Corint that they would not look out of place in a New Delhi slum. The green Michelin guide diplomatically reports "sand and pebble beaches alternate and tourist development is negligible". Someone is playing flamenco chords on a guitar. I listen for a few minutes and chastise myself for playing the class game. Nothing wrong with lower middle class or lower class, I remind myself. They keep the tourists away.

The sun remains bright, the sea calm and the beach pebbly until Sagunto, where an attack by Hannibal led to a mass suicide by villagers and the onset of the Second Punic War. Today the accompanying industrial zone includes gigantic SolMed and GalMed steelworks plants, large trucks, ship berths, bad smells and more lower class housing. The only relief during an hour-long detour from the sea are fruit-laden orchards of orange trees and a completely empty parking lot at an oddly-placed multiplex cinema. When I arrive on the sea and look back at the monstrous plant and port, I welcome the walk on the lower middle class rocky beach front with shabby housing and an unpaved road.

Two Guardia Civil officers stop me near Pucol and examine my passport. They're not unfriendly, nor are they particularly impressed that I correctly pronounce Moncofa and Xilxes. It's dark when I find a strange hotel called the Residencia del Tiempo Libre El Puig. Though theoretically for retired people, I talk my way into a room. Once again, the oldsters dance until midnight.

I leave the retirement home the next morning for Pobla de Farnals where the seaside walk is again getting a facelift with those ubiquitous European Union funds. Nine kilometres from Valencia, a speedy dual carriageway is on my right and a long dike made of large boulders abuts the sea on my left. A colourful pack of cyclists is racing along the *autopista* escorted by motorcycle cops. In the distance is an Oz-like apparition of pastel-coloured high rises.

Oz turns out to be Alboraia, a modern development that includes massive blocks of ochre and sienna-coloured apartments amid a ring of Venice-like canals. But what makes this place different than Port Grimaud, Empuriabrava and other built-from-little-or-nothing ports is that it's inhabited, animated and going strong, even in winter. There's even a seaside commercial zone, complete with a Carrefour hypermarket and a McDonald's.

I enter Valencia on a beach that, on this Saturday at noon, has a wonderful mix of walkers, lovers, dogs, horses, sandcastle builders, kite flyers, topless bathers, smoking teens and everyone else.

Then I reach the gigantic El Grau de Valencia. Unlike most ports, this one includes attractive restored pavilions and gigantic cargo-loading cranes that have been converted into 'sculptures'. There are artists working on the quays and families out with their kids. I lunch on *tapas* near the Avenida del Puerto, which heads towards the city centre about five kilometres away, before hiking through the entire port, amidst ships from China and containers from Taiwan, until I cross the bridge over the Turia River. Not a bad way, I think, for a port to present itself, especially compared to the tightly closed Zona Franca in Barcelona.

Across the Turia, I'm on the Pinedo beach and in the Albufera National Park that, like the Camargue and the Ebro Delta, consists of marshes, rice fields and wildlife. The naked men lounging on towels amidst the dunes and reeds don't try to conceal the fact that I'm also in another gay cruising zone. A couple of them make it clear that they really like my headwear. I'm so embarrassed by all of the attention that I take off my 'Happy Sailor' cap and stick close to the water's edge.

Had I bothered to read the Michelin guide, I would have realised that this stretch of coast is "a 30 kilometre ribbon of fine, pale sand stretched along the sea's edge". And that's not all: "The excellent beaches have attracted the modest development of small seaside resorts, the villages in the past were built inland for greater security from raiders. Most resorts are accessible only along dead end roads through orange groves." Or by walking on the sand with a 'Happy Sailor' cap.

A paved walk between the dunes and the reeds, rice and marshes features an array of educational signs that explain everything about dunes, reeds, rice and marshes. Then I approach two-dozen high-rise apartment buildings that look bombed out and are inhabited by squatters. Finally, after a 34-kilometre day, I arrive at the five-storey, five-star Hotel Sidi Saler. I get a room, clean up and catch a ride back to the centre of Valencia, about ten kilometres away, in the hotel minivan.

Valencia has been inhabited by nearly everyone – the Greeks, the Carthaginians, the Romans, the Visigoths and the Arabs–and its fertile agricultural countryside is partly due to an irrigation system first laid down by the Romans. I light an electrically timed candle in the Cathedral, which is built on the site of a former mosque, and have an exquisite coffee scented with chocolate before I return to my luxurious $70 room.

21. MadTrekking with René, Cassandra, Leonardo and Warrior Girl

"My dear child, I can have no fears for you, no doubt about your conduct or your heart, if, at your age, the gods are your companions." — The Odyssey

René, a French swimming buddy who's been tracking my progress since I launched the MedTrek, drives down from France and joins me at the Hotel Sidi Saler. We've travelled to a number of swimming competitions together, including the French nationals in Vichy, and get along pretty well. He's a tall, stocky man and, like many Frenchmen of his era, is very well read and has forgotten a lot more than I'll ever know about the annual Tour de France bicycle race. Also like many of his countrymen, he's convinced that Lance Armstrong is a walking pharmaceutical company.

"I thought you'd quit when you got to the Spanish border," René admitted when I invited him to walk with me. "But now I've got to get a taste of whatever it is that keeps you going."

The next morning we're on the Devesa, a sandbar between the Mediterranean and an expansive freshwater eel-and-duck-filled pond called La Albufera, Spain's largest lagoon that gets its name from the Arabic word for 'small sea'. We soon run into some high-rise buildings and I mention to René, an architect in his early 60s, that this is typical of the coast around Valencia.

"The sandy beaches are interrupted, every ten kilometres or so, by these distinctly unattractive and too-tall apartment blocks," I tell René in French, as we walk amidst scores of sandpipers dancing in the sand. "There're also lots of infrastructure projects underway, especially seaside promenades and sewage treatment facilities, financed by the European Union. Our taxes pay for all this!"

"What's really remarkable is that all this building occurs in a place with so few permanent people," René says as we walk by fishermen who've caught bucketfuls of sea bass in a nature reserve that, says a sign, permits 'only professional fishermen to enter'. "It's all for summer tourists."

"The Spanish go wild building and renovating during the autumn, winter and spring before the tourists, mainly Germans, return in the summer," I reply as we enter El Perellonet.

René eagerly launches into a lengthy commentary on Spanish construction methods and the traditional role of European governments in promoting urban development. That keeps me quiet until we lunch on cheese, biscuits and cookies in El Perelló near a five-metre-long sailboat 'parked' in the middle of a street. No trailer. No benches. Just a boat.

We walk on an EU-financed promenade and sandy beaches that continue to Cullera at the mouth of the Xuquer River. I splurge on a taxi back to the hotel because I want René to have a painless introduction to MedTrekking. Along the way we pick up some local lore from the driver.

"The thatch-roofed cottages with whitewashed walls along the coast are called *barracas* and house the North Africans who work in the orange orchards during the picking season," he explains. "And you'll regret leaving town without eating the lagoon eels cooked in garlic and green pepper."

I convince René, a shower kind of guy, to take his first bath in 15 years after I describe its soothing effect on his soon-to-be-sore leg muscles. I explain that the bottom of the bathtub indicates the degree of difficulty of the day's hike.

"My tub looked like a Normandy beach after the D-Day invasion," he tells me when we take a seat to order lagoon eels and orange soufflé for dinner.

I throw out a toast from *The Odyssey* to get our first MedTrek meal together underway: "They made libation to the gods, the undying, the ever-new, most of all to the grey-eyed daughter of Zeus."

René, who once asked me to explain the Buddhist philosophy to him in less than five words (my response was "Do no harm"), gets a little philosophical as he sips a Courvoisier cognac and smokes a Cuban cigar after dessert.

"I recall some of the great travellers and my childhood heroes – Marco Polo, Jules Verne, Magellan and even Captain Cook, whose journals are a powerful read on exploration – and sometimes I reckon it would have been better to have been born 500 or 1000 years ago when there was a lot more potential for adventure into the unknown than there is today," René says. "There's just not that much room for novelty and completely pristine experiences now, though I admit that walking the Mediterranean isn't too bad."

His references, and don't ask me how my mental leaps work, move my mind forward in time to the 20th century.

"Actually there was still room for adventure in the 1900s," I reply. "Look at your own countryman Gontran De Poncins, who wrote the travel masterpiece *Kabloona* in the 1930s after he lived with Esquimaux (as he spelt it) in the high Arctic for a year. Or the Australian Leahy brothers who were the first white men to enter the Highlands of Papua New Guinea about the same time and capture it all on a Leica camera. All that was less than a century ago."

"And more recently I remember how my friend John Keeney deliberately chose to arrive in Paris with only five dollars in his pocket and see if he could survive," I continue. "I guess that, like me, he was inspired by George Orwell's *Down and Out in Paris and London*, which was published in 1933. Anyway, he arrived at the doorstep of winter in early November armed with rudimentary French and was determined to prosper from the ground up without drawing on funds from home. He lived with Laotian refugees, quit smoking due to lack of money and scrambled to find a variety of illegal jobs. Within a few years he had a well-paying profession as an advertising exec and, once he'd succeeded there, left Europe to create yet another existence in Sydney. Now about our age he has, I hear, reverted to staying in backpacker hostels instead of flashy hotels. I think the message is that if you want continual excitement in life, stay on the move."

Then I think of another dear friend, Catherine Domain, who owns a travel bookstore near my former apartment on Ile Saint-Louis in Paris. Her shop, appropriately called Librairie Ulysses, is still crammed to the ceiling with the best array of travel books I've ever seen in one place. She frequently left the store for months at a time and invented her own travels. Once she sought out an extremely remote dot of an island in Polynesia and lived with a small tribe that was nearly untouched by modernity. A diminutive woman, Catherine, who'd frequently get up and swim with me at the pool near the Panthéon at the break of dawn, always travelled alone and was experienced, fearless, sensitive. When I asked her about her least favourite country, she said it was Colombia: "The minute I crossed the border, I could literally smell the violence."

For some reason a fine piece of poetry from Gary Snyder's *Riprap and Cold Mountain Poems* pops into my head. Snyder was much more than a Beat Generation poet who frequently composed poetry while working/living in a forestry fire lookout in the North Cascades in Washington State. He studied Zen for years in Japan, won a Pulitzer Prize for Poetry and became a scholar, lecturer and an environmental activist who's been described as the 'laureate of Deep Ecology'. A verse comes back, that of a true traveller with a Buddhist perspective, and just before we order, after I think I've got it right in English, I translate it for René:

"In my first thirty years of life
I travelled hundreds and thousands of miles.
Walked by rivers through deep green grass
Entered cities of boiling red dust,
Took drugs, but couldn't make Immortal;
Read books and wrote poems on history.
Now I'm back at Cold Mountain:
I'll sleep by the creek and purify my ears."

"I better start reading Gary Snyder (he pronounces it "Needs-aire") to provoke a little more adventure and reflection in my life," René says as he orders another cognac.

The next morning it's time to abandon taxis and fine food. After all, this is a MedTrek, not an American Express tour. Our zigzagging day begins when we encounter the Xuguer River and head upstream to a bridge. A few kilometres after we return to the sea there's another slow-moving river with jumping fish, flying ducks, boated fishermen and riverside restaurants amidst delightfully smelling orange groves. René is tempted to rent, or even buy, a boat to get across. But again we spend over an hour heading upstream and, once we find a bridge, walking an hour downstream. The detour adds less than a hundred metres to the day's distance. There's another delay when we run into a large kennel of barking dogs.

"Did I tell you that I have a serious fear of dogs?" René says. "Whenever they're around, you've got to walk ahead of me."

"Don't worry," I say. "Like most of the people I encounter, dogs tend to be wary of hikers. Visualise yourself walking like a tiger. Slowly, slowly."

"I think we're going slowly enough already," he replies. "And not getting very far."

He's got a point. We've walked 18 kilometres in four hours but, as the cormorants fly, are only six kilometres from our starting point. Still I feel compelled to dish out some MedTrekking philosophy.

"Just take it a step at a time and remember what a sage once told me," I counsel. "'Keep it with faith, practice it with keenness, perfect it with faithfulness—then though the task be great, you will surely succeed.' It doesn't really matter how far we go."

That shuts him up and we continue through the nearly vacant resorts of Torre de la Vall and Xeraco. At dusk we stop to watch a competition on the Tavernes Beach involving a dozen fishermen, lined up 20 metres apart, each using the same type of bait and line weight to see who can hook the biggest fish. We watch for half an hour and no one gets a bite.

We get two rooms at the Bayern II hotel in Gandia and René takes the next day off. "I think I'll drive down the coast to investigate Benidorm, which is supposed to be the Saint-Tropez of Spain, and then pick you up at the end of the day," he says the next morning.

"Let's meet at the northern edge of Denia," I tell him. "I should be there by 7pm."

The solo hike along the manicured Gandia beach is peopled with promenading Sunday Spaniards until I arrive at the fishing dock and a larger port in El Grau de Gandia, used to export tons of local oranges. After hiking up the Serpis River to a bridge and returning to the sea, I traverse Daimus, Bellreguard and Miramar, a string of beaches on a seaside punctuated by uniformly unattractive apartment complexes. But after René's lecture about the poor quality of Spanish seaside construction and the lack of urban planning, I've taken a neutral moral and philosophical position on the pros and cons of both construction and urban development. I no longer judge whether the buildings are unattractive or beautiful. In fact, I try not to notice them.

I'm probably too kind about the many unattractive buildings and urban blights on the Spanish coast, but the fact is I simply don't find much point in constantly harping about them. Still I can't blame René. It's normal that someone coming on the MedTrek for the first time, perhaps driven by the need to develop a sense of perspective, is going to be thoughtful, analytical and vocal about what he observes. Whereas I, now firmly in the stride of things and perhaps too enmeshed by my own thoughts and transfixed by my own steps, have a duller sense of observation or, perhaps, simply less brain power. I'm still capable of freaking out when something offends me, but I find that I'm much more accepting than I was a few months ago. This is a big sea and, overall, it's much more attractive and alluring than it is ugly or diseased, disfigured, scarred, stained, blotted or afflicted. Or so I think.

The sky is darkening when I reach Oliva, the last town in Valencia province, and embark on the Platja de Denia. It takes me over three-and-a-half hours of steady speed walking to meet René.

We have dinner at a pizzeria called Clima where, once we're seated, the owner comes by and sprays the area around our table, and only around our table, with a lavender-scented aerosol disinfectant.

"You stink!" he says to me.

Glad he wasn't around after the hike through the Ebro Delta.

I used to know a swimmer in California who talked to his feet and encouraged them to kick harder just before each race. Then he'd pray to Nike, the Greek goddess of victory. The next morning I'm praying to Nike as I soothingly speak to my tired feet after yesterday's forty-klick sand trudge.

We march towards Cap de Sant Antoni and the majestic El Montgo hill on the Baetic Cordilera chain of mountains, which continue under the sea and reappear as the island of Ibiza. After a coffee at Arenettes, René pulls ahead of me and we separate. I walk along a cliff so steep that, due to the wind, I keep well away from the edge. I finally have the courage to shimmy to the precipice on my stomach and stare, transfixed, directly down the vertical rock face at the crashing sea below. I always imagine, at these heights, that my glasses will fall off and be lost forever in the sea. To help prevent that, I toss a coin into the sea as an offering.

René is not at the lighthouse at the tip of the cape, where I spend fifteen minutes giving breadcrumbs to a banded homing pigeon. I figure that, if he hasn't fallen off the cliff, he's ahead on the trail to the port of Xabia. A sign at the edge of Xabia says "Welcome to the Costa Blanca" but René's neither on the Tango Beach nor in any of the cafes. As I turn away from the coast two kids on a motorcycle yell out "*Hola loco!*" (Hey, crazy man!).

"Excuse me," I ask a man in Spanish. "Can you tell me where to find the bus stop?"

"No, I'm afraid I either walk or use my car," he said in American-accented Spanish.

It turns out that I've just met Leonardo who's not only a sixty-something American but also (1) offers me a lift up the hill to the bus station, (2) invites me to spend the night at one of the houses he's built since coming to Spain to avoid the draft almost 40 years ago, (3) says that if I don't mind waiting while he checks his email at an Internet café he'll give me a ride to Denia, (4) introduces me as "Joel, my friend who's walking around the Mediterranean" and (5) takes me to his home near what he calls "the mystical El Montgo hill that's the focal point for my daily meditation".

During our two hours together, Leonardo and I discuss my MedTrek, the '60s, the Vietnam War, women, marriage, kids and the time he spent in jail as an international drug trafficker.

"I first left the US to avoid being sent to Vietnam but after a while I felt completely comfortable living in self-imposed exile in Spain," he tells me when we reach his car. "It's a slower pace, everyone is more relaxed and back then there was much less stress about the government, money and prestige."

"As I look at America today it resembles an alcoholic on a dry drunk, like chickens on bad acid running around with their heads off," I agree. "It's an extraordinary place but everyone's always careening towards the extremes, whether the issue is war, sex, rock and roll, or the legalisation of marijuana. But maybe it looks that insane because I'm older."

"Whatever it is, I'm very happy that I raised my daughter abroad and at least exposed her to some other options," Leonardo adds. "Americans tend to forget that there are other ways to live, that we don't know everything and can learn valuable lessons from countries that have been around longer than us. Or even countries that haven't."

"Do you go back much?" I ask. "Can you go back?"

"I'm a free man but I've got some bad memories that still make me prefer Spain," Leonardo says with a smile as he describes his time in the clink which, for people of my generation and for that type of crime, might be a badge of honour but still tends to create a bad impression among some of the head chickens.

As we drive towards Denia, we run into René walking along the road. He's been wandering around the top of the Cap de Sant Antoni all afternoon and, besides spending thirty minutes with the homing pigeon, imagines that I'm the one who plummeted over the cliff.

I hug Leonardo when we part, which somewhat startles more formal René, and tell him that I'll return in a few weeks and we can walk together.

René gives me a lift back to the south of France and, after a break, I make the 1150-kilometre return drive to Spain with Cassandra, a forty-one year old Bostonian with bright red toenails who'd read an article I'd written about the MedTrek and contacted me about her own project.

"It's called a MedCrawl and I'm hiking from the Italian border to Toulon with a friend," Cassie explained. "Any advice?"

I met Cassie a few days later at the Carlton Hotel when she MedCrawled through Cannes. I appreciated her enthusiasm and invited her to join me for a stint of MedTrekking. We're now on the way to Spain with a movable feast that includes tapenade, stuffed grape leaves, rice cakes, granola and Maltese oranges. Along the way we pick up James, a 21-year-old hitch-hiking English student and wannabe hippie who'd read everything written by Beat Generation guys in the '60s, including Ezra Pound, Richard Brautigan and Ken Kesey. He loves hearing my tales of a Thanksgiving at the Keseys' in Oregon and the shenanigans surrounding the Woodstock music festival.

"And now you're hiking the Med?" he says. "That's pretty adventurous for someone your age."

"Did he say 'someone my age'?" I ask Cassie.

They both laugh.

We drop James in Valencia and arrive in Xabia. On the way to Leonardo's, who's promised us a feast of fish tagine, I show Cassie the dramatic clifftop view from the lighthouse where I'd met the homing pigeon.

"Did I tell you that I don't do particularly well with heights?" she wonders.

The next morning Leonardo, Cassie and I resume hiking at the Playa de l'Arenal near the mouth of the Jalon River. Things begin auspiciously near Cala Blanca when a security guard lets us walk through a private villa to get beyond the first cliff blocking our access along the sea. Leonardo, who's now a cook on tall-masted sailing ships, regales us with tales of his life since he left the US as we scramble down a cliff to the rocky beach and continue to the tip of the Cap Sant Marti.

It's a joy running into a raconteur that I liken to a Middle Ages minstrel. The walking is slow going and I often go ahead to check the path. I use a line from *The Odyssey* the first time I do some scouting. "I'll find out what the mainland natives are– for they may be wild savages, and lawless, or hospitable and god fearing men." At one point I walk a little over two kilometres before returning to let Cassie and Leonardo know that it's possible to proceed along the sea.

"What's the secret to walking long distances?" Leonardo asks.

"A lot of hikers consider this to be a type of meditation, walking mediation," I reply. "It's nothing very mysterious. A Vietnamese Buddhist monk says 'walking meditation is meditation while walking'."

"That's it?" asks Leonardo.

"The monk simply encourages his students to 'walk slowly, in a relaxed way, keeping a light smile on our lips'," I add. "He says that when we practice this way, we feel deeply at ease, and our steps are those of the most secure person on Earth. All our sorrows and anxieties drop away, and peace and joy fill our hearts."

"Sounds like the '60s all over again," Leonardo smiles. "Bring it on."

We reach the lighthouse at the tip of the Cap de la Nau, the westernmost of Valencia's capes and a traditional telltale sign for navigators. Then we cross the cliffs to La Granadell beach, where a narrow path extends up a nearly vertical cliff, and arrive at the hillside Cumbre del Sol, which a billboard calls 'Paradise on the Costa Blanca'. An Algerian worker offers us a lift back to Xabia. "*Chokrane, chokrane,*" I thank him as I give him ten euros.

That night, after a 35-kilometre day, we have a fresh fish dinner with Leonardo and his daughter China Moon on the port in Xabia.

Leonardo takes the next day off as Cassie and I virtually fall down the mountainside from the German-built Cumbre del Sol to the Platja del Moraig, best known for its nudist beach. There, besides the nudists, we find elaborate caves with multicoloured rocks and a kaleidoscopic array of colourful fish.

We work our way along the sea until a steep, crumbly-rock path heads up the hill towards a Middle Ages tower on the Cap de Moraira promontory. The going's too tough and we're again tumbling downhill, leading Cassie to decide she's having a "Kathleen Turner moment" due to the avalanche of small rocks. Like the actress in the Michael Douglas film, she slips and lands in a particularly embarrassing pose.

Cliffs dominate the coast and we walk a mix of main road, villa'd roads, cliffside paths, seaside paths and forested paths into Calpe where the 332-metre Penyal d'Ifac, a towering Gibraltar-like rock, dominates the town and dwarfs large apartment complexes occupied primarily by Germans. I suggest to Cassie that she take the next day off in Calpe, where our two rooms at the Hotel Porto Calpe look onto the sea, the port and the Penyal d'Ifac.

The Penyal d'Ifac is an ideal spot to start the next trekking day with Leonardo and Warrior Girl, a thirty-something former American stripper with eight tattoos and multiple piercings who's now a performance artist (and is definitely not a member of the San Francisco Warriors basketball team's cheerleading squad called The Warrior Girls). A friend of China Moon's, she's just arrived in the area and is crashing at Leonardo's for a few days before she starts work with a circus in Barcelona.

"I'm game for anything you've got in mind," Warrior Girl told me when I invited her to join us and mentioned that we'd be hitting some difficult terrain. "Lead the way!"

We walk the four kilometres to the top of the Penyal d'Ifac as screeching seagulls swoosh down on us like fighter jets to protect their young. Then we hike to the end of the Calpe promenade and tackle a cliff that makes yesterday's Kathleen Turner moment look like a slide in the park. I feel like a somewhat irresponsible guide during the next two hours as we encounter slippery rocks, vertical rock faces and steep mountainsides that we frequently traverse using guide wires left by some mountaineers. There's one particular chasm that we can cross only by dangling in mid-air for a few seconds, which scares the hell out of me not to mention my companions.

Neither Leonardo nor Warrior Girl (aka Kate McGlynn) are experienced enough for this type of climbing and I'm a fool for encouraging them to continue to hike, painfully and slowly, up the steep, steep mountain. Before we descend to the port of Olla, we pass some rock climbers going up a face called 'Coming Back to Life'. They look at us like we're idiots to be on the mountain without any equipment.

"This isn't just walking, hiking or trekking," Warrior Girl says to me when we stop for a much-needed breather. "This is extreme bouldering and it's very dangerous. It scares the shit out of me."

"I'm afraid you're right because it scares the shit out of me too," I agree without hesitation. "One of the unfortunate things about walking on unexplored turf for the first time is that the conditions are unpredictable. If it's any comfort, I'll take full responsibility for getting us into this."

"Well, that makes me feel a lot better," says the feisty and sarcastic street artist. "If I fall and die please make sure that my parents and my fans know that it was all your fault."

This isn't the first time I've found myself in a troubling position of leadership and responsibility. I led a group up Mount Whitney, the largest mountain in the mainland United States, which had to be climbed during the night due to hazardous weather conditions that would prevent a summiting the next day. We were well-equipped but you can only see so far, and so much, with headlamps and flashlights. After reaching the summit at 5am, enjoying the rising sun and then making the descent in daylight, I realized that on the way up I'd occasionally led my buddies off the trail and just a few feet from the edge of a precipice. I didn't mention to my comrades then, and I'm not mentioning it to Warrior Girl now, but dicey circumstances like this make my stomach feel like it's in a dizzying free fall. Fortunately, we made it up and down Whitney and today we make it alive to back to the sea. But people could have been injured, and it would have been my fault, in either situation.

"That was very stupid and it might have been dangerous but it was very cool," Warrior Girl admits when we collectively make a sigh of relief. "I'm going to find a way to use it in my act."

Well-constructed promenades, a sandy seaside, some rocky beaches and coiffed paths lead into Altea. The only slightly disconcerting moment occurs when we run into a guy at a gay beach who is ferociously masturbating in the middle of the path. He casually says "*buenos dias*" as we walk by without any display of self-consciousness about the task at hand.

"I've got a friend who puts walnut oil on his cock, get its hard and points it at the sun all afternoon," comments Warrior Girl. "He says it's rejuvenating. It's a free world."

"Sounds like the '60s," I say to Leonardo.

"Girls and guys were always naked in the '60s, and there was a lot of sex, but beating off to the sun is definitely New Age," Leonardo says. "I'll try it tomorrow and let you know what I think."

The next day Cassie and I start off on a seaside road that climbs to the lighthouse at the end of the Punta de la Bombarda. But after yesterday's experience, I forgo a pathless cliffside walk over the 435-metre-high Sainte Geleda Mountain in the direction of Benidorm. Instead we walk on a dusty road lined with villas and Cassie discovers a gold ring with eight diamonds on the sidewalk in front of 69 avenida de Monte-Carlo.

"This is a real omen," she says. "Finding a ring on the Spanish coast. Know what that means?"

"That we probably aren't going to turn it in to the lost and found," I reply.

Actually, Cassie makes it clear that she's thinking along more intimate lines.

"This portends that we are meant to be together as a couple above and beyond the MedTrek," she says, smiling as though a thunderbolt from Zeus had just transformed us into a peripatetic Romeo and Juliet with a fairytale ring. "It's only right because I have walked with you more than anyone else."

I obviously hadn't made it quite clear enough that, at this stage in my divorce, I'm not looking for anything more than a fit and intelligent Scrabble-playing MedTrek hiking companion, though I admit that I didn't completely reject intimacy. However, I proposed a 'don't ask, don't tell' policy about other relationships either of us might have in an attempt to prevent things from getting too serious. Cassie is a wonderful companion, and a decent Scrabble player, but it took me a few more kilometres before I realised that, from her perspective, only 'No' means 'No'. Anything else is synonymous with 'Yes'.

Benidorm has the most eclectic collection of high rises I've seen anywhere on the Med. Surrounded by lovely ochre-tinted mountains, the overbuilt city features two immense sandy beaches on either side of a tiny rock promontory, as well as five-star hotels, British pubs, all-you-can-eat fast food joints, cyber cafes and dozens of nightclubs. Even out of season, its 'tourist-dotted beaches', as one guidebook calls them, are packed with human flesh as tight as sardines in a tin.

We have a secluded picnic lunch near the blue-domed church on a terrace that looks onto Plumbaria Island, which according to legend was severed from Mount Campana by Roland with a single stroke of his sword.

We chat about the health of our parents. My father and her mother both have Alzheimer's disease and we discuss the ultimate release and relief that death will bring to them both. There are not a lot of positive things about that insidious disease but my father's situation did prompt me to get involved with a longitudinal research study that monitors my own mental abilities and, if it occurs, will track my decline. I initially had MRIs and various cognitive tests performed to establish a baseline and now update the exams and data on an annual basis. The results will enable researchers to track the course of the disease, if I ultimately get it, to better understand how it progresses. And I've given permission for the lab to dissect my brain and conduct further analysis after I die.

While there are some drugs on the market that arrest or slow Alzheimer's, and it looks like there may one day be medication to completely eradicate it, I'm not in this just for the science. I'm also doing it for selfish reasons. Should I be diagnosed with Alzheimer's, I want to be able to make some life-changing decisions before the disease has me completely in its clutches. I'll never forget my father attempting to futilely explain that he'd been afflicted by something that initially kept him from driving, counting change and recalling names. To paraphrase Bob Dylan, he knew something was happening but he didn't know what it was. He was cognisant that numerous of his skills were slipping away but he could neither describe nor fully comprehend his progressively deteriorating state. Had he been aware of the nature of his gradual decline, he might have chosen to pull the plug at some point.

Though I already have a living will that spells out what to do if I lose certain mental and physical capacities, receiving an early warning that I've got Alzheimer's will enable me to give very specific instructions about when and how I'll exit the stage. And make some very specific plans before I'm incapable of assessing my own deterioration. I'm not trying to be a god, but simply want the opportunity to exercise some free will and choice before the disease nails me.

After this pleasant rumination, I walk Cassie briefly through a visit Odysseus made to the "land of the death".

"It's remarkable that long before Christianity Homer already had a view of the afterlife," I say. "He suggests that 'no one has ever sailed to the land of the Death' but then Odysseus goes there and meets some 'shadows,' including his mother."

"What did he call the place?" Cassie inquires. "The Underworld? Purgatory? Heaven? Where was it?"

"The title of that particular book in *The Odyssey* is called 'A Gathering of Shades' and takes place in 'the cold homes of Death and pale Persephone'," I mention, noting that Persephone is the daughter of Zeus and the goddess of the Underworld. "Odysseus' mother calls it the 'gloom at the world's end' and it's located 'down dank ways, over gray Ocean Tides, past shores of Dream and narrows of the sunset'. But just think how fantastic it was for Odysseus to have a chat with his after-death mom!"

"Odysseus doesn't die, does he?" Cassie asks.

"No, Zeus says that 'his destiny is to see his friends again, under his own roof, in his father's country' and he's told by the prophet Teirêsias that 'a seaborne death soft as this hand of mist will come upon you when you are wearied out with rich old age, your country folk in blessed peace around you'. But sometimes Odysseus wants to die. He says once, when he's really depressed, that 'I should have had a soldier's burial and praise from the Akhaians–not this choking waiting for me at sea, unmarked and lonely'."

We traverse the second stretch of Benidorm's beaches, a total of ten kilometres from start to finish, and head to the Cala Finistrat Vilajoyosa.

"Ah, no more neon signs or fat sunburned German tourists," says Cassie. "We've left the shadows behind."

The next day the three of us – Cassie, Leonardo and myself – hike beyond Vilajoyosa, where I'm so intimidated by one steep incline that I make my companions plunge into the water to get around a cliff. The sea, so cold and refreshing, seems the best way to travel and as we're drying on the rocks Cassie says she'll never forget "diving into the cool, sparkling Med".

Drenched with sweat, we arrive at the top of a hill to find the luxurious El Montiboli hotel. Cassie has tied her bikini to her backpack to dry after our swim in the sea and Leonardo graciously offers to wash out the salt in the hotel fountain.

"Don't sniff them," I counsel as he grabs the bikini bottoms.

"Sniff them?" he replies. "I want to wear them!"

"Just like the '60s," I say as, despite our exhaustion, the three of us crack up and laugh until tears come to our eyes.

We're on mountain-top white dusty paths and reach one of many towers, relics of a Middle Ages defence network that punctuate the never-ending hills. As we descend we run into some caged rabidly-barking dogs. Cassie calls my method of trying to calm them a 'Vulcan mind melt'. It doesn't have much effect.

Stymied by a sheer rock wall that will require more gymnastics than Cassie can muster, we all walk back up the hill and run into a pueblo style hotel. We refresh ourselves under a very cold outdoor freshwater shower before buying a few litres of bottled water at the bar.

Then, against the advice of the concierge who tells me that it's "impossible" to walk through the hills to the next town, we head up the next hill.

When we arrive at the beach in Calapiteres, I hit the 2000 kilometre mark and anoint my lips, Cassie's lips and Leonardo's lips with seawater. A few days later Cassie gives me a tiny, varnished rock taken from the beach that says, in red nail polish, 'K 2000'.

"You are the most decent and the most patient MedTrek guide of the new millennium," she tells me. "You always seem to smell the right path by talking to and communing with the sea."

Now that, for me anyway, is about the best compliment I've been paid as a hiker and MedTrek guide, though I'm not sure Warrior Girl is going to give me an equally ecstatic review.

22. Shadow Dancing on Spain's Sandiest Shores

"And I myself should hold it to shame for any girl to flout her own dear parents, taking up with a man, before her marriage." – The Odyssey

A sign at the railway station in Calapiteres indicates that from September 15th until June 15th, after and before the oppressive summer heat, a 'Walker Train' promotes guided hikes every weekend from different stations. This, unfortunately, is a Wednesday and Cassie and I guidelessly follow some moderately challenging up-and-down paths to a sprawling tourism complex called Poblé Español. Beyond is a tiny promontory known as La Illeta where a team of archeologists is exploring some first century Ibero-Roman ruins. In the water, a German tourist spears one of the smallest fish I've ever seen taken out of the Mediterranean. He's ecstatic.

The beaches in Campello and San Juan are relatively empty and concessionaires at the two-star San Juan Beach hotel aren't having any luck renting mattresses or beach chairs. I buy some gazpacho, ham, cheese and bread at a mini-mart before we head out of town past a just-completed astonishing sand castle. It's a replica of Brussels' *Manneken Pis*, or Pissing Boy fountain, with the 'piss' supplied by a bucket of seawater. Another practical use of the Mediterranean. I enthusiastically toss some coins in the artist's basket and applaud his exacting execution.

It's so hot at the tip of Cap de l'Horta that we seek shade in a little cave with barely enough space to throw our heads back to sip the gazpacho. "This reminds me why I don't hike much in the summer," I tell Cassie. "There's more daylight but it's much too hot to walk, except at dawn and dusk."

"How did Odysseus cope with weather like this?" Cassie asks. "He must've gotten sick of the heat."

"You know, nature is omnipresent in *The Odyssey* but most of the comments about weather have to do with the state of the sea rather than the temperature," I tell her, admitting that I'm unsure what the weather was like almost 3000 years ago. "A typical description is that Zeus sent out a 'gloom over the ocean', which once is called a 'weary waste' and another time 'unmarked and lonely'. Odysseus didn't like terrible storms or layovers due to bad weather, but he didn't complain too much about the heat."

"Maybe it wasn't this hot back then?" Cassie continues. "Check that out, would you!"

"Actually it must have been warm. When Odysseus visits the land of the dead Teirêsias asks him 'why leave the blazing sun … to see the cold dead and the joyless region?'" I tell her. "And Odysseus talks about how he yearns for his wife 'as the sun warmed earth is longed for by a swimmer spent in rough water where his ship went down.' So the general climate may have not changed too much since then."

We're on a rocky path through the middle of a nudist beach where everyone is in much better shape than the white-skinned and swim-suited British tourist crowd here on a discount holiday. We round a cape on an ooh-and-aah scenic walk to La Albufereta on Alicante Bay and continue parallel to the railroad tracks to the tourism capital of the Costa Blanca.

The Greeks called Alicante 'Akra Leuka', or the white citadel, because of the large fort that still dominates the town's sole hill. The Romans renamed it Lucentum, the city of light, and Alicante is justly renowned for its luminous skies, as well as its natural harbour, sandy beaches, and the palm-treed Esplanada de España promenade with wavy multicoloured marble pavement. The tiles create optical illusions for arriving MedTrekkers and we both start hallucinating after our 31-kilometre day.

I head into the gigantic Melia Hotel, which is priced beyond my MedTrek budget, and thumb through a booklet that claims the beaches between Alicante and Cape Palos 'are Spain's sandiest shores'. There we check into the Hotel Alfonso el Sabio before dining on the esplanade where we play a game of Scrabble as we sip aperitifs. Between moves, Cassie asks another practical question.

"What did Odysseus think about extramarital affairs?"

"His wife Penélopê appeared to be faithful, put off her many suitors and 'let no man take Odysseus' honored place'," I say. "But Odysseus certainly met and bedded women, including goddesses, on his journey. He stayed with a couple of them, notably Kalypso who 'clung to him in her sea-hollowed caves – a nymph, immortal and most beautiful, who craved him for her own', for a long time."

"Did he tell Penélopê?" Cassie asks, as though I'm supposed to know everything about Odysseus' private life.

"He did mention Circe and Kalypso to Penélopê but it's not clear if he gave her details about the sexual liaisons," I tell her. "He's told by Agamemnon, whom he meets in the 'dark where the dimwitted dead are camped forever', that 'some things a man may tell, some he should cover up. Not that I see a risk for you, Odysseus, of death at your wife's hands.'"

"Nothing's changed," Cassie laments. "Men get away with it, women don't."

Our hotel undoubtedly has the two noisiest $25 hotel rooms in Spain. I awaken at 5am, after just a few scattered minutes of sleep, to the combined clamor of garbage trucks, drunks and screeching cars. Cassie and I are among the first customers at the nearby fruit and vegetable market, joining produce sellers and street sweepers for early morning coffee and rolls. She tells me that she plans to take the day off and read a walking meditation book written by Thich Nhat Hanh.

She randomly turns to a page and reads an excerpt: "As you begin to arrive with each step, you become more solid. As you become more solid, you become more free. Solidity and freedom are two aspects of Nirvana, the state of liberation from craving, fear and anxiety."

It looks like Cassie's made a sensible choice to skip the day's hike because the walk out of Alicante is hardly on Spain's sandiest shores. The trudge along the town's port abuts an industrial zone, railway tracks, an Alcoa factory and a Holiday Inn Express Hotel. It's ten kilometres to a beach in Urbanova, a dramatically congested and stark group of high rises.

The scores of apartment buildings are apparently a nesting place for British vacationers, perhaps because Urbanova is in the flight path of the Alicante airport and they want to feel close to their transport home. But Urbanova Three, the latest addition, features some decent condos and villas.

There's a paved promenade in Els Arenales del Sol that leads to the Cap de Santa Pola, which has nudist beaches and a view of the Tabarca Island. Numerous boats leave Santa Pola harbor for Tabarca and I briefly consider an outing to visit its Roman ruins. Instead I decide to stay still, cool down and wait until mid-afternoon to resume my walk. Even then I have to shadow walk, jumping and dancing from one bit of shade to the next, to the Llisa beach and the Vinalopo Delta salt flats, where there are gigantic brown and white hills of salt collected from nearby flamingo-filled marshes. I take a therapeutic MedSwim, letting the waves lap over me as I lay naked in the warm water, and then walk buck-naked to the Plata del Pined. After 35 kilometres, I plop down on the shaded terrace of the rustic and airconditionless Hostal Galicia that is 2068 kilometres from Antibes and wait for Cassie to join me by bus from Alicante.

The next morning I anticipate a quick and easy 17-kilometre walk along the seaside to the beach in La Mata where Cassie's found a room in the pastel pink Lloyds Club. But I hit the mouth of the Segura River that, though not as intimidating as the Ebro, is too wide and deep to swim. I head inland on a white, dusty road and pass fishermen catching *pequeños* fish until, tired and sweaty, I finally cross a bridge.

I'm rewarded by two novel observations. The first is Drometour, a corral and snack bar based on the premise that people want to go for camel rides. It looks like the wrong entrepreneurial venture because there aren't any cars in the parking lot and ten camels are lazing contentedly inside the corral. The next surprise is a topless woman juggling three balls on the beach, a scene that seems straight out of the film *King of Hearts*.

I take a plunge in the sea near Guardamar del Seguar and, experiencing a strange sensation, break into a jog despite the heat. I stop briefly to investigate a man who is completely, and inexplicably, covered with tar before I run into Cassie, who's decided to shift from MedTrek to vacation mode, tanning on the Lloyds Club beach.

The following day I set off barefoot on a carpet of sand past Torre del Moro and Lomas Altas to Torrevieja, a town that thrives, says the Michelin, "off fish, salt and tourists" presumably intrigued by saltwater lagoons that form the Salterns of Torrevieja.

An EU-financed walkway features a number of manmade swimming pools, complete with cement steps and ladders, amidst the rocks on the sea. There are some superb beach benches, colourful urban flower displays, garbage cans for organic refuse, a splendid port and a rare Santa Monica-like wooden pier. Fittingly, a seaside retirement home lets residents tool around the promenade with their wheelchairs and walkers.

Sandy beaches are mixed with cliffside paths in this southern version of the Costa Brava. Sunbathers frequent the palm-adorned beach in La Veleta but almost no one descends to tiny beaches tucked beneath the cliffs. One patch of sand, a steep walk down a red-coloured precipice, is completely vacant and immediately becomes my favourite. No, I don't recall the exact location but the sand is constantly being washed and, as Deng Ming-Dao wrote, "is free of lingering impressions". So is my mind.

At one point I'm on a manmade stone walk that winds enchantingly around Cap Roig to Dehesa de Campoamor, Torre de la Horadada, El Mojón and San Pedro de Pinatar. Ahead is an intriguing sandbar that separates the big Med, which is called the Mar Mejor, from the little Med or the Mar Menor, a placid 'inland' sea.

I'll figure out how to negotiate the sandbar between the two seas tomorrow but am exhausted and anticipating a decent sleep when I get to bed at 10 p.m., long before most Spaniards have dinner. But it's Saturday night and a band on the Lloyds Club terrace plays raucous tunes like *La Bamba* and *You Can Leave Your Hat On* until 2am. At one point, I sit outside on my terrace and attempt to listen beyond the music to the welcome noise of the sea waves. It doesn't work. The next morning the hotel offers us our suite for free due to the impossible-to-sleep-through noise. I chuckle again. 699,999 times out of 700,000 things turn out just fine without my intervention.

The sandbar separating the flamingo-filled Mar Menor from the Mediterranean is 500 metres wide and continues for just over twenty kilometres to the town of La Manga del Mar Menor. There's a break, of course, where the Mar Menor is fed by the Med, but a park official tells me there's one point, and only one point, where I can get across the chest-high water.

"It's possible to wade across the 400-metre gap that separates the northern and southern parts of the sandbar," he tells me. "The water will never get above your chin and you can carry your pack on your head. But stay near the tall wood poles securing the fish nets or you'll have trouble."

The crossing turns out to be a 15-minute wade walk. I move cautiously, sticking close to the fishnet-holding poles, and emerge on the other side to the amazement of two sunbathers who look like they've just seen someone walking on water. I step into tar, which has presumably washed ashore after an oil spillage at sea, for the first time on the MedTrek. I continue along the sparsely populated sandbar and horseshoe-shaped Playa del Pudrimal, taking a therapeutic dip before arriving in Tomas Maestre where I cross a drawbridge to officially enter the elongated seaside resort of La Manga del Mar Menor. Though there are some small houses on stilts, the dominating trend is high-rise apartment blocks called Las Vegas, Hawaii, Miami Beach, Monaco and Euromira.

My good deed of the day involves moving someone's clothes when they're about to be hit by a wave before I leave the sand to walk on the Gran Via, a two-lane road that stretches 19-kilometres to the centre of La Manga. Each kilometre is marked with a vertical surfboard, apparently a contemporary kilometrestone, and I'm particularly intrigued by 'Wonderland Circus' posters advertising Los Dakotas with two pictures of American Indians. The wavy Med on my left contrasts with the glass-smooth surface of the Mar Menor on my right.

Cassie's taken the Alicante-Cartagena bus line to a place called Los Alcázares, or The Fortresses, about halfway down the inland coast of the Mar Menor. It's not far from Santiago de la Ribera, the seat of Spain's air academy, and she gets two quiet rooms at the Hotel Cristina.

She's also got a present for me. She gives me a 'Life is Good' baseball cap to replace my weathered 'Happy Sailor' headgear before I walk out to a little promontory called Cabo de Palos, which is mentioned in *The Nautical Chart*, a novel I'm reading by contemporary Spanish author Arturo Pérez-Reverte. I pass the vibrant and picturesque port, make my way through a few housing developments and shout with glee when I find a GR that goes through the stark mountains ahead.

I strip down and take a swim at the 15 K marker, casually floating on my back with an 'Ah, this is the middle of nowhere' feeling. But I briefly lose the GR when it meanders through an expanding housing development near the Alamaria golf course. Fortunately, one of the builders knows its location and skirts up the hill with the speed of a mountain goat to show me the way.

The GR, with four-star views that would impress the most jaundiced outdoorsman, cuts inland before I arrive at an out-of-use military base at Cenizas where I spend fifteen minutes absorbing the view from the top of a cliff. Deng Ming-Dao ("Knowing things in advance is possible with a high vantage point") and Lao Tsu ("With a high vantage point, foretelling the future is elementary") were right about heights.

I look back at La Manga before heading downhill to the lighthouse, port and beach at the Playa El Lastre where a honeymooning couple from Madrid give me a lift to Los Nietos at the Mar Menor. There, in a bar, a Moroccan agricultural worker offers to take me back to the hotel.

I tell him that I've just completed a stupendous leg of the MedTrekking that I'll use to promote my hiking venture to potential hikers. The 24-kilometre sandbar that separates the Med from the placid Mar Menor is a unique natural setting; the high-rise sandy beach environment in La Manga and the homey fishing port in Cabo del Palos are contrasting urban areas; the seven-hour hike mixes demanding 300-plus metre mountain climbs with steep cliffs, wave-battered rocky coves and sandy beaches in a completely stark and isolated natural environment; and it all ends at a little lighthouse and tiny marina in the middle of nowhere.

"Have a beer on me," says the Moroccan.

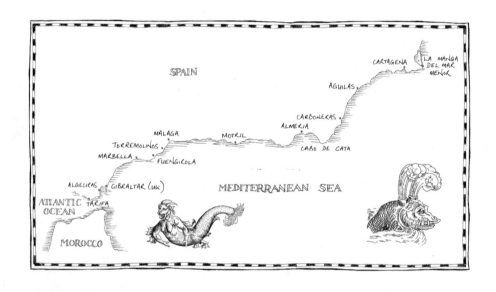

SPAIN

CARTAGENA

LA MANGA
DEL MAR
MENOR

AGUILAS

CARBONERAS

ALMERIA

MALAGA

MOTRIL

TORREMOLINOS

CABO DE GATA

MARBELLA

FUENGIROLA

MEDITERRANEAN SEA

ALGECIRAS

GIBRALTAR (uk)

ATLANTIC
OCEAN

TARIFA

MOROCCO

Part Six

The End of Spain: Travels With a Sorceress and a MedCrawler

23. Trembling on the Beach

"When men lack a sense of awe, there will be disaster." – Lao Tsu

I fly into Alicante on a mid-June afternoon after a nine-month break from MedTrekking and the plane cruises over Calpe, Altea, Benidorm and other coastal towns that I've already visited on foot. The longest interruption since the project got underway was due to working trips to Ghana and Tunisia, a foot fractured while rock climbing in France, and a lengthy jaunt in the US with my kids. I murmur a contented "ahhh ommm" when I return to the exact spot I left off. The sea and the path can obviously survive without me. As Thich Nhat Hanh says: "The beautiful path is patient, always waiting for you to come back."

I start off, striding across a one-kilometre reed-covered beach towards Puerto de Portman. Ahead are a dozen peaks, each slightly over 300 metres high. As I approach the first hill, I recall a conversation the night before with my friend Alison at her apartment in Antibes.

"I've finally learned to avoid playing around with cliffs and rock faces that look like they could cause trouble," I told her as we sat on her terrace and watched the powerful beam from the lighthouse on Cap d'Antibes play on the sea. "I've resolved to take the sensible, easier road. No more dashing through briars and daring detours on cliffs faces for me! I'm going to act my age."

Then I discover a rusting pipeline that abuts the seaside cliff and is topped by a catwalk about three metres above the spraying sea. Who could resist? I carefully crawl on my hands and knees for 400 metres, simultaneously getting drenched by waves and admiring the sheer rock face towering above me.

"Yes, this is why I MedTrek!" I say to myself. "I cherish the unknown and slightly dangerous nature of the path."

The pipeline dead ends and I'm forced to climb the first rock face of the day. I playfully scamper up and over the hill to reach a beach populated by thousands of seagulls hypnotically fixated on an offshore fish farm. They don't even bother to move, much less fly, as I walk past them. They look like they're all on Prozac and don't have a care in the world. I'm so concerned about the possibility of an avian Jonestown (you might remember that this is the name of the place in Guyana where Jim Jones led 900 members of his People's Temple cult/sect/ congregation in a mass murder-suicide in 1978) that I rush towards the birds to assure myself that they're neither dead nor decoys. One or two reluctantly take flight and give me a look that seems to say "Leave us alone, we're tripping." I know the feeling and utter a silent apology for wrecking their high.

In six kilometres I encounter another steep hill with skin-cutting scrub bush and prickly pines that seem intent on blocking my way. There are no trails, either on the hills or along the sea, and I move at a snail's pace through the increasingly challenging overgrowth. After gingerly hovering over the edge of each clifftop to admire the sea below, I pass an out-of-use carabineers station, a former military camp, and some uninhabited high-rise apartments. The buildings, and their inhabitants, apparently all gave up battling the proliferating vegetation and these inanimate structures appear, like the birds, to have overdosed on antidepressants. If there is something in the air causing this widespread somnolent state, or maybe a mysterious force that's cast a comatose spell on the entire coast and transformed both animate and inanimate objects into nearly lifeless beings, then I might be the next to go. The words I write right now could be my last. So, if that's the case, I'll end this paragraph with one of my favourite phrases: 'This too shall pass'.

A few minutes later, still alive, I dance down a steep pathless hillside to take a dip, cool off and soak my cuts in saltwater. But I'm still sweating profusely after my swim and there's no way to make any progress on the seaside. Somehow I clock 28 kilometres without taking a too-nasty fall, losing my pedometer or getting frustrated to the point of actual tears. But I've run out of water and am parched by the time I reach a dirt road winding downhill towards a port below.

I apparently didn't notice the first signposts indicating that I'm walking in a 'Mined Military Area'. When I do see the numerous markers, I figure that I've come too far to turn around. But at least I have another explanation for the Rip Van Winkle state of this place. Maybe it's the mines that prevent birds and humans from flying, walking or living here. Maybe it's the mines that have created an undisturbed environment that has lulled even usually neurotic seagulls into a sense of smugness and complacency.

I make it unscathed to the Escomberas tanker port and refinery complex where a clerk working in a tiny office at a company called Praxair takes one look at me and, not even bothering to let me spurt out the details, hands me a two-litre bottle of chilled water and invites me to sit in his air-conditioned office. He's an actual human being and his movements and chatter end my Jonestown reverie. But it's so odd to see a balding man wearing a tie and working in relatively normal circumstances that I feel like I've just walked from the land of muted zombies into a Kakfa novel.

Then I relax and realise that this guy is simply the god of the day. He's taken to heart the words that Eumaios utters to Odysseus: "Come to the cabin. You're a wanderer too. You must eat something, drink some wine, and tell me where you are from and the hard times you've seen."

"Did you really come over that mountain on foot?" he asks. "Didn't you see all of the 'No Trespassing' signs? You're lucky you weren't killed. I hear explosions all the time."

"Do you think the noise is so intense that it's wrecked the sea gulls' hearing and knocked them out?" I ask. "They look so tame that I could have picked them up."

"No, don't worry about them," he smiles. "They're all on Prozac. Want some?"

This is becoming too Kafkaesque for even Kafka to fathom.

I tell him about my project and then, refreshed, continue into Cartagena, a sprawling naval and commercial port that exports lead, iron and zinc ore. The city, at the back of a deep bay, was settled in 223 BC by the Carthaginians and further developed by the Romans. Then it was neglected by the Arabs, who favoured Almería further down the coast, and the Christians, who preferred nearby Murcia. Cartagena returned to prominence during the reign of Philip II, who fortified the surrounding hilltops, and Charles III, who established an arsenal. A submarine invented by a local in 1888 decorates a roundabout near the Plaza del Ayuntamiento and Fort Concepcio.

Things start nicely the next morning with an elaborate breakfast at the Cartagena bus station where, anticipating a hot hiking day, I splurge on two coffees and a chocolate croissant. It's easy walking around the port to the local lighthouse where I begin an uphill climb through brush and briar to a rocky road with a panorama of yesterday's walk through the 'mined military area'.

Today's exquisite terrain presents me with radically steeper cliffs and sheerer escarpments, even more up-and-down walking, yet another half dozen off-limit military installations and dizzying dramatic drops to the proverbial deep blue sea. The GR 92 runs through here but, though there've been some attempts to keep the hiking paths marked, I frequently lose my way due to overgrown brambles and bushes. After a dozen kilometres I realise that I've been looping around in the hills and am still within spitting distance of Cartagena.

I finally head in the right direction and approach the peaks of the Sierra de la Muela mountain range, each over 500-metres in altitude and covered with pitch-smelling mastic aromatic trees that produce a resin used for lacquer and varnish. It's a perfect locale for eagles, foxes and wild boar but not a great place for casual walkers.

I begin a determined march to the very distant lighthouse at the tip of Cabo Tiñoso. Again the brush pricks me and my shorts become completely shredded when I slide on my ass down a rock-and-gravel 300-metre escarpment to the nudist camp at Portus that, I'm amazed to learn, is only 11 kilometres from Cartagena. It's taken me hours to get this far and I'm so frustrated that I relax, swim and remove splinters on the Playa de la Morena nudist beach until I have the strength to inquire about the conditions of the path across the mountains to La Azohia.

A thirty-something Spaniard, with a long ponytail and a substantial beer gut, introduces himself as Armando and insists that it's a well-marked three-hour hike to my destination. For some reason, and tell me if you've ever had the same reaction, I presume this fellow has some credibility and knows what he's talking about just because he's an aging hippie.

"You'll easily make it by nightfall," Armando says with authority as I refill my water bottles.

"Thanks so much for letting me know," I reply. "I've had a rough day and it's nice to know that it'll soon be over."

It turns out to be a 7.5-hour hike on a primitively marked path to Cabo Tiñoso, which a guidebook correctly describes as 'the wildest and most solitary aspect of all the coast of Cartagena with a powerful automatic lighthouse with a range of 24 miles'. By 9pm, after I've walked 12.5 hours and 47 kilometres, I still haven't neared civilisation and am running out of light, energy and water. I take a dip to cool down and explore my options. It's a 20-kilometre walk inland on a narrow dirt track to the main road and, not in the mood to make the hike in the dark, I decide to crash on a sandy beach. I hadn't anticipated this and am not carrying a sleeping bag. But fortunately it's summer.

"Let me lie down tonight as I've lain often, many a night unsleeping, many a time afield on hard ground waiting for pure Dawn," I say to myself, echoing a line from Homer.

I'm awakened throughout the night by constant noise produced by waves crashing on the rocky beach. Sand? Forget it! I'm sleeping on pebbles and only get a few hours sleep. A line from Homer haunts me around 1am: "Rag of man that I am, is this the end of me? I fear the goddess told it all too well – predicting great adversity at sea and far from home."

Then I remember a response from Odysseus when he had the blues. "Where is your valour, where is the iron hand that fought at Troy for Helen, pearl of kings, no respite and nine years of war? How many foes your hand brought down in bloody play of spears? What stratagem but yours took Priam's town? How is it now that on your own door sill, before the harriers of your wife, you curse your luck not to be stronger?" Get a grip, Joel. This too shall pass.

After some predawn meditation and stretching in the dark, I start walking at first light. The summer solstice sunrise is spectacular and I'm sweating profusely by the time I finally reach the Campillo de Adentro military fort atop Cabo Tiñoso. I learn from a sign that the structure, which is an imitation of a medieval building, dates from 1929 when it was part of a Plan for the Defence of Naval Bases by Primo de Rivera.

But who cares?

I'm so relieved when I see a town in the distance that I collapse on the flat bunker near one of two colossal Vickers cannons and fall asleep for an hour. Then I descend to the sea and begin scavenging for water. There's a little left in a plastic bottle, some Sprite in another and a Styrofoam green water cooler has some condensation at the bottom. I mix them together and it's the best cocktail – I'm even comparing this to my drinking days – I've ever had.

I put my pack in the mouldy water cooler, shed my clothes and jump into the sea. I plan to kick/swim around the jutting point towards the Gulf of Mazarrón because I'm tired of dealing with escarpments, climbing and cliffs. I'm in the water for about 20 minutes when a Frenchman, who turns out to be an underwater photographer, insists that I jump in his motorboat for the 500-metre final sprint to the edge of La Azohía. I hesitate, thinking this might be a violation of MedTrek ethics, but then, truly fatigued, I climb aboard. When he drops me at a little fishing port a few minutes later, I immediately head to a bodega and drink a litre of water and two cups of coffee. A lackadaisical fisherman insists that the sea here is rich with tuna, bonito, melba and lecha and that the nearby Tower of Santa Elena was built in the XVI century to give protection to local fishermen and guard against pirates. Reassured, I walk on the thank-god-it's-flat road for a few kilometres and check into the four-star La Azohía Hotel near Isla Plana.

It's only noon but I decide to call it a day. I want to rehydrate, bathe, sleep, and recuperate.

The next day I stroll along La Costa Calida and am overwhelmed by acre after acre of tomatoes being grown under sheets of plastic that create a growth-provoking greenhouse effect.

I'd noticed in the market yesterday afternoon that there are ten different types of local tomatoes at ten different prices. "The area around Mazarrón is famous for its tomatoes and only its tomatoes," a hotel receptionist had told me.

I pass through the Puerto de Mazarrón on a palm-lined promenade and walk barefoot on the sandy beaches into Bolnuevo where I buy lunch, including more tomatoes. At two, feeling more than a bit like a Greek god, I'm sitting naked on a beach with chilled gazpacho, fresh tomatoes, bread and a banana. Walking barefoot, buying tomatoes and having a naked lunch are three simple things that were impossible during my two gruelling days in the Sierra de la Muela Mountains.

I return to a dirt path that takes me into Punta de Calnegre where I climb a steep hill just beyond the village and descend into the best-maintained isolated beach resort I've run into. Apparently this is the first stage of an industrious scheme to develop this completely undeveloped area for tourism.

I bypass the next string of mountains by concentrating, a step at a time, on walking and jumping on seashore rocks underneath the cliffs. It would probably be impossible to make this passage at any other time of year but it's doable at the onset of summer. After 42 kilometres, worried about reaching the next village before dark, I begin walking on a dirt track that parallels the sea.

Then, seemingly out of nowhere, I see a Chrysler SUV churning up dust on the dirt trail. The driver, a woman in her 40s, stops when she sees me and offers to take me four kilometres to a paved road. Once we get there, she offers to take me a few more kilometres to a bigger paved road. And once we get to the bigger paved road she says she'll take me all the way back to the Hotel Azohia.

My chauffeur turns out to be French but has been living in Spain for a decade. She tells me that she'd been sunbathing on a beach and heard me walk by. I tell her about the MedTrek and in a while we're discussing the physical and spiritual aspects of hiking.

"Religious people definitely have written a lot about walking as a way to create a balanced life," I said. "But I do it for all sorts of reasons – physical, spiritual, emotional, enjoyable."

"Christ always walked," she said. "And so did Buddha."

"Well, they didn't have Chrysler SUVs back then," I smile.

I take my book of Tao daily meditations out of my pack and turn to page 42. Then I translate the words of Deng Ming-Dao into French: "Walking may be a good metaphor for spiritual life, but there are times when simple hiking is literally the best activity. When one walks in the woods or climbs mountains (or strolls alongside the Mediterranean, I add for effect), there is a wonderful unity of body, mind and spirit."

Then I quote a phrase from Thich Nhat Hanh: "When we walk as the Buddha did, we continue his work. We nurture the seeds of Buddhahood in ourselves and show our gratitude to the Buddha, not by what we say, but by the way we take peaceful happy steps on earth. To have peace, you can begin by walking peacefully. Everything depends upon your steps."

I've been in the car for 30 minutes when I see a gas station and offer to put 20 euros worth of gas in her petrol-guzzling SUV. Actually, I have a hidden agenda. The Chrysler's windscreen looks like it's just survived a red-and-yellow bug-launched terror attack.

"That's a really dirty windscreen," I nonchalantly remark, as though it hadn't been bugging me for the entire drive, when we pull up to the pump. "Mind if I clean it while we're gassing up so we can have a clearer outlook on life?"

"Are you complaining about the cleanliness of my windscreen after I've given you a free ride?" she laughs.

When she drops me off, she asks if she can walk with me.

24. Encountering a Sorceress

"Her ladyship Kalypso clung to him in her sea-hollowed caves – a nymph, immortal and most beautiful, who craved him for her own." – The Odyssey

The next day's theme is cadavers, five of them in fact. In order of discovery they are: a dead man, a dead dog, a dead turtle, a dead fish and a dead seagull. All on a seashell-and-fossil speckled 30-kilometre stretch of beach. I'm accompanied by Jacqueline, the 45-year-old Spanish-speaking French woman I met yesterday whom I consider a guide put in my path by Zeus "who gives what fate he pleases to adventurous men".

The fisherman's body was being pulled ashore almost directly beneath Jacqueline's penthouse terrace in Aguilas before we started our walk. And we literally stumble upon the remains of the dead dog and the dead turtle as we approach the base of the majestic Cabo Cope Mountain after returning to the exact spot where she'd picked me up.

"This is very unusual," I tell Jacqueline. "It's abnormal to see this much death on a MedTrek."

"Once death begins to appear, it's all over the place," Jacqueline replies, as though there are some days that you encounter death and others that you don't. "One reason I'm studying sorcery with a very old Danish woman living in the hills outside town is to make sense of things like this."

Danish woman? Sorcery? The last thing I need is some New Age neophyte. But I keep my mouth shut and let her continue.

"She's been here for decades and everyone respects her power," Jacqueline adds. "But don't worry, I'm a novice. It's just a mid-life project, like your MedTrek."

Many people I run into are godlike. And Jacqueline–with her lithe body, long blonde hair and sharp features–seems to me to bear a distinct resemblance to Circe. If she's a goddess, she didn't even bother with a disguise.

"Watch out," I reply. "Or I may, as Odysseus told Nausikaa when she saved him on the beach, 'invoke you as I would a goddess, princess, to whom I owe my life'."

"That would be a big mistake," she said. "I'm just another human being and confusing me with a goddess would be really dumb."

Jacqueline, who is wearing sparkling white Reeboks, has no trouble negotiating the coastal trail and initially confines her comments to the state of the sea and the remarkable colour of the landscape. Nothing personal, just general observations as we climb the staircase of the built-from-stones Cope Tower before tackling the climb up and around the Cabo Cope. The dizzying ascent on almost non-existent paths up a vertical mass of slippery rock is a bit precarious and atop of one peak Jacqueline plaintively squeals in French *"Je veux ma mère!"* (I want my mother). She calms down when we find a trail downhill to the sandy beach in Calabardina, where we see the dead fish and the dead seagull.

"See what I mean!" Jacqueline said. "When death is around, death is around."

We have a coffee in Calabardina and a dozen people at the bar insist that it's impossible to hike further along the sea. They're wrong. Although we occasionally have to wade, the 10-kilometre stretch into Aguilas is relatively easy. Jacqueline, once we get wet the first time, hikes in a sexy red bikini.

When we reach El Hornillo district of Aguilas, I check into the $25 Hotel Bahia on the port. I shower, put on a clean t-shirt and change my hiking boots for sandals. Built on two sides of a rock promontory, Aguilas dates to 1765 and we continue strolling along the seaside promenade past its crumbling but still-dominating castle to Jacqueline's place. She gets cleaned up and we head out for a midnight dinner of steamed vegetables and a fish stew that, if we can believe the unshaven waiter at El Faro, consists of grey mullet, meaty monkfish, cod, tuna, squid and mussels.

During dinner, Jacqueline mentions that she's a widow and describes her grief and anger following her husband's early and completely unexpected death over a decade ago. "He was there one moment and gone the next," she explains. "I learned very quickly about the impermanence of life."

She makes it clear over dinner that she's content living alone and doesn't want the complications of a man or a relationship.

That, of course, makes me even more intrigued by this simple, self-contained and seemingly content woman with whom I'm just beginning to launch a friendship that, I hope, will mature with each step we take.

Jacqueline recuperates the next day while I head towards the province of Andalucía, which begins six kilometres south of Aguilas. The well-marked GR92 traverses beaches congested with sun-worshipping and generally overweight Spaniards. The Sunday crowd includes some serious day trippers who bring tables, chairs, tents, refrigerators, beds and books to the sea. My first kind act of the mid-morning occurs when I see an elderly woman who appears to be drowning in the surf. I shout to alert a nearby family who, busy setting up camp, don't seem too enthusiastic about coming to her assistance. They don't even look too happy when I pull her out of the water. Maybe they're not related. Maybe she's just trying to commit suicide without bothering anyone.

"I just saved this woman," I shout. "Does she belong to you?"

No one seems in any hurry to admit ownership or a relationship. But one very fat man looks like he's just been cheated out of his inheritance.

"Yes, she's my mamma," says a thin woman who appeared to be in the unfortunate position of being married to El Gordo, the fat man. "We think she wanted to kill herself which is why we put her in the water in the first place."

"My apologies," I say to El Gordo y la Flaca. "But please don't put her back in the water or I'll report you to the police."

It's slightly overcast, there's a steady breeze and I'm ready for any terrain that Mother Med might throw at me. I run into some low mountains, numerous little capes, and dozens of beaches before I spot my first 'Puerta de Andalucía' sign in San Juan de los Terreros. Billboards announce that I'm on the Costa Tranquil and the Costa de Almería.

The pleasant stroll between El Pozo del Esparto and Villaricos is on a two-lane blacktop above a rocky coast punctuated with an occasional luxurious home. After 30 kilometres I cut down to the coast through a gigantic tomato and melon patch, then walk barefoot along a three-kilometre Playa Naturista in Vera Plage. Jacqueline joins me in Garrucha the next day to continue towards Mojacar. She insists that she lost three kilograms during our first outing and I resolve to treat her to a decent lunch.

We reach the Indalo Hotel at the end of the seven-kilometre long Mojacar beach and chat with the owner of a *chiringuito*, a snack bar on the sand selling drinks and sandwiches. Then we trek along shoreline stones, cliffs, creeks and beaches until we arrive at the English-run Obscure Bar, where we take time out for a long lunch of scrumptious fresh *rougets* and tiny baked potatoes to the tunes of the Traveling Wilburys and Duran Duran. Before we leave I politely ask Jacqueline to dance under the straw roof at the cabana restaurant.

"I could never dance in public, especially in the middle of the day," she says. "I'm a very reserved and prudish woman. Don't try to change me."

I ask her what she'd like me to do if she doesn't want me to ask her to dance.

"Teach me!" she says. "I realise I can learn something from you. You're like one of those ancient sages walking around and imparting tidbits of knowledge to people. Teach me, teach me. But please don't try to make me dance."

We climb, scamper and frequently swim as we proceed along the many isolated beaches. Then, because Jacqueline is sensibly unwilling to attempt a jump off a fairly high rock, we make a high, sweaty and hard climb inland. When we return to the sea, it's taken us an hour and a three-kilometre walk to cover the equivalent of 25-metres on the coast.

"This is the type of detour that adds distance and time to the MedTrek," I tell Jacqueline. "Though it's not as bad as getting stuck on an island with Kalypso for seven years, like Odysseus did."

"It was a lovely detour and we're in no hurry," she replies. "It would take a lot more time if either of us got hurt jumping when we shouldn't."

We reach another beach where, frustrated by an insurmountable abutment that runs into the sea, we escape from the heat by taking shelter in a deep cave to chill out before attacking the steep, tower-topped hill on the outskirts of Carboneras.

At sunset we're having *tapas* at a bar called La Esquina and, having long ago told Jaqueline that I can't/don't consume booze because I'm an alcoholic, she directs the conversation to my drinking. Like most normal drinkers who can take it or leave it, she has little comprehension about how troubling and life-threatening alcoholism can be.

"You're such a balanced guy that I can't believe it could have been too bad when you were drinking," she says as she orders a *cerveza* and I get a glass of fresh orange juice. "Just how crazy were, or are, you?"

That kicks off a half-dozen colourful stories about my behaviour when I was on the sauce, from the wild '60s in California, through the irresponsible '70s in Africa and Europe, and into the transitional 1980s when I finally recognised and admitted that I'm an alcoholic and tried to do something about it.

"I divide my life into three periods: childhood years of innocence, a reckless era of indulgence until I was thirty-five, and my current time in recovery," I begin. "The '60s were a wonderful time to get strung out on booze and drugs and the area around San Francisco, where I went to college, was the place to do it because everyone was encouraged to reach for the extremes. And I took that to heart."

"Give me some examples," she requests.

"I went to the San Francisco Airport in 1968 to pick up a female friend and parked my white Toyota Corolla, which I'd named Roxanne, in the red zone in front of the arrivals hall," I start out. "There were open cans of beer on the front seat, a case of beer and a bottle of Chivas on the back seat, and a cartoon drawing I'd made of cops looking like pigs on the dashboard. When we returned fifteen minutes later, the car was surrounded by police cars with flashing red lights and it was obvious that a few cops with flashlights had already looked inside."

"I quickly told Marty to pretend to be my sister and start bawling which, to my amazement and relief, she did. When we reached the cops I immediately admitted that it was my car, that I'd been drinking and that 'Look, our mother just died and I've got to get my sister to the funeral home. You can arrest me if you want but let her go say goodbye to our momma's corpse. I really don't care what happens to me.' For some reason, and this is absolutely indicative of the times, they let me drive away. No ticket, no reprimand, no nothing. In fact, they were much more upset about the picture of the pigs than the liquor."

Then I tell Jacqueline about the time I drunkenly broke into a store in Big Sur, stole 60 cloth purses and handed them out to all the women on the Stanford campus. And the time I was in court on a speeding charge and took LSD before I told the judge that I'd rather serve seven days than pay $70.

"When they took me into the cell I told the cop that 'I'm going to get you when I get out of here', which is perhaps the stupidest thing to say a cop when you're going into jail, or even when you're coming out," I continue. "He threw me into a cell with a guy who kept telling me how easy it is to kill people. But because I was a middle class white guy I got a phone call and had a friend come pay the fine and get my completely stoned body and soul out of jail."

I continue with a few more titbits from my interminable drunkalogue and mentione the hangovers, blackouts and periods of humiliation that gradually made me realise that I was completely out of control. Alcohol might have made me slightly creative and amusing in the early days but it was now ruling and wrecking my life.

"I went to a dinner party in Rome where, already drunk on arrival, I apparently insulted everyone, tried to pull the tablecloth away without upsetting the fine china on the table (I was later told that my magic trick didn't work at all) and pissed on my date shortly after we got into bed back at the Hotel Angleterre," I calmly recollect. "The next morning, with a thrashing headache, I didn't remember a thing about it. And that type of blackout occurred dozens of times everywhere in the world, from Zaire in 1974 where I was covering the aborted Muhammad Ali fight to Zanskar in Kashmir after a Himalayan trek in 1980 and at the 10,001 Knights club in Munich in 1982.

"I'm amazed, today, that I got away with so much without killing myself or anyone else," I conclude, admitting that I made amends to a number of people, and the Big Sur store, when I first got sober. "I definitely consumed enough liquor for this lifetime."

"Weren't people a little freaked out when you quit?" she asks. "After all, it sounds like you were the life, or death, of the party."

"I remember coming back to Europe after a trek in the Himalayas and showing up at some of my old haunts in Rome with my buddy Michael Erleigh, who's since died from his addiction to alcohol," I recall. "Most people didn't even notice that I'd quit drinking and I was a bit reluctant in those early days to tell my friends what was going on. When I didn't feel like spilling out the whole truth, I just told people that I'd had a spiritual awakening in Ladakh, was now a practising Buddhist and was following a suggestion that I not drink any more alcohol until the next lifetime. That usually shuts them up. And my belief that it was true kept me sober for 18 months."

"What happened then?" Jacqueline inquires.

"I was back in Rome in late 1983 and met a lovely Australian woman working with an Italian telecommunications company," I continue. "We went to a nightclub where a friend of hers was celebrating a birthday and, without thinking, I took a glass of Champagne. Within a few minutes, I was pulling at tablecloths and knocking over bottles just like the bad old days. I went to my first AA meeting two years later and haven't had an intentional sip since."

After dinner and the end of my story, Jacqueline heads home with a couple who offer her a ride in an air-conditioned Jaguar.

The next morning I head down the seaside promenade looking like a Boy Scout in clean clothes and a new black baseball cap. I pass the towering thermal power station at the edge of town and jump gingerly from rock to rock below the cliffs. I slip and there goes the Boy Scout look after only nine kilometres. Everything is wet. My thick socks probably won't dry for days and my credit cards and map are soaked.

I head up the hill to the Faro Roldan lighthouse and a 14th century Moorish tower to follow a *sendero* or path chiseled into the hillside that's blazed with circular piles of small rocks. I'm immediately reminded of something written by Deng Ming-Dao: "Even a little circle of rocks beside the trail – who put them there, or did any hand arrange them, and no matter which, what are the secrets of that circle?"

The coastal path meanders into the Cabo de Gata-Níjar *Paraje Natural,* or natural park, where a remarkable array of cacti, dwarf fan palms, a strong wind, austere hills and arid terrain have served as the set for *Lawrence of Arabia* and dozens of spaghetti westerns.

Just beyond San Pedro a motley crew of contemporary hippies have set up house, including a large tribal teepee, in an old tower and a dozen caves. I turn down their offers of drugs and a game of chess but do follow their directions to a spring where I fill up my water bottles. One young woman assures me that the water is potable.

"I've been drinking it for six months and haven't gotten sick," she tells me, pointing to a sign that encourages hikers to take their garbage to Las Negras rather than leave it here. "You can bed down here, if you'd like, we've got extra food. Or it's about an hour to Las Negras."

There's something alluring about their set up. For some reason I recall New York Mayor John Lindsay telling a television interviewer back in the 1960s that he was thinking giving up politics to join some hippies living in the caves in Crete. That seemed like such a revolutionary idea for a politician that it's always stuck with me.

Everything, me included, changed very dramatically in the mid-60s, of course.

Drop out of pre-med, make booze and drugs my gods, and major in religious studies and creative writing at Stanford? Then spend over thirty years working as a journalist in Africa, Asia and Europe? Raise bilingual and bicultural kids and try to teach them about compassion, gratitude, humility, impermanence, moderation and unselfishness? Walk around the Mediterranean? Moi?

When I get to Las Negras I enter a little boutique and launch into a complicated conversation in Spanish with a woman about my age. Explaining my plight and wondering if there's a spare room around, I tell her I only have 20 euros in cash and that my credit cards have been drenched and might not work. After letting me spiel on for a few minutes, she responds in perfect English.

"My father's Spanish and my mother's Irish," she says with a broad smile. "And I've got a room you can have for ten euros. Don't worry, we'll take care of you."

I call Jacqueline, who never goes to sleep before 2am, and arrange to meet her further down the trail at noon the next day.

After sleeping nine hours (it's so rare that I sleep nine hours that I feel compelled to mention it whenever it happens), I continue on the *sendero* through a *paraje natural* populated by hawks and snakes. I run into a French hiker and we agree that we could be at a wadi somewhere in the Jordanian desert. I manage a pleasant up-and-down 14 kilometres before I meet Jacqueline in La Isleta del Moro.

We're discussing walking meditation when we stumble upon a memorial tombstone with a picture of a 17-year-old German girl on a horse. How, we ask each other simultaneously, could she have met her death in this isolated spot?

"It's nice that they've given her such a splendid little tomb," says Jacqueline, as we eat our lunch on a high, rocky outcrop called the Punta de Loma Pelada. "And I guess it doesn't really matter how she died."

We follow a road through the park that continues into San Jose. My feet, irritated by the itchy sea-wet socks, are sore and my thighs, irritated by the itchy sea-wet shorts, are chafed. When we get to Morrón de los Genoveses we stay at a hotel with a lobby decorated with photos of Peter O'Toole, Richard Chamberlain and other actors who've shots films here. The next morning we see scores of cats, presumably to remind us that we're about to head to the tip of the Cabo de Gata.

25. "No Job—No Money—No Worry" on the Costa del Soul

"And no adventurer could beat Odysseus at living by his wits – no man alive." – The Odyssey

The vast Cabo de Gata park is devoid of people, cars and cats due to a strong wind and impending rain. A sail-less catamaran is anchored in the bay but otherwise it's me, the sorceress, the sea, the sand, the mountains and lots of multicoloured ochre-tinted rocks. I haven't been to the moon yet but I wouldn't be surprised if this turns out to resemble a moonscape.

The wind is so intense at the tip of the orca-shaped point that it almost bowls us over. We walk like overloaded sherpas, bending over to hug the narrow, rocky path to avoid being scooped up and pitched into the sea. At the flat top of one hill, we make an eerie MedTrek discovery. There are packs, clothes, shoes and other belongings strewn across the rocky peak. Their owners, or former owners, have disappeared, perhaps driven off the cliff by the wind. Most of the labels are in English and we speculate about a collective suicide or lemming-like drowning.

A dirt road, barricaded to prevent automobile traffic, gradually winds up to the highest peak in Cabo de Gata. We're wearing rain gear and are completely wet and extremely wind-beaten when we finally arrive at the top. But the striking limestone cliffs, rustic coves, stark hills and isolated beaches make the three-day hike from Carboneras one of my MedTrek favourites.

The turbulent sea looks more like the Pacific Ocean than the Mediterranean today but Jacqueline is content to acknowledge the stunning vista with a meagre and noncommittal *"Pas mal!"* (Not bad). No *"magnifique"* or *"super"* for this French woman. We pass the nondescript village of Cabo de Gata, which definitely lacks the majesty of the cape, and continue to Retamar, one of those modern built-but-never-completed developments.

Jacqueline returns to Aguilas that night and, exhilarated by the promise of a sunny day, I eagerly prance along a beachside dirt road the next morning towards Almería. Typically, the day begins with a surreal MedTrek image: two teams of three Alaskan Husky sled dogs are pulling two bicycle-riding Spaniards through sand that's so white it almost resembles snow. The dogs don't appear to notice the difference.

By mid-morning I've changed from jeans to shorts. Everyone – fishermen, cyclists, joggers, walkers, cars – seems to be out. I pass a small airport, a university and an EU-financed water treatment plant before I get to Almería, where the Alcazeba Arab fortress dates from 800 AD and the Cathedral was built in 1524 to replace a former mosque. There's a municipal theatre, a spic-and-span seaside promenade, a portside Club de Mar sports complex, vestiges of the old port, a sparkling new port with ferries to Morocco and the dramatic cliff-hanging *autopista* precariously perched above the middle of town.

I continue to Aguadulce, or Sweetwater, on a new road, an old road, beaches and rocks and, after some succulent salmon-and-ham *tapas* at a beach restaurant, cruise into town through a port with an eclectic mix of retail outlets, like the 'American Rock Café' and 'Kangaroo Australia Grocers Store' that obviously cater to foreigners arriving on sailboats and yachts. A road sign indicates that it's 213 kilometres to Málaga.

I check into the three-star Hotel Andarax and the next morning head out of town past newly built palatial villas and 37 Costa del Sol construction cranes. Then I see the first GR92/E10 sign since Aguilas. How could the GR gods have ignored the extraordinary Cabo de Gata yet reappear amidst a flurry of construction projects that includes a mammoth building topped by twelve garish green cupolas?

After the Costa del Cranes, I walk a few kilometres on spiffy promenades and clean beaches through Roquetas de Mar and enter the peaceful and serene Ponte Sabinar natural park. A signpost informs me that it's a five-hour walk to Almerimar and, on a sandy beach between marshes and the calm sea, I figure they could change the name of the coast to Costa del Soul or Costa del Sole.

It's a 12-kilometre hike to the Sabinar lighthouse and I run into two German couples, swim-suited and barefooted, walking in the opposite direction. They think it'll take an hour to get to Roquetas. I tell them it's taken me three to walk from there to here.

"*Drei Stunden, Schutz!*" one husband says to his wife.

They thank me for the reality check and turn around.

I stop for lunch at the Nautilus restaurant in Almerimar before continuing through Guardias Viejas, Balerma and Balanegra alongside the tomato-squash-and-bean-filled greenhouses that line the coast. The sea, often separated from the greenhouses by rock breakwaters, has little niches of sand but the smell of fertilisers and piles of plastic and containers aren't very inviting, though paradoxically this is a very well marked segment of the GR92/E10 trail. I eat some fresh peppers to pep myself up for the final run into Adra, where the seaside promenade abuts greenhouses and pens of sheep. Both vegetables and beasts are meant for human consumption but they seem like an odd tourist attraction to be found after walking more than 80 days, and precisely 2622 kilometres, from Antibes.

When I arrive by bus back at Jacqueline's late that night, there's a steaming bath awaiting me. I feel like Odysseus when Homer wrote "And soon a call came from the Bathing Mistress who led him to a hip-bath, warm and clear – a happy sight, and rare in his immersions after he left Kalypso's home – where, surely, the luxuries of a god were ever his."

Two days later, within minutes of setting out, Jacqueline and I stop to watch a father and son successfully snare wild canaries using some of their already-caught birds to lure them into an unpretentious trap made from cardboard boxes. We quietly sit down to enjoy the game of cat-and-mouse, or man-and-finch, won by the patient duo.

"The head of a biotech company in Sophia Antipolis told me that the Spanish generally use five times the legally permissible amount of pesticides on their tomatoes in this particular area," I whisper to Jacqueline as we prepare to exit the scene of ensnarement. "It's amazing that there are any canaries left. But these guys are geniuses and we should help them patent and sell their simple but effective bird-catching process."

Seaside cliffs force us onto the main road between Almería and Málaga and we walk next to zooming-by traffic for an hour before returning to the dirt path between the sea and omnipresent greenhouses.

Jacqueline, very put off by the malodorous state of agro affairs, launches into a discourse on the environmental destruction caused by greenhouse agriculture. Then, visibly perturbed, she quietly begins collecting symbolic heart-shaped rocks until she feels "synchronised and balanced" again.

We have an outdoor lunch in La Rabita that consists of gazpacho and *tamales* stuffed with heavily seasoned chopped lamb before marching through La Mamola, where we see fish drying on nets in the sun. Anchovies, says Jacqueline, who's never seen this sight in Spain.

Then there's another MedTrek surprise. The main road heads inland for the next nine kilometres and we're on a nearly abandoned seaside lane until we arrive in Castelló del Ferro.

During dinner that night Jacqueline devises a way to secure my pedometer to my pants to avoid it falling into the sea.

"Your deft needlework reminds me of the goddess Athena," I tell her. "She wasn't only the goddess of wisdom, the daughter of Zeus and probably the reason that Odysseus stayed alive during his travels. But she also presided over all of the useful and ornamental arts of men and women, including spinning, weaving and needlework."

"Don't start thinking I'm a goddess just because I can keep your pedometer from falling in the water," Jacqueline says. "If I were a goddess, we wouldn't need a pedometer."

Her comment reminds me of a remark by Odysseus when Alkínoös suggested that he might be a god.

"You may set your mind at rest," Odysseus told him. "Body and birth, a most unlikely god am I, being all of earth and mortal nature."

He still didn't need a pedometer.

The next morning the cliffs and terrain force us back to the main road.

Fortunately, it's Sunday and, because anytime before noon is early for Spaniards in this part of the country, there's no serious traffic during eight kilometres of road trekking above the calm sea, gurgling creeks, tranquil coves, steep cliffs and inviting beaches.

"There's no better time to walk than early on a Sunday morning because it's invariably so peaceful," I tell Jacqueline. "Before everyone gets to the beach, even the sea and the shore look like they're getting a day off."

"And the Spanish habit of big family gatherings for lunch on Sunday keeps many away until late afternoon," she adds.

Then, in a rare burst of levity, Jacqueline says she thinks I should write a story about a man hiking the Med, meeting a sorceress in Spain, falling in love and then learning that the sorceress has been hired by the man's former wife to kill him before he changes his will. Sounds like one of the sagas or parables from *The Odyssey* but like Odysseus, I figure the hero, or anti-hero, will survive.

We take a trail into Calahonda, or Deep Creek if you want the English translation, and I regale Jacqueline with an account of Ken Kesey's antics in La Honda, California, while I was attending Stanford.

"I read *The Odyssey* at Stanford but was much more influenced by Kesey's *One Flew Over The Cuckoo's Nest* and *The Electric Kool-Aid Acid Test*, Tom Wolfe's book about Kesey and his merry pranksters who were on a two-decade acid trip," I say. "*The Odyssey* was part of a Western Civilisation course but the instructor didn't have any reverence for mythic voyagers and nearly forgotten gods. Somehow, despite him, I developed a fondness for Homer's epic and a bit of wanderlust."

"Did you ever meet Kesey or any of those other '60s authors?" asks Jacqueline, who'd seen the Milos Foreman film of Cuckoo's Nest starring Jack Nicholson.

I tell her about spending Thanksgiving at Kesey's place in Oregon in 1968 and mention that I first spoke to Norman Mailer when I called him in 1969 and offered to fly east to help him campaign for mayor of New York City.

"I guess the two things I remember most about Kesey's farm is that I'd baked some cookies and gave them to his kids the moment I arrived. When Kesey's wife Faye saw their smiles she looked at me and said 'You've got the gift,'" I recall. "The weirdest thing about the spread wasn't the weathered Merry Pranksters' bus or Kesey's incessant energy, it was a toilet just off the main room with nothing to shield the person using it. I called it The Naked and the Head."

Jacqueline doesn't get the joke until I explain that Mailer wrote *The Naked and the Dead* and that another English word for toilet was head, which came into being because toilets were traditionally located near the bowsprit, or head, of a ship.

"Mailer told me that 'Son, this is a tough part of the country and it isn't the place for a clean-cut California boy like you', when we spoke on the phone," I went on. "I ran into him dozens of times after that – during graduate school in

New York, at a conference at the Sorbonne in 1983, at the Cannes Film Festival in 1987, and in Los Angeles just before he died – and consider him a major influence on my attitude if not my writing, though I frequently stole many of his techniques in my early days as a reporter."

"Who else influenced you?" she asks.

I recount my run-ins with poets like Richard Brautigan and Lawrence Ferlinghetti in San Francisco in the late 1960s and described my fascination with the works of Kenneth Patchen, the author of *The Journal of Albion Moonlight* who lived in Palo Alto. I mention that my favourite contemporary screenplay is William Golding's *Butch Cassidy and the Sundance Kid*, which she'd also seen; that my favourite book of criticism is D.H. Lawrence's *Studies in Classic American Literature*; that I love, and frequently recite, Oscar Wilde's puns and witticisms; and that I'm still in awe of Bertrand Russell's *A History of Western Philosophy*.

Some of the names don't mean anything to her but it was authors like these – and I've got to add Homer, Chaucer, Herman Melville, James Joyce, Hart Crane, Malcolm Lowry, Jack Kerouac, Ernest Hemingway, F. Scott Fitzgerald and J.D. Salinger to the list – who inspired me to travel and write.

"One of the intriguing things about *The Odyssey* is that every translation can almost be considered a different book because the choice and use of English words is so different," I go on. "I can't read the original Greek but love the lyricism of both *The Iliad* and *The Odyssey* which, of course, were first passed down by story tellers that the Greeks called bards or rhapsodists."

"Have you thought much about the deeper meanings of Homer's books?"

"I haven't written or read an academic critique of Homer since college, when I wrote a nonsensical and pretentious paper about Odysseus' pride and prejudice," I reply. "I have a superficial understanding of *The Odyssey* but it expands a bit with each reading and I could probably hold my own in a debate because I know the story so well. It would be worth writing about my MedTrek if it could inspire one person to get as excited about making his or her own unique journey as I did after reading *The Odyssey*."

"Well, you've already got me excited just by taking me on your walk and talking to me," Jacqueline says as we got to the other side of Calahonda in just a few minutes. "If you write a book in French or Spanish like you speak French and Spanish there's no telling what it might encourage people to do."

"Like?" I ask.

"Like improve their French or Spanish," she smiles.

We leave Calahonda for Carchuna near greenhouses where cleanliness and recycling are more impressive than the stench of fertiliser. There's even an advertisement with the telephone number of a company that will take away used plastic for recycling.

"This is a sign of progress," I tell Jacqueline. "I'm going to call these people to congratulate them."

"They don't want congratulations," she says. "They want plastic. Call him if you find some."

"Well, let's start picking up stray pieces and we'll give him a ring," I reply. "Remarkable to think that there wasn't any plastic when Odysseus was on his journey."

Once out of town, the sea cliffs are impassable and we circle around the lighthouse on Cabo Sacratif, which we figure means either 'sacred' or 'sacrifice', on the road. There are exceptional views down on translucent bays, where the water is so clear that it's impossible to tell whether it's deep or shallow, until we descend into Torrenueva and follow a rocky, gravelly and sometimes sandy beach to the Gran Hotel Elba in Motril.

Jacqueline spends the afternoon at the hotel and I head out on the spic-and-span promenade to Playa Granada, where a sole horseback rider appears between the sea and sugarcane fields against a backdrop of the setting sun. Beyond the Guadalfeo River I follow a rock-hewn seaside trail to La Caleta where Jacqueline picks me up at dusk. She immediately notices that my white T-shirt is covered in blood.

"What happened?" she asks. "Did you get in a fight without me along to run interference?"

"No, I got my first nosebleed in twenty years," I respond. "I was just walking along and it started spurting blood. I've blocked my nostril with toilet paper, the panacea for any MedTrek injury, and I'm sure it'll heal by tomorrow."

We leave La Caleta on a seaside path but after 500 metres the hike turns into a playful scamper along the rocks. The going is slow and in a few hours, without once leaving the coast, we reach Almunecar. The first group of modern apartments resembles a ghost town, but things liven up in the centre of town where there's a Yankee Clipper restaurant. We pass a nudist beach and reach a cove where I swim around a point to the yacht-filled Marina del Este. Getting out of the water I'm severely needled by sea urchins but continue into La Herradura, which has an aging wooden pier once used to transport goods from rail to ship.

A massive construction project is underway on the steep hillside out of town. As we gaze into a vat of pudding-like concrete, I mention to Jacqueline that one thing I've always wanted to do is swim in concrete.

"That will be the denouement of my murder story," she says. "I'll drown you in cement."

There's a dramatic view towards Nerja from the hilltop but we then find ourselves walking nine kilometres on a noisy, truck-filled *autopista* that parallels the natural park. When we finally arrive in Maro, an hour after dark, we're both bushed but I manage to belt out a few lines of *To Maro*.

That night, as she removes urchin needles from the bottom of my feet, Jacqueline decides to return to Aguilas and leave me on my own to advance towards Málaga.

Though we'll later meet to hike the Robert Louis Stevenson trail in France, this is the last stint of our MedTrekking. During the next month Jacqueline will sell her apartment in Spain and move back to an isolated village in central France.

Easily the least pretentious and perhaps the most calming person I've met on the MedTrek, encountering no-nonsense Jacqueline has been a very pleasant and instructive experience. Besides being a willing walker, she's droll and so unlike most French women of her age that it's a joy just to watch her flout traditional values and conventions.

"I want to thank you for 'opening' me up to a type of walk that was so full of marvelous discoveries and deliciously shared moments," Jacqueline later wrote to me in flowery French. "It enriched both my senses and my memories."

I wonder if Odysseus kept in touch with Circe, Kalypso and his other acquaintances after he left them. Or whether they simply became mythic memories. Whatever happens, I found Jacqueline so special that, as Homer said, "The very gods themselves will sing her story for men on earth."

I hike through little Maro and pass two old viaducts, which contrast nicely with two modern bridges on the *autopista* high above, before cutting into some dark green avocado groves. I run into a farmer plowing the rich edible-looking earth and ask if I can walk through his property to get to the coast.

"You can try but it's very dangerous," he said.

'Danger' turns out to be a 100-metre high escarpment that, as I gingerly make my way along it, stretches into Nerja a few kilometres away. The way is made particularly difficult because dozens of fenced-in gardens abut the edge of the cliff. After an hour, I'm on the Nerja beach and realise, as I look back at the cliffs, that I could have fallen a dozen times–and that the drop was much further than I imagined.

I climb up to Nerja's Balcony of Europe, reach the centre of town and admire the many white-washed plazas. Then I drop into the 17th century San Salvador church to light a candle in gratitude for not having fallen over the cliffs, for Jacqueline's presence, for balance, for everyone and everything else.

The town not only has a bustling local market but is also the first of many international resorts on the Costa del Sol. There's everything a foreigner needs: a newsstand with international newspapers and magazines, a new age boutique, a spa, real estate agencies, bars and pubs, and a high-speed *autopista* to Málaga.

For the second time in three days, I get a serious nosebleed. The nose bleeding, or gushing, is probably only a minor medical issue, but I feel especially self-conscious walking around with bright red toilet paper hanging out of my right nostril. That's because there's an anti-cocaine poster campaign on almost every billboard that shows an addict with blood dripping from, you guessed it, his right nostril. I reach Torrox which, says a big sign, has the 'Best Climate in Europe'. But it's cloudy and windy when I stop in a pub where the English owner tells me most people here in the summer are English, German or Dutch.

I take a break at a little restaurant in El Morche and change my toilet paper bandage in the bathroom. I'm now sure that my bloody nose is due to a brain hemorrhage. As I look in the mirror, I say a quick prayer to Apollo, the god of prophecy and healing. Although death is presumably imminent, I continue walking through Algarrobo, Lagos (yes, Lagos), Mezquitilla, and the port of La Caleta de Velez into Torre del Mar where a sign indicates that it's a mere 30 kilometres to Málaga. I check into the Mainake, the town's pleasantly sophisticated hotel, for a long bath and a room service meal.

I ask the receptionist, after a hearty MedTrek farmhouse breakfast of eggs and ham and toast, about the origin of the name of the hotel. She tells me that Mainake was a Phoenician village somewhere in the mountains. The local newspapers all predict rain and I pull out my red poncho, surprised that it isn't completely in shreds after all the wind on the Cabo de Gata. Then I stick to the grey-sanded, wild-waved, dark-skied coast.

The day definitely has a winter feel to it. The many *chiringuitos* on the coast, like the 'Island of Pleasure', are closed, the sea is looking gruff and the waterfowl in the cane marshes aren't moving. A storm is definitely coming.

Fortunately it's an easy coastal walking day through Benajarafe to Chilches, Roncón de la Victoria and Cala del Moral. The Castillo del Marques is a marvelously restored 18th century coastal fort in Puerto Nina. A sign, with the 'o' in Puerto written as a sun symbol, indicates the distances to Gibraltar and Tarifa, where the tip of Spain is the demarcation between the Mediterranean Sea and the Atlantic Ocean.

Málaga is another major kilometrestone on the MedTrek and I feel exhilarated as I walk past *La Farola*, or lighthouse, and the port to the *corrida* and cathedral. There's something magical, almost African, about the city and the many boats preparing to depart for Melilla, one of two Spanish enclaves in Morocco. Or maybe it's the simple reality that I've almost walked Spain's entire Mediterranean coast that causes me to let out a yodelling yelp in the centre of town. Two policemen walk by and act like this is something every American does when he arrives in Málaga.

The next day I start walking on the Pasillo del Matadero next to the Guadalmedina river. Málaga's seashore is being completely revamped with new walkways, new palm trees and even new brownish sand. There are certainly enough apartment complexes to justify the investment. After three kilometres I enter an 'industrial coast' and then cross the sprawling and muddy Guadalhorce River before I reach Torremolinos, the well-known symbol of over-built tourism on the Costa del Sol.

Dozens of British-named pubs are open and there's serious capitalistic competition regarding the price and content of a 'big British breakfast'. There are nicely appointed lounge chairs, each outfitted with pillows and clean towels, on the beach despite the foul weather and there's no shortage of hotels, bars, discos and cyber cafes. The hot teen spot seems to be a *salsateca*, which is right next to one of the numerous discotheques.

I'm feeling like a teen myself until I get another nosebleed and decide that it's time to drop into a medical clinic. A young, English-speaking Spanish doctor, another plus in a cosmopolitan place like this, examines me and concludes that there's a broken blood vessel. No, he says, the bleeding was not caused by stress, blood pressure, too much coffee or a brain hemorrhage. I will live.

"Your heart is ticking but you should walk a bit more slowly for the next two days," he said, as he puts some sophisticated netting in my nose to stem the bleeding. I start off slowly on the remaining 13 kilometres to Fuengirola along the coast through Benalmadena Costa and Torreblanca del Sol.

The sea, though, is becoming wilder and wilder, its colours changing from sandy brown to pea green to turquoise to cobalt blue to coal black. The wind whips my eyes, causes them to tear and I get a whiff of an overpowering tang of sea salt that clears my nasal passages like a blast of undiluted menthol. There are only a few places where I can walk on sand and rocks without getting wet so I stick to well-tended sidewalks along a road that features everything from McDonald's and Burger King to Body Shop, massage parlours, gigantic hotels and pubs like Kitty O'Shea's.

Late that afternoon I see another Forrest Gump-like weathered backpacker wearing a T-shirt that reads 'No Job – No Money – No Worry'. He's reading the anti-cocaine billboard and doesn't see me as I walk by. But I get a close look at his backpack and he's written 'No Woman – No Cry'. More messages from the path.

When I enter Fuengirola, half a dozen surfers are testing the waves and I check into the four-star Hotel Villa del Laredo. My fifth-floor room, easily the best of the trek this week, looks over wild waves that are illuminated by floodlights throughout the night. The thrashing, beating and clapping sound of the waves doesn't, like you might imagine, keep me awake but instead inspires a very deep sleep.

I dream that I've just skied down a long *hors piste* run in Val d'Isere with either Princess Caroline or Cameron Diaz, I'm not sure which, and visualise us taking off our skis before entering a chalet with a brightly burning fire and an odour of strong apple cider mixed with warm rum. Hmm. I'm offered a glass of something and discover, the second I take a swig, that it contains alcohol.

Princess Caroline or Cameron Diaz gives me a wry smile and a wink that encourages me to swallow the whole concoction in one gulp before she gives me a long, lingering kiss. One thing leads to another and I wake up unable to remember exactly what's happened. It takes me a few seconds to remember where I am and sense the relief that, whatever my feelings might be about Princess Caroline or Cameron Diaz, comes when I realise that I was deep in a pipe dream and didn't actually pick up a drink. Whew.

The next morning, after I make a call to get the times and locations of some English-speaking Alcoholics Anonymous meetings, I'm joined by an atypically large number of Spanish morning walkers. All of us, as we pass the lighthouse and fortress, marvel at the ferocity of the rolling waves, silently thankful that, for the moment, there's no rain.

The waves are slamming with such intensity into the seaside rocks that I'm forced to trek on the national road to the California Beach Resort. There I'm struck with another nosebleed and, madly frustrated, I plop down on the sand for 15 minutes and stuff enough cotton up my nose to double its size. Again, I'm self-conscious. I can feel that everyone thinks I'm a coke addict.

"For Christ's sake, don't worry about me!" I feel like shouting at them. "I'm just a run of the mill alcoholic, not a coke addict. I didn't get drunk last night, I didn't have an affair with Princess Caroline or Cameron Diaz, and I'm going to an AA meeting later today. Don't worry, this too shall pass!"

The sea spray has completely clouded my glasses when I stop at a *chiringuito* for some freshly grilled sardines. The waiter tells me that it's a seven kilometre walk on the sand to the Marbella Marina, which has a new blue-tinted administrative building financed by, you guessed it, the European Union. When I arrive at one of the most upmarket places to be seen on the Mediterranean, the pedometer lets me know that I've MedTrekked 237 kilometres in seven days, though according to the signs on the road I've covered 225 kilometres.

I board a bus and every little kid begins pointing at my nose, then at the anti-cocaine advertisements. It's obvious, their looks seem to say, that I'm the target of all of the publicity. It would be fruitless to attempt to explain my medical predicament and proclaim my innocence. A good walker leaves no tracks or bloodstains, I remind myself.

But I'm ready to go to an AA meeting that will enable me to spin the tales about my bloody nose and my latest drunk dream. And I'll quit walking for a few days to let my broken blood vessel adequately heal.

26. Reaching Europe's Southernmost Point

"The enchantress in her beauty fed and caressed me, promised me I should be immortal, youthful, all the days to come; but in my heart I never gave consent though seven years detained." – The Odyssey

> "Here is the story of Hsuan Tsang.
> A Buddhist monk, he went from Xian to southern India
> And back—on horseback, on camelback, on elephantback and on foot.
> Ten Thousand miles it took him, from 629 to 645,
> Mountains and deserts,
> In search of the Truth,
> The heart of the heart of Reality.
> The Law that would help him escape it.
> And all its attendants and inescapable suffering.
> And he found it."
>
> – Charles Wright

Remarkable, I thought. The same distance as my intended MedTrek in only 16 years. There must have been fewer distractions back then. Or maybe it was due to the camel and the elephant. I'll have to ask Charles Wright, the Pulitzer Prize-winning poet from Tennessee who frequently mentions Buddhist monks in his work.

My haemorrhaging nosebleeds have stopped and I'm about to finish the walk along the Spanish coast. It's only about 150 MedTrekking kilometres, less than a week's walk, from Marbella to Tarifa, Iberia's southernmost point. That's on the edge of the Atlantic Ocean and just across the roaring Strait of Gibraltar from Morocco and Tangier, an intriguing city on the edge of another world.

The Marbella promenade, as befits an upscale and jetset resort, is paved with shiny marble, decorated with ornately tiled benches and flies a rainbow of flags representing European Union member nations. There are enough Saudis in town, including Prince Alwaleed bin Talal, one of the world's richest men, to make the place look like Jeddah on the Red Sea. There are also scores of inviting restaurants, upscale hotels, well-appointed villas and a sandy beach that looks like it's been fastidiously raked by a troop of monks. The next town, Puerto Banos, is equally rich. I mean, really, Armani shops on a port?!

The affluence doesn't distract me as I traverse sandy and rocky beaches until I reach El Saladillo, where I have a gazpacho and salad lunch on the seaside. It would be hard to find a completely isolated beach in this part of Spain but there's almost no one walking on this one. Despite the usual morning meditation, my thoughts are in a wandering and cluttered mode. I'm reflecting about whether I'm handling my ongoing divorce as well I could.

This round began when I awoke next to my wife very early one Saturday morning to discover a stranger in my bed.

Physically this was the still-lively, still-beautiful, still-brazen blonde with whom I'd fallen in love in Paris over two decades ago. It was the same feisty, same fashionable Franco-American woman I had first kissed, when I was 30-years-old and she 25, on a cobblestone quay of the Seine on the very autumn afternoon in late 1978 that *The Paris Metro* dissolved into bankruptcy. My arms were wrapped around her petite shoulders when, exchanging hugs and kisses while we walked along the riverbank, we returned to my apartment on Ile Saint Louis to make love for the first time. (I didn't dip the pen in the company ink while we were in business, but bankruptcy and Chloé's own recent divorce ended that constraint.)

"*Je t'aime*," I said in my accented French as things got underway.

"Please," she replied. "Don't even try. Keep it in English."

I knew then, with that single memorably candid and amusing comment, this woman was for me.

During the subsequent years Chloé, so seemingly bedrock strong and secure, blossomed as my wife and friend as she helped me recover from bankruptcy (she translated the weekly column I wrote in English into French for *Le Matin*), suggested I get sober and took me to my first-ever meeting of Alcoholics Anonymous in 1980, gave birth to our two glorious children, tolerated my workaholism and most other character defects, and journeyed both around the world and through the up-and-down cycles of marital life with me.

But now – emotionally, physically and spiritually – I was lying next to a woman who wished she were somewhere else with someone else.

Chloé had returned the night before from a five-day trip to London. Remarkably, she did not look too much different than when I first saw her in the cobblestone courtyard of an 18th century *hotel particulier* in the Marais when she'd come for a job interview as an advertising salesperson at *The Paris Metro*. At that time I told her that advertising director John Keeney (I pronounced it 'Queenay' to make him seem French) had not yet arrived and urged her to be patient.

"Presence not patience," she replied, giving me a look that would have titillated greater men.

Her first words to me on her return from England were much less witty.

"We've got to talk," she said in a provoking and determined tone. "I've got to tell you what's happening with me."

I immediately sensed the possibility, no make that the certainty, of impending misfortune, no make that disaster. I was right. Chloé informed me that she had a 24-year-old male lover, a nightclub bouncer half her age, who not coincidentally had accompanied her to London while I'd been at Sogyal Rinpoche's lamasery receiving teachings about impermanence from the Dalai Lama. She wanted a separation.

"We've got to split up!" she said with finality. "I've been seeing him for nine months."

"You must have known there was someone else," she continued. "Couldn't you see that I wasn't with you when we made love? Couldn't you tell how cold I was when you said you loved me? You knew, you had to know."

I didn't. I was completely unaware of the magnitude of her discomfort and discontent and just a few weeks before had told her that I was still 'happy and content' in our marriage.

The decline and demise of almost any long relationship is complicated and, as any student of Greek literature will tell you, even the gods had problems with their wives. But Cyclops was not as blind as I was.

Naturally, I was initially shocked, furious, hurt and confused – and maybe even a little embarrassed. Although I wanted to talk some sense into my wife and vomit on her asshole boyfriend, I took (and I attribute/blame this to/on my recent exposure to the Dalai Lama and a weeklong retreat at Lerab Ling) the higher road.

"Please know," I wrote to Chloé, whose version of our breakup obviously differs from mine, "that I want you to do whatever is best for you to get over this considerable hurdle and make yourself 'whole'. Take your time.

"Stay sane and accept the love and support I can give you after having seen you struggle and progress during the past 22 years. You are a very fine woman and, whatever happens, you have my love."

During the next few weeks I accepted my expanded parental role created when I kept the house and the kids. I decided not to quibble about money (a 50-50 split seemed fair to me) and had no reason to fight about sharing custody of our two teenage children. I was not grovelling (I may be sober, but I'm not stupid!), but I didn't do anything foolish and decided to simply give Chloé some time. I placated myself with the maxim that it's 'better to have loved and been hurt than never to have known love at all' and the certainty that 'this too shall pass'.

I wasn't able to pull off this love-her-and-support-her attitude without considerable weight loss and an internal torment that, thank the gods, I was able to discuss and share with a number of friends, therapists and family members. I'm sure I bored many of them with repetitive remarks concerning my marital dilemma, but I owe them all my lifelong gratitude for being there and pulling me through the mire.

I'm pleasantly surprised, as I think about it now, that I accepted the situation with such equanimity because I was boiling and exploding inside. Perhaps, it was a psychological ploy. Maybe I expected that Chloé would see the light, appreciate my Zen-ish reaction and move back into the house with the kids and me. That never happened.

The blunt announcement of Chloé's desired separation and intention to have a relationship with a man just a few years older than our daughter also led me almost instantly into a painful period of self-examination. I felt obligated to define my own role in the disintegration of our marriage and, besides coping with all of the emotional and practical challenges of single parenthood, learn something about myself. After all, as Graham Greene once said, "failure is the point of self-knowledge". He also added "success is the point of self-deception".

The ordeal prompted me to question and analyse my own extramarital philandering (and in this department I admittedly made Chloé, whom I'd once left for six months to take up with a younger spiritual goddess, look like a saint), my personal flaws, my shortcomings and even some of my 'better' qualities. What made me so blind to my wife's troubled inner self and external life? Was I ducking real intimacy? Hadn't I developed enough to truly know the person closest to me? Why didn't I see what was going on?

It didn't take too long for me to realise that both Chloé and I had changed considerably since we married. And maybe, as she herself pointed out to me, that we initially got together for all of the wrong reasons.

She chose me as a partner at a time when, beginning with a beer in a Paris café in the morning and ending with a Cognac or Calvados in my living room at night, I was an active alcoholic—a very wild madman unable to see beyond the next drink as I obsessively pursued different women and believed the cocktail party success stories concerning *The Paris Metro*. I was living like a golf ball teed off in a tile bathroom. Zing-zang-whop-whiz-zip-whap-bap-bang. And I had so many varied interests that, despite all my chitchat about an intimate 'I and thou' relationship (I'd read Martin Buber in college when I was, for a year, a religious studies major), I probably wasn't capable of participating in a true partnership.

In retrospect, Chloé and I also seemed to have unwittingly created an unwritten contract that stipulated that we were not to get too close to each other. Discovering any of her pain or inner turmoil would not only have violated the agreement but also would have destroyed my image, however erroneous, of a happy marriage to a strong, independently minded woman. I completely missed the elephant in the living room though, of course, that could be one reason she married me.

During our 20 some years together, I got sober, which is a guaranteed life-changing experience that puts a lot of relationships and marriages into play, and spent a considerable amount of time helping other alcoholics and addicts. Although we lived together, had a lot of fun and were pretty good parents, our paths gradually diverged.

During a period that included weeks of sexual abstinence (look, for a guy like me, who's as addicted to sex as anything else, weeks IS a big deal) followed by months of extreme sexual indulgence, the initiation of the long French divorce process gave me an opportunity to put years of meditation and AA meetings to work by staying calm, not picking up a drink and doing the next right thing. I began giving long massages, which I'd learned how to do during two years of weekly classes in the mid-90s, to a few friends each week to take care of my touch deprivation syndrome. I got regular exercise, gradually regained the weight I dropped and stayed close to home, my children and my day jobs.

The debacle gave me an opportunity to illustrate to Chloé – who seemed to have my personality and character locked in a time capsule dated circa 1980 – that I had dramatically improved and progressed during our years together. I convinced myself that the whole point of everything I'd been doing on a spiritual level – from morning readings, meditation and prayer to retreats, community service and AA meetings – had been geared towards enabling me to act like a decent human being in precisely this type of agonising and trying situation. And I wasn't worth much if I didn't.

I thought I'd been coping and rebounding fairly well until, five months into the grieving process provoked by the separation, my Buddhist acupuncturist/ homeopath judged it time to needle the area around my heart. A few hours after the prickly treatment I felt like a boil had been lanced. I sensed an overflowing release of the pent-up anger, frustration, pain, pus and resentment that I was unwittingly concealing deep inside. My dam burst. During the next few days, which included a long crying session with my daughter, I simultaneously experienced an overwhelming sense of loss, love and liberation. As pleasant and instructive as that might sound today, it was a major pain in the ass.

As I gradually began to rebound – in the midst of what still seems to be a reasonably amicable divorce with everyone's health intact – the MedTrek emerged as a paramount passion. I figured it would, among other things, provide me with an opportunity to restore my self-confidence for the next stage of life.

It seems to be working. And, for the record, I never asked Chloé or the kids about the other guy.

By the time I reach Estepona, the MedTrek mindset takes over and I've purged most of the real and imagined stress.

My most immediate problem is that there's so much construction on the road in Estepona that I wonder if I'll have to spend the entire day amidst dust, tarmac, traffic jams and tractor noise. But after a kilometre I'm on a lovely little strip that protects the Mother Med from the pollution-spewing machinery.

I continue at a fast clip until I stop at the Eastender, one of the many British pubs in the homey port of San Luis de Sabinilla, where breakfast is served until 4pm. I'm lost in a meditative MedTrek reverie until the smooth contour of the sand is altered by a just-dead tortoise. Then I encounter 20 men manually and gracefully raking a beach with the attention usually paid to a Japanese

Emperor's garden. They're collecting everything, from plastic to seaweed, in a mindful manner that would make any Buddhist environmentalist beam. I stop and thank them for their efforts.

"I want you to know that you've made this the cleanest beach I've seen in all of Spain, in all of France and Spain in fact," I shout to the bunch of men. "I want you to appreciate how extraordinary your work is and that I consider you much more creative than Picasso or Cervantes. And I want to give you some money for a coffee or a beer. It's not a lot, I mean your work is worth thousands of euros, but please take it."

They all crack up, though I'm not sure if this is due to my Spanish, my sentiment or my offer. Whatever. I felt a great sense of satisfaction when I gave one of them a 20 euro note.

Gibraltar, which the locals tend to refer to as either Gib or The Rock, emerges impressively from the sea to become the dominating focus of my afternoon. The majestic, solitary and unyielding Pillar of Heracles, which was first settled by the Phoenicians around 950 BC, rises 1398 feet. I can make out the tree-covered slopes covering the western side of the chunk of off-white Jurassic limestone when I walk through Sotogrande, which seems to have more bank branches than downtown Manhattan, and when I cross the Guadiaro River. With each barefoot step during the next 14 kilometres, Gib gets closer.

I put my shoes on when I reach La Atunara, a suburb of La Linea de la Concepción. Then I reach the edge of Gibraltar, which gets its name from Djbel Tarik, or 'the hill where Jabal Tarik landed' in 711, and am greeted by a fortified border fence with spikes, barbed wire, razor wire, flood lights and other not-too-subtle deterrents. A sign says 'MOD (Ministry of Defence) Property – Entry by Unauthorised Persons is Prohibited – Warning: RAF Police Dogs on Patrol'.

The warning and threats look serious so I skirt the fence and end a 45-kilometre day at the sole official border crossing, which is open 24/7. With my mission accomplished, I head across the Spanish street to enjoy a McFlurry on the terrace of McDonald's. As I pick out the red M&Ms, I recall a recent newspaper story concerning this anachronism of British colonialism.

"British troops temporarily invaded Spain when a landing exercise on Gibraltar went wrong," read a subhead in the *International Herald Tribune*. The story continued: "About 20 Royal Marines landed in bad weather on a Spanish beach, thinking they were on British territory. They hastily retreated after locals told them of their error. Gibraltar has been a contested area between London and Madrid for 300 years. The two European Union and NATO allies, though once great foes, are negotiating a deal to resolve their tussle over Gibraltar, which British marines seized from Spain in 1704."

That spate of ill weather in Spain didn't just trouble the Marines. Tony Carey, a friend of mine who's keen on serious sailing, encountered rough seas and high winds while heading to the Atlantic to cross to the United States. He emailed me a vivid description of 'the furious Levanter wind and the funneling effect of the Med entrance at the Estrecho de Gibraltar'.

Then, once the weather cleared, he spoke of 'the joy of dolphins playing on the bow wave'.

The ongoing negotiations between England and Spain regarding the future of Gibraltar definitely rankle 28,000 locals overwhelmingly in favour of remaining British. It's easy to understand why they're outraged. After all, in 1713 the King of Spain ceded sovereignty to the place in perpetuity to the Crown of Great Britain after the War of Spanish Succession. Things will certainly change during the 21st century but nothing dramatic is likely to happen until Gibraltar's tailless Barbary macaques die off. One of the world's most familiar legends has it that Britain will hold Gibraltar as long as the ape colony survives.

Cassie is back. She's flown in from the US and gotten us rooms at the well-equipped AC Hotel in La Linea. The next morning she accompanies me across the Spain/Gibraltar border and within a few minutes we have 'Welcome to GIB' stamps in our passports and are on British soil to walk its 12-kilometre coastline.

It hasn't always been this easy. The border was closed in 1969 by General Franco when telephone lines were cut, mail to La Linea was sent via London and cross-border communication was accomplished by shouting through the security fences. It reopened in 1985 but Spanish customs agents still diligently search cars coming into Spain to ferret out any smugglers carrying smokes and booze, which are less expensive in Gibraltar.

Immediately upon entering the isthmus we cross the airfield runway that, sensibly, is closed to human and vehicle traffic when a plane lands or takes off. Although Gibraltar receives no direct subsidies from London, there are Union Jacks hanging from many apartment terraces, the Queen's monogram is on post boxes and gasoline is priced in British pounds. We get a UK-on-the-Med feeling when a more-polite-than-a-London-bobby at the first roundabout informs us that a landslide has closed the tunnel on the eastern side of the island.

"The area's closed to pedestrians and there's no way you can walk around Gibraltar until the tunnel reopens," he insists in a Gibraltarian accent often referred to as Spanglish, a mix of Spanish and the Queen's English.

Then he provides simple instructions about how to get to the zenith of Mount Misery, the highest point of the colony.

"Just walk up, up and up," he advises.

Cassie and I walk down the high street to the tourism office where a uniformed official reconfirms that a landslide and steep escarpments make it impossible to walk around Gibraltar. She, too, pleasantly describes how to get to the top of The Rock.

"Once you get to the cable car, just keep going up, up, up and see how many of the 530 species of flowering plants you can identify," she says, telling us that Gibraltar is exactly five kilometres in length and that the Spanish have controlled it for only 266 years during the past 12 centuries.

The duty-free High Street is typically British with pubs, chemists and 'shoppes'. Cassie buys some Gibraltar stamps featuring John Lennon before we begin our hike to the top of the 423-metre high Misery Hill, which is capped by the ruins of Moorish fortifications and more modern military paraphernalia. It is known to many as one of the two Pillars of Heracles (Hercules).

Odysseus and other Greeks considered Heracles, who was said to wear a lion skin and carry a club, as a godlike version of Superman who successfully travelled to the ends of the earth. Every Greek was aware that this son of Zeus and Alcmene had completed 12 labours after being driven mad by his stepmother Hera, the queen of the gods.

The labours included a trip to the underworld where Heracles triumphed over the forces of death. He also held the sky on his shoulders, destroyed monsters to make the earth safe and cleaned the Augean stables by diverting the Alpheus and Peneus rivers. That labour, the sixth, was challenging because the stables contained 3000 cattle and hadn't been mucked out for 30 years. Heracles is also credited with plundering Troy 79 years before the Trojan War and is said to have fathered 51 sons.

The Pillars of Heracles, which were called Abyla and Calpe by the Greeks, are on either side of the Strait of Gibraltar. One myth gives Heracles credit for creating them during a labour that involved capturing the Red Oxen of Geryon, a monster with three bodies. Instead of climbing the Atlas Mountains, he purportedly split the mountain range in half with his indestructible sword to create the strait. Not a bad story, even if it's impossible to verify.

The Pillars are not just considered the entry to the Mediterranean but also gates, or portals, to different locations on earth. Travelling between them wasn't always smooth sailing. A report by Himilco, a Carthaginian admiral, said "many seaweeds grow in the troughs between the waves, which slow the ship like bushes ... here the beasts of the sea move slowly hither and thither, and great monsters swim languidly among the sluggishly creeping ships."

Our uphill walk, frequently shaded by greenery, is a pleasant stroll, though most tourists prefer to take the cable car or a bus to the top of the hill. The view at the peak looks over the entire Bay of Gibraltar, which the Spanish call the Bay of Algeciras. On this clear day we can see Morocco and the other Pillar of Heracles on Almina Point in the Spanish enclave of Ceuta.

We also see lots of apes around the Great Siege Tunnels, the Moorish Castle, Saint Michael's Cave and Gorham's Cave, which was first inhabited by humans 100,000 years ago. Above us are some migratory birds sensible enough to fly far enough south to cross the western Med at its narrowest point.

We spend a few hours sightseeing before we traipse back across the border to Spain and celebrate with a multinational Coca-Cola at McDonald's.

"Forget Britain, Spain and the United States," I tell Cassie. "McDonald's is now the world's most successful contemporary colonial power."

The city of Algeciras is across a bay full of tankers waiting to load products from the refineries in San Roque. As I leave La Linea I see a wheelchair tossed into a small creek entering the Med. Did the owner, perhaps due to some religious miracle, begin walking again and throw it away in disgust? Did his family junk it in despair after his death? Maybe someone got a new wheelchair and didn't know where to recycle the old one? Anyway, if you know someone who needs a wheelchair they can find it here.

I attempt to circumvent dozens of fenced-in petrochemical and electricity facilities but am thwarted by the omnipresent and labyrinthine industrial complex.

"How do I get to the beach?" I ask some workers leaving one of the factories.

"There is no more beach," they say almost in unison. "The beach is part of the plant. Walk on the *autopista*. It's the only way to Algeciras."

I ignore their advice and hike through a field of blossoming flowers. My legs are cut to shreds by the thistles, a wild rose bush catches me in the mouth and I wind up on a long-disused railroad track. I get over the first river by straddling the elevated rails on a decrepit trestle. But to cross the larger Guadarranque River, I'm forced to cut inland to the *autopista* where a sign proclaims 'Algeciras – 10'.

I cross a third river by swimming 20 metres on my back and then walk into a town occupied by the Moors from 711 until 1344. They called the place Al Djezirah, or 'Green Island', after the Isla Verde that's now connected to the mainland. There are dozens of *téléboutiques*, which cater to visiting North African workers making international telephone calls, and lots of souk-like markets peddling everything from couscous and henna to kaffias and kaftans. Besides the tanker traffic, one of the port's mainstays is the almost constant ferry service to both Ceuta and Tangier. I pick up a ferry schedule before I catch the 9pm bus back to La Linea. The guffawing passengers have a ball during the half-hour ride as the local comedy king tells amusing joke after joke in spitfire Spanish. These people might have been working at labour-intensive jobs for the last 12 hours but they act like they're going to a fiesta.

Cassie is here primarily to relax and isn't interested in the glorious march from Algeciras to Tarifa, an outing that any MedTrekker would include in his home video highlights. Within an hour I'm bare-footing it past La Sirena bar on the Getares beach. Beyond Punta del Carnero the hike is along sloping green hills that lap the Mediterranean Sea. It's fitting that the hills are occasionally topped with industrial windmills that resemble quixotic stick figures.

Except for some horses, cows, sailboats and the tanker traffic, I'm alone until I've walked 20 kilometres and run into some teenagers skinny dipping. During a late picnic at an ornithological observatory, I see two blue wooden boats wrecked on the rocks below. These are typical Moroccan fishing boats and could have been beached while trying to smuggle illegal immigrants into Spain. That was one good thing about Homer's day. The sea was equally threatening but there were few borders, visas and customs to impede travel.

The Tarifa lighthouse is behind a locked gate that says 'Military Zone'. Beyond it is the expansive Atlantic Ocean and a wide, sandy beach. Across the way is Morocco, though only Europeans are permitted to travel there from Tarifa, which is not considered an 'international' port. I drop into a hippie-like candle shop on a cobblestone street in a colourful town encircled by medieval ramparts. Then I stumble on La Sacristia, a boutique hotel on a back street run by an ex-New York stylist. As I wait for the bus back to Algeciras and La Linea, I notice that ads warning about cocaine use no longer adorn the bus stop billboards.

MedTrek MileStone #3 – Tarifa, Spain

I've just completed my 2993rd MedTrekking kilometre on arrival in Tarifa, the southernmost point on the Iberian peninsula. I'm sitting near a lighthouse, the Mediterranean Sea on one side and the Atlantic Ocean on the other, staring across the 8-mile wide Strait of Gibraltar at the barely visible Moroccan coast.

I plan to swim across the Strait of Gibraltar, but it looks impractical today because of the currents and boat traffic. I'll contact the Gibraltar Strait Swimming Association tomorrow and determine the best time to make the crossing. Or maybe I'll walk across in order to more miraculously kick off the MedTrek transition from Europe to Africa.

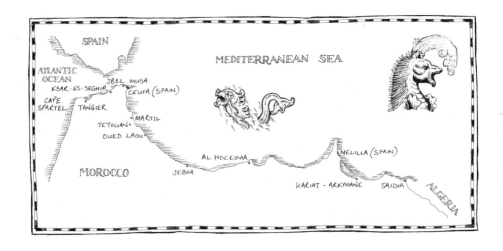

SPAIN

ATLANTIC
OCEAN

MEDITERRANEAN SEA

JBEL MUSA
KSAR · ES · SEGHIR
CEUTA (SPAIN)
CAPE
SPARTEL   TANGIER
MARTIL
TETOUAN
OUED LAOU

AL HOCEIMA
MELILLA (SPAIN)

MOROCCO
JEBHA

KARIAT - ARKMANE   SAIDIA

ALGERIA

Part Seven

Morocco: Walking on Water, Stuck in the Sand

27. Where Does the Med Begin?

"I don't suppose you walked here on the sea." — *Telémakhos in* The Odyssey

Cassie and I are among only 73 passengers on the *Atlantic*, a gargantuan multi-storeyed ferry that's crossing the Strait of Gibraltar from Algeciras to Tangier. During the three-hour trip I walk back and forth, my pedometer recording each step, on every level and deck of the ship until I've gone eight miles. Not only am I walking on water but the two-hour time difference between Spain and Morocco also makes me feel like I'm walking out of time. Whatever's happening, it's much easier than swimming.

Although one Moroccan woman gives me the evil eye when I stride by her family for the fourth time, the highlights of my MedSeaTrek include the sight of scores of diving dolphins and a cinemascope panorama of both Spain and the surprisingly mountainous North African coast. Once we cross the strait, which the Arabs call the Bughaz Jabal Tarik, the *Atlantic* docks and we're immediately confronted by the fixers, guides, black market moneychangers and taxi drivers found in most North African ports.

"I speak seven languages and can find you anything you need," boasts one fixer wearing a light blue *djellaba* and weathered yellow *baboosh*/slippers. "Want to meet Paul Bowles?"

He's referring to the American author Gertrude Stein first inspired to go to Tangier in the 1930s. A composer and author of books that include *The Sheltering Sky* and *Days: A Tangier Journal*, Bowles stayed in Morocco for over fifty years and wound up living in the *kasbah* near the sultan's palace here.

Cassie coincidentally read *The Worlds of Tangier*, a travel piece written by Bowles in 1958, during our crossing. When I passed by her after my first circuit around the ship, she screamed out a line.

"'Beginning with the first day and continuing through all the years I have spent in Tangier, I have loved the white city that sits astride its hills, looking out across the Strait of Gibraltar to the mountains of Andalucia'," she shouted as I wandered by. "This is really getting me excited!"

On my next round Cassie was slightly critical of Bowles, who also wrote nine plays that were performed at the American School of Tangier.

"Wait, he's not completely enamoured of the place!" she yelled as I huffed past. "He writes 'What do I show visitors? Not very much, I'm afraid. Aside from the so-called Sultan's Palace, an 18th century construction which now houses a small museum, there are no 'points of interest' or historic monuments.' I thought you told me there was a lot to see in Tangier. Are you saying Bowles is wrong?"

Her enthusiasm had been restored when I finished my walking-on-water meander.

"I want to visit the Paul Bowles room in the Tangier American Legation in the medina," she said when I returned to my seat. "Are you aware that it's the oldest US diplomatic property in the world?"

Actually, I wasn't. And I doubt that our prospective guide knows that. In fact, I'm not even sure he's aware that Bowles died in 1999.

"He's been dead for years," I reply with a you-can't-trick-me twist of the head. "He's not even buried here."

"But I can show you his old apartment, take you on a tour of the medina and drive you out to the beaches on the Atlantic Ocean," the guide continues. "My name's Choukri. Your wish is my wish."

"Let me think about it for a minute," I say, fully intending to hire a fixer to get us to a decent hotel and help me find the right spot to start the MedTrek. "I've got to make an important tactical decision before I do anything else."

I'm in the midst of a debate about precisely where the Mediterranean, which the Moroccans call the Al-Bahral-Mutawassit, actually 'starts'.

"The closest place to Tarifa in Morocco, the place where the continents were joined eons ago before they were perhaps separated by Heracles, is Ksar-es-Seghir," the *Atlantic's* first mate insisted when he showed me detailed maritime charts during our crossing. "To the west of Ksar-es-Seghir is the Atlantic, with Atlantic temperatures and Atlantic fish. To the east is the Mediterranean. This, the narrowest point between Europe and Africa, is where the Mediterranean begins."

According to his calculations, there's no reason to begin hiking at the Atlantic Ocean or even in Tangier. If he's right, I can legitimately skip about 70 kilometres of Moroccan Mediterranean seaside and kick things off in Ksar-es-Seghir. Or at least that's what I thought before I spoke to one of the immigration officers.

"The Med starts, for all sorts of historical reasons, at Cape Spartel, the cape on the Atlantic Ocean where you'll find the Caves of Heracles," said the officer. "Thinking that the Med starts at Ksar-es-Seghir is nonsense. No one in Morocco would ever refer to the sea in front of Tangier as the Atlantic. It's the Mediterranean. Just look at the different colours of the water when you get to the lighthouse at Cape Spartel."

I ask Choukri, whom I speak to in French, to think about where he thinks the Med 'begins'.

"But first I'll give you five euros to take us to the most comfortable hotel on the seafront and we'll dump our luggage," I say to my guide-to-be. "Then please don't show me Paul Bowles' apartment but take us to the place where you think the Mediterranean commences."

"That's not enough money and everyone knows the Mediterranean begins in...," he says.

"That's what I'm offering," I interrupt. "Take it or leave it. And think very hard before you decide where the sea starts. It's a very serious matter."

Choukri shows us to his black Mercedes. The sedan looks like someone without a driver's licence has carelessly chauffeured it around the entire Mediterranean once or twice. But the debate about where I'll take my first steps in Africa isn't easily resolved because everyone in Morocco seems to have an opinion.

"The Med actually starts at the port in Tangier," says the receptionist when we arrive at the Movenpick Hotel about six kilometres east of town. Although I would have preferred a cheap hotel on the port, I wanted something upmarket and comfortable because Cassie was, understandably, apprehensive about being a western woman alone in Tangier. I wanted her to feel as secure as possible while I was out walking.

"It definitely doesn't start in Rabat," adds a Moroccan woman who's checking in at the same time. "That's about the only sure thing. That's definitely the Atlantic."

The dilemma would have been easier for Odysseus to resolve because the Greeks rarely travelled past the Pillars of Heracles, which they considered the limits of their world. Beyond, the common thinking went, was a desolate and destructive sea called Mare Tenebrosum by the Romans and Bahr al-Zulamat by the Arabs, that contained the underworld and the lost continent of Atlantis. It wasn't to be toyed with.

I have to come to a decision. It's indisputable that the underwater Gibraltar Ridge officially dividing the Med from the Atlantic is east of Tangier, as are the Pillars of Heracles. I could start walking in Ksar-es-Seghir and defend myself if anyone cared to argue about it. But I decide to start at Cape Spartel. Then, wherever the Med might actually start, nobody can challenge the 'authenticity' of the MedTrek just because I skip a few kilometres. Besides, I've always thought that the Med's a state of mind. And if that state of mind wanders a bit out of bounds into the Atlantic Ocean, then that's where it starts.

"That's the right decision, sir," Choukri says when we return to the car. "That's precisely where I was going to take you."

Yeah, right.

Cape Spartel and the nearby Caves of Heracles are 14 kilometres west of Tangier. There were once Phoenician and Carthaginian settlements in nearby Lixus, where the well-preserved Roman ruins include an amphitheatre and baths. And if I were a ship captain steaming up the African coast from Cape Town, I'd feel like I've entered the Med the moment I take a right at the cape.

Choukri skirts around the back of Tangier, which he pronounces Tanjay like the French, and we arrive at the Cape Spartel lighthouse around noon Moroccan time. This is the northwesternmost tip of Africa and I jump out of the car to look down on the 'border' between the Atlantic and the Mediterranean. I'm somewhat embarrassed to tell Choukri that the water looks pretty much the same on both sides of the lighthouse.

"You've got to let your eyes adjust," he says. "Keep looking and you'll see the difference. The Atlantic is always a darker and more brooding blue. Watch, watch. You'll see a line form, a demarcation. This is where the Med begins."

Maybe. But I don't see it.

Before we start walking we make a quick visit to the Caves of Heracles that, according to the age of excavated bones and flint stones, have been used as dwellings since Neolithic times over 8000 years ago. They haven't always been given the respect they might deserve. They served as brothels in the 1900s until locals determined that tourism was a more lucrative pursuit.

Choukri, Cassie and I return to the ridge near the lighthouse and I'm still unable to make out any visible 'border' in the water. But Cassie and I head to Tangier without worrying whether we're on the 100 percent Med, the 100 percent Atlantic or a mélange of the two.

"You should stick to the pavement if you want to get back to Tanjay without any trouble," Choukri counsels. "The coast is very rocky and there's a lot of thick brush on the hilltop. You'll never make it. Everybody, even the shepherds and their sheep, walks on the main road."

I ignore Choukri's advice and half-carry Cassie down an overgrown trace of a one-time track to the seaside. She complains constantly during our descent, takes one look at the rock-strewn shore and within seconds proclaims that she's going to boycott this route.

"This is not only impassable but it's slippery, dangerous and stupid," she says. "Help me get back up the mountain."

I don't even bother arguing with her. We slowly climb back up to the lighthouse and begin a ten-kilometre walk on an unpaved hillside road through the area known as the Mirador de Perdicaris. One group of kids taunts us, or perhaps taunts the idea that we are walking to Tangier, as we pass, and I frequently climb to the top of one of many gigantic boulders to gaze across the sea to Spain and out at the Atlantic. When I hear the loud blare of a cruise ship's horn heralding its entry from the ocean into the Strait of Gibraltar, I realise that it's time for a serious commemoration. I've just reached the 3000-K mark of the MedTrek. Cassie, who was with me at the 2000-K kilometrestone, refers to this as KKK.

"Did you ever think you'd make KKK when you started out?" she asks as she gives me a congratulatory hug. "Or that you'd be walking with me in Morocco?"

"I'm a bit surprised, and pleased, about both occurrences," I admit as I excuse myself to mount a tall boulder to sit for a few moments of quiet reflection. "Walking from Europe to Africa, even the northwesternmost tip of Africa, does feel like an accomplishment."

The last few kilometres into Tangier, which is built on a shelf of limestone, run along the paved road that passes in front of King Mohammed VI's summer palace on the Med – if, indeed, he considers it the Med.

We arrive at the Grand Socco, the large souk that was so completely renovated in 2006 that there's no longer a scent of the erstwhile snake charmers and storytellers who once gathered here. Taxi ranks and bus stops have, I'm afraid, replaced romance and folklore in this part of a booming metropolis with over 700,000 people. But when we head into the narrow alleyways that typify Tangier's dark and leather-smelling medina, it's clear that we're no longer in Spain. The maze-like passages lead uphill through a confounding labyrinth with babbling tradesmen in front of bustling shops selling everything from handbags, spices and multicoloured cloth to produce, pastry and meat.

"I feel like I've just entered Narnia and wouldn't be surprised if that sheep starts talking," Cassie says, apparently unconcerned that the sheep in question was on prominent display at a butcher shop. And was, of course, dead.

I mention that a friend of mine doesn't bring his watch whenever he visits Tangier, not because it's a different time zone, but because he says it's a different time, or outside of time entirely. It's definitely not Europe.

We head through the Bab el-Aassa gate to the Place de la Kasbah, the highest point of the city dominated by the Dar el-Makhzen, the former palace built by Sultan Moulay Ismail and abandoned by his successors in 1912.

"Well, Paul Bowles definitely knew a 'point of interest' when he saw one," Cassie says as we enter the first of two inner courtyards. "Just look at that!"

She's admiring the wooden ceilings, marble fountains and arabesque patterns on the walls.

"Do you know that the arabesques are not just geometric forms but also express a view of the world?" I ask as we approached one wall. "To Moroccans these are very spiritual designs and represent the infinite creations of Allah."

We decide to skip the museum, which is devoted to Moroccan arts and archaeology, and leisurely amble down myriad pathways to the port. I exchange some euros for dirham on the very visible black market before dropping into a hookah bar, where most customers are sucking on elaborate water pipes, for a fresh mint and heavily sugared tea.

When I first came here during the summer of 1970, I found myself in a teahouse called Baba's, which was perched somewhere on a hill with an open-walled courtyard looking across the sea. A young boy dressed up in bright colours carried a bronze platter full of dates and sweet things, including a treat made of hash, honey and nuts. As everyone sat on cushions and smoked their hookahs, the boy began dancing and clapping along to the sharp tones of the clay tom-tom drums. This fellow understood rhythm.

"Do you know that the word 'hookah' is thought to have originated with the Arabic *uqqa*," I tell Cassie, "which means 'jar' and refers to the water chamber that cools the tobacco as it's inhaled?"

"That might be true, but I'm so tired that I'd pass out immediately if I took a puff," she say. "Why don't I go back to the hotel, unpack and get cleaned up."

One customer, who claims he's smoking herbal tobacco (yeah, right!), is a somewhat responsible-looking English-speaking taxi driver who agrees to take Cassie to the hotel. I pay in advance, let him see me taking down his licence plate number and hand Cassie a mobile phone.

"Pretend to speed dial the police if you have any problem at all," I whisper as she gets into the cab. "Settle into your room and I'll be there within two or three hours."

I return to the café for another mint tea and recall my own close encounter with the Moroccan police during a hashish-induced drug experience here during my first visit over three decades ago. I'd bought a chunk of *primero kif* that had been made by Berbers in the Rif Mountains and was looking forward to indulging with Henrietta Dax, my Franco-British-American girlfriend, in our dark room at the Hotel Continental on rue Dar Baroud in the medina.

Henrietta had insisted we stay there because Prince Alfred, Queen Victoria's son, was among the first guests when the hotel opened in 1888. I got enthused about the place, even though it was way above our hitchhiking budget, when I learned it was also where William Burroughs wrote *Naked Lunch* in 1957 with the assistance and support of Jack Kerouac, Allen Ginsberg and Peter Orlovsky. I figured some of their drug-induced visions, and maybe a few revelations, were still hanging around the lobby.

I have to admit that back then I didn't know or care that the Phoenicians, the Romans, the Vandals, the Byzantines, the Visigoths, the Arabs, the Portuguese, the English, the Spanish and finally the Moroccan Berbers had all played a part in the history of Tangier. Or that the town's name was presumably derived from the Berber goddess Tinga. Her son Sufax laid the first stones in the city, though the Greeks claim Sufax was the offspring of Heracles. And I was only slightly impressed that Tangier was a renowned hub for international spies and smugglers.

The allure of illicit and addictive Oriental pleasures was considerably more important because I thought they would transport me to a higher spiritual realm than dribs and drabs of historical trivia.

Before we scored the dope I'd already had a bit too much *mahia*, the Jewish Moroccan fig brandy, at the Café Central. We'd gone there for a drink because Henrietta, who now runs a classy bookshop specialising in Africana and rare books in Cape Town, knew that Barbara Hutton, Somerset Maugham, Truman Capote, Gore Vidal, Cecil Beaton, Malcolm Forbes and the Rolling Stones had all been seen there cavorting amid *djellaba*-dressed Moroccans. Then somehow we continued our drinking spree at the Gran Café de Paris in the Place de France.

To be honest, I'd completely forgotten about the second watering hole on that outing until I saw *The Bourne Ultimatum* in 2007. For some reason Nicky Parsons/Julia Stiles, who was seated at a terrace table at the Café de Paris to exchange cell phones with the film's arch villain, looked just like Henrietta did almost 40 years ago. The scene not only spurred my recollection of our drinking bout but also had me imagining myself as Jason Bourne/Matt Damon, flying across rooftops and bounding into the medina's alleyways during the most riveting cinematic chase scene ever filmed in Morocco.

In any event, after our various café stops, Henrietta and I were in the midst of an evening of confined debauchery in our room at the Continental when there was a loud knock on the door.

"Police!" shouted a voice in French.

"Shhhh!" I indicated, putting a trembling finger in front of my lips as I grabbed the hard brownish block of dope, stuffed it in a plastic bag, tiptoed into the bathroom and tossed it into the hole-in-the-floor toilet. My ingenious plan was to flush it if the police broke down the door.

"Police!" said the voice again.

We didn't budge. Then, a minute later, we heard footsteps marching down the stairs. We stayed still and silent for half an hour before I had the nerve to plunge my hand into the toilet and retrieve the chunk of hash. It was dry but I was scared and flushed it down the drain. We took the first ferry to Algeciras the next morning.

"You know, I'm not sure they really were cops," I said as we looked back at the Moroccan coast during the crossing. "I think they were the guys who sold us the dope just trying to scare us."

I'll never know, I remind myself, as I casually walk along the seaside for six kilometres to the Movenpick. When I look back at Tangier, the sun is setting over the Atlantic. Or is it the Mediterranean?

The next morning Cassie watches me start the day with a swim before a leisurely breakfast of muesli, bananas and dates. I'm paying over $100 per room, a MedTrek high, but I baulk at buying the hotel's over-priced bottled water for 35 dirham when I can get it for five at a local shop. A guy's got to have some principles.

Once I start walking, I immediately chastise myself. Not having water, especially in a place with questionable tap water, violates a key hiking rule and common sense. I'd already sworn never to walk without ample water. But here I am again. Waterless.

I round Cap Malabata, where dozens of fishermen are congregating with their extraordinarily long poles, and make decent time despite being hobbled by the right knee injured yesterday when I jumped from one big rock to another. After 13 kilometres, still without water, I reach some houses and ask the first person I meet if he's got "un verre d'eau".

"Follow me," he says in French.

He's a mason, takes me into a home he's building and introduces me to the owner who offers, without any hesitation, some bottled water. This retired businessman from Rabat wants to hear everything about my little adventure and we swap stories for fifteen minutes before I get to the second most pressing issue of the day.

"The Med starts right there," he says, pointing at the sea below his house. "They're planning to put an undersea tunnel to Spain not far from here because it's the shortest distance between the two continents. Incidentally, you must have a great cardio-vascular rhythm."

He asks if I want lunch but I decline, thank him profusely for the water and continue along a seaside that is now definitely the Mediterranean. But the countryside is so verdant and fertile that the rich dark soil reminds me of the green hills of Kenya. I stay inland until I cross the Oued (River) Aliane and see a sign indicating the day's destination: "Ksar-es-Seghir 12".

I move from beach to path to road until I reach the Ksar-es-Seghir taxi rack, where an out-of-place new PT Cruiser is parked amidst the old Mercedes that have a lock on the automobile market in Morocco. A sign indicates that it's 38 kilometres to Sebta, which is what the Spanish enclave of Ceuta is called in Arabic. I chat long enough with the locals to learn that Ksar-es-Seghir means 'little castle ruins' and that a shared taxi to Tangier will cost me 12 dirham, or just over one dollar. I grab a communal cab and ignore the startled stares of my four fellow passengers when, 30 minutes later, I ask to be dropped off at the exclusive-by-local-standards Movenpick.

My knee is sore and swollen and I'm in no mood to walk the next morning. But Cassie's booked herself a birthday bikini wax on me at the hotel spa and I have no desire to lounge around the place. I limp to the main road, flag down a communal taxi and return to Ksar-es-Seghir, promising myself that this will be a short Sunday stroll.

My companions include a Moroccan in his thirties who's extremely proud to be working as a cook in a McDonald's in Bonn. Mamdouh explains in German that he's on a one-year sick leave due to a severely pulled muscle, two intestinal operations and mental stress. Leaving his wife and two kids in Bonn, he's come back to his *Heimland* to recuperate.

"The German doctor told me that the Moroccan light, air, forests, heat, sea and lack of stress would help me return to good health," he says as the cab skirts the Med.

"Want to quietly walk with me to take off some more of the pressure?" I ask.

"I'm not quite up for it yet," he grimaces as we get out of the cab. "But thanks for asking."

I saunter past the Ksar-es-Seghir 'castle' and immediately run into a remarkable number of fishermen on the shore whose wives are preparing intricate vegetable dishes to accompany the anticipated catch. Ahead is what I think is the second Pillar of Heracles, the African half of the Rock of Gibraltar, which I reach when I round a corner into a valley that, were it not for the minarets and mosques dotting the hillside, could be in Ireland rather than northern Morocco.

The village of Wa Musa sits in the shadow of the steep and towering Jbel Musa mountain and there appears to be a path that runs along the sloped seafront to the Spanish/Moroccan border at Ceuta. According to a poll of the local populace, the distance ranges from four to 15 kilometres. Two villagers insist that Jbel Musa is the true African pillar of Heracles. This latter claim is not without some dispute, as others say Mount Hacho in Ceuta is the correct choice.

I'm too sore to continue today and hitch a lift part way up the hill on a tractor, giving the driver my spare pair of tennis shoes as a gift. Then I get another ride to the main road with the head of the local jet-ski business and jump into a communal cab that gets me back to the Movenpick at the end of the afternoon. Rachid, the receptionist, informs me that Musa means Moses and that the mountain has a colony of Barbary apes.

"Jbel Musa, not the mountain in Ceuta, is the Pillar of Heracles," he insists. "That'll be clear when you climb it and look at Gibraltar."

"I'm taking a break for a few weeks," I tell him. "When I return I'll find the real pillar just like I found the real starting point of the Med."

My knees are in such pain when I return to France that I immediately head to the emergency room at a hospital in Mougins.

"You've been walking too much," says the ER doctor when he looks at the X-rays and pokes at my knees. "Take some anti-inflammatory medicine and don't hike for a couple of weeks."

28. How to Get Arrested Three or Four Times in One Day

"Leave jesting to the gods who do it better." – The Odyssey

My son Luke decides to join me on the next segment of the MedTrek and I book us passage on a ferry from France to Tangier because it seems appropriately funky. We'll leave from Sète, where I saw gigantic Africa-bound ferries when I walked through the town millions of steps ago, and steam south along the European coastline.

"My dad trekked through the whole of Spain without me and now I'm taking a few weeks off to join him in Morocco," I overheard Luke tell a friend before the trip. "There's no way I'm going to let my old man venture through that place on his own."

The *Marrakech*, the large ferry liner dominating the Sète port when we arrive on a Friday afternoon in early December, certainly looks capable of making the crossing. Before we board I give Luke a walking tour of town and show him the canals, the fish market and the beaches that I'd MedTrekked.

"We'll be docking in Tangier in just 36 hours," I say as we board.

I immediately shift into relaxed ferry mode, though just as we depart Luke learns that he has to fly back to Nice the following Monday for an unscheduled day's shoot on a feature film he was in that starred Matthew Modine. He'll have less than 24 hours in Morocco before returning to France by plane in business class. A funky way to travel, indeed.

At breakfast on Saturday morning, with a calm sea and a do-nothing sunny day at our disposal, I talk to a Moroccan traveller who owns a bar in Tangier, which he pronounces Tanjah.

"This boat is packed in the summer and you're lucky to be travelling with so much free space," he says. "You're also lucky that the sea's so calm because it's often impossible to keep your tea from spilling. Incidentally, I've got an apartment you can rent in Tanjah if you want it."

That evening during dinner I chat with another Moroccan who's lived in France for 20 years but now resides in Fez, Morocco's third largest city that, he points out, is twinned with Montpellier. He makes a living by taking the ferry to Sète once a month, buying electrical goods and returning to sell them at his shop in the alluring Fez medina.

"I enjoy France but it's much less stressful to live in Morocco," he tells me. "Everything's much slower and more relaxed."

The other passengers include some guest workers returning home from Germany and 30 African agricultural students from Montpellier who will be studying in Meknes for ten days.

Time drifts as the ferry passes Cap de la Nau, Calpe, Benidorm and other places that I'd walked through in Spain. We spend the second night listening to live Moroccan music and the passengers' staccato clapping in the lounge where, without a doubt, the best dancer is an African student from Chad. Otherwise we play Scrabble, read and slowly sip Moroccan mint tea, which costs one euro on the boat compared to 30 cents in a Moroccan cafe.

I'm out of bed on Sunday morning at seven and spend half an hour meditating on the deck as the sun comes up. I wake Luke to show him the stunning Rock of Gibraltar on this glorious sparkling-bright winter morning and point out Tarifa, Ceuta and Jbel Musa in Morocco.

"That's where we'll be starting the hike," I say, stretching my arm in the direction of Jbel Musa. "Gibraltar is one of the Pillars of Heracles and either Jbel Musa, or Mount Hacho in Ceuta, which is that peninsula you see jutting into the Mediterranean, is the other. There're arguments both ways."

"What's Ceuta?" Luke asks. "That doesn't sound very Moroccan."

"It's not, it's a Spanish enclave and the Moroccan name for it is Sebta," I tell him. "It's actually part of Spain and the European Union, though Morocco wants it too."

"Remarkable!" Luke says as he spins around on the top deck. "I can see Spain and Britain (Gibraltar) and Spain and the Atlantic and the Mediterranean and Morocco and Spain (Ceuta) and Morocco and the Med just by turning in a full circle."

The ship docks a few minutes late and I tell Luke that we should be able to make the climb up Jbel Musa this afternoon and reach Ceuta by nightfall.

"*Inshallah,*" I add. "If that be the will of God."

I attempt to show Luke that I'm in control of things by dismissively rejecting the first few offers from the contingent of fixers at the port. Then I barter with one driver, whose name is Ssossi, to get us to Wa Musa in his decent looking Mercedes. Ssossi explains that he has to stop at a police station to get permission to travel beyond Tangier to the 'forbidden' Spanish enclave. Once we show our passports, mention that we're tourists and obtain the permit, we speed to the sea-viewing Hotel Ibis at Fnideq on the Moroccan side of the border with Ceuta to drop our baggage. We don't get the favourable room rate reserved for Moroccan citizens and residents, but it's still a lot cheaper than the Movenpick.

On the way back to Wa Musa, we stop to look at Isla Perejil, an insignificant island a couple of hundred metres off the shore, that has frequently been the scene of territorial tussles between the Moroccan and Spanish governments. Before Ssossi drops us off, we arrange for him to pick Luke up at the Ibis the next morning and get him to the Tangier airport.

We walk from Wa Musa along a mountain path that features extraordinary views of the Med, the Strait, Spain and Gibraltar. Then we trek through some typically down-to-earth seaside villages with whitewashed homes surrounded by tons of refuse that, unfortunately, is a feature of many Moroccan villages on the Med. The hike's a physical piece of cake until we hit the seaside border with Ceuta, which is open only to a certain type of foot traffic.

"This border entrance is closed to everyone except Moroccans entering for the day to work in Sebta," we're rudely informed by a Moroccan customs agent.

"But we just want to walk through Sebta and return to our hotel in Fnideq on the other side," I explain, quite calmly and sensibly I think.

"You'll have to get back to the main road and take a taxi," he says gruffly. "That's the only way for you to get into Sebta. This is not a border crossing for just anyone."

"Actually we're staying in Fnideq tonight," I tell him. "Can't we just walk through Sebta and come out the other side? *Inshallah.*"

I threw in an *inshallah,* which many Arabs use incessantly in conversation, to illustrate that I'm not completely ignorant of Arabic and local customs.

The uniformed officer looks at us like we're terrorists readying to invade the place. I try, still quite politely, to reason with him but he says he'll confiscate our passports and detain us if we don't move "*now!*" He doesn't even add an *inshallah.* There's not much we can do because a serious razor wire fence, separated from another serious razor wire fence by a 15-foot wide service road, surrounds the entire enclave. The Spanish have constructed it to let everyone know that no clandestine and illegal Moroccan workers, smugglers or MedTrekkers should try to get into Ceuta/Sebta, either for the day, in an effort to sneak into Europe or just to walk through the place.

After ignoring the agent's suggestion that we walk back to the main road, we somewhat surreptitiously climb up the hill along the fence. It's steep, we start sweating almost immediately and within a kilometre we're approached by a troop of Spanish Guardia Civil aiming their rifles at us through the fence.

"*Manos arriba. Arriba!*" one of them shouts quite loudly.

We raise our hands as five young men outfitted in Spanish military uniforms swing open a gate in the fence and approach us.

"You're not allowed to walk near here," another officer says in Spanish. "Keep going and you'll be put under arrest."

"But we're not trying to get into Ceuta," I tell them. "We're just trying to walk around it to Fnideq."

They tell us we can't walk along the border unless we want to be detained.

"The Moroccans are always causing trouble trying to get on Spanish soil," said the oldest member of the troop. "Either head back down the hill and walk up to the main road or cut into the hills where you'll find the *camino de los aduaneros* (customs path)."

"There are no signs indicating that the walk along the fence is off limits," I reply.

No one seems to think this a pertinent observation. But I continue to haggle and they agree to let us walk another 200 metres along the fence before cutting into the bush. Once we get to the agreed point, we head down into a gully and back up the hill for a mountaintop walk on the customs path. We're now about half a kilometre away from the fence and have glorious views of Tangier and across the Strait to Spain. Most people refused entrance at the border post probably don't take this uphill option, but it's definitely the way to go if they haven't changed the regulations by the time you get here.

"This is spectacular," Luke says as he points to a large ship leaving Tangier. "And, look, there's our ferry making the return trip to France."

We meet a lone Moroccan soldier as we continue along the *camino de los aduaneros* and he asks to see our passports.

"What nationality are you two?" he asks in French. "French? American?"

"American? No, I'm Icelandic, *inshallah*," I reply. "And you?"

He tells us that he's a member of Morocco's Force Auxiliaire, the Auxiliary Force that patrols the mountainous seaside and has small lookout camps on almost every hilltop. One of their main jobs is to prevent Moroccans from trying to sneak across the Mediterranean into Spain.

"You should always check in with us and let us know where you're heading," he says. "There are outposts every few kilometres between here and the Algerian border almost three hundred kilometres away."

"We will," I said. "But don't worry, we're not going to defect."

He kind of smiles, kind of laughs and lets us go without looking at our passports. Luke, who's carrying both French and American passports, doesn't like my remark about defecting or being Icelandic. Or my constant use of '*inshallah*'.

"You could really get us in trouble and that guy has a gun," he says. "This is the third time we've run into trouble in an hour. I don't want to get shot or spend the night in jail."

"We'd be lucky if it's just one night," I reply. "But a bit of polite and mild intimidation never hurt anyone. Homer often described Odysseus enduring the 'odds he met on land from hostile men' and that's what we're doing. We haven't done anything wrong."

"Yeah, but Odysseus wasn't a blond-haired kid walking in an Arab country after 9/11," Luke says. "He was a fighter who'd just returned from a decade of battle. Anyway, they didn't have guns or border patrols back then."

We descend towards Fnideq along the omnipresent barbed wire fence just a few metres to our left. As we trip down the hillside, there's a set of Moroccan military, police and customs officers waiting for us at the bottom.

"Do you know that you're in an off-limits Moroccan military zone?" says one officer. He's completely uninterested in my explanation that there are no signs indicating that the area is off-limits or that we spoke to a Force Auxiliaire officer thirty minutes earlier. He insists that we follow him into the office of Fnideq's top customs official.

Two officers caress their carbines as we cool our heels in a waiting room before we're shown into a small, cluttered office and offered seats on two collapsible chairs. I spin a tale in French about our travels to the Moroccan customs officer, who's about my age, and he loosens up considerably when he finds out that we're American. He doesn't seem at all concerned that I'm a journalist and laughs when I tell him that I'm walking around the Mediterranean.

"You're doing all this walking at your age?" he says in amazement. "And you're not worried about being robbed or arrested? Do you know what people will do to get an American passport? You better smarten up or you'll never make it through Morocco, much less around the sea."

I tell him that Odysseus was probably just a little younger than us when he travelled on the Med.

"This is a perfect project for middle-age guys like us," I tell him. "And so far the only trouble we've had today are run-ins with Moroccan and Spanish military officers and customs officials. *Inshallah.*"

It's twilight when the interrogation is concluded and the Moroccans let us out of their country and into Sebta. We show our passports to the Spanish border guards and customs agents and are immediately, with no questions asked, allowed into Christmas-decorated Ceuta.

Our hotel in Fnideq is less than a kilometre away but I wanted Luke to get a taste of the strangely situated Spanish territory before he flies back to Nice. After an outdoor dinner of *tapas* and a stroll around the city, he mentions the blatant differences between this odd Gibraltar-like piece of Spain and the tiny bit of Morocco that he's seen today.

"That razor wire fence separates two completely different worlds," he says as we walk through streets filled with fashionable Spanish *chicas* and well-stocked stores. "Developed and undeveloped, Europe and Africa, black and white. And so close to each other. No wonder they want to keep the have-nots out of here. And no wonder the Moroccans want to get in."

"It's definitely odd that the Spanish, who make such a big deal about the British staying in Gibraltar, insist on maintaining this little place," I said. "They claim that it's an integral part of Spain while Gibraltar is a British colony rather than part of the UK. I'll bet it costs a fortune to keep Ceuta afloat."

We cross back into Morocco around 10pm, filling in the required immigration/ emigration cards after standing in a line for 15 minutes. When we're back on Moroccan turf, a guard waves, smiles and says "Ah, the monkey men of the Musa Mountain have returned."

We head down the dark road towards the Ibis, open the window and fall asleep to the sound of the breaking waves.

I'm on my own the next morning and leave before Ssossi arrives to pick up

Luke. It's a chilly, grey wintry dawn and my first steps are through litter, garbage and oil on the pot-holed road into the unbustling and unlike-Ceuta village of Fnideq. I head to the sandpiper-populated beach and maintain a steady pace on the packed, flat sand for two hours until I stop at a hole-in-the-wall store near a very closed Club Méditerranée resort.

I stock up on water and call Luke to ensure that he's awake and ready to go. I tell him that if he looks out the window with his binoculars he might see me outside a *téléboutique* near the large white Club Med.

"I can see a big white place but it's miles away," Luke replies. "I can't see you but keep walking, man! I'll be back on Wednesday afternoon and meet you here."

"I'll keep the room until you get back," I said. "Break a foot."

Cabo Negro, the dark-looking camel-humped cape in the distance, seems close enough to touch but I've walked 23 kilometres by the time I near it and drop into the Golden Beach Hotel in M'Diq for a mint tea. The seaside near this town is much more upscale than Fnideq. There are two yachts from London in the Marina Marbella Maroc and I pass a Royal Golf Club, a riding stable and a restaurant called La Langouste. But there's no seaside path around the protruding Cabo Negro.

"The only way to go is up, then down, then up, then down," says the owner of a travel agency. "Nobody walks up there unless they're grazing sheep or goats."

Although the sun is still hidden by the clouds, it's an arduous and sweaty climb. When I finally reach the top of the Black Cape I hear two or three different *muezzins*, or recordings of two or three different *muezzins*, making the azan call to prayer at nearby mosques. The prayer times are listed in local newspapers but it's the screeching calls that alert most Moroccans five times during the day. Despite the thick and challenging underbrush, I scurry down the hill and wind up amidst seaside villas that would be considered luxurious even in Spain or France.

Further along the coast in Martil, kids are kicking soccer balls, younger men are pulling in fishing nets and older men are sitting in cafés. There's a bit of courtship underway on the sand between a scarfed young woman and her suitor. After another hour I hit the Oued Martil and a ferryman offers to take me across the river for three dirham. But rather than get stuck on the other side as dusk falls, I approach a car and ask for a ride to the main road where I can catch a lift into the nearby town of Tetouan. It turns out that I'm speaking to some plainclothes cops investigating a carjacking and they want to see my papers. I've left my passport and credit cards in the hotel safe, a usual MedTrek precaution, but tell them where I'm staying, explain what I'm doing and show them photocopies of my documents.

When I describe my walk they give me a ride back to the main road and I catch a communal taxi into Tetouan. I've survived my fourth brush with the authorities in 24 hours without getting arrested. *Inshallah*.

Tetouan, the capital of Northern Morocco, is a town of over 300,000 buzzing with students and many more young women than I've seen in Tangier or along the coast.

"Know where I can find an Internet café?" I ask a jeans-clad female student.

"There are quite a few of them but the computers are incredibly slow," she replies. "If you're as impatient as most tourists you'll go crazy. You'd have more fun walking to the edge of town and catching a view of the Rif Mountains. They're almost 3000 metres high and home to 10,000 Berbers."

Tetouan, which was called Tamouda in the 3rd century BC, definitely isn't a high-tech type of town. But there are myriad varieties of citrus fruit in the market, a cigarette manufacturing plant, lots of white houses and a gigantic pomegranate orchard.

After an hour, I catch a communal taxi back to Fnideq. To celebrate the day's successful walk, I buy two fares for $2 each so I can have the front seat all to myself rather than squeeze in with someone.

One Mercedes communal taxi takes me to Tetouan the next morning, then I catch another back to Azla where I left off last evening. I explain to my fellow passengers that I'm resuming a hike that will take me to Alexandria in Egypt. They all think I'm out of my mind as I get out of the car to walk on the dizzying road along the cliffs above the beachless Med in the direction of a place called Jebha.

There's rain and grey skies but the smooth calm-before-the-storm sea, the distant cloud-shrouded mountains, the narrow road curving along the coast, the tiny strips of sandy beaches, the pine forests and the bright red earth are inspiring. This coastal stretch surpasses the ruggedness of the Costa Brava, largely because there's almost no development or infrastructure. It's the most glorious part of the Med that I've yet walked.

In Asma, where I have to cross a brook, I find a tree trunk, a remarkably thin and wobbly tree trunk, across the stream at its narrowest point. I know I'll fall without some kind of support. I'm about to look for a stick when a toothless woman starts screaming and shakes a long piece of thick cane at me. I walk over, take the branch from her, half bow and say "*chokrane*", or thank you.

I cross the brook and during the afternoon use her staff to brace myself on many downhill paths, fend off dogs, wend through mud and even take a few golf shots using pebbles as golf balls. At one point I jokingly shake it at an adolescent goat herder friend when he holds out his hands and says "*Dirham, Dirham*".

When I end the walk in Oued Laou an hour later, tired from 33 more-up-than-down kilometres, I hide the staff behind a wall and book a reservation for a shave the next morning at the local barber's. Then I wait for a communal taxi to fill with passengers and head back to Tetouan (50 minutes) and from there to Fnideq (35 minutes). I tell the second driver what a superb walking day I've had on the coast.

"You'll be seeing even more natural beauty between Oued Laou and Jebha," he says just before he drops me at the Ibis. "And then you'll run out of road."

After a leisurely shave I visit the one very dismal hotel in Oued Laou and immediately abort my plan to book a room as a base camp for Luke and myself. The accommodation, basically a few mattresses on the floor in a room with no heat, would be torturous, especially after Luke's upmarket trip to Nice. Instead, I find my hidden staff and head towards the river on the edge of town. The water is far too cold and deep to cross but when I hike upriver there's no bridge or crossing in sight. I return to the mouth of the river, strip down and use the staff to determine whether it might be possible to cross. It's definitely too deep and, having accomplished nothing, I put my clothes back on and again head up a river that snakes through the countryside.

Two hours later I realise that I've gone nowhere, if winding up where I started can be considered nowhere. It's frustrating and I have to remember, as I repeat a mantra ("By the power and truth of this blessing, may all sentient beings find happiness and the power of happiness. May they ..."), to stay calm, that the goal is the path, that the path is the goal. Walking around in a circle, I try to convince myself, is some form of progress. I stroll through the *souk* in Oued Laou, where an array of local fish are being sold, and jump on a bus heading inland. I ride it for half an hour to the bridge in Kas Asras. Crossing the river, I make it back to the sea and walk for ten kilometres to Targha. I meet a Moroccan Dutch couple on the beach who tell me they flew from Amsterdam to Oujda for Christmas vacation, even though there's really no Christmas in Morocco. Then I begin the slow trudge uphill until I reach a Force Auxiliaire military station on a hilltop and again gradually drop down to the sea.

I scamper over rocks, tease the sea, admire the hills and avoid the steep road until I reach the village of Stehat. The last fifteen minutes are in the company of a hooded Moroccan fisherman who, if I correctly catch his drift, tells me that he thinks a Frenchman is building a hotel in Stehat. No one seems to know anything about it when I inquire at the local café, but the word spreads that an infidel is looking for a room and I'm immediately invited to check out a few 'apartments'.

The brother of a mason working on a hotel that a Frenchman actually is building offers me a room with beds, sheets and pillows for 200 Dirham, the equivalent of $10 when I was there, a night. I can't wait to see Luke's expression when he gets a look at our base-camp squat. Then, in the dark, I get a lift back to Tetouan in a van carrying nine soldiers before riding on the gearshift of a

Mercedes taxi back to the hotel. The three-hour journey makes the move to the squat look very sensible and I plan to take tomorrow off until Luke returns. Then I'll convince Ssossi to take us to Stehat.

I spend the next morning in Ceuta and admire the views of Gibraltar, the Med and the Spanish enclave from the top of Mount Hacho, which many non-Moroccans consider the other Pillar of Heracles. I decide that, for me anyway, it's the towering and more majestic Jbel Musa that's my second Pillar of Heracles.

The Spanish Army is in firm control of the enclave and a soldier tells me "the Autonomous City of Ceuta is on European Union territory and has a population of just over 70,000". In fact, Ceuta would look at home in Andalucía or Cadiz, though its economy is pegged to the military base, some tax-free trade, visiting ships and fishing. But the Internet connections are much faster than in Tetouan and there's a pleasant little supermarket where I buy essentials to equip the squat for a few days.

"Ah, the monkey man of the Musa Mountain has returned again," says the guard Luke and I'd run into a few days ago when I cross back into Morocco. "You should just stay in Morocco. It's much better than that place."

Luke arrives around three with Ssossi, whom I immediately 'encourage' with a wad of *dirham* to take us along the *corniche* to Stehat. When we get there I take the two of them on a tour of our spacious apartment and jabber about the electricity, hot water, gas stove, view of the sea, shower, hole-in-the-floor toilet and other conveniences. I promise Ssossi that I'll get in touch if, at the end of this adventure, we need a lift back to Tangier.

"Not a bad base camp, huh?" I say to Luke after a gazpacho dinner and a game of Scrabble. "There's no heat but otherwise we're in great shape."

"Gees, D, you sound like you've been away from civilisation for a long time," Luke says as we both freeze through the first part of the first night. "I know that we managed to get through the first day without winding up in jail but, trust me, this ain't the Hilton."

29. A Death-Defying Fall: The Goat Is the Path

"You ought not to practice childish ways, since you are no longer that age." –
The Odyssey

"In adulthood, childhood can return." – Deng Ming-Dao

It's so cold that we've both slept fully clothed. Progressively awakened by a rooster, a *muezzin*, a donkey, and then more roosters, I gradually force myself to get up, light a fire, boil water, make tea and wait for the sun to rise before arousing Luke. He studied the map last night and thinks we can make it to Jebha today.

"Jebha sounds so cool that it should be our next goal," Luke said before we turned in. "But there are no roads on the map once we get there. What lies beyond it?"

"A very mountainous coast too steep for roads," I replied.

We're about to head through downtown Stehat, about a two-minute walk from our squat, to the sea when the owner knocks on the door. He informs us that we must be 'interviewed' by the chief of police.

"I mentioned that I had two Americans staying here and he wants you to fill out some papers," he tells us. "Don't worry, there's no problem. *Inshallah.*"

It's Friday the 13th and we pass a newly-dead dog in the middle of the road as we approach the police station. We enter a large courtyard, then a small office where a uniformed Danny de Vito lookalike spends 40 minutes interrogating us amidst enough piles of paper to make a recycling plant look profitable. He painstakingly writes down every detail in our passports, even adding the birthplace of my mother and father.

"I want to be sure that I've got absolutely everything absolutely right," he smirks. "In case you disappear on your ridiculously irresponsible adventure. Now please autograph this."

We both sign the document, which is written in Arabic, apparently to vouch for its accuracy. We finally get to the seaside and the walk progresses from a pebbly beach to a rocky hillside path in the shadow of the cloud-covered Rif Mountain range. It's soothing, soulful, spectacular and savage. I feel blessed, yes 'blessed' is the appropriate word, that I can bring my son on such a wondrous jaunt and casually chat about stuff – his acting, the future of our family home in France following my divorce, my own undefined plans – as we carefully avoid waves and slippery sea-washed stones. Just before breaking for lunch we're cutting along the escarpment on a narrow trail used primarily by shepherds and their goats.

Then it happens.

After trekking over 3000 kilometres, the earth finally moves. Or, rather, the unstable ground beneath the dangerously narrow goat path on this steep mountainside perched above the glistening sea moves. Then crumbles. Then collapses. Then disappears.

I fall off the cliff, bouncing off boulders like a pitched pebble. Just before I hit the rocks below, I hear Luke screaming, "Oh no, Dad! Oh, my God!"

When I come to, sprawled on the stony seaside, I don't notice the blood running down my face, the gash in my left hand, a scraped right shoulder, twisted left ankle or my badly bruised body. I don't even realise that I'm still in danger, lying right in the path of an oncoming rockslide initially caused by my descent and worsened by some curious goats. For some mysterious reason, I remember that goats were symbols of fertility in ancient Greece. Don't ask me why I think these things at moments like this.

"I'm still here," I cry to Luke, but my voice surprises me by how weak it is. Luke is already scrambling down the rocks to find what he was sure would be a dead dad. "I'm still here," I say again as Luke slides down the scree and scurries towards me.

"Find my glasses, find my glasses," I mutter, stuttering slightly as soon as I see the look of sheer panic on his face. "I'll be okay if you give me a few minutes to catch my breath. Just find my glasses. I don't think I'm hurt too badly."

That gives me a few seconds, despite my obvious state of shock, to compose myself. I begin to realise that my bleeding hand and throbbing shoulder broke my fall and reduced the impact of my head bashing unimpeded against the rock. Otherwise, my skull would have been cracked open like a coconut smashed by a baseball bat.

"Here's your cap, Dad, but I can't find the glasses," Luke says in a deflated voice from just a few metres away. "You don't realise how lucky you are. A big rock just missed your head."

"I think I'm okay, I think I'm okay," I say as I sit up and remove my backpack. "Just give me a few more minutes to get it together."

It takes us an hour to apply first aid from my inadequately stocked medical kit, stop the bleeding with makeshift compresses from a shredded T-shirt, find my splintered glasses and smashed pedometer, and clean off blood and dirt with bracing fish-cold seawater. As my state of shock gradually subsides, we have a bite to eat and then hike, limply but with a renewed respect for nature and the importance of staying on the path, back up the sheer mountain.

Luke carries the backpack and I put my good arm over his shoulder for support as we slowly begin the arduous trudge up from the sea.

"That was one of the worst falls I've taken in my life," I admit as we move at a snail's pace.

Just before we reach the potholed road high above the smooth cerulean sea, we encounter half a dozen mocha-skinned Jabala tribeswomen. Clad in colourful red-and-white blouses and skirts, they carry bundles of sweet-smelling brush for their nightly fires. They keep their eyes low, pretending not to notice the bloodied middle-aged European and the tow-headed teen trudging along their inhospitable coastline.

"They look like they've just seen a ghost," Luke says. "Maybe you're in worse shape than you think."

"I really thought it might be all over just before I hit," I reply, as we reach the roadside in the late afternoon winter sun to hail one of the rusted Mercedes taxis that sporadically sputter down the little-travelled *corniche* road between Oued-Laou and Jebha. "The fall comes with the territory but I'm glad someone wanted to keep me alive. And I'm certainly glad that you were there to help me!"

"The gods are on your side," Luke says. He probably doesn't know that Athena once told Odysseus "A god could save a man by simply wishing it – from the farthest shore in the sea.'

I consider that for a few moments before I say anything.

"I'll be sure to thank them," I reply, as a taxi appears in the distance. But the Greeks always acknowledged man's fragility and the very thin line between life and death. Homer made it clear that "miserable mortals who, like leaves, at one moment flame with life, at another moment weakly perish". He also contended that "the gods may love a man, but they can't help him when cold death comes to lay him on his bier".

"Call it a mix of luck and fate, it just wasn't my time. It's lucky Friday the 13th after all."

We flag down a taxi which rounds bend after bend at a torturously slow speed. I tell the driver, whose full moustache and thick horn-rim glasses make him look like an Arabian Groucho Marx, a bit about my hike and recent tumble. He translates the story from French to Arabic, doubling the drama and danger from what little I can understand, for the five Moroccans, three men and two veiled women, sitting in the tattered back seat and smelling like a musty blend of mildewed clothes and burnt wood.

"Allah is with you," one man says in Arabic, pointing to the nearby cloud-shrouded Rif Mountains. "*Inshallah.*"

After a bumpy half-hour drive, the taxi drops us at the outskirts of Stehat and we head to the village infirmary. As we walk past an outdoor market selling the leftovers of the morning's catch of glittering silver sardines, a *muezzin* makes his melodic call to worship from the minaret above the town's simple but sprawling wood floored mosque. Then we step inside the whitewashed clinic, consisting of small rooms around an open-aired patio. The receptionist takes one look at me and immediately leads us to a cubicle with a metal chair, a collapsible bed, a stethoscope and a wire waste can full of blood-stained cotton.

"Well ... it's not the Pasteur Clinic," I whisper to Luke. "Let's just hope they use new needles."

It takes less than 20 minutes for a young French-speaking female doctor to assess my various injuries, stitch and staple my cuts, shoot me full of antibiotics, and fill out some prescriptions. She adamantly refuses my attempts to pay for her care, explaining that the Moroccan government finances the infirmary for local shepherds, farmers and fishermen. No one, not even a foolish foreigner who tumbles down a mountain, has to pay.

"You're incredibly lucky to have walked away from a fall like this," she says, asking me to return the next morning for a check-up. "*Allahu Akbar*. God is great."

I can see Luke grimace, probably wondering what he'd be doing right now had Allah not interceded. Homer captured his feelings when he wrote "What a dear welcome thing life seems to children whose father, in the extremity, recovers after some weakening and malignant illness: his pangs are gone, the gods have delivered him."

Before heading back to our humble squat, Luke and I stop at the café in the main square for some fresh mint tea. As we join locals watching a soccer match between Morocco and Tunisia on a small flickering TV, the short and beefy police chief stops by our table. Seems word spreads quickly in these parts. He's already heard about my fall.

"I warned you this morning that it's very dangerous to walk on this coast," he says smugly. "After Jebha there's no road at all along the sea and the terrain is even more hostile. There are Riffi Berber tribesmen, al-Qaeda trainees and *kef* dealers who would love to get your money. And your son," he adds ominously.

As he walks away shaking his head, I silently sip my tea until Luke asks the inevitable question: "Dad, are you sure you want to keep walking the Mediterranean?"

"*Inshallah!*" I say. "A fall like this comes with the territory and I would have felt much, much worse if you'd taken the dive. I feel fortunate that things turned out as well as they did." Luke shakes his head.

Despite my injuries, I tell Luke that if I can walk tomorrow I'll be happy to try to reach Jebha, which is 35 kilometres from site of The Fall, before we catch the ferry back to Sète.

I have the bandage changed at dawn the next morning and we take a bus heading to Djedniche, the 'Garden of the Apricots', and ask the driver to drop us on the *corniche* road just above The Fall. The sea below is a syrupy brown near the shore due to last night's rain, though it sparkles bright blue a few hundred metres off the coast.

Luke carries the backpack and I wear a glove to protect the stitches and staples in my battered left hand. My ankle's well enough to enable me to scurry through the brush and butt slide down the steep rocky hillside to a beach where

waves are crashing against boulders and churning the pebbled shore.
"You're pretty stupid to be doing this the day after that kind of fall," Luke
says. "And now you're wrecking the environment by causing a rockslide."

"Better causing it than under it," I reply.

We reach Amtar where some kids ask us for a few dirham in exchange for
showing us where to cross a brown and swollen river. Then one invites us into
the most luxurious villa, minaretted and temple-like, this side of the king's
palace in Tangier. A twenty-something Swedish girl reading on a chaise longue
introduces herself.

"I'm Eva and wound up here when I met Youssef, whose father owns this
house, six months ago," she says in English, closing her copy of *The DaVinci
Code*. "I've been here ever since."

A young man dressed in jeans and an ironed white T-shirt walks into the
garden. Without introducing himself, and before I say a word, Youssef tells us
that the family made its obvious fortune "from the sale of Mercedes cars and
Moroccan hashish". Then he invites us to stay "for tea, dinner and the night".

"I'm afraid we've got to be in Jebha," I reply. "But a mint tea would be great."

We all sit around a gigantic garden table shaded by an umbrella made from
the fronds of local palms. Within a few minutes, I realise that Youssef and Eva
are moderately stoned and can't say much more than they already have. Luke
takes a toke on a cigar-sized joint and I enjoy the very sweet cup of tea.

"Are you having a good time here?" I ask Eva, thinking that maybe she's
been kidnapped or is here against her will. "Or would you like to leave?"

"Actually, I'm getting used to being treated like royalty," she smiles,
indicating that she caught my drift. "But I appreciate your concern."

We strip down completely to cross another river just before we reach Jebha,
which is the closest thing to a bustling metropolis in this undeveloped part of
the country. A three-storey hotel has just opened, trees have been planted on the
main drag, a taxi is waiting to head back to Tetouan and half a dozen cafés are
filled with dozens of hanging-about men.

Dusk is approaching as we climb towards the sand-coloured Pointe des
Pecheurs beyond the town. Just beneath us is a large horseshoe-shaped bay
with two little coves. "Paradise," Luke says softly. "Real paradise."

We walk a kilometre down the beach towards Al Hoceima. There's no longer
a road but there does appear to be a trail that presumably leads to some villages
in the distance. Then we return to Jebha where I have a shave and explore the
local market until there's a taxi with enough passengers to head back to Stehat.

The next morning Ssossi drives us to Tangier through the mountain towns
of Talembote and Chefchaouen, where we immediately encounter goats, dope
sellers and market hustlers. "That's how the place got its name," Ssossi explains
as he simultaneously negotiates the narrow streets and points at the top of the

mountain. "Those two peaks resemble goat horns and Chefchaouen means 'look to the horns.' Makes sense, doesn't it?"

He says the town is important to the Berbers, the government and trade in the Rif Mountains. "This is one of the main producers of cannabis in the whole country," Ssossi says proudly before we continue to Tangier. "You can buy it in the market when you pick up your tomatoes."

"*Inshallah*," says Luke.

30. "There Are No More Roads in this Country"

"Men grow old soon in hardship." — The Odyssey

"This is going to be a serious mission," Luke says when we meet Ssossi at the Tangier Airport to return to the MedTrek on the rural, roadless and trailless countryside beyond Jebha.

It's now August and the summer climate has completely altered the seaside landscape. The trees and roadside fields on the coastal road to Jebha are ripe with figs, melons and corn-high marijuana plants. Tents, umbrellas, parasols and sunbathers dot the beaches but the Jabala tribeswomen are as colourful and omnipresent as ever in their body-covering garments.

Although I keep it to myself, I embark on 'the mission' with some trepidation due to my fall and the unpredictable terrain. But we're now armed with two mobile phones and two 60-litre, 15-kilogram backpacks with a serious first aid kit, sleeping bags, a tent, water purification tablets and the usual MedTrekking paraphernalia.

Once in Jebha, Ssossi talks me into paying twenty euros more than our agreed 100-euro fee for the ride. "What do you expect?" he asks. "You've come to the end of the road. You're in the middle of nowhere. Most taxi drivers wouldn't come out here for 1000 euros. Most taxi drivers wouldn't come here at all."

"*Kif kif* ('Same old, same old')," I reply as I hand over some extra cash.

Our second floor ten-euro-a-night hotel room looks onto the province's largest mosque and we immediately hit the town to seek information about the next stage of the MedTrek. We start with the hotel owner, who's honest enough to admit total ignorance about the state of the seaside, and then talk to two Royal Gendarmerie officers on patrol near the port.

"We're walking to Al Hoceima and I'd like you to keep this photocopy of our passports," I say as I hand over a copy of our documents. "Incidentally, do you know anything about the condition of the trails?"

"What trails?" replies the older officer. "The seaside paths through Chefchaouen province are full of dope addicts and thieves. You'll be lucky to survive. You should take the bus out of here to Targuist and go by road from there."

Then we meet Said, the owner of the Caroline Café, who tells us that he's hunted game in the area since he was a kid.

"Al Hoceima is three days walk from here," he explains. "There are no roads but there are paths, wells with water and friendly people. The rivers will be dry and the only problem you'll have is hiking the rough terrain of the Massif des Bokkoyas escarpment. *Inshallah.*"

I estimate that it's a two-day hike to Torres El Kala and, well stocked with water and supplies, we leave at sunrise. We again hike up the trail to the exhilarating Pointe des Pecheurs and, despite our very heavy packs, enthusiastically work our way along the cliffs down to the pebbled beach. After 11 kilometres we hit a hole-in-the-wall shop and replenish our water supply. Then we pass through field after field of cultivated marijuana being weeded – yes, the weed is being weeded – and Luke is absolutely amazed at the splendour of the grass.

"Wait until I tell the guys about this during the next poker game," he says as he grabs some leaves to smell and chew. "This is a doper's paradise."

A weed weeder approaches us and we ask him whether it's smarter to continue along the coast or head over the mountains.

"*La playa es mejor*," he tells us. "Stay at the edge of the water."

This innocent and grizzled old man definitely didn't try to lead us astray. But he obviously isn't aware that, eight kilometres away, a landslide has propelled a 30-metre slab of rock into the sea to form an impassable barricade. Getting there along the sandy coast is a breeze and, letting things get ahead of me, I didn't expect any problems on what appeared to be an uneventful day.

"Well, this is easy," I remark to Luke. "Even your grandma, who's just had a knee replacement, could handle this stretch."

Then we hit the whale-shaped, ten-storey chunk of mountain/rock/earth that has literally slid from its towering perch into the sea.

We try traversing it, climbing it and moving past it in the water before finally backtracking to take a steep trail up and around it. We're drenched with sweat by the time we reach a house with marijuana drying on the roof and the sound of goatskin bongo drums and tambourines emanating from inside.

"If you're looking for a party," says a teen with 'Chill Out' inscribed on his T-shirt. "This is it."

"Actually we just want to get some water," I reply.

"It's all yours," he says.

We fill our empty water bottles with dirty well water, toss in an excessive number of purification tablets and move across a dry, cracked riverbed into another shoulder-high meadow of marijuana. Then we arrive in a little village with a mosque and the usual hole-in-the-wall shop selling drinks and staples.

As we luxuriate with cold sodas, a Force Auxiliaire officer approaches us. We talk for half an hour and, though he's chagrined to hear about the rockslide, he directs us to a faucet with nearly clean water. Then he takes us into the room next to the mosque where grade-school children are chanting verses from the Koran.

"Mosques are still the traditional form of education in rural areas like this," he explains. "They are also key to giving village people a spiritual program that leads to an ethical life."

We're tired and the packs are heavy. But we continue on the pathless beach until we get to Masstasa where we immediately check in with another Force Auxiliaire team.

"We'd like to pitch our tent near your camp and spend the night," I tell the officer.

The French-speaking officer looks at our passports, then smiles at me and says "*Vous êtes âgé!*" ('You're old!') as we pitch our tent between the sea and a field of marijuana.

I'm building a fire the next morning when our Force Auxiliaire contact, who kept our passports during the night, offers me a gas stove. Who could refuse? I brew some tea and as we drink it he suggests that we follow a dirt path over the mountain.

"The coast is inaccessible and impassable after another kilometre," he tells us. "But go that way for nine kilometres and you'll reach a little village. It's got a fishing port, a campsite and a trail that goes across the mountains to Al Hoceima."

We arrive in Torres El Kala at the base of a plateau that reminds me of Table Mountain in Cape Town. At the seaside Café Méditerranée we chat with an English woman who's wearing a headscarf and sitting with her Moroccan husband. We learn that it's a two-hour walk to Bades, where the Spanish control a tiny island called Peñón de Vélez de la Gomera just off the coast.

"King Mohammed VI's aunt has a summer palace just a few metres from the island," she says as we leisurely dine on grilled sardines, olives, chickpeas, Moroccan bread, bottled water and mint tea. "But there's never been any problem between them."

The bill for lunch is less than three euros and we embark on a stunning up-and-down cliffside walk to Bades. The compact Spanish fort is almost within spitting distance of the beach and, equipped with a helicopter-landing pad, looks like a villain's lair in a James Bond film. The princess's palace resembles the movie set of *Topkapi* and there are enough moving vans, tents and military trucks to easily stage an invasion of Bades.

Our arrival at a shop near the palatial digs immediately causes a crowd to gather and one brazen teen quizzes us about our walk, our mission and our condition. He says that the vertical Bokkoyas Mountains just ahead completely block access to the sea. I leave Luke with the packs and climb the first peak to evaluate the terrain. There's no seaside and not even a trail along the top of the escarpment. We decide to follow an inland road that the princess uses to access her seaside digs.

We gradually increase our distance from the Med as we hike through countryside that, like the Cabo de Gato in Spain, is strikingly beautiful, oddly mystical and full of changing colours. We gather plump and sweet figs and stop frequently to rest our shoulders, now bruised by carrying the heavy packs.

When it becomes clear that we're not going to see the sea, we hitch a ride to the main road, grab a communal cab to Al Hoceima and check into the rundown four-star Hotel Mohammed V. As we dine on a lamb *tajine* served in a conical clay pot on a terrace overlooking the bay, the waiter tells us we made the right decision.

"Those mountains are too steep unless you're a goat," he said. "But you could take a motorised Zodiac back along the cliffs and get off at the Boussakour beach. Then it's a fairly easy 15-kilometre walk to Al Hoceima."

Two Moroccan skinheads, obviously on vacation from France, make snide remarks about us in French during dinner. And when we take an after-dinner stroll into the main square we run into a group of guys wearing 'I Love Oussama' T-shirts.

The town is getting spruced up in anticipation of King Mohammed's upcoming visit to inaugurate a ship and evaluate some state-funded projects. New paint has been applied to every curb side, patriotic posters and photos of the king are plastered on every wall, and the red Moroccan flag, with a green pentangle Seal of Solomon in the centre, is hanging from every lamppost. I keep my mouth shut rather than talking to Luke about the monarchy, terrorism or the fact that the colour red symbolises the descendants of the prophet Mohammed.

"Let's keep a low profile," I tell Luke. "Colin Powell, the US Secretary of State, came here just after 9/11 and the King asked 'What are you doing here? This country is not safe for Americans!'"

The next morning I hire a Zodiac and a man my age to skipper it.

"I don't like missing a big chunk of hikable coast," I tell Luke. "Anyway we should get out of town before the 'I Love Oussama' gang gives us a second thought."

As we motor along the coast, the cliffs are much steeper than I'd imagined. And just past the Al Hoceima lighthouse is one of the most disturbing MedTrek sights I've encountered. There's a large garbage dump, smoldering from an ongoing fire, that covers the face of one cliff and spills into the sea.

"Jesus, that stinks," I complain. "I hope they'll show it to the King. He's probably the only person who can do anything about it."

The skipper takes us beyond Boussakour and it's clear that the coast, with vertical cliffs diving straight into the water, is unhikable. The water's also too rough to enable us to land the Zodiac on the Boussakour beach and Luke and I both get soaked when we jump onto a large rock just offshore. Fortunately we've left our backpacks at the hotel in Al Hoceima and are carrying only one lightweight daypack. I tell Luke that Lao Tsu once said, "Have little and gain; have much and be confused."

We kick off the day by eating a dozen wild figs before we begin a pristine walk along the vacant and pebbled beaches beneath the uninhabited Bokkoyas Mountains.

We walk four hours, passing just a few Moroccan shepherds living in tents, until we arrive at the Plage Tala Youssef that can be reached by car from Al Hoceima. And what a surprise. The Complex Touristique Chafarina's Beach has a hotel with four royal suites, 16 regular suites, a bar, a pool, tennis courts and a terraced restaurant. We eat heartily on the outdoor terrace – me spaghetti with grouper kebab, Luke a *gratin de seafood* (sic) – before we tackle a steep hill leading to Al Hoceima.

A Moroccan in a Mercedes with Spanish plates asks us if we want a ride and is surprised to see that we choose to walk. Then a college student from the university town of Oujda near the Algerian border approaches and says he wants to practice his English. "I'm really sorry about 9/11 and the virus of terrorism that it's caused," he says when he learns we're American.

Our amble through a small hillside village leads to a road with the smelliest collection of garbage and other foul-smelling waste that I've encountered anywhere, on or off the MedTrek. I'm not surprised to learn that it's the approach road to the smoldering garbage dump.

Luke decides to head directly back to Al Hoceima but I continue up the mountain to the lighthouse and military lookout post. I'm stopped by the guards, my passport is examined and I'm politely told to head back down the hill to Garbage Drive.

I don't see Luke during the trudge down, but expect him to be at the hotel when I get there. However, he's not around and no one's seen him. I tell myself not to worry. I take a bath. I tell myself not to worry. I walk around the hotel. I tell myself not to worry. I walk to the main square. I tell myself not to worry. I walk towards the hill where we separated. I tell myself not to worry.

After an hour of this, I tell myself to worry and am prepared to contact the police, the Force Auxiliaire and the King to report that the "I Love Oussama" gang has kidnapped my son. As I sit in the lobby and let my imagination create the worst possible scenario, Luke nonchalantly walks in.

"It's all cool," he says when he notices my stress level. "I was just chilling near the port."

We have a chicken dinner on an outdoor terrace overlooking the bay before I fall asleep reading *Quarantine*, the novel by Jim Crace. It's about Jesus and some others spending forty days and forty nights in caves in the scrub. The setting could have been the Bokkoyas Mountains.

After breakfast on the terrace of the Hotel Mohammed V, and a delay while we wait for the maid to return our damp laundry, we head out of Al Hoceima. We kick off the laundry-drying hot day with a ten-kilometre walk up and down mountains with steep inclines and sharp drops to clear-watered coves inhabited by tarantula-like spiders, sea turtles and pomegranate trees.

"How do you know that's a pomegranate?" Luke asks, pointing to a tree about eight feet tall with bright red flowers.

"We used to have a couple in our yard in the house on the Sacramento River in Redding," I say, alluding to the town where I grew up in Northern California. "There's no fruit now but I always loved pomegranates because they're filled with berries that explode in your mouth."

This warm-up's followed by a ten-kilometre stroll on sand-and-pebble beaches with a narrow band of tall shady birch trees. Moroccan women don't wear bikinis, or even one-piece bathing suits, but we see a few fully clothed women wade into the water.

We pass a closed Club Med near the tiny Spanish-occupied island of Peñón de Alhucemas and plant ourselves underneath a palm tree for lunch. We're almost immediately joined by Moustafa, a self-described 'former hashish salesman and unemployed truck driver'. He tells us that Peñón is now a Spanish military prison and claims that 80 percent of all Moroccan men are unemployed. Then he tries to sell us some hashish.

"And just what does 'former' mean?" I ask.

"It means selling *kef* used to be a job," he replies. "Now it's just a hobby."

We're finally far enough away from Al Hoceima to no longer see the smoke rising from the smoldering garbage dump. We pass through a small village and are joined by a young man walking to his parents' house. Luke, chatting with him in Spanish, learns that he's a student in Madrid and that a large road is being built to open up this entire area to people, development and tourism.

Apparently a few years in advance of the opening of the road, we stop at the Force Auxiliaire outpost at a clifftop in La Sib and ask if we can pitch our tent on the rocky beach below. An hour later, as we watch dozens of fishing boats from Al Hoceima heading out for their nightly troll, a Force Auxiliaire officer climbs down to the beach to check on us. He says that if we're up at sunrise we'll see the fishing boats heading back to Al Hoceima.

I'll remember this particular day because everyone's been making comments about my age: "You look tired," said the young student from Madrid. "Do you think we're the same age?" a 75-year-old toothless man shopkeeper asked. Then the Force Auxiliaire officer called me *El Viejo*. Even Luke claimed that during the last stretch of the hike I looked like "a dying camel".

I resolve to tell everyone that I'm Luke's grandfather. That should shut them up.

Luke climbs the cliff to the Force Auxiliaire outpost the next morning to retrieve our passports and they offer him tea.

"I just want you to know that, in this land of delightfully scented and sugared mint tea, that was the worst liquid I've ever tasted," he tells me when he returns. "I should have used a purification tablet. I'll probably get dysentery."

"Well, it's very rude to refuse tea," I reply. "*Inshallah*."

We head out on a sculpted seaside path to Cap Ras-Turf, where an extended Moroccan family has taken up residence in a deserted office block at the base of a lighthouse. We're sick and tired of carrying the heavy packs but there's nothing we can give away. And we stock up on water just to add some more weight.

Then we meet a French-speaking donkey rider who takes 15 minutes to tell us that the nearby town of Olad Hmghar Tamsaman "has a *grand magasin* (department store) where you can get anything you want".

I imagine all sorts of delights when I hear 'you can get anything you want' and *'grand magasin'* in the same sentence. But the *grand magasin* turns out to be the usual non-descript dark bar with a dozen men sitting around tables. We buy three 1.5-litre plastic bottles of Sidi Ali (*sidi* is water and *Ali* is one of the many Moroccan brands), and some rock-hard Mars bars that have long passed their expiration date. We learn that we're in Nador province and will soon run into the 'large road'. But the most exciting event in Olad Hmghar Tamsaman during our visit are two cocks fighting in a *téléboutique*. Somehow they've both been thrown out on the dirt path in front of us as we walk past. But just as in a western movie when the bad guys get tossed out of a saloon, they immediately head back in for another round.

I presume that a 'large road' means two-lane blacktop. But it turns out that what we've been hearing about is the multi-million euro Route de la Méditerranée, also known as La Route du Nord, that will ultimately run along the Moroccan, Algerian, Tunisian and Libyan coasts. Once we've waded through swarms of gigantic jumping grasshoppers, we're walking alongside the future North African link that is being surveyed and graded on the moon-like landscape.

After a much-needed dip to take a break from the mid-day heat, we continue to Sidi Driz and look for someone who can speak English, French or Spanish. We meet Mohammed who tells us how some 40 years ago he was "lucky enough to cross the sea, *inshallah*" and work as a mason in France. Then he describes his injury on the job in 1978 and his frustrating, and frustrated, attempts to reclaim his French visa and obtain some type of compensation. No one, not the doctor nor the authorities, will give him any help, he tells us, hiding his rotting teeth beneath the omnipresent moustache worn by 99.99 percent of Moroccan men. But he's so pleased to be speaking French with someone that he wants to walk with us to Tizirhine where, he says, "you can get anything you want".

When we arrive I buy Mohammed a 'Moroccan whiskey', which is what he calls mint tea, and he helps us negotiate a place to crash for the night and the rental of a donkey to carry our backpacks tomorrow.

We sleep in the back room of the Tizirhine Téléboutique and the manager, who lost his left hand in a building accident, treats us like we're his long-lost cousins. I'm so pleased with the concrete-floored accommodations and happy to learn that we've got a donkey reserved for tomorrow's walk, that I buy a $5 blow-out dinner for three at the town's best restaurant.

"You're very lucky, a father and son, to be on an adventure like this," says Mohammed. "And you're the first tourists that many people around here have ever seen."

We do realise we're lucky. And we're not even upset when Luke's tennis shoes, which he left outside the *téléboutique* to air out, are stolen. But the mayor, who gives us some mats to sleep on, takes the theft a bit more personally.

"It's the attitude that led to the theft, which is very non-Moslem, that bothers me," he says. "They'll think that 'Hey, if I can get away with stealing shoes then I can get away with stealing money.' It's not how Moroccans, especially in a rural area like this, think and act. We all take our shoes off when we go off in mosques and stealing shoes from there, or anywhere else, just really infuriates me."

"*Inshallah*," I reply.

We wake up in the well-locked back room of the *téléboutique* to learn that our donkey deal has fallen through because, the owner claims, "You'll be walking through some dangerous territory and I can't risk losing the beast." I stubbornly look around town for another mule to carry our packs to a village called Aazanen, which is pronounced 'Zen'. Nothing materialises and we start off with our backpacks which, despite the loss of Luke's stolen shoes, seem to be getting heavier each day.

When we stop at a café for drinks, I concoct a major change of plan. I decide that Luke and our packs will hitch a ride on a truck parked outside while I walk backpackless for precisely seven kilometres. The truck is one of many working on the 'large road' and the workers are pleased to help us out. We meet up in an hour and, pleased with our strategy, I again put Luke on a truck transporting men and material for the new road. We agree to meet in exactly seven kilometres.

I head to the cliff-lined beach and trek along dozens of coves and tidal-like pools, even encountering a bearded mystic meditating in one of the caves. As I approach, he waves me away. "So much for passing on wisdom," I say to myself. But after seven kilometres, I'm unable to climb the towering cliffs to head inland. Along the way, above me, I can hear noise from the heavy construction equipment at work on La Route du Nord. But my only option is to continue walking.

After a total of ten kilometres, I finally reach a long beach. I'm not too concerned that there's no sign of Luke and hitch a ride with two Arabic-speaking Force Auxiliaire officers who've just come down to the beach from their hilltop camp. I realise that Omar and Mohammed are on the wrong road long before we arrive in Dar-Kebdani, a congested market town an hour's drive from the coast. I very slowly convey, using a napkin and pen to vividly illustrate the situation, that I'm separated from my son, that Luke's lost on the coast, that I'm passportless and penniless, and that I'm not where I should be.

They spend an hour in Dar-Kebdani buying supplies, everything from meat and rice to hashish, to last them for a few weeks.

"They've got super hashish here," Omar, who comes from Casablanca, tells me. Meanwhile Mohammed, a local boy, stops in to see everyone he's known since birth.

Omar and Mohammed offer me a beer, ice cream, money and a joint. I refuse everything except money and water, telling them that I'll eat after I find Luke. They can see I'm getting worried and blow smoke in my direction.

By the time they're ready to leave Dar-Kebdani, Omar is calling me 'Father' and insists "*Inshallah*, Allah is watching over you both." He invites me, using an increasingly comprehensive sign language, to return to the coast and spend the night on a cot at the Abdouna outpost.

"We'll find your son!" he says with his fingers. "Someone will be taking care of him."

I try to appear relaxed and in control. But I'm frantic. I use the money to try to call both our cell phones from a *téléboutique* but get no response. I'm completely baffled about how we're going to find each other in the middle of nowhere. Lacking a better plan I agree, as dusk falls, to ride back to their seaside camp with Omar and Mohammed.

It's dark when we get to a newly made access road and within minutes we literally run into a pickup coming the other way. We blink our lights, they stop and Luke is sitting in the back of the truck with three hard-hatted road construction workers. It turns out that he's been hanging with the French-speaking crew for the past few hours.

He tells me that, after waiting an hour, he presumed that I couldn't climb the cliffs and got a ride with the construction crew to the Force Auxiliaire outpost. An officer told him that "an older European" had gotten into the car with Omar and Mohammed a few hours earlier. Luke knew that had to be me.

"That calmed me down because I knew you were in good hands with the Force Auxiliaire," Luke says, as we head back to Dar-Kebdani with Mohammed Bouchiha, the foreman for a 25 kilometre stretch of La Route du Nord. "Everyone's been overwhelmingly nice."

We spend the night with Mohammed, his chauffeur and an architect at their apartment. Mohammed not only gives us a room with two beds, but also washes our clothes, lets us take showers and cooks the best fish, lamb and vegetable dinner we've had in Morocco. He speaks French and English, describes the highway project in great detail and talks about various traditions in rural Morocco. He tells us about the Berbers and lets us watch Arab video clips on his satellite TV. The chauffeur from Taza tells us he was married at 14 while still-unmarried Mohammed says there are bars in Al Hoceima and Nador that he occasionally visits in hopes of finding a wife.

"Would you like to come out with me, Luke?" he asks. "You probably won't find a wife but it'll be a unique experience."

Luke gives me a 'Well, why not?' look.

"Thanks for the offer but I think we've had enough drama today," I tell them both.

31. The Med Takes Our Passports, Money and Sanity

"I have my eyes and ears, a pair of legs, and a straight mind, still with me." – The Odyssey

I wake up at Mohammed's and everything, except my clean laundry, is stiff.

"Can you go another day with these heavy packs?" I ask Luke. "What can we dump?"

"We could be very Zen and give everything away," Luke suggests, "but that's probably a bit extreme."

"Yeah, we shouldn't go overboard," I reply. "Homer said 'Measure is best in everything. To send a guest packing, or cling to him when he's in haste – one sin equals the other.' Let's stick to the middle road and slightly lighten up."

We could also use a day off, but it's not going to be today. I take some homeopathic medicine and a handful of vitamins to prepare me to walk the middle road. Psychologically anyway.

After we feast on an enormous construction man's breakfast, we give Mohammed our 'exquisite Mexican/Cuban coffee blend', our Italian-made coffee brewer, some books and a few tidbits that have gradually become less essential as they weigh us down. Mohammed, who's given us a detailed rundown on the terrain between here and the Algerian border, presents Luke with a pair of slightly used tennis shoes to replace the ones stolen at the *téléboutique*. Then we all return to the coast.

"I really want to thank you for all that you've done," I tell Mohammed when he drops us near the Force Auxiliaire camp in Abdouna. "Without you and the Force Auxiliaire, I'm not sure if Luke and I would have found each other."

"The Force Auxiliaire know what they're doing," Mohammed says "Keep in touch with them! And come back and use the road in a few years."

We walk up the hill to the Force Auxiliaire camp and I address Omar as "mon fils", pay back the money he lent me and give him some presents I picked up at the morning market in Dar-Kebdani. After parting hugs, Luke and I head down the steep path to the beach where I jumped into the car 18 hours ago.

"It's too bad that we screwed up the meeting place but you've got to admit that it was a pretty cool adventure," Luke says. "I told you this would be a mission."

"Fortune shined on us and we should remember how generous and helpful everyone's been," I reply. "We'd have been in big trouble if they hadn't helped us out."

Voyaging Greeks benefited from the same type of assistance.

Lord Meneláos, the King of Sparta, says in *The Odyssey*: "Could we have made it home again – and Zeus give us no more hard roving! – if other men had never fed us, given us lodging?"

The answer is no.

And the people they met frequently offered gifts.

"Let me see what is costliest and most beautiful of all the precious things my house contains: a wine bowl, mixing bowl, all wrought of silver, but rimmed with hammered gold," Meneláos said to Telémakhos. "Let this be yours."

"I wish we could think of another way to thank Mohammed," I continue. "I don't know what his motivation was but, like most Arabs, he was a perfect host. I'm sure he was inspired by his religion."

Eumaios, the swineherd, once said to Odysseus "If I receive and shelter you, it is not for your tales but for your trouble, and with an eye to Zeus, who guards a guest."

It's probably Allah, Mohammed's Zeus, who saved the day for us. In any event, our host knew better than that mystic in the cave that it's more rewarding to give than receive, that the more you give away the more will come to you, that you should be compassionate to others.

Earth and rock from La Route du Nord being dumped over the steep cliffs short circuits our stroll along the sea. We meet a Moroccan gathering seashells, for jewellery he says, and the three of us climb a nearly vertical slope to reach the new road. I'm so worn out by the time we approach the top that I not only feel like Luke's grandfather, but also accept an offer from our recent acquaintance to carry my pack. It's the first time on the MedTrek that I need help meeting a physical challenge.

The Moroccan portion of La Route du Nord, we learned from Mohammed, involves 560 kilometres of coastal road between Tangier and Saidia "to break the isolation of this mountainous region and open some 200 kilometres of beaches to tourism." Scheduled for completion before 2010, it's estimated to cost over $272 million. The European Union is contributing $72.7 million, the United Arab Emirates are giving $70 million and key bilateral benefactors include Japan, France, Italy, Spain and Portugal.

We continue walking with the Moroccan, who claims he never drinks water, along the unpaved foundation for La Route du Nord until he heads inland to make necklaces from his collection of seashells. Luke and I arrive at Schimla Beach and run into Ahmed, a guest worker from Germany who immediately offers to buy us some 'Moroccan whiskey'.

Ahmed's got a new Mercedes, the kind frequently brought back on summer vacation by Moroccans working in Europe. The cars give Morocco an affluent feel, but their nouveau riche drivers are responsible for many serious accidents when they attempt autobahn speeds on Moroccan blacktop. However, Ahmed says he's in no hurry and let's us in on a secret.

"Just walk eight kilometres along the beach and you'll run into a completely new village that's got everything–hotels, restaurants, taxis, you name it," he tells us in German. "This is the type of infrastructure that will be everywhere on the coast when the large road is completed. Incidentally, don't try to walk along the sea to Melilla because it's a military zone. But definitely go there because the Spanish enclave is just like Europe."

Still weighed down by our packs, I offer the owner of a donkey twenty dirham to take our packs for three kilometres but he refuses.

"There's obviously something intimate going on between these men and their asses," I tell Luke. "Heck, I'd carry our packs for what I just offered him."

"Why bother when you can carry them for free?" Luke jokes.

By the time we've walked 23 kilometres we're exhausted, footsore, and pack weary. Even if it weren't a military zone, we don't have the energy today to walk around the Cap des Trois Fourches into Melilla, the second Spanish enclave on Morocco's Mediterranean coast.

There's a lot of building underway in the village, but not even the taxi stand has been completed. Still it's clear that we're in another part of Morocco, the Morocco of tomorrow maybe, when the café owner dramatically overcharges us for two drinks and a delivery truck driver offers to take us to Melilla for a whopping 50 euros.

"We're obviously out of rural Morocco," I tell Luke. "These people are clearly used to seeing, and overcharging, Europeans. Let's go to Spain."

We cross the border into Melilla after a brief interrogation by a Moroccan customs agent who, when he learns I'm a journalist, gives me a long lecture about the evolution and relevance of Islamic thought. We instantly lose an additional two hours when we enter Melilla because it's on European time and, presto, 6pm becomes 8pm when we check into the five-star Hotel Puerto Melilla. Sore, blistered, tired and bearing a rash due to a brushing against some type of poisonous bush, we agree to take a full day off tomorrow. We toss our packs in the closet to get them out of our sight.

The bathtub residue aptly illustrates the tenor of our 202-kilometre effort during the past seven days. Despite Melilla's European lights, we're too tired to do anything but eat some over-priced *tapas* in the air-conditioned lobby. And enjoy a room that not only has a telephone but also air conditioning and toilet paper.

The next day we investigate what a brochure calls 'a slice of Spain with an African touch' and it's immediately clear that Melilla is, as many Moroccans told us, 'Europa'. It actually does have everything.

We walk and bus around the town, which was founded in 1497, and feel, as the brochure promises, 'safe in the knowledge that we are in an exceptionally beautiful Spanish location'. We tour the fortifications in Melilla la Vieja, or the old town, where we learn that another name for this part of North Africa is Kelaya, the 'place of castles'.

"Historians contend that these are the only Mediterranean maritime fortifications that have not been attacked from the sea in the modern age," one guide tells us before we lunch on squid paella in the port. Then we walk through a cordoned-off part of town that will explode in a few hours with the annual *feria*.

"Don't even think of making me feel bad about this type of relaxation!" Luke says as we take it easy. "This is how normal people travel all of the time. They tour, they eat, they sleep."

Melilla, which the brochure claims is the European city closest to the desert, is a 12.33-square kilometre semicircle with a twenty-kilometre perimeter and a population of about 70,000. "It's 50 percent Europeans and 48 percent Berbers," another guide tells us. "Jewish and Hindu communities account for the remaining two percent. European markets are just down the street from *souks*."

Although we didn't MedTrek to the end of the military controlled peninsula of Cap des Trois Fourches yesterday, I justify this lapse because troops and fenced barriers would have forced us to backtrack. Despite this, I feel guilty that, for the first time since I left Antibes, I've intentionally cut out a few kilometres of the MedTrek.

"I feel like I've cheated," I tell Luke.

"You didn't skip that much and we can walk out to the point this evening," Luke replies sympathetically. "Don't beat yourself up over nothing."

Another Melilla guidebook contends that the town "separates the low coast of fine sand situated to the east", which is where we're heading, from the "strong cliffs dotted with small coves and isolated beaches" to the west from whence we've come. I look forward to walking on smoother, flatter terrain.

We hit the *feria*, which has taken over the central plaza and surrounding tree-lined streets, and munch on a variety of foods, including a delicious stuffed baked potato.

The next morning I debate the wisdom of abandoning our fine hotel in order to again trudge the path towards Algeria with our heavy backpacks. I decide to keep the room, leave the backpacks, and walk 2.5 kilometres to the border along the clean, raked and ordered Spanish sandy beaches. Then, wherever we wind up in Morocco, we'll make our way back to Melilla for another night of comfort.

After a quick ten-minute passport check at 8:30am in Melilla, we enter Beni-Enzar in Morocco where, bingo, it's 6:30am.

"How many of these people have even been into Melilla and experienced the comparative luxury next door?" Luke asks as we survey the crowd at a café. "What's it feel like being unable to keep up with the well-off Spanish family right next door?"

When we reach Nador after sixteen blissfully backpackless kilometres, construction on a *corniche* and seafront walk is underway while goats and sheep munch on every available bit of greenery. We walk out onto a Coney Island-like rotunda café built on stilts for a freshly squeezed orange juice and a fresh mint tea. The Spanish consulate across the street is besieged with visa-seeking Moroccans.

We spend the next four hours hiking on a marshy lagoonside coast where a newly developed neighborhood with streetlights and paved roads is waiting to be inhabited. We've run out of water when a Moroccan farmer counsels us to head inland to the road running from Nador to Kariat-Arkmane along the sea.

Once on the tarmac we pass a number of bootleggers selling Algerian gasoline in small containers at about a third the price of a Moroccan filling station. We walk alongside a bearded *babu* who looks like he makes this trek every day. As we pass Kariat's ornate mosque, the *muezzin* begins his call to prayer. By the time we get to the seaside it's Luke's longest-ever hiking day – 41 kilometres, or 54,812 steps, at an average of 4.8 kilometres an hour.

As we finish a mint tea, scores of worshippers leave the mosque. Then we find a taxi driver who, for ten euros, will take us straight back to Melilla. During the drive, I negotiate a fare for the next day. The driver agrees to take us from Melilla to Saidia on the Algerian border, where we'll dump our backpacks, and then drive us back to Kariat to resume the hike. We arrange to have him pick us up at a pre-arranged spot in Beni-Enzar that's down an alley and out of sight of other taxi drivers.

"They would not be happy with our arrangement," says our driver. "This is a very competitive business."

That night we head out to the *feria* for another baked potato but don't have the stamina to hit the casino.

"MedTrekking really doesn't make for an exciting night life," says Luke.

We leave Melilla at 8am and gain the usual two hours when we cross the border. But we don't get to the Hotel Manhattan in Saidia until 10:30 Moroccan time. The delay is due to a registration stop at the Royal Gendarmerie where, besides conveying our passport details and getting a pass to enable our driver to go further than the permitted 50 kilometres from Nador, we see a Mercedes with German plates that was completely destroyed the night before by a *Gastarbiter* making the drive to Kariat.

"It looks like Ahmed's car," I say to Luke.

"These Mercedes all look alike," he replies.

Saidia is the Saint-Tropez wannabe of the north coast. There are, for Morocco, a surprising number of clubs, discos and restaurants with enticing names like Le Patio, Caracas, Les Pyramides and Toscane. There are also spacious vacation compounds for employees from the national telecommunications and electricity companies and a campground owned by a leading Moroccan long-distance runner. Although not nearly as well-kept as the beach in Melilla, there's an expansive sandy beachfront and jet skis for rent. It looks, eerily, like La Route du Nord has already arrived.

The Manhattan Hotel is especially surreal. Opened in July 2002 by a Moroccan woman living in Amsterdam, it features not only photos of the New York City skyline circa 1936 but also dozens of pictures of the World Trade Centre. Our sea view room costs 375 dirham, or 37.50 euros a night, and a maid says she'll do all of our laundry for five euros. But, we both agree, the shots of a New York that's been destroyed seem in remarkably bad taste.

"Don't worry," one of the waiters whispers to me. "They're going to rebuild it just like it was."

Before we return to Kariat for a packless hike on 'the low coast of fine sand', I take all the cash out of my pack and put it in Luke's money belt with our passports and credit cards.

The drive from Saidia through Cap de l'Eau and the town of Ras Quebdana is right along the sea and the only potential problem appears to be the wide Mourouya River. The bridge across the river – the only bridge across the river according to the driver – is about three kilometres from the sea. Otherwise, I say to Luke, "This should be a piece of cake."

But the terrain changes dramatically when the road cuts inland. Deep gullies, valleys and hills now separate us from the Med. We could be stuck if we don't complete the whole hike, which by road is forty-one kilometres, in one shot.

We pick up a small blue pack, six litres of water, two loaves of breads, a pound of olives and some cakes in Kariat. Then we start speed walking along the villa-filled Kariat Plage to a path that initially takes us up and down gullies and hillsides. We're having a blast getting completely soaked as we make our way along the pebbly, rocky and sandy beachfront.

"This is what MedTrekking is all about," I tell Luke. "Being kids getting dirty and wet."

As we approach the Spanish-controlled Chafarinas islands off Cap de l'Eau, I'm confident that we can make it to Saidia before dark. There's just one last cliffy part of coast before the terrain levels off. Unfortunately, we're at an impasse and, because we can't climb up the cliff, we have to swim around it. The water is rough and our plan, once I swim to the other side, is that Luke will toss me the small pack and make the swim himself.

Not a great idea, it turns out. The pack, which Luke seems to toss carelessly as a cigarette dangles from his mouth, doesn't make it to my outstretched arms and falls into the water. I'm aware, as I watch it drop in slower-than-slow slow motion, that I'd transferred the contents of Luke's money-belt back into the pack, and it now contained our cash, credit cards and passports.

"Get it! Get it!" I scream to Luke.

Luke jumps into the water and surfaces in a few seconds.

"I can't find it," he yells. "I can't see anything."

We both search for 45 minutes before coming to the conclusion that the pack has disappeared. It's getting dark and we're in the middle of nowhere with no identity papers or cash.

"Sheeeeeeeeeeeeet!" I scream.

"It could be worse," Luke says once I conclude my rant. "It's just money and passports."

We head uphill to a Force Auxiliaire outpost. There's not much they can do, of course, and they don't have any form of transport. We walk another five kilometres until we're picked up on a dusty, dark road by a car that takes us to the Gendarmerie Royale in Ras Quebdana.

Wet and bedraggled, we report the loss to the gendarmes but are told to return in the morning to make an official declaration. The very helpful police chief arranges a lift for us to Saidia where, in my heavy backpack at the Manhattan Hotel, I've got one remaining credit card, a California driver's license, photocopies of our passports (I'd taken the originals because I was worried about theft) and a mobile phone.

The next morning, not quite able to accept our loss, I hire a cab driver to take us back to Boufadiss beach. Watched by Luke, the driver and a Force Auxiliaire officer, I spend an hour diving, eyes wide open, searching for the submerged pack. I'm thrashed as the waves toss me into the rocks and then punctured when I reach for rocks and come up with sea urchins. I recall a line from *The Odyssey* when Odysseus is challenged by the sea: "Here are sharp rocks off shore, and the sea a smother rushing around them; rock face rising sheer from deep water; nowhere could I stand up on my two feet and fight free of the welter." Odysseus left the skin of his great hands torn on that rock-ledge as the wave submerged him. So did I.

After an hour, I give up and we return to make the *déclaration de perte* at the Royal Gendarmerie, call the US Consulate and figure out a way to get to Casablanca to get our passports replaced.

"The bag was obviously swept out to sea by an underwater current before you could do anything about it," declares Mohamed Lameharem, the head of the brigade. "But the sea never keeps anything. It will turn up somewhere and, who knows, you might even get your documents back."

Fat chance, though one officer claims he is going to lead a diving expedition when he learns that we lost 500 euros in cash.

It takes five hours to complete the *déclaration de perte* and when we finally return to Saidia, we walk to the barbwire barrier on the Moroccan side of a 500-metre no man's land extending to the Algerian border.

"This is a *zone interdite* and I can't let you cross," warns the friendly Moroccan guard who climbed down from his watchtower to talk to us. "Anyway the Algerians won't let you in. You'll have to try the border crossing in Oujda."

I thank him and stare at the no man's land for a few minutes. Then I turn to Luke.

"These are just minor setbacks and tests," I tell him. "We can't quite laugh at them yet but we'll be able to in a few days. After all, losing the passports was our fault and not being able to cross the border is really beyond our control."

"Yeah, we've got our health," Luke jokes.

"Well, remember what Homer wrote when Odysseus got out of a bind."

He gives me a look that said 'Oh, God, what's the old man going to spoon out this time?'

"And what was that?" he asks.

"Few men can keep alive through a big surf to crawl, clotted with brine, on kindly beaches in joy knowing the abyss behind," I say, quoting a passage from one of the last of the twenty-four books in *The Odyssey*.

"Well, if he could do it then so can we!" Luke says as we turned away from the sea.

Algeria, I tell Luke, doesn't look that good anyway. The domestic violence, kidnappings and killings have not abated, as I projected they might when I started the MedTrek. In fact, things have gotten worse. And the Algerian authorities in Washington, DC, Nice and Algiers have refused to issue me a journalist's visa.

I sit on the sandy beach and reflect on our perambulatory options. Swim around no man's land at night and enter Algeria illegally; try again to get a journalist's visa from the Algerian Embassy in Washington; try to enter with a simple tourist's visa; or skip Algeria and resume the hike in Tunisia.

Or I could return to my starting point in Antibes, head the other way around the Med through less-dangerous Italy and save North Africa for sometime down the road.

As we head back to Ras Quebdana, we stop at the Al Jazira restaurant to thank the man who gave us a lift to Saidia the night before. Then I buy a gift for the guy who picked us up in the dark to take us from the seaside to Ras Quebdana.

When the official stamps arrive and our declaration is finally complete, we get a taxi to the train station in the centre of Oujda, a remarkably clean university city in eastern Morocco. We have just enough time to pay a visit to the animated *souk*, send a card to Mohammed to thank him for his hospitality, and have a traditional Moroccan dinner before taking an overnight train across the country to Casablanca.

After a coffee on arrival at the aptly named Café d'Arrivée on a Sunday morning, we get a cab to show us the locations of the French and American consulates. Then we have the driver take us to the Hassan II Mosque built by King Hassan II for his 60th birthday. Finished in 1993, it's the world's largest mosque with the world's tallest minaret.

"Muslims with means are expected to build a mosque during their lifetime and I guess if you're a king you've got to make it a big one," I tell Luke.

We check into the opulent Hyatt Regency Hotel, spend the day getting massages and hire a photographer to take new passport photos.

That afternoon, I make a serious mistake. After getting powerful, joint-cracking massages on the marble slab in the centre of the *hammam*, I tell the masseur to give Luke's skin a thorough rubbing with a camel-hair glove.

"My first Turkish massage in Istanbul when I was your age is one of my fondest memories," I tell Luke. "This takes off your outer skin and makes you ready for a new life."

In Luke's case, though, the rub-off almost immediately spreads a mysterious rash all over his body and he looks like he's thoroughly infected with poison oak.

"There's an old French adage that goes, '*Qui cherche, trouve*,' or 'Seek and ye shall find'," Luke later reflects. "Well, if adventure is what I was seeking, in Morocco, adventure is what I found. Indeed, the most pivotal moment occurred in the early stages of our Moroccan escapade when my dad's life was nearly taken before my eyes. That the boulder skipped over his head was a miracle – one that reminded me how much I loved and still needed my father.

"From that day forth I approached the trek under a new light," he continues. "I now saw every day walked as a chance to share precious time with the man I most admire. The value of each step became unquantifiable. I decided that, if I weren't going to finish the walk around the Mediterranean for my old man, I'd be by his side the day it finished him."

The next morning we arrive at the consulate at 8am to get replacement passports.

"Get there early and you'll have new passports in an hour or so," advised Amy Tachco, the duty weekend officer, when I called her from Ras Quebdana on Saturday.

But the bureaucratic process takes the entire day and makes me ready to complain enough to cause a diplomatic incident.

I initially wait patiently in the embassy waiting room reading the US tax code. I notice that an 'America – Catch The Spirit' poster published by the US Department of Commerce includes a photograph of the World Trade Centre. And I thought the Manhattan Hotel was behind the times.

I look at the consulate's schedule of services and fees and, as the hours pass, realise that it's easier, and cheaper, to die and be sent home than to get a new passport. That night I write an inventive, incensed and indignant note of complaint and send it to everyone from the Secretary of State to the head of the consulate in Casablanca. As a working journalist who has visited over 100 countries and not lost a passport during the past forty years, I make it clear that a Moroccan employee treated us like, and I'm being polite here, homeless scum. He wouldn't give me his name 'for security reasons' but his extension is #4149.

I get an email a few days later from one US official telling me that my letter will "be a catalyst for change … don't give up on your government". The Consul General wrote that "You are entitled to expect a more compassionate and effective service from the US Consulate. As a result of your letter, the contents of which I have shared with the entire Consulate staff, I have again underscored to Consulate employees the importance of our contact with American citizens and again re-emphasised that our primary mission here is the protection of Americans."

I write back that "My hope, of course, is that future American travellers will not be as frustrated as I was with the passport replacement procedure in Casablanca. *Inshallah*."

Another MedTrek service.

Odysseus would never have made the round trip to Troy in only two decades if he'd encountered this type of bureaucracy. It would have taken him at least twice as long, even with the help of all those gods.

MedTrek MileStone #4 – The Morocco/Algeria Border

There's no question that my 531-kilometre trek across northern Morocco to the Algerian border, after walking continuously on the decks of the ferry during the crossing from Spain and determining that the Mediterranean begins at the shores of the Atlantic Ocean, has been the most physically challenging part of the MedTrek to date.

I fell off a cliff and was badly cut up when a goat path collapsed. I was almost arrested three or four times in one day. I was separated twice from my son, once sure he'd been kidnapped by a guy wearing an 'I Love Oussama' T-shirt. We lost our passports and money in the sea. And, the worst blow, I was accused of being 'old' by a guy two decades my senior.

The Moroccans certainly weren't responsible for any of the mishaps caused either by the gods or myself. Indeed, the locals, both military and civilian, were among the most helpful people I've met. They had a sense that, as Homer wrote, 'fair dealing brings more profit in the end'.

Now, finally armed with a new passport from the US Consulate in Casablanca, I'm at a crossroads and border crossing. I can't legally get into Algeria and, with the civil war, am reluctant to proceed under false pretenses. But I'm definitely not ready to abandon the MedTrek. I'll let you know what inspiration floats my way. *Inshallah*.

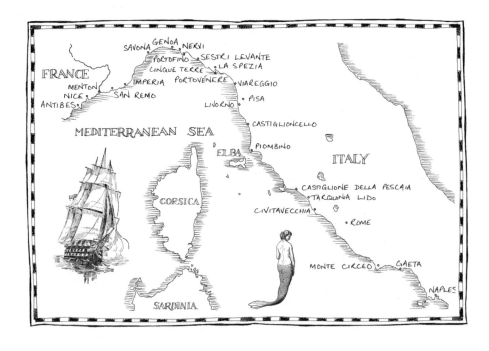

Part Eight

An Italian Roam and Ramble

32. The Return to Antibes and a Nice Promenade

"In life there's nothing worse than knocking about the world, no bitterness we vagabonds are spared when the curst belly rages." — *The Odyssey*

"I didn't set out on the MedTrek to get killed," I tell Elissa, an American journalist who's become a very close friend, as we discuss the logistics of the walk from Antibes to Nice. "It would have been vainglorious, if not suicidal, to enter war-torn Algeria. I'll tackle it from the other side after I walk through Monaco, Italy, Albania, Greece, Turkey, Syria, Lebanon, Israel, Egypt, Libya, Tunisia and a few other countries."

"I feel a lot better now that you're back in Europe instead of bouncing around North Africa," says Elissa, who lives in Los Angeles but has begun making frequent visits to the South of France, as she prepares for her first stint of MedTrekking.

We're in a very relaxed mode and mood as we inaugurate the next segment of walking the Mediterranean after my 3524-kilometre journey through France, Spain and Morocco. Meanwhile, acknowledging that this little adventure is taking much more time than I'd initially figured, I'm simply following Lao Tsu's instructions: "It is important to examine both the short-range and the long-range. If you want to go far in a decade, you have to go far each year. If you want to go far each year, you have to make sure that you do something significant each day."

Moving back to the cultivated Riviera from Morocco is a considerable change of pace and space. This time around I keep my plans to myself and don't bother sending out invitations to attract fellow hikers. It's just the two of us starting off at high noon on a slightly windy, somewhat sunny autumnal day.

Despite the distance I've got under my belt, I'm as enthused about taking off with Elissa as I was setting off with Bogart and Delphyne. Perhaps because I've realised that Thich Nhat Hanh was right when he said "The path is you." And that my motivation to continue the MedTrek echoes Deng Ming-Dao's precept: "Only when wisdom, courage, timing and perseverance are combined can one have a basis for initiative." Simple Buddhist banter.

Though we have together hiked bits of the Riviera coast and camped in the Vallée des Merveilles in the nearby Maritime Alps to examine the mysterious Bronze Age engravings around Mount Bego, Elissa admits that she's not a natural outdoorswoman. She was so put off by the crowded conditions in the refuge on our mountain hike that she almost got out of her bunk to walk down the hill in the middle of the night.

"You probably wouldn't want to hike in Morocco," Luke said when Elissa related how unpleasant it was to sleep amidst 90 snoring Italians. "But to hike the Riviera all you need is some sun block, a hat and a credit card. It's civilised, pleasant and peaceful."

And away we go.

"This is where you'll find the Picasso painting of Odysseus and his crew that I mentioned," I tell Elissa as we amble along the ramparts behind the Picasso Museum. "This spot was first a Roman camp in the Antipolis acropolis. It became a castle in the 12th century, then Picasso's atelier, and finally the museum that bears his name."

As we edge past Heidi's Bookstore through the sailboat-and-yacht-filled Port Vauban, I spin tales about the topless swimmers I encounter during workouts at the municipal pool on avenue Jules Grec. I recount another story about a ferocious breed of turtle kept in a sanctuary at Marineland just east of town and explain that we're now walking along the Baie des Anges, or the Bay of Angels, that stretches from Antibes' Fort Carré to the other side of Nice.

I'm carrying a small daypack, about the size of the one I lost in the sea in Morocco, and no one would guess, or perhaps even care, that I've recently walked from here to Algeria. We look like just another couple nonchalantly admiring the mistral-cleared sky, brilliant turquoise sea, and cloudless views of the Alps and Nice. As we pass the Siesta casino and discotheque, I mention how I fell into one of the outdoor pools here in 1977 after I'd been drinking heavily and failed to negotiate a dance step with chic French cartoonist Claire Bretécher.

"That incident wasn't as embarrassing as you might think because earlier that evening I'd won 6000 francs at the Casino Ruhl in Nice, was flying high on Champagne and coke, and had a voluptuous friend from North Carolina, whom I'd nicknamed the 'woman of a thousand questions', waiting for me back at the Hôtel Negresco," I sheepishly tell Elissa. "I did fail to accomplish the evening's main objective, which was to promote *The Paris Metro* to some potential investors. But, hey, you can't be good at everything."

For better or worse my *modus operandi* in those days was more inclined toward booze, broads (that was still a politically correct word 30 years ago) and backgammon than business, though I'd pretentiously convinced myself that I was the era's Rupert Murdoch. I recall being tremendously relieved when, sopping wet, I was able to split from the Siesta early and get a cab back to Nice for dry clothes, more gambling and a night of lascivious carousing.

I don't tell everyone this part of the story but I lost the 6000 francs during ten minutes of blackjack and not too politely suggested to the 'woman of a thousand questions,' who interrogated me about everything from the weather and sexual positions to Jimmy Carter and Brigitte Bardot, that she try to make it through one night without ending a sentence with a question mark. She lasted 12 minutes.

"I don't remember much of what I did in Cannes, Nice and Monaco when I came down here on assignments from Paris in the mid-to-late 70s," I admit, mentioning that I covered a spectacular bank robbery in Nice during the summer of 1976. "It was an era of liquid business lunches and drunken dinners that invariably ended in a daze or blackout at a nightclub or a casino. Now the most exciting thing I do in life is walk."

"And you even manage to get into trouble doing that," she laughs.

Elissa, whom I contacted frequently when Luke and I were getting into and out of a number of jams in Morocco, has gradually come to know more about the MedTrek than anyone who hasn't walked the walk with me. She sensed the moment I called from Jebha that something dramatic had happened the day I took that death-defying fall. And she immediately got in touch with the State Department in Washington and the US Consulate in Casablanca when Luke and I accidentally drowned our passports and other important documents. She's heard my tales about Delphyne, Marie, Jacqueline, Cassie (whom I no longer invited to MedTrek after I met Elissa), Leonardo, Bill and other people who'd been out on the trail with me. She was also familiar with my history of alcohol abuse, the many years I'd devoted to staying sober and my truncated marriage.

Though not a MedTrek participant until today, Elissa respects how much I value the undertaking and, as a fellow journalist, completely understands its personal and professional allure. She's smart, funny, gorgeous and a witty writer. And my kids have become very fond of both Elissa and the stability her companionship brings to my life. As our friendship gradually developed, we have discussed the baggage that we each carried into a relationship at this stage in our lives and made a simple but solid pact: complete fidelity. One strike and you're out.

"Well, the kind of trouble and problems I encounter on the MedTrek are insignificant when compared to the rampage I was on when I was drinking constantly and abusing everyone I met," I continue. "You wouldn't be speaking to me if I were still getting juiced."

"You're right about that," Elissa immediateyl agrees.

Developing her own MedTrek esprit, Elissa picks up two-dozen sea-smoothed pebbles as we move along a stone-covered beach adjacent to the freshly blacktopped two-lane road.

"The rocks on this beach are the smoothest I've seen in the world," she explains when we stop for lunch at a beachfront restaurant in Villeneuve-Loubet, not far from the house where the renowned chef Auguste Escoffier was born. "But I still think it's weird that all these people want to sunbathe on rocks right near a highway. Why don't they go to one of the sandy beaches?"

The mostly elderly, mostly French sunbathers have indeed all set up umbrellas, towels and cushions on the hard and glossy stones. A tribe of homeless folks, who have the darkest tans of anyone around, keep their eyes glued on a prospector searching for buried 'treasures' with a high-tech apparatus.

During lunch, Elissa decides which stones to keep and stuffs them in my pack before we continue to Marina Baie des Anges. That complex, which consists of four towering pyramid-shaped blocks of luxury apartments, has become a symbol of the French Riviera and a landmark, or eyesore, on the flight path into the Nice Côte d'Azur International Airport. It includes a dozen restaurants, half a dozen massage and thalassotherapy spas, a shoe store and supermarkets open 24/7. But it's definitely not everyone's cup of *chai*.

"We left the Riviera and moved to Paris when we saw them building that," Warren Trabant, a Homer-loving journalist who lived here in the 1960s, told me. "If that was the future, we didn't want anything to do with it. To paraphrase a line in *The Iliad* 'it was built against the will of the immortal gods, and so it will not last for long'."

Yet here it is four decades later.

A sign claims there are 2.9 kilometres of beachfront walking ahead and I admire the Zen-like cleanliness of the area underneath the bridge over the Loup River near Cagnes-sur-Mer. There's no trash and the gravel has been raked as carefully as the garden of a well-tended Japanese monastery. I'm definitely not in Morocco anymore but this spot is eerily clean for the French Riviera.

We cross the bridge and pass the gated Cagnes-sur-Mer hippodrome before arriving at a McDonald's that was built, after much contesting and public outcry, right on the rocky beach.

"There's a little cubicle with two tables inside that surprisingly has the best sea view of any restaurant on the Riviera," I tell Elissa as I lead her to my favourite Big Mac vantage point. "But the real action on this part of the coast is actually up in the hills in La Gaude, Saint-Paul-de-Vence, Tourettes-sur-Loup and Saint-Jeannet.

That's where most of my friends, artists like Nall and Mitch Waite, live."

They like the Riviera as much as Auguste Renoir, whose former estate near here is renowned for its splendid olive grove, but find the coast too congested during the summer.

We share a McFlurry with M&Ms before continuing to Cros-de-Cagnes where, after 14 kilometres, I'm revitalised and pleased to be on the way to Monaco and Italy. I tried not to let it upset me too much when McDonald's, and other restaurants on this same stretch of coast, were deemed 'illegal' by a city ordinance and destroyed in 2006. At least the MedTrek enabled me to get one last sea view from my favourite table and share it with Elissa.

Few things beat an early, breezy, wave-crashing-in-the-dark pre-dawn start to the MedTrek after I drop Elissa off at the airport for her flight to Los Angeles the next morning. As I begin walking on the beach in Cros-de-Cagnes at 6:30am, it's brisk enough that I'm wearing gloves, though I'm optimistic enough to have on shorts.

An unlit 'Handiplage' sign indicates that a nearby sandy strip of sand is 'Accessible for the Physically Challenged'. The chatter of fishermen emerges from the port in Saint-Laurent-du-Var, their Provençal accents a pleasant contrast to the din of cars taking their drivers to work in Nice, which was presumably named after Nike, the Greek goddess of victory. The paved seaside promenade continues behind the Holiday Inn and past Cap 3000, the closest thing in these parts to an American shopping mall. A sign at the Var River informs me that I'm in 'a little Camargue' with all sorts of flora and fauna.

Ah, the Var. The people in Nice, the Niçois, consider crossing the Var like the Greeks felt about making a trip beyond the Styx, one of the five rivers of Hades. And people like me living west of the Var are often reluctant to cross it to get into "The Big Olive", which is what I've called Nice since I coined the expression, or took credit for coining the expression, in an article in the 1980s.

The Var actually is a key boundary, psychologically if not physically. And though the river is usually quite harmless, it occasionally lives up to its mythic reputation. One winter it overflowed and not only destroyed dozens of cars in the underground airport parking lot but also soaked important documents and records in the basement of headquarters of the Alpes-Maritimes General Council. It was of greater importance when it was the border between France and the Kingdom of Sardinia run by the House of Savoy before Nice became part of France in June 1860.

No one seems to know what people felt about the Var when Greeks living in Marseille moved here in the fourth century BC to found the village of Nikaia. But there's nothing to indicate that they made a big deal about it. The most important river back then was the Paillon, on the other side of town, and the Romans later built their settlement a bit uphill and inland in Cimiez rather than on the riverbank.

Today the Var is much more important than the Paillon, which runs mainly underground, though Cimiez has much more to offer than Roman ruins. There's a very relaxed annual summer jazz festival held amidst remains of the arena and amphitheater and two worthwhile museums, the Musée Matisse and the Musée Marc Chagall. I particularly enjoy the latter, which I first visited shortly after it opened in the 1970s, because of the way the Mediterranean light illuminates Chagall's lyrical canvases, including the 17 that make up the *Biblical Message* which took him 13 years to complete.

After crossing the Var I almost immediately encounter the airport, which has grown dramatically since it was a walk-down-the-steps-of-the-plane-cross-the-tarmac-and-exit-through-a-little-building operation when I first moved here. Today Nice boasts the second most important international airport in France and there's a fence along the Var that prevents me from accessing the landing strip and walking on the seaside.

The airport was certainly more important to me psychologically than the Var in the 1980s and '90s when I was travelling constantly on assignment for various magazines and newspapers. The first word uttered by Luke was "Daddy", but he said it when he was looking at a plane above our home in Castellaras near Valbonne.

As I walk parallel to the airport I notice that Nizza, the city's Italianised name, is written just below 'Nice' on the sign indicating the western city limit of the second largest city, after Marseille, on the French Mediterranean coast. Across the street near a business centre called Arénas is the vast Parc Phoenix botanical garden where I've taken numerous walks amidst areas recreating seven different tropical and sub-tropical climates. It's worth a visit just to hear loudspeakers that bark out the sounds of birds and animals found in each particular ecosystem. In the African area, it's a gorilla; in 'India' there's the roar of a tiger.

The Parc's pyramid-shaped roof camouflages a gargantuan greenhouse that reflects the rising sun. But the sun does more than just rise this morning. A gigantic orange-red ball emerges from the sea and pours an incredibly bright light on the seaside Promenade des Anglais that stretches along the seashore. Joggers, bikers and walkers come to life, as though awakened by the sun-triggered alarm. Perhaps some hear Homer whisper "You'll be awake to see the primrose Dawn when she goes glowing from the streams of Ocean to mount her golden throne."

A sunrise like this, when the sun explodes like a dolphin launched from the bowels of the Med, makes it clear why the Greeks created so many myths to explain the solar movement. Right now, it's easy for me to imagine Helios, the god of the Sun, riding across the heavens with the solar ball in his chariot. Or Atlas, the Titan whom Zeus made hold up the sky in punishment for challenging the Olympians, turning the heavenly sphere on its axis to provoke a new sunrise. I feel bathed, cleansed and protected.

That's not my usual reaction when I arrive in Nice. As I said, like many people who live west of the Var, I'm often intimidated by the place. The traffic can be traumatising and the narrow lanes on the Promenade des Anglais, which got its name when it was constructed by the city's English colony during the 18th century, would be more appropriate for bumper cars. I've always dreaded coming to the colourful but congested Carnival celebration that brings flower-bedecked floats, fireworks and a procession to the city each February and culminates with a packed parade aptly called the Battle of the Flowers. I remember driving my infant children to school near Nice years ago and making them howl with laughter when I used various accents and contorted facial expressions to blurt out the phrase "Too many cars!"

But walking into the city this morning gives me a totally different perspective. Though rush hour traffic is at a crawl, I'm blissfully unaware of the 'too many cars'. Everybody else strolling on the Promenade seems to be in a similarly relaxed let's-ignore-the-stress state of mind. I stop to admire a group of Japanese tourists meticulously examining pebbles on the beach – all of the Nice beaches along the Promenade are pebble rather than sand – with the same intensity that Elissa did a few kilometres ago.

I get flashbacks of my many past visits to Nice as I pass various buildings. There's a Casino supermarket (rebuilt after its roof collapsed on shoppers), the offices of France Conseil (where I did some copywriting work), the Lenval Hospital (where Sonia saw a very good doctor and Angelina Jolie gave birth to twins in 2008), and the Elyseés Hôtel (where I once took Bogart to lunch). I walk by Elizabeth Billhardt's apartment on the Promenade. She's a photographer friend who published the photo-rich *Coastal Pleasures – Perusing the French Coastline* that included shots from the abbey off Cannes, the Camargue, Nice and other scenic spots.

I'm frequently criticised for rarely carrying a camera on the MedTrek to record the entire outing from a visual perspective. Though I've taken some digital snaps, I feel that taking photographs is a time-consuming activity that distracts me from the present. I also plan to return to my most treasured spots on the Med with a professional photographer and Elizabeth is a candidate. I particularly like her photographs depicting light dancing on the surface of the sea, her enthusiasm about the change of light between dusk and dark, and the fact that she frequently takes midnight swims when there's a full moon.

I pass the baroque Hôtel Negresco that is to Nice what the Carlton, Majestic and Martinez are to Cannes. But I'm not thinking baroque when I see the hotel. Instead I recall the time I stayed here after one Cannes film festival in the '70s and met an American woman taking a break from her life in Paris. We took an afternoon drive to the perched villages behind Nice and she told me that her ex-husband had published a letter in the *International Herald Tribune* claiming that

Paris "destroyed my wife's moral fibre". He called the City of Light "the Sodom and Gommorah of contemporary civilisation". Another reason to move south.

Beyond the renovated Palais de la Mediterrannée Hôtel with its stunning 1930s façade, I stroll through the Jardin Albert 1ᵉʳ before continuing into the labyrinthine old town and the Cours Saleya. Once the city's elegant walkway, the Cours Saleya is now a vibrantly active flower and vegetable market beginning each morning at daybreak. I buy green olives, *socca* made of chickpea flour, and homemade ratatouille.

Then I stare at a nearby building on rue de la Préfecture where, in the penthouse apartment, former mayor Jacques Médecin and his American wife Ilene resided before they were forced to leave the country due to political and financial shenanigans. The wealthy mayor, who frequently acted like royalty because he inherited the title of the Count de Medici, often assured me that he didn't need to embezzle public funds. Obviously, I learned over the years, he lied.

I frequently interviewed the conservative Médecin, who succeeded his father as mayor and ran France's fifth largest city for over a quarter century, and was impressed with his charisma, stamina and successful dictatorial approach to politics. I vividly recall the first time I met Ilene in 1984 on the night of the US presidential elections. I was wearing a Jimmy Carter mask at a bash at the Acropolis, a lavish conference centre where the salons and rooms have Greek names like Agora, Hermes, Athena, Rhodes and Muses.

"Look, Jacques, can you believe someone has the audacity to wear a Democratic mask at one of our parties?" Ilene, who's my age but my political antithesis, said to her cigar-puffing husband in her adopted but authoritative Countess de Medici voice. "Should we have him shot?"

"Ma'am, perhaps you should be asking 'Who is this masked man and why is he here?'" I said in my best Georgian accent.

I left without taking off my mask. But that exchange launched a friendship that almost led to my death. I was appointed an "Eagle of the Acropolis" which, though there were really no responsibilities, involved attending a number of black-tie dinner functions. Ilene, always stunningly attired like an over-dressed Barbie doll at these events, asked me to be the first to dance with her at one gala. I could feel the entire ballroom waiting to see whether the mayor's entourage, in retribution for a dastardly violation of protocol that requires her to first dance with the mayor, would sweep me off my feet and take me to a back alley. I tried to carry on a conversation nonetheless.

"What attracted you to Jacques?" I asked.

"We met when I was 28 and he was the French Minister of Tourism," Ilene began. "When we shook hands there was an electrical current that flowed through my entire body. What really hooked me was the way he kissed my hand. It was so French, so much out of a movie, that I just swooned. After an hour of playing around in the bucket seats of my Porsche, we spent the night in his suite at the Beverly Hills Hotel.

"By the time the night was over I thought I'd met God. I certainly didn't care that he was a government minister and the mayor of Nice because I hated politicians. I told him that all of his titles made him sound like he was the head of a banana republic. But I'd never seen anyone with so much sexual stamina."

"And what attracted Jacques to you?" I asked.

"My blow jobs!" she said, maintaining her picture-perfect Barbie smile as the crowd looked on. "I give the best head in LA – but this better be off the record."

Ilene, who recently agreed to put her quote on the record, didn't have a hard time adapting to life in Nice, where she had chauffeurs, servants and everything else at her fingertips. And extramarital affairs, though not with me, were part of the lifestyle.

"Mediterranean men make me feel like I'm the centre of the world," she gushed. "They drip with charm, have savage animal-like eruptions and are emotional volcanoes. Every American woman should sample the Latin lover at least once."

During the next year the two of us worked on a book about her amorous and political experiences as an American princess on the French Riviera. The oral sex comment was one of her milder remarks and, to be safe, we showed the first draft to Jacques before turning it over to our French publisher.

"If any of that ever gets out," he told his wife, "you'll be dead and I'll make sure that your American co-author always walks with a very noticeable limp."

We cancelled the project but Jacques and Ilene were forced to flee France to Uruguay in 1990. Médecin – who compared himself to Napoleon, Victor Hugo and Charles de Gaulle – stridently argued that he was "in exile" and not on the lam. But before he died, or was murdered, in 1998, he served time on charges that included tax evasion, abuse of confidence, fraud, misuse of public funds, violation of exchange controls and corruption. No one, not even Ilene, claimed he'd been framed.

The city of Nice threw a big funeral for their former mayor and he remains a popular figure, a French Odysseus, on the corruption-is-a-way-of-life French Riviera. Ilene, who's not allowed back into France unless she wants to be put in jail, looks back in awe on their time together from the top to the bottom.

I buy a postcard to send Ilene in Beverly Hills and scribble a phrase uttered by Agamemnon. "But that woman, plotting a thing so low, defiled herself and all her sex, all women yet to come, even those few who may be virtuous."

I know she'll laugh.

I walk past the Chapelle de la Misericorde, which is overseen by a group called the Black Penitents, to the Cais de Pierla Palace where the omnipresent Picasso lived from 1921 to 1938. When I reach the massive church at the end of the Cours Saleya, I admire its colourful bell tower before continuing on the Promenade des Anglais and climbing the steps behind the Hôtel Suisse. I watch the arrival of a ferry from Corsica from my perch at the top of the 300-foot high Château, as the hill I'm on is called. Then I descend to walk around the rectangular port and alongside the ferry docks towards the *sentier littoral* that will take me out of town.

I pass the apartment complex of an English-speaking psychologist, one of a handful on the Riviera, that Chloé and I saw before our divorce. We were sitting on the terrace at the family home in Valbonne when the telephone rang a few hours after our last session. To protect the psychologist, and the profession, I'm calling him Mr X.

"This is Mr X and I'm calling to find out if I know you," he said. "I see your name and number in my book but I just don't remember if we've ever met."

"My wife and I were at your house two hours ago discussing some intimate aspects of our relationship and marriage," I said. "You've got it all down on tape."

"Oh, my gosh, I don't remember," Mr X replied.

My wife looked at me in astonishment and then burst out laughing.

"Maybe that's a professional trick," she said. "He figures it'll jar us into some type of reconciliation."

"I suppose he could be some kind of wizard," I laughed. "As Homer said 'though you have your wits about you, still it is hard not to be taken in by the immortals.' If so, he's pretty smart. If not, he's missing some circuits."

There was no reconciliation, we never saw Mr X again and I don't feel like dropping in on him this morning. Instead, after the wilds of Morocco, I just enjoy my safe saunter along a manmade seaside path that continues around the Cap de Nice and passes directly underneath the seaside Restaurant Coco Beach that's been serving extraordinary bouillabaisse and fish dishes since 1936.

I rest on a rock atop a well-known local swimming hole and then, because there's no longer a path on the sea, walk along the *basse corniche* road to Villefranche-sur-Mer. One of three roads from Nice to Monaco, the *basse corniche* is closest to the sea and, as the name implies, is at the bottom of the hillside beneath the middle, or *moyenne*, and high, or *grande, corniches*. Above all of these is the *autoroute* that runs through frequent tunnels from France into Italy.

I don't officially get out of Nice/Nizza for quite a while but by the time I reach the city limits I decide that, in the Mediterranean-wide scope of things, the city should rank much higher on my list of destinations. It takes a MedTrek to change my impression of the place with 'too many cars' reached by crossing the contemporary equivalent of the River Styx.

I trample around the cobblestone streets in Villefranche-sur-Mer before sitting on the ramparts at the edge of the deep bay. Considered one of the most beautiful harbours on the Med, today there are two large cruise ships, dozens of yachts, some multi-masted sailboats and a French naval vessel docked in the natural harbour. This was an even more popular port, and a favourite for the Russian fleet in the 1800s, before the port in Nice was dredged.

The town's Citadelle contains the remains of a wreck that sunk in the 1600s but wasn't excavated until the 1980s and four Swedes are swimming in the cool but still soothing seawater on the sandy Plage des Marinieres. Beyond them is the Cap Ferrat peninsula and the blue-roofed villa that appeared in *To Catch A Thief*, which I once featured in a story about the most expensive house for sale on the Riviera.

Considered an historic local monument, 'The Palace with Blue Tiles' sits on 2.6 hectares with 300 metres of waterfront, layered gardens and a view of Villefranche. Originally built between 1899-1901 by an American named Ralph Curtis, the mansion and its marble columns, frescoed ceilings, Venetian roofs and medieval chimney was going for $30 million in 1995.

Personally I find the house, whose guests have included J.P. Morgan and Sarah Bernhardt, a little too large. I wasn't surprised that the then-owner told me, as we toured the cavernous kitchen and examined a heating installation that resembled the engine room on the Queen Mary, that he'd never been able to get a correct count of the bedrooms.

"I think there are 40 but I always lose count," the Turkish proprietor said. "However, I know it takes a staff of a least ten people to run the house because I once tried to do it with only nine."

The villa presumably influenced Somerset Maugham, who wrote about life on the Cap when he lived in the nearby Villa La Mauresque, the priest's house on King Leopold II's former 12-acre estate that Maugham renamed because of its Moorish style. Maugham thrived on the Cap from 1928 until, as a British agent during World War II, he was forced to flee with one suitcase after the collapse of France to the Germans in 1940.

I leave the Palace with Blue Tiles and head to the sculpted stone seaside trail that wends around the cape. On my left are a restricted *terrain militaire*, villas owned by the likes of Sir Norman Foster and the Grand Hôtel du Cap. As I near the port of Saint-Jean-Cap-Ferrat I arrive at Place David Niven. I was first here in 1971 to seek out Niven in his pink home, La Fleur du Cap, where the actor and author of *The Moon's A Balloon* lived until he died in 1983.

"Mr Niven isn't here today," a man who looked exactly like Mr Niven had told me. "He's in Bora Bora and won't be back for a month."

After that polite and amusing rebuff, I walked up to the lighthouse on the Cape before visiting the Villa Ephrussi-de-Rothschild, the 17 acre architectural folly inspired by renaissance residences in Venice and Florence. Its seven Belle Époque gardens have Spanish, Florentine, Japanese, Provençal, Oriental, exotic and classical *à la française* inspiration. I've only been to the gardens twice since then, but I never miss an opportunity to climb the 164 steps to the lighthouse and enjoy a view of the Alps, Italy and the French Riviera.

At the Baie des Fosses, I head out to Pointe-Saint-Hospice to rub the well-polished foot of the 11-metre high bronze statue of the Virgin. Rub it, I was told decades ago, and you'll always be in good health when you come to Cap Ferrat. So far, so good.

After the Plage Paloma, the sculpture-decorated port and the Promenade Maurice-Rouvier, I continue to Beaulieu-sur-Mer. There are exceptional views of Eze and the Tête du Chien, the dog head-shaped peak above Cap d'Ail and Monaco, and for the first time I notice that this part of the *basse corniche* is named after Gordon Bennett. He's the eccentric American newspaper publisher who sent Stanley in search of Livingston and was absolutely smitten with Beaulieu, where he lived in the seaside Villa Namouna.

Then the Villa Grecque Kerylos on the Impasse Gustave Eiffel, a fairly faithful reproduction of an ancient Greek villa that was built less than 100 years ago, holds me up. I spend an hour walking around the estate admiring the frescoes, sculptures, marble, alabaster, mosaics, vases, lamps, statuettes and even a Grecian urn. I call it a day at La Reserve de Beaulieu, where I have tea and call Luke.

"Did you happen to find the pack we lost in Morocco on the seaside there?" he asks.

33. Marching Through Monaco to Italy

"When there is no peace within the family, filial piety and devotion arise." — *Lao Tsu*

It's another week before I return to Beaulieu. I'd planned to MedTrek every day but have been thwarted by incessant rain. Precipitation and dramatic thunderstorms are not a rarity on the Riviera. But one of the delights about the climate in the south of France is the rapidity with which the weather changes. Many times, right before my eyes, sombre gray skies have become brilliant blue within seconds. But not this week.

Today, barring mishap, will be historic. For the first, and perhaps only, time, I'll walk in three different countries—France, Monaco and Italy—within just a few hours. Beyond Beaulieu's seaside sidewalk and rocky beaches, steep cliffs rise to the perched Eze village on my left and, in this area of expensive and exclusive real estate, I stumble upon an eclectic mix of ornate, luxurious villas next to dilapidated ruins. The most unkempt home is paradoxically called Shangri-La.

The Nietzsche Trail heads uphill from Eze-sur-Mer to Eze village and I briefly consider making the vertical climb to have an existential *café au lait* on the terrace of the Château de la Chèvre d'Or, where Elissa and I recently spent a romantic weekend. But I stick to my three-countries-in-one-day agenda, remain on the *basse corniche* and pass La Petite Afrique snack bar before strolling onto the grounds of the Hôtel Cap Estel.

Recalling a lunch here 20 years ago reminds me that I've probably written more stories about this part of France than anywhere else in the world. Not just about Sophia Antipolis and numerous Cannes film festivals, but also dictators (Mobutu Sese Seko had a villa on Roquebrune-Cap-Martin), royalty (my daughter Sonia was born on the day Princess Grace died and I covered Monaco for *People/Who*) and prestigious events involving celebrities, yachts, music, tennis, casinos and, even, duty-free shopping.

Typically, the *sentier littoral* around Cap d'Ail is a namedropper's delight. Greta Garbo frequented one home while Winston Churchill was a guest at the Villa Capponcina, which was owned by Lord Beaverbrook, after World War II. The Marriott Hotel, which is officially on French soil, sits near the Monaco border and beyond it I gawk at the deluxe seaside apartments near the heliport in Fontvieille. The five-minute helicopter ride from the Nice Airport is, if you don't want to walk, a sensible and speedy way to get here. The low-flying copter not only hugs the coastline but the pilot, if you ask nicely, may also fly over Monaco's exotic gardens, royal palace, cliff-side aquarium, yacht-filled harbour, serene Japanese garden, plush hotels, ritzy restaurants, classy casinos and ultra-modern spa.

Monaco was once a Greek settlement and later a Roman port. But not everyone is aware that Fontvieille, where I'm walking, didn't even exist a few decades ago. Completely built on reclaimed land, it literally rose from the sea during the

1970s and now consists of apartment complexes, light industrial companies, a church, a bustling port and a mall. There's even a 20,000-seat football field on the seventh level of the Stade Louis II Stadium, which also contains a 50-metre indoor swimming pool.

The territorial addition instantly increased the size of Monaco by 25 percent and reigning Prince Albert II has plans to further urbanise his country's 4100-metre shoreline. But, no matter what he does, the 'postage-stamp sized principality' will always be synonymous with adjectives like 'diminutive' and 'Lilliputian' because it's still smaller than New York's Central Park. And the well-mannered, law-abiding Monegasques will probably always remain distinctly different in behaviour from the pastis-drinking, truffle-hunting, boule-playing Frenchmen that surround them.

Beyond the Princess Grace Rose Garden, which contains more than 5500 rose bushes of myriad species, is the Fontvieille port. From there I crane my neck to get a look at the cliff-top palace on the Alpine-like Le Rocher, or The Rock, a rough-cut diamond-shaped hill jutting 800 metres into the Mediterranean that overlooks the entire principality.

The Rock can't be climbed from the Fontvieille side and steep cliffs prevent a seaside stroll around it. So I casually and briefly visit a museum that features 105 superbly restored antique automobiles collected by Albert's father Prince Rainier, who ran Monaco for over 50 years until he died in 2005. I'm sure that some locals have put the 1903 De Dion Bouton and a gigantic 1928 Hispano Suiza Coupe Chauffeur on their shopping lists.

On the other side of The Rock is La Condamine where steep steps lead to the salmon-coloured Palais du Prince that's been home to Albert's family, the Grimaldis, almost continuously since 1297. Encircled by a parapet, the palace's cobblestone courtyard is flanked by cannon bequeathed by Louis XIV. Monaco's flag is not flying above the palace today, an indication that the prince is not in the country. But just a few minutes after my arrival, at precisely five minutes to noon, bells chime to signal the changing of the guard—mostly handsome, mostly young men attired in light blue helmets, dark blue trousers and even darker blue coats with red trim.

After watching this symbolic daily exercise, I creep to the ramparts and look down on the central market in La Condamine and across the port to Monte-Carlo, where the imposing Monte-Carlo Casino epitomises La Belle Époque. The view is not always this peaceful, especially during the annual Formula One race each spring when the principality resembles a noisy, albeit upscale, NASCAR race track.

Guy de Maupassant once said Monaco attracted "the scum of continents and society, mixed with princes or future kings, with women of the world, the bourgeoisie, money lenders and exhausted girls, a mixture unique on earth." But that's not how the rich city-state, which now relies on gambling to bring in only about five percent of government revenue, looks today. It's easily the cleanest spot on the Riviera, if not the entire Mediterranean, and the only exhausted girls I see at this time of day are those cleaning the expensive hotel rooms.

Money laundering aside, the folks here are so law abiding that when I first visited in the late 1970s I would regularly leave a 50-franc note, worth about $10, on my dashboard with the windows open and the keys in the ignition. Neither the bill nor the car were ever taken, which made for a good story, and the jewels women wear are still the real thing.

One reason Europe's second smallest independent country after the Vatican is so spic-and-span is because, although the royal family doesn't like the phraseology, Monaco is a benevolent dictatorship and a benign police state. There's one police officer for every 71 inhabitants to maintain law and order in a place that's only 482 acres in size and has a Disneyland-like mix of quaint cobblestone streets, lavish hotels and hideous high-rise apartment residences. Security is one of the reasons that Anthony Burgess, Helmut Newton, Karl Lagerfeld, Claudia Schiffer, and half of the world's Formula One racecar drivers have lived here. Another reason might be that there's no law in Monaco requiring anyone to wear seat belts.

After his father's death, Prince Albert II became the 32nd member of the family dynasty to run the country. I first met the son of American actress Grace Kelly, whose full name is Albert Alexandre Louis Pierre Grimaldi, in the early 1980s. The prince, who signed a letter to me 'Albert de Monaco' and whose secretary refers to him as 'His Highness', said a few things in our initial interviews that have stuck with me.

The first was that he claimed "it often happens, particularly in the US, that someone will refer to me as Mr Prince". That's funny. The second was "I'm straight and always have been". That was quite candid, especially in view of the then-constant rumours that Albert, who's since fathered at least two illegitimate children, had to be gay. The third was that "When I bring women here they are either so awed that they don't know how to react, or so overwhelmed that they are frightened. Some say 'Uh, this is all very nice but it's a bit too much – give me a call if you want to go to the beach or skiing'." And the last was "The black tie functions, chauffeured cars, hotel suites and public activity might look glamorous to an outsider but it is all hard work." Uh, okay.

Among other things, these comments illustrate that Albert, like Odysseus, is bound to his destiny.

Being Monaco's constitutional monarch is, if you're in the driver's seat, not a job to take lightly. Executive power belongs solely to the reigning prince, who is said to derive his power from God, and he appoints the government and proposes all laws to an 18-member National Council. To a great degree the prince is Monaco and Monaco is the prince. Monaco Inc, as the principality is sometimes called, is run like a family business.

Albert, whose mother was killed in a car crash in 1982, had a multilingual, multicultural upbringing and his reign brings a much-needed breath of fresh air and youthful vision to the country. And of all the world's leaders, he'd be the first to endorse the MedTrek: the athletic Amherst-educated prince participated in the Winter Olympics and has competed in a few of the marathons run through Monaco, France and Italy.

Beyond the palace are the National Assembly, the Ministry of Justice and the neo-Romanesque Saint-Pierre Cathedral, where Princess Grace and Prince Rainier are entombed. Then I saunter by the homes of Albert's sisters, Princess Caroline and Princess Stephanie. Stephanie's four-storey-high Clos Saint-Martin, a garish orange colour with Florentine balustrades, adjoins Princess Caroline's more modest Clos Saint-Pierre across from the Oceanographic Museum and gardens. I reported on the lives of the sisters for 15 years and, while I enjoyed tracking their peccadilloes and growing pains, I don't miss them. Nor, I'm sure, do they miss me.

Past the national jail, where contrary to rumour few cells actually have sea views, is the descent to the port and Stars 'N' Bars, the principality's hot sports bar and night club. Located in a revamped industrial section of the principality near the Monaco Yacht Club, Stars 'N' Bars was launched by Kate Powers, a Saint Louis-born American raised in Monaco, in the early 1990s. It used to be a de rigueur late-night stop for Prince Albert, whom Kate frequently encouraged to sing and dance on her stage.

Monaco's port has been enlarged by an impressive 600 million euro project that included the placement of a 352-metre dike tugged up the Mediterranean from Algeciras. This unique floating breakwater further protects the harbour from the sea, doubles the number of pleasure boats berths, and enables large cruise ships to visit Monaco so passengers can spread their wealth.

"Almost every big infrastructure project in Monaco is innovative, unique, expensive and complicated in conception, planning, technology and execution," boasts Patrice Cellario, the director of the government's department of urban management. Cellario tells me about the blasting required to create the cavern for the underground railway station and the dam built to hold back the sea during the construction of the Grimaldi Forum conference centre. The port expansion, he says, adds another few hectares to Monaco's land mass. Hmm, maybe the place will even be bigger than Manhattan someday.

These projects combine to improve the plethora of athletic, business, cultural, residential, scientific, social and tourism-oriented facilities that contribute to the image of luxury and glamour in revenue-rich Monaco. There are still occasional, and usually justified, accusations of financial shenanigans but Somerset Maugham's claim that Monaco is a "sunny place for shady people" is less and less apropos. It's now a sunny place for made and moneyed people.

Since I'm not one of them, I grab a five-euro lunch of calamari and rice from an outdoor vendor and sit on a bench just above the gigantic outdoor saltwater pool on the port. Up the hill is the Casino that made the principality synonymous with glitter, glamour and gambling almost from the moment it opened in 1856, though it wasn't until 1878 that the building designed by Charles Garnier, the architect behind the Paris Opera, was inaugurated. Today the main Casino is considered an architectural curiosity and its marble columns, decorative murals, cabaret and adjoining opera, which was 'authentically renovated' between 2003-2005, attract over one million tourists a year.

Nearby is the celebrated Hôtel de Paris. If I were to spend the night here I'd check into the Churchill Suite, the only room on the eighth floor. That spacious complex, where Prince of musical fame and Michael Jackson used to hang out, is definitely not where I'll be bunking tonight. But I do enter the hotel lobby to, like other Monacophiles, rub the right foot of the bronze horse carrying Louis XIV for some additional good luck.

My fondest Monte-Carlo memory doesn't have anything to do with the horse's foot, gambling, or even the time I asked chef and restaurateur Alain Ducasse to prepare a private menu for 20 to be served in the Churchill Suite. It dates from a memorable faux pas I made when I interviewed Princess Caroline for the first time in a small office above the opera. As things got underway, I politely tried to light her cigarette with a long fragile wooden royal match. The slender stick broke and set my notebook on fire. It could have burnt down the entire building which, of course, would make this a much more interesting tale. But I'll never forget Princess Caroline's immediate reaction.

"This is a hot interview," the princess joked without missing a beat.

An elevator whisks me from the hotel lobby to sea level where I enter a glitzy five-storey glass-enclosed seaside complex called Les Thermes Marins de Monte-Carlo, or the seawater thermal baths. The centre is based on the centuries-old practice of thalassotherapy that employs ingredients from mineral-rich seas and oceans for prevention, healing and relaxation through marine hydrotherapy. Though the algae are imported from Brittany and some mud comes from the Dead Sea, seawater is obtained from a pipe extending 600 metres into the Mediterranean.

About my only claim to fame here is that I had treatments in the same tub as Caroline and her father Prince Rainier, though not at the same time. Ritual bathing is traceable to both the Egyptians and the Greeks but was it anything like this?

"This is the state-of-the-art of thalassotherapy," says Dr Yves Tréguer, the spa's creator, as he shows me through the complex. "The Romans, Greeks and Egyptians never had it so good."

I walk through the tunnel underneath the Fairmont Monte-Carlo Hôtel and try to imagine what the sea to my right will look like once a Fontvieille-like sea reclamation project is completed around 2015. It's just a few steps to the serene Japanese Garden where I stand for a few moments on the Taiko bridge that, according to Shintoists, illustrates the difficult journey towards the gods. Then I pass the Grimaldi Forum, two-thirds of it below sea level, built between 1992 and 2000.

The big surprise of the day occurs on Larvotto Beach where two bodiless legs are stretched on the sand. I blink, scratch my eyes and take out my binoculars for a better view. Maybe, I think, the sunbather's upper torso and head are buried under the sand. Or maybe this is the bottom half of an invisible man. It turns out that a legless woman nearby has taken off her two prosthetic limbs and put them a few feet away while she tans. Absolutely surreal.

The Summer Sporting Club, where I've attended more concerts, dinners and gala benefits than I care to count, is the next seaside attraction. The two most regal charity events here are the summertime Red Cross Ball and the springtime Rose Ball. And which one should you attend if you're forced to accept just one invitation?

"I feel much more motivated and concerned by the Red Cross Ball than most other official black-tie events in Monaco," Prince Albert told me one night before heading to nearby Le Jimmy'z discotheque. "I even choose the menu. If the food's no good, it's my fault."

I take a quick walk through the new Monte-Carlo Bay Hôtel and Resort and, a little further along, enter the Monte-Carlo Beach Hôtel that is, despite its name, located just across the Monaco-France "invisible" border in Roquebrune-Cap-Martin. The only way to spend a decent summer afternoon here is to rent a private tent or cabana, which has a chest of drawers, lounge chairs, tables, towels, mattresses and other amenities. Unfortunately the experience costs more than an expensive hotel room in Spain.

The hotel's sandy beach is adjacent to a 50-metre saltwater swimming pool and the venue, especially the setting of La Vigie restaurant, is so ideal that it's difficult to quibble with the brochure's description of "luxury, calm and sensual pleasure, in endless sunshine, alongside one of the Mediterranean's most beautiful shores."

Outside the hotel lobby is a trail heading up past the Villa de la Vigie, once occupied by designer Karl Lagerfeld, to the *chemin des douaniers* leading to Cap Martin. I've known Lagerfeld since 1979 when I convinced him to appear on the cover of *The Paris Metro* in a John Travolta-like pose at Le Palace discotheque in Paris. It's unfortunate that the philosophic designer, who's a good friend of Princess Caroline's and still lists Monaco as his official residence, isn't around today because I'd love to get his Germanic take on the MedTrek.

My next stop, Cap Martin, is not only particularly renowned for its castle built in the 10th century to rebuff the wily Saracens and the procession held every August that depicts the Passion of the Christ, it's also the location of President Mobutu Sese Seko's former luxurious estate. This was fastidiously maintained for impromptu visits when the dictator tired of war-torn Zaire and its down-in-the-dumps capital of Kinshasa, where I first interviewed him in 1974. Mobutu's palatial home in this town of 14,000 featured everything from security cameras and armed personnel to neatly swept walks that flow down the steep hill past his pool to the Mediterranean.

One entrance to the three-storey ochre-coloured mansion called Villa del Mare is at the dead end of the regally named but narrow Avenue Imperatrice Eugenie in the private Domaine du Cap Martin. Behind the gates are thyme-and-lavender scented flowering gardens containing pine, bamboo, olive, lemon and eucalyptus trees. The villa, marble driveway, ubiquitous garden lights, sculpted plants and imperial looking crests above windows protected by electric white shutters were financed by funds Mobutu stashed away in foreign accounts during over two decades in power. The place is worth about $50 million and used to cost the people of Zaire about $12,000 a month to maintain.

"His staff were very friendly when they shopped and the bills were always paid promptly," Marsou Viano, who owns a local café, tells me. "There were probably some very good reasons that he was so well guarded but he provided a lot of work for people living here."

The Zairian president is hardly the town's most celebrated resident. Churchill, Coco Chanel, William Butler Yeats and Christina Onassis were probably more prominent. But the contrast between Mobutu's stark African reality and his Riviera fantasy reality was so extreme that I think of Mobutu whenever I'm in town.

The popular footpath around Cap Martin passes beneath Mobutu's old haunt but, since he's dead, I have no desire to see the place again. I round the headland to get my first view of the Italian coast and approach Menton, often called the 'Pearl of France' and the hot bed of European aristocracy in the 19th century. Menton, which like Nice became part of France in 1860, claims to be the warmest spot on the Riviera and a billboard contends that the 'city is a garden', which is why its annual Lemon Festival is one of the prime tourist attractions.

Foreigners, particularly the English, are credited with developing many of the Belle Époque gardens here. Sir Lawrence Johnston, the renowned landscaper who created Hidcote Manor in England, laid out the Serre de la Madone garden between 1919 and 1939. The 'water stairways' at Le Clos du Peyronnet were designed by garden designer and landscape sculptor Humphrey Waterfield and the Villa Fontana Rosa with its Jardin des Romanciers was created in 1920 by Spanish novelist Vicente Blasco-Ibanez.

I walk up the steps from the sea to the Parvis Saint-Michel in the old town and admire a mosaic of the Grimaldi coat of arms, a reminder that Monaco's royals ruled the place at one point in the Middle Ages. Then I recall a simple description of Menton by Katherine Mansfield, the New Zealand novelist who lived here in the 1920s: "My house faces the sea: on my right is the old town with its little port and pepper plants growing on a tiny quay. This old town … is the loveliest place I have ever set my eyes on."

The march towards Italy is on the broad Promenade de la Mer that edges along the port past the Plage des Sablettes. I admire the collection of palm trees at the Jardin Maria Serena and make a quick side trip to Val Rameh to check out a *Sophora toromiro*. That tree, which was purchased by Lord Radcliffe at the beginning of the 19th century, was common in the forests of Easter Island until wood carvers wiped it out in the 1950s.

When I finally reach the Poste Frontière Saint Ludovic Mentho, the dilapidated border checkpoint and customs office is now completely closed due to the frontierless Europe. Though there's a functioning custom's office a kilometre up the hill, there's no formality, sense of accomplishment or anything else at this one-time bustling seaside border. I do think, because I could use a McFlurry about now, that the old customs building would make a great drive-through McDonald's.

Once across the border, I have a cappuccino and spend a few minutes listening to Italians croon, which is what they do whenever they open their mouths. Ah, there's still an Italy. It's dusk but I managed to MedTrek in three countries in one day and, for the record, can tell you that it's precisely a 3595-kilometre walk along the seaside from the French/Italian border to the Moroccan/Algerian border.

34. Strolling Along the Lungomare to Genoa

"You know they go in foreign guise, the gods do, looking like strangers, turning up in towns and settlements to keep an eye on manners, good and bad." — The Odyssey

It's a windy, blustery, cloudy morning and the wintry sea is in a thrashing, waving, barking and whiny uproar as I repeat the steps taking me from France into Italy. I want to reassure myself that, in this era of a borderless European Union, crossing this particular border is a non-event. Yet it doesn't take too long to realise that I'm in another country amidst a different mindset.

Every woman over 40 is wearing a politically incorrect fur coat, colourful cadres of cyclists are out in force despite the weather, and everyone still speaks pleasantly demonstrative Italian. The more sober and sombre French are flocking into Italy to buy booze and smokes at a supermarket in Latte for significantly less than they pay in their more highly taxed country. In fact, my daughter Sonia and her boyfriend, who dropped me at the border this morning, claim they "pay" for a trip to Italy just by buying a couple cartons of cigarettes and a few bottles of whiskey.

I'm entering crescent-shaped Liguria, the Italian region that extends to Tuscany and includes the provinces of Imperia, Savona, Genoa and La Spezia. It's named after the pre-Roman Ligurians who flourished around the Mediterranean in the first millennium BC. And this part of the sea is known, to Italians anyway, as the Ligurian Sea.

Assigning names to various parts of the Mediterranean off their coast has always been an Italian passion. The Med off southern Tuscany, Lazio and Campania is called the Tyrrhenian Sea. Go further and you'll run into the Ionian Sea. Along the other side of the country, the Adriatic Sea separates Italy from the Balkan Peninsula, Slovenia, Croatia, Bosnia, Herzegovina, Montenegro and Albania.

My Italian MedTrek begins on the Riviera di Ponente, which means 'the spot on the horizon where the sun sets'. This stretch is also known as La Riviera dei Fiori, or the coastline of flowers, because of omnipresent greenhouses and the fact that cut flowers are among its most lucrative exports. Even the high-speed toll road, the Autostrada dei Fiori, has an appropriately flowery name. But I'll be walking on the *lungomare*, or seaside, and the Via Aurelia, the road built in the third century to connect Rome with Liguria.

Just before Capo Mortal, I'm almost driven into the Ligurian Sea by the whooooooosh of a gigantic flock of small birds that skydive in unison right at me. The first three kilometres along the *lungomare*, the railroad tracks, the rocky seaside and the Via Aurelia are a jumble of construction calamities that include ramshackle terraced greenhouses and randomly dumped building debris. I'm reminded that 30 years ago, like many people, I considered Italy the 'India of Europe'. The country was so disorganised that the acronym ALITALIA, the national airline, stood for 'Always Late In Take-Off, Always Late In Arrival'. Nothing ran on time and the Red Brigades threatened the entire nation with a gory reign of terror.

Italy – whatever the status of punctuality, litter, terrorism and a permanent state of ordered chaos – will always be Europe's cultural gem. I pass two museums during my first hour in the country and enter the city of Ventimiglia on the aptly named Corso Arturo Toscanini. The importance of composers and opera is again emphasised when I reach Via Giuseppe Verdi.

And then there's the coffee. I stop in a bar for an it-can-only-be-made-in-Italy cappuccino and gaze over the beach back towards Cap Saint-Martin and Monaco. One wall in the place has a blown-up photograph of summer sunbathers on the same beach, but there's no one here today. Even the city's famous fields of flowers – the carnations, jasmine, hyacinths, narcissi, violets, tulips and not-yet-blooming mimosas – are hibernating.

Waves crash against the seawall along the Ventimiglia *lungomare* and I'd be drenched were it not for a breakwater of gigantic rocks. This border town on the Roia River, which the Romans knew as Albintimilium, is filled with French shoppers who pour into town for the weekly market. Its economy, I figure, has got to gradually tank due to the borderless Europe that will ultimately lead to more balanced prices in European Union member countries. But today the market's still selling fashion rip-offs and faux Rolex watches at comparatively inexpensive prices, though the town's also making an effort to promote its 1000-year-old Cattedrale dell'Assunta as a focal point for tourism.

After another four kilometres I'm in Vallecrosia that, like most coastal towns, combines a seaside resort with a medieval *città vecchia*, or old town, that's usually a few kilometres inland. Unfortunately, the olive groves that once made the Romanesque San Rocco Church here so romantic have been replaced by apartments.

Near the beachside railway station in Bordighera, a museum displays facsimiles of the Bronze Age rock carvings from the Vallée des Merveilles. Apparently Claude Monet once spent a few weeks painting landscapes here and this is where the Vatican buys its palms for Holy Week.

Battered by the incessant wind, I consider calling it a day and checking into the four-star Hotel Parigi on the Lungomare Argentina. It's one of a number of decent-looking establishments that have made the Italian Riviera, once considered the poorer sibling of the posh French Riviera, a hot place to stay. After the British Cemetery, the winter-closed Grand Hotel del Mare has sculpted life-like bronze lions strategically placed throughout a garden set above the sea at Capo Migliarese. I vaguely consider breaking into one of the rooms and camping out until the weather improves.

Instead I scramble around the Cape Nero beyond Ospedaletti, which got its medical-sounding name because the Knights of Rhodes founded a hospital here in the 14th century. On the outskirts of San Remo, a band of *Romas* have circled their state-of-the-art caravans around a fairground not yet open for business.

"Wait for two hours and you can be our first customer," suggests one carnie. "I'll let you have ten tickets for the price of five."

"I'd love to, I really would," I said. "But I'd go crazy sitting around in this wind for two hours. I'm moving on."

Then I stumble upon another marvel: a baseball diamond complete with a scoreboard and outfield distances marked in metres. I love the tranquility of baseball parks anywhere but finding one here seems particularly karmic. All of a sudden the jingle for Riviera Radio, the Monaco-based station that used to let me spout off about politics and current events with my daily 'Critical Comment' program in the early 1990s, starts running through my head: "From San Remo to Saint-Tropez–Riviera Radio!"

San Remo, the self-proclaimed capital of the Riviera of Flowers, features dozens of florists, greenhouses, nurseries, garden shops and the Corso dell' Imperatrice, an avenue famous for its canary palms. A sign at the shimmering Teatro del Mare indicates that it's 143 kilometres to Genoa. Next to the seaside theatre is a closed and shuttered railroad station and a billboard indicating that the tracks have been moved inland 'to put the seaside to better use'.

"I used to think disorganised Italy was Europe's India too," Tony Rocca, a British journalist who renovated a farm and vineyard in Tuscany, told me recently. "But they're very progressive. The foresight of moving and burying the railway line near San Remo will, despite the expense, save that coast. And the new hotels are as good as any in Europe."

The first Chinese Tibetan restaurant that I spot on the MedTrek is also in San Remo. Apparently there's a colony of Tibetan refugees here, as well as many more Africans, South Americans and Indians than are visible along the Med in France. As I walk through the town, which was another favourite destination for the Victorians in the 1800s, I get the feeling that representatives from the entire world are intermingling on the shores of the Ligurian Sea.

I visit the flower market the next morning and discover that over 20,000 tons of flowers, a large albeit relatively incomprehensible figure, are shipped from here each year. In the old town, called 'The Beak' because of its pointed shape, I light a candle at the baroque Madonna della Costa, the Church of Our Lady of the Coast.

Past the port is a rocky beach covered with seaweed and detritus, presumably washed ashore or tossed by tourists and the town's Italians, European, Tibetans, Africans, Asians and South Americans. The narrow beach runs into an old railway tunnel going under a greenhouse-covered hillside called Capo Verde.

Although chilly, it's a perfect day to walk. The sea is calm, the sky is blue and there aren't too many Italians out and about. Italians, unlike the Spanish, do not speed stroll but bring a distinctly nonchalant and lackadaisical approach to walking. They meander and frequently stop to chat for extended periods when they want to get a point across. Sometimes, when everyone stops to get a point across at precisely the same moment, it seems that a movie director or a policeman has yelled, "Freeze!"

Another distinguishing feature of the Italian Riviera is the colours. Each town, from Arma di Taggia to San Bartolomeo al Mare, is part of a colourful rainbow that exemplifies Mediterranean character, history, lore and romance. Different shades and tints of the palette bring a distinctive character to almost every building, from the obligatory church to tall and narrow apartment houses rising above the tight cobblestone streets, between the azure sea and the snow-capped white hills. The cast of earthy colours – brownish-red terracotta, maroon, sienna, saffron, Dragon's blood, red jasper, emerald green and *verdaccio* earth – are produced from natural mineral pigments like ochre, sienna and umber.

It's hardly a recent phenomenon. Ochre, derived from the Greek word *ochra* which means pale yellow, is found close to the earth's surface and our prehistoric ancestors mixed it with blood, grease, gum or water to draw figures and create compositions. And sienna influenced the tone of cities like Pompeii, as well as artistic frescoes created during the Italian Renaissance. "Sienna is as Italian as pasta," Andrea Dolci, whose family company commercialises sienna, umber and other earths in Verona, told me when I was writing an article entitled *Earthborn Hues: Painting With A Mediterranean Palette*.

Pasta or not, the specific shades are amplified by what Vincent van Gogh affectionately called "the different light", the unique radiance responsible for the pleasing palette of comforting and chatoyant colours synonymous with the polychromatic Mediterranean. The impact is heightened, especially in Liguria, by *trompe l'oeil* three-dimensional illusionist façades that trick the eye, or my eye anyway, with their uncanny perspectives. It's often difficult to determine whether the pastel-coloured windows, curtains, flowerpots, balconies and ornamentation on some buildings are real, an illusion or a momentary acid flash.

Then there are the sounds and smells. Liguria beats to the insistent peal of church bells and a rhythm of waves that, depending on the state of the sea, create a rolling 'Om', a gentle lapping or a rocky roar. The smells blend the scent of morning coffee and pasta sauces with an odoriferous floral bouquet and a salty breeze.

I'm not the only one to appreciate this confluence of sensations. An old guidebook states that the "enchanting Ligurian Riviera, washed by the blue waters of the Mediterranean, offers all the spell of colour and beauty under skies which are always clear. From Ventimiglia to the Gulf of La Spezia the coast describes an arc backed by the attractive slopes of the Ligurian Apennines."

I buy a detailed map of Liguria in Arma di Taggia to better calculate where I am amidst the coast, slopes, sounds and colours. After Riva Ligure – 'riva' means bank and 'riva del mare' means seashore – and Santo Stefano al Mare is another unused railroad tunnel that goes through the mountain beneath the perched hilltop village of Piani. Although the entrance is blocked by a formidable fence, I climb over the barricade to enter an increasingly dark two-kilometre tunnel. The knowledge that I won't get hit by a train, and the apparent lack of man-eating rats, doesn't prevent me from being a little on edge as I carefully sidle forward, once or twice on my knees, in the pitch black. I remind myself to buy batteries for my flashlight.

When I finally reach the proverbial light at the other end of the tunnel, I again climb over a barrier and a pair of octogenarian Italians walking on the promenade simply stare at me, a dirty and bedraggled apparition. Fortunately, the municipal police car doesn't show up until I've begun heading into San Lorenzo al Mare. When the *carabinieri* do arrive I'm speaking to two different octogenarians who are remarkably polite about my mangled Italian. They confirm that the railway line has been out of action for years.

"Now we can walk without the *disturbo* of the *ferroviario treno*," one says as he stops walking and freezes to make his point.

The old train track goes through San Lorenzo and I decide to use it as another shortcut when, without any warning, I suddenly find myself on an activated track. When an engineer blows a warning whistle, I cut down to the restaurant-lined promenade in Porto Maurizio.

I'm famished and choose the terrace at Sailor's, a restaurant in the marina, for *tagliattini al mare* and grilled vegetables. I eat slowly and watch sunbathers and paddleball players enjoying themselves on the long sandy beach. Italians, if the glances from the sultry waitress and fur-bedecked diners are any indication, aren't used to seeing scruffy backpackers buy a meal. I admit I'm a bit grubby after the tunnel escapade and doubt that a decent tip will improve my image.

In Imperia there's a building with five gigantic letters on the rooftop spelling PASTA, which presumably is manufactured inside, and two olive oil museums, each tracing the history of olives and touting the fruit as 'the lubricant of the health-inspiring Mediterranean diet'. I also learn that the word Christ is derived from the Greek *christos*, which means 'the anointed one', or one anointed with olive oil. But the real delight of the day is a spectacular seaside romp from Oneglia around the Capo Berta to Diano Marina.

If I had to invite someone to the Ligurian Med for some civilised, family-style hiking this is where I'd start. The rocky hillside has been secured by steel 'spaghetti' wiring to prevent a landslide, an old stone house has been charmingly renovated, and there are scores of Italian cyclists, families, kids and older couples strolling on the paved road-sized but closed-to-vehicles path.

There's a soothing view of San Bartolomeo al Mare, a hillside village in the direction of Genoa, from my room at the Arc de Ciel hotel in Diano Marina. The next morning I awaken to the smooth, reassuring resonance of dawn waves breaking on the sandy beach. It's like a meditative aural massage.

"This is obviously the type of sound they try to put into those wave machines to make people imagine that they're in a calm and supportive environment," I tell a very blonde Norwegian couple during breakfast. "But there's nothing better than the real thing. I could stay here forever."

Instead I head east towards San Bartolomeo al Mare and Cervo, once an important control point on the Via Aurelia. Only a few people, all of them substantially older than I, are out for a morning stroll and their stares imply that I'm too young to be walking amongst them. "Your hair's not gray enough!" they seem to be saying. Whatever they're thinking, it's nice to be the youngest person on the path rather than be, as I was in Morocco, considered almost too old to walk.

Despite the aging population, a beach construction frenzy is underway. New pipe is being laid, tractors are moving rock and earth to create additional dikes and breakwaters, even the church steeple in Cervo is completely encased in scaffolding.

In Capo Mimosa, I move from the steep and rocky coast to a narrow seaside road into Marina di Andora. The town, which promises visitors '365 holidays a year', is full of aging walkers who stop to gesticulate and emphasise a point as they discuss everything from the prime minister's rumoured facelift to the latest construction scandal. There must be a pan-national government program to send the entire population over seventy to the many Promenades degli Pensioners in Liguria. Maybe I should make a reservation.

After all, even Odysseus was encouraged to acknowledge that he wouldn't be forever young. "Must you have battle in your heart forever? The bloody oil of combat?" Circe said to him. "Old contender, will you not yield to the immortal gods?"

Of course, he could be excused for being confused about the aging process because Athena frequently transformed him into a younger man. When he returned to Penélopê "Athena lent him beauty, head to foot. She made him taller, and massive, too, with crisping hair in curls like petals of wild hyacinth but all red-golden."

The goddess was very skilled at this particular task. When Odysseus first appeared at home she dressed him in rags and made him ugly and decrepit. "These tatters that he wore hid him so well that none of us could know him when he turned up, not even the older men," said one observer. "We jeered at him, took potshots at him, cursed him."

Sometimes, though, the real man was almost identified despite his god-given disguise. "Strangers have come here, many through the years, but no one ever came, I swear, who seemed so like Odysseus – body, voice and limbs – as you do," he's told.

Odysseus had a sense of humour about his altered appearance. At one point he even promised that "if Odysseus fails to appear as I predict, then Swish! let the slaves pitch me down from some high rock, so the next poor man who comes will watch his tongue."

Who can think too much about aging and mortality with this going on?

"*Divieto*" (Prohibited!) is the most prominent sign I see as I scamper, jump and climb along the rocky shore towards the lighthouse at Capo Melo, which is at the end of a road with numerous private campgrounds each advertising their ferocious guard dogs. There's a picture postcard perfect view of Isola Gallinara, a whale-shaped little island off Albenga that could easily waylay a contemporary Odysseus for a few years.

The 11-hectare island, which gets its name from wild chickens that once resided here, is now a nature and marine reserve with southern cliffs populated by one of the largest colonies of seagulls on the Tyrrhenian Sea. The surrounding seabed is the burial ground for wrecks dating back to the fifth century BC, but I'm instinctively fond of the church-topped island because it was a refuge for Saint Martin of Tours in the fourth century and later became a Benedictine monastery.

Further along a billboard just outside Laigueglia promotes a *Bandiera Blu* award from the European Union that certifies that its seawater is clear and its coast is clean. Despite this reassurance, I wonder what a long pipeline extending off the coast might be depositing into the Ligurian Sea. I also notice, as I go through an under-the-street passage for pedoni, or pedestrians, that Via Aurelia briefly changes its name to Via Roma.

I stop for a cappuccino and a pastry in a restaurant in Laigueglia decorated with dozens of mirrors that reflect my wind-blown hair and wind-beaten face. Thinking how delightful it would be to have Athena change my appearance, I stare into the mirror, expecting some kind of god-sent alteration, and recall how Odysseus described such a transformation.

"As for my change of skin, that is a charm Athena, Hope of Soldiers, uses as she will," he explained. "She has the knack to make me seem a beggar man sometimes and sometimes young, with finer clothes about me. It is no hard thing for the gods of heaven to glorify a man or bring him low." When he finally arrived home it was said that "this man comes with a certain aura of divinity into Odysseus's' hall. He shines."

No such luck for me. I'm still staring, transfixed but as dishevelled as before, at the mirror when I hear a voice.

"It's filled with warm chocolate," explains a very tattooed Italian bartenderess who licks her lips to describe the taste as she hands me a chocolate-filled croissant. "You'll feel like a new man."

I thank her and then ask: "Do you think my hair's grey?"

"I'd say it's more brown than grey," she diplomatically replies without missing a beat. "You're certainly not as grey as most people around here. Anyway it looks fine, like you've just been skiing all day with a mask over your head. And remember the Bible says that 'gray hair is a crown of glory attained by a life of righteousness'."

The *lungomare* that links Laigueglia with nearby Alassio is called the Riviera delle Palme, obviously because of the maritime pine and palm trees decorating the walk along remarkably clean beaches of fine sand, even at an amusing 50 metres of no man's land between the two resorts.

Everyone is in I-don't-have-a-care-in-the-world stroll mode as lunchtime approaches. I try to imitate their lackadaisical pace as I glide through Alassio's cobblestone streets, but I gradually regain speed until the Sacro Al Caduti del Mar chapel. I toss my pack on the stone bench and meditatively sit for 15 minutes to munch on a chocolate-filled croissant and admire another perspective of the Isola Gallinara and the bay.

An archeological walk starts here and continues to Albenga, following a footpath that retraces an old Roman road, but I keep to the coast and even jog, quite quickly, through a 220-metre 'live' train tunnel to get under and beyond one steep hill.

The Cathedral of San Michele in Albenga, a busy port and regional capital in bygone days, features a Gothic bell tower and a surprisingly pleasant medieval old town. The Roman Naval Museum contains amphorae taken from a ship sunk about half a mile from the coast in the first century BC. My meander back to the sea is through a maze of greenhouses and fields where farmers are at work watering and cultivating artichokes, broccoli, lettuce, flowers and other crops that prosper in the silt-rich earth on the alluvial plain.

The sea is separated from the fields by a railway track perched atop a large-rocked breakwater. I prance from rock to rock for a few kilometres until I reach Ceriale. By then I'm definitely ready for cereal, or something to eat, but wind up, after a few more kilometres, making do with a pistachio and coffee ice cream cone in Borghetto Santo Spirito.

"This is the real Mediterranean diet!" jokes the old man running the ice cream stand. "That's how I've made it to 84."

Loano, where I start the next day by investigating an 'anti-seismic iron dome' added to the San Giovanni Battista church after an earthquake in 1887, is the next popular resort. I'm intentionally wasting time on the palm-lined waterfront because it's a wet, dreary Mediterranean morning and *La Repubblica* predicts snow.

But, as though the gods have something to do with it, the clouds clear, the sun shines and the light-splashed sea is smooth and tranquil by 10am when I reach Pietra Ligure, a shipbuilding centre with a beach that's become a depository for out-of-season construction paraphernalia that includes plastic orange fencing, machinery and stacks of massive pipes. A barrier makes the seaside unapproachable. Not just for me but also for a habited nun.

"*Bon giorno, suora,*" I say. "A wonderful day for a quiet walk."

"Every day is a wonderful day for a quiet walk," she says with a smile that would have impressed Jesus. "We should each be grateful not only that we're able to walk but also that we're still breathing. *Pax Vobiscum.*"

We're not the only ones breathing. Fishermen are bringing in their overnight catch, a pack of bikers buzz by on Via Aurelia and there's a thriving morning market, though the closed and fenced-off Cantiere di Mediterreano shipyard adds a depressing touch.

A splendid seaside sidewalk called the Lungomare Migliorini stretches from village to village into Finale Ligure. I wonder if this connotes the final bit of the Riviera of Flowers. After all '*finalità*' does mean 'finality' and the town's surrounding boroughs are called Finale Borgo, Finale Marina and Finale Pia. All important-sounding names to my ears.

It turns out that Finale, a mecca for rock climbers due to the steep Ligurian Alps that roll into the city, has always been the town's name. But it must be somewhat prominent because a sign announces that it's been twinned with Ocean City, Maryland, since 1968 and has a youth hostel located in a 19th century castle.

Beyond Finale is the formidable Capo di Noli, a towering promontory that, my map illustrates, has even forced the railway line inland. I approach a rock climber and try to get some information.

"How do I get beyond the Capo di Noli?" I ask.

"Actually this isn't the Capo di Noli," he tells me. "This is just a big rock called Caprazoppa. Take the road, the Malpasso, but don't worry about the name; the road once had a reputation for banditry. It's safe."

The 145-metre high Rock of Caprazoppa (try pronouncing that quickly a dozen times!) dominates the Saracen Bay and is itself a prelude to the Capo di Noli, the cape between Varigotti and Noli, the ancient 'Neapolis' dominated by a 12th century castle.

The stunning cape reminds me of the dramatic cliffs near Xabia in Spain and I'm so awed that I simply sit and stare at the sea for fifteen minutes. Then I notice that a fisherman has dropped his line at least thirty metres from the top of the cliff to the water below. I wish him luck reeling in a catch of any size.

I stop in Spotorno for lunch at the Sunshine Café. Unfortunately the high-rise apartments, the result of what a guidebook calls "mass tourism and unchecked property development", make this town much less attractive than Noli. Most hotels are closed for the winter and there are so few people that I feel I have the whole coast, as well as the many citadels perched on the nearby hills, to myself. I leave Spotorno and pass the Isola de Bergeggi, part of a 'protected environmental area' and another stellar MedTrek attraction. Then I hike up to the village of Bergeggi to get an overview of the coast and a better look at the remains of two Middle Age churches and an even older Roman tower on the eight-hectare conical island. I consume the view because, as Deng Ming-Dao suggested, "There are a thousand meanings in every view, if only we open ourselves to see the scripture of the landscape."

After this scenic stretch, civilisation. Even the map has removed the green lineage on the seaside road from one end of Savona to the other. Power station funnels, dilapidated buildings, ramshackle construction sites, you name it. Here Italy is still India.

I arrive at the REEFER (it's written in VERY big letters) Terminal and check out the size and origin of the various containers. Ferries are leaving for Sardinia and Corsica from Porto di Vado, which exports crude oil, coal, and Italian cars. Another shipping terminal has rail cars destined for Switzerland. One plus: innovatively designed blue benches on the promenade are shaped like traditional fishing boats.

After an hour I'm wondering why Savona hasn't yet recovered from the last war. What war, you ask? I know, there hasn't been a war here for over 60 years. That's precisely why the place should be a little more spruced up. The Michelin guide, being diplomatic and polite, calls Savona "austere and somber". Another book says the city "keeps its treasures jealously guarded, revealing them only to those who are prepared to dedicate some time to discovering them". Although I'm impressed with the 16th century Priamar fortress, every other treasure in Savona is either non-existent or well hidden and I'm in no mood for a scavenger hunt.

It's Sunday and the promenade in Albissola Marina is congested with walkers who nonchalantly stroll through an out-of-use train tunnel without flashlights. I just can't get over the casual way that Italians walk! Unlike me, they don't need courses in walking meditation. It's genetic. They look at me as though I'm absolutely demented when I speedily stroll past them.

The sunset seaside walk continues into Celle Ligure where, after 42 kilometres, I ask a ten-year-old girl whether I should take a bus or train to Genoa, where I plan to spend the night.

"Train," she says. "Always the train. It's more reliable."

"But the schedule says the bus will be here in ten minutes," I reply.

"This is Italy," chuckles the young girl. "If you add a zero to the ten and get *cento minuti* you might be right. Take the train."

She'd used that line before.

I check out the schedule at the train station and decide to stay near the station at the Pension Sylvie, which is owned by a woman called Henriette. Michael Moore, or a guy who looks like Michael Moore, is checking in at the same time and I'm amazed that he speaks excellent Italian.

The Pension Sylvie has very little heat but a great sound system broadcasting the clamour at the nearby train station. Hey, what can I expect for 30 euros? I sleep fleetingly, in each of my room's three different beds, and by 6am, when it's still dark, am ready to get on the path. But when I head across the courtyard to the breakfast room, it's raining and very cold. *La Repubblica*'s prediction of snow could be on the mark, though a day late. No wonder Michael Moore skips breakfast.

I slowly sip three *cappuccini* before donning rain gear to tackle the day. My bright blue poncho, when stretched over my baseball cap and pack, makes me look like a one-man Blue Man Group, the creative trio of mute performers that appear on stage in blue grease paint and black clothing and have been the rage in the US for 20 years.

I don't like hiking in the rain, primarily because my glasses get wet and blurry, but decide that, although Zeus has "sent a gloom over the ocean", it's Genoa or bust. The last time I walked in rain like this was near Sète, thousands of kilometres ago, and I start off with only minimal gusto and a lack of enthusiasm.

"What's a little bad weather when Genoa's on the horizon?" I ask myself as I scan my brain for a few comforting words of wisdom to revive my spirits.

Bingo, I come up with the appropriate aphorism just as I pass a road sign indicating 38 kilometres to Genoa, which is often called the "toilet of Italy" by Italians due to the considerable amount of rainfall.

"Ideal circumstances are seldom given to anyone for an undertaking," Deng Ming-Dao said. "Wanting everything in life to be perfect before you take action is like wanting to reach a destination without travel."

Maybe, but there's no one else walking on the *lungomare*. Not even the most ardent Italians are out today. But their working countrymen haven't tossed in the wet towel. There are deafening construction noises emanating from a port project in Varazze and when Elissa calls from California I can barely hear her due to the combined noise of traffic and construction.

"And this is supposed to be meditative?" she asks.

Again impermanence reigns and conditions change as I hike through Varazze on the Lungomare Europe into Invrea and Cogoletto, where the Arresta River signifies the end of Savona province and the beginning of Genoa province. The promenade includes half a dozen tunnels that create an umbrella-like passageway on a very rainy day.

Long impressed by the hill-hugging roads the Italians built in Ethiopia and other foreign outposts, I'm particularly fascinated by the Autostrade dei Fiori with its multitude of tunnels and spectacular bridge spans. This little walkway is of equal stature and, although the weather makes it seem more like the English Channel, I'm wet but still in one piece when I get a coffee and pastry in Cogoletto.

By noon, the rain has stopped and snow seems unlikely. I remove my poncho in Arenzano after walking through a mini-tunnel cut through a large rock on the beach. I'm so titillated by this Tom Sawyerish discovery that I say "Cool" over and over again but pronounce it like a pigeon – "Coo-ell, Coo-ell!" I keep repeating. A young couple watching me start flapping their arms and yell "Coo-ell, Coo-ell!" This comical display marks the midway point between Savona, 23 kilometres behind me, and Genoa, 24 kilometres ahead.

Just after noon I pass a sign indicating 'GENOVA' in GIGANTIC letters. I stop, sit on the ramparts and again notice that there's no green road on my map until the other side of the city.

"Coo-ell, Coo-ell," I say to myself as I overlook a port with a breakwater that's a whopping five kilometres long. Beyond it are ships, the airport and other parts of the city. But it must be another twenty kilometres to the town centre and I assume that 'GENOVA' signifies the very extensive Greater Genoa.

It's six kilometres through the suburb of Voltri to the gigantic commercial port in the suburb of Pegli, where I stop for a pizza. The chef tells me that 'downtown' is about twelve kilometres away.

"Just go past the Olympic canoeing workout centre, past the Sestri shipbuilding plants, past the petrol port, past the airport, past the new Sheraton Hotel, past dozens of gutted old factories, past a new commercial centre and past lots of garbage," he says, speaking so fast that I can barely keep up with him. "Then you'll reach the towering and renowned Lanterna lighthouse, the most famous symbol of Genoa."

As I walk there's building, booming, blasting and bustle everywhere. I wonder why Genoa, like Savona, doesn't look more robust and clean. True, the 117-metre Lanterna, built in 1543 with a flashing light that now has a range of 53 kilometres, is impressive. And the names of the quays and bridges – Etiopia, Eritrea, Somalia, Libia, Mogadiscio, Tripoli and Benghazi – are reminders of Italy's expansionist past. But everything I see indicates that Genoa is best approached from the sea.

One local guidebook says that "the coastal strip to the west of Genoa is often unfairly described as little more than one big industrial estate. This is an over-simplification that ignores much of the history and culture of the area." Maybe, but trust me, west of Genoa is right up there with a few other harbouring eyesores on the Med. And it's intensified here because the ring of mountains around the city has forced excessive industrial development on the coast.

Other parts of Genoa, the bustling seaport that Petrarch once called the "mistress of the sea", did get a much-needed facelift in 2004 to spruce up Liguria's most important city for its role as the European Capital of Culture.

"The city was teeming with activity because we were determined to regain a leading role in Italy and the world," Giuseppe Pericu, the mayor and president of the Genova 2004 committee tells me when I call in at his office. "Many international tourists still think of Genoa as a dilapidated port, but we've become a revitalised and dynamic centre of art, life and tourism."

And what about the area I just visited on my walk?

"There's always much more to do," Pericu says. "But go to the top of the Apennine hills that surround the town and you'll better appreciate Genoa's beauty."

I walk past the renovated bustling Sottoripa arcade, a trading place for fish and spices since the Middle Ages, and visit five museums, including the Museum of the Sea and Navigation and a museum network that connects three medieval palaces on via Garibaldi. Then I end the day's walk at Europe's largest aquarium, one of Italy's most popular family destinations that showcases an intriguing underwater reconstruction depicting the bottom of the Med.

After intentionally getting lost in the alleyways a few blocks back from the sea, I follow the mayor's suggestion and take the Sant' Anna Funicular to the top of the hill. There's a picturesque overview of Italy's sixth largest city, which the Ligurians founded in the 6th century BC, from my table on the terrace of the Montallegro restaurant. The city stretches some 30 kilometres from east to west, on either side of the Lanterna lighthouse that symbolises its reputation as a crossroads for languages, religions, commercial goods and ideas.

And how long will it take to clean up the area I just walked through?

"We Italians are slow to get going until after our morning coffee," says Gianfranco Castagnetti, the President of the Genova Convention Bureau and owner of the Best Western City Hotel where I spend the night. "But there's a new conference centre near the airport named after Christopher Columbus and once we hit our stride, we'll finish fast. It's the Italian way. Keep coming back and you'll see."

35. Surmounting Portofino and Embracing the Kissing Path

"The Lord Odysseus walked along, debating inwardly whether to whirl and beat the life out of this fellow with his stick, or toss him, brain him on the stony ground. Then he controlled himself, and bore it quietly." — The Odyssey

Elissa, who's flown in from Los Angeles with her French poodle Mera, is understandably nervous about the constant chaos and crowds on Genoa's streets as she chauffeurs me in a rented Peugeot 206 from our dilapidated hotel in Nervi, just south of town, back to the aquarium on a cloudy Sunday afternoon. Motorcyclists fearlessly criss-cross lanes, cars dash in every direction but straight ahead, jaywalkers look like they want to get hit and big buses try to caress our bumper. There's no rhyme or reason to the traffic.

"I'm not sure how good a chauffeur I'll be if it's going to be like this until we get to Rome," Elissa says when she drops me off. "This traffic's going to wreck my vacation."

"Don't worry," I reply confidently. "This is just a Genoa thing. Once we get to Cinque Terre and into rural Tuscany it'll be like driving on a farm in North Dakota. Except there won't be any snow. Trust me."

I affix my pedometer to a worn pair of Levis and head out of Genoa, planning to walk only a few hours into the Riviera di Levante, or the Riviera of the East Wind, until I reach our room in the weathered five-storey Hotel Bonera. Our top-floor room looks onto the Med but the once-elegant seaside resort and the dowager-like hotel have seen better decades.

"This hotel is like a woman whose makeup has crusted in the creases of her face," Elissa remarks about the Bonera's distinctly down-and-out appearance.

"Hey, it's MedTrekking," I say. "Dumps like this are part of the adventure and charm. I promise that you'll love the coast down the road with its charismatic villages, multicoloured villas, isolated coves and terraced olive groves."

The Italians haven't changed the pace of their *en masse* strolls. Despite the gray sky, incessant wind and a slight chill factor there are roller bladers and skaters amidst the local promenaders and baby strollers as I pass the Piazzale Martin Luther King. Offshore two wet-suited jet skiers dash among the kayaks and sailboats on a just-before-the-storm quiet sea. About half a kilometre from the aquarium the congested traffic has thinned and, as I buy some cheese and olives from a roadside vendor, the chaos has assumed a more normal Italian cadence.

Elissa, who insists that we have mobile phones and back-up mobile phones to keep in touch after the many melodramas in Morocco, calls me when she's returned to Nervi. We agree that the traffic mess is just a downtown Genoa thing and I follow a red brick path that winds through fishing ports where kaleidoscopically colourful private *castelli*, or small castles, have endearing names like Villa Carina.

All of the bathhouses and changing rooms on the coast are closed and no one is serving sandwiches at the shuttered *paninotecas*. But the Portofino Diving Club is selling tickets for excursions to the fishing holes in romantic coves between Genoa and chic Portofino.

I pass an American International School, the Iglesia Santa Maria Assunta and an empty Simón Bolívar Garden where a plaque describes Bolívar as a 'Venezuelan politician', a rather humbling epitaph for the man who liberated six South American countries from Spanish rule and is known as *El Libertador* in many other places.

I'm so engrossed walking on the Passeggiata Anita Garibaldi, with extraordinary views of Mount Portofino and its finger-out-into-the-sea promontory, that I miss our hotel. I surface a kilometre later near the Gropallo Tower in the Nervi gardens, a nine-hectare park shared by three villas decorated with elaborate *trompe l'oeil*, and backtrack.

The overnight gales, and the celebratory teen-to-twenty-somethings that awoke us at 3am when they returned from clubbing, have calmed down as dawn dawns with grey skies, a light sprinkle and quietly breaking waves gently lapping the rocky coast. I see two large birds, an omen that again evokes a line from *The Odyssey:* "Now Zeus who views the wide world sent a sign to him, launching a pair of eagles from a mountain crest in gliding flight down the soft blowing wind."

I expect to get beyond the 2000-foot-high Mount Portofino today and have my first social interaction of the morning when I thank two street sweepers, dressed in vibrant green uniforms, for collecting debris that's accumulated during the recent wind. They seem bemused. Not only because I'm talking to them, which few people do, but also because I'm wearing a bright orange fluorescent smock. Elissa wants me to wear this fashion accessory, found in the glove compartment of all Italian rental cars for use in case of an accident or emergency stop on the *autostrada*, to "alert the crazy Italian drivers from Genoa" and, in the case of a fall, "enable rescue teams to find your body".

The Museo Giannettino Luxoro at the edge of Nervi is closed, reinforcing a winter mood on the Mediterranean that many potential tourists find so gloomy and sinister that they stay away. At the end of the seaside passage I return to the omnipresent Via Aurelia. Beyond Nervi is a sign indicating that I'm finally getting out of Greater Genoa.

I encounter another street crew whose uniforms are the same bright colour as my orange smock. They look at me as though I should pick up a shovel or get rid of the glowing vest. Okay, I'm a fraud. But I keep the smock on because walking on the sidewalkless Aurelia Way is actually a potentially treacherous pursuit. After Bogliasco, Sori and Recco, and just before Camogli, Elissa pulls up next to me in the car. She catches me finishing a *fugassa al formaggio*, the pie made with *prescinseua* cheese that's a specialty in Recco and, I tell Elissa, a necessary staple for all hearty MedTrekkers passing through town. We make necessarily vague plans to meet for a late lunch in Santa Margherita Ligure.

"I'll call you at high noon and let you know where I am," I say. "It shouldn't take me more than two hours to get to Portofino from here. After all, it's only a 15-minute drive. Just take a right when you get to Santa Margherita and wait for my call."

"I expect that by the time we talk I'll have found a comfortable hotel for us somewhere on the coast," she replies.

"Sounds like a plan," I say as I kiss her goodbye.

Portofino turns out to be *molto* further by foot than by road. The first warning that I might have been a bit optimistic occurs in Camogli, where an amphitheatre-shaped port is under construction and the owner of a brightly coloured bar on the Via Garibaldi describes what's ahead as I casually sip a *caffè*.

"It will take you at least three hours to round the Portofino cape and it's a *brutto* walk, especially in this lousy weather," he informs me. Apparently I'll be traversing the heart of the 4680-hectare Portofino Regional Nature Park which includes the municipalities of Camogli, Chiavari, Portofino, Rapallo, Recco, to Santa Margherita Ligure and Zoagli. "It'll take five or six hours," he adds.

"It certainly doesn't look that far on the map," I reply, showing him the Carte Stradalí Delle Regioni.

"Trust me, not the map," he advises.

He's right. It is a 'brutal' five hours to Portofino on a very slippery path. I cut my face to shreds going up terraced slopes through thorn bushes and untrimmed olive groves. Unfortunately I don't have a mirror in my first aid kit to evaluate my damaged face. Instead, I use my fingers to feel the cuts and apply Band-Aids to stop the bleeding. When I finally get a look at myself, my face resembles a quilt knitted by a blind dog. Again, I swear to myself, "Quit getting into these ridiculous situations, idiot!"

How wild is it out here on the three-kilometre wide and 600-metre high cape? The overgrown terrain is certainly appropriate for a regional nature park and the few picnic sites all have green garbage cans suspended from tree branches some five metres above the ground. How ecologically conscientious and civilised, I say to myself. Then I realise that they elevate garbage or food to keep away the bears. Great.

The challenging walk from the hillside village of San Rocco goes along a hilltop path that abuts dizzying steep cliffs. An occasional vertical trail leads down to dazzling coves and isolated inlets near Chiappa Point and the Cala dell' Oro but I ignore them in an effort to more quickly reach Portofino. Next time! At one tricky spot, where there's a straight drop into the sea, linked chains enable me to get around a rock face. I do slip once and invoke a line from Homer: "Ask help from Athena, Zeus's daughter, she it will be who saves this boy from death."

I call Elissa at noon just as I arrive at the Romanesque church of San Nicolo di Capodimonte, which dates to 1141.

"I've got to scrap our lunch date," I say. "It'll take me at least another two hours to get to Portofino."

"I stopped there and the seas are raging," says Elissa. "I had to leave because I thought the car would be blown into the water. Be careful."

"It's rough here too but the views are astounding, beyond belief almost," I tell her as I look over the Bay of San Fruttuoso. "I'll call from Portofino."

I love the idea of having a chauffeur but I'm not sure how much the chauffeur is going to like the constant unpredictability of MedTrekking.

The chapel of San Fruttuoso, which was inhabited by the Bishop of Tarragon in the 8th century after he fled Spain to avoid the Moors, has been splendidly restored. I run into a group of school kids who've just arrived by boat and listen to their teacher describe the place.

"Benedictine monks were here in the 10th century," she says. "And the Doria family built the abbey in the 13th century in exchange for the right to put the family tombs in an adjoining crypt."

Although scuba diving has apparently been restricted since the creation of a marine reserve in 1999, the teacher tells her class that there's a bronze statue known as *The Submerged Christ* sitting at a depth of about fifty feet just off shore. "It was created by sculptor Guido Galletti in 1954," she says. "And it's worth breaking the law when you get a bit older to dive down for a look."

That's the educational spirit.

Some German tourists offer me a lift back to Portofino when their boat leaves. "It's too slippery and muddy to walk today," one man tells me. "Come back with us after you wash your face and get all that mud off your boots."

"Thanks for the offer but I love the walk," I said. "It's easier than washing my face and cleaning my boots."

The detour to Castelló di San Giorgio features dozens of postcard-worthy views of Portofino and the Gulf of Rapallo beyond it. I'm so impressed that I take a photograph with my telephone camera and send it to Elissa before walking by the lighthouse on Punta del Cao and dropping into the Churches of San Giorgio and San Marino as I head into town.

Portofino, perhaps the most photographed town on the Ligurian Sea, is deserted in mid-afternoon when I sit on a bench near the wind-blown port to change my muddy socks and shoes. Looking at the sailboats and yachts blowing in the wind, I remember that a German officer was so impressed by Portofino during World War II that he refused to carry out orders to destroy it. Good decision by a wise man! Then, as I leave a town that's existed for over 800 years, I make a little pilgrimage to the Benedictine Monastery of Saint Jerome of Cervera where Richard the Lionheart stopped on his way to Syria.

To get to Santa Margherita Ligure, I take a sea-hugging road that's so narrow that even my orange smock doesn't provide much reassurance. I almost immediately turn left on the Salita Baratta to drop into the Hotel Splendido, a former 16th century monastery where the Duke of Windsor was the first to sign the visitor's book in 1901 and where Richard Burton proposed to Elizabeth Taylor...the first time. Most of the hotel's clients traditionally arrive by yacht and there's a rumour that the width of the seaside road into and out of Portofino is due to a decree by the duke. Apparently, he wanted it kept narrow to discourage commoners and their cars from visiting the resort.

"I'm not sure that's a true story," says the concierge, "but it's *certo* that nobody complains that the road is too wide."

After Santa Margherita I walk around the Gulf of Tigullio to Rapallo, a popular vacation spot for non-royals like myself. I buzz Elissa and tell her that, after 39 kilometres, I'm ready to call it a day. She tells me that she's about twenty kilometres further down the coast in Sestri Levante.

"Mera and I will get there as quickly as we can," she says.

Very few boats appear to have left the port to brave today's sea and there are dozens of hotels on the flower-filled Lungomare Vittorio Veneto. Elissa picks me up just outside the city limits and I'm not upset to learn that, having skillfully executed her role as chauffeur and aide-de-camp, she's got us a luxurious room in Sestri Levante.

The Grand Hotel Villa Balbi sits on a peninsula between the Bay of Fables and the Bay of Silence and we're treated to dinner by a journalist from the Danish Broadcasting Corporation who's driven over from Monaco to interview me. Mette Fugl and her cameraman drove four hours to discuss Prince Albert, get the latest Monaco gossip and pick up a dose of Mediterranean lore.

"Lone Kuhlmann, who went to Columbia Journalism School with you, told me that it was worth a five hour drive to pick your brain," Mette says after I finish my veal scaloppini and am about to order a *gelato alla fragola* for dessert.

"Did Prince Albert agree with Lone?" I ask. "After all, this is a long way to come for two minutes of air time."

"He's not talking to us," she replies. "That's why we came to you."

The Bay of Fables apparently got its name from Hans Christian Andersen when he was here in 1833, but nobody's talking about the origin of the Bay of Silence. I presume there are mafia connotations and tell the journalist that the bay is probably full of victims in concrete shoes. Or, I say, maybe the name is more profound. "The deepest sound is silence," I tell her.

In fact, I learn the next morning that the Baia del Silenzio was named by poet Giovanni De Scalzo because it's so, you guessed it, quiet and was a favourite working locale for Byron, Goethe and Wagner.

Elissa drives me back to Rapallo the next morning and I charge up a steep hill on Via Aurelia to Zoagli, a quiet seaside town that manufactures velvet and damask. Along the way I see a plaque indicating that 'The Incomparable Max' Beerbohm, the English writer and caricaturist who was married to American actress Florence Kahn, resided at 250 Aurelia Way from 1910 until his death in 1956. Acquiring this completely unexpected bit of literary knowledge is precisely why I walk, because I certainly didn't see the plaque the two times we drove by.

Beerbohm, whose presence encouraged a number of his English peers to move to Rapallo, was occasionally self-effacing. He claimed simply "My gifts are small. I've used them very well and discreetly, never straining them." But V.S. Pritchett made an amusing comment about him: "Among the masked dandies of Edwardian comedy, Max Beerbohm is the most happily armoured by a deep and almost innocent love of himself as a work of art."

Is that what I'm becoming, a work of art?

I consider my aesthetically mobile persona for a moment and attempt to visualise how I must appear to people who see me on the MedTrek. Most of us have a fair idea what our family and friends think about us, but it's difficult to assess how we come across to complete strangers in a foreign land during a fleeting encounter. For one thing, we each carry a heavy load of national baggage that can create an unfavourable bias before we say more than a few words.

Americans are still frequently categorised as boisterous, naïve and lamentably unfashionable. One thing that really bothers me is that the recent breed of loud-mouthed, newly-rich and rowdy Russians, who frequently get drunk and make real asses of themselves as they toss their money around in fleshpots in Monaco and on the French and Italian Rivieras, still have not replaced Americans as the most caricatured or ridiculed group of world travellers. Hell, these rogues make most of us look like meek monks. Yet we're the ones who continue to get the most flak.

Appearance and apparel are actually a bigger deal than nationality in fashion-conscious Italy. When I'm here to work I fastidiously wear a Dolce & Gabbana suit, a well-chosen silk tie from Valentino or Versace, and freshly polished John Varvatos shoes (one of the first things they look at is the shoes!) just to go out for my morning cappuccino. That type of attire also puts me on an even footing with anybody I'm going to interview.

But the MedTrek isn't a business trip and I never carry fancy or fashionable togs. Although I'm not quite as scruffy as the Forrest Gump character I met in France or the dishevelled hippie on the train in Spain, no one is going to mistake me for an English dandy, a suave Italian or an inordinately well-attired American. So I might as well cave in and, adorned with my orange smock and a baseball cap, hope they at least consider me a decent example of a walking work of American art. Maybe I can sell myself on eBay.

I cut down from Via Aurelia to the sea on a walled walk between some large private villas. After Zoagli, though, a sheer cliff face puts me back on the curvilinear Via Aurelia with vertical drops to rocky beaches. I take a snapshot of the under-renovation Castelló San Benelli, where a sign says that the work is scheduled for completion in 2003. They missed that deadline by a few years and I'd say 2013 seems a bit more realistic. In Chiavari, I remove my bright orange street-walking smock and attempt to get some information.

"*Buon giorno,*" I say to a man my age. "How many people live in Chee-avari?"

"It's Kee-avari not Chee-avari," he replies, with an expression that seems to indicate that I'm the first person in history to mispronounce the town's name. "This is one of the oldest towns in Italy and is usually given a great deal of respect. It was founded in 1178, but there's a necropolis near here that dates from the Iron Age in the 8th century BC."

Past the Kee-avari archeological museum, I notice that the statues on the façade of the Cathedrale di Nostra Signora dell'Orto are surrounded by chicken wire to protect them from pigeons. I buy lunch at the fruit and vegetable market in Piazza Mazzini before cutting down past Mike's American Bar that's not far from the first significant sandy beach since Genoa. Across the Entella River is Lavagna, a medieval-aged city that's the blackboard capital of Italy. There are quarries of black slate here and the Italian word for blackboard is, you guessed it, *lavagna.*

Lavagna's other claim to fame involves a party every August 14 when the townspeople, and thousands of tourists, dress in medieval garb to eat a 1500-kilogram cake. Yes, that's over 3300 pounds of cake. The ceremony commemorates a wedding in 1230 when a local count insisted that the wedding cake be large enough for every villager to get a piece.

I'm thinking about the screech made by fingernails on a blackboard when I get a panicked call from Elissa. Apparently she, Mera and the car are stuck on a steep hill in Monterosso al Mare, the northwestern most of the five villages in the Cinque Terre National Park.

"I'm at the end of a one-way street, a hotel owner screamed 'Animale!' when he saw Mera and kicked me out of his garden," says Elissa, who doesn't speak any Italian. "Now I'm getting hit on by every guy in the country. Help!"

I call the Hotel Suisse Bellevue, where we booked a room online, and the owner promises to have Elissa picked up by a taxi.

I cruise into Sestri Levante after walking 20 kilometres, just one kilometre more than Elissa had clocked in the car for the same trip. There are multiple signs of wind damage and another clan of street cleaners, dressed in bright green this time, are cutting broken tree branches and raking fallen pine needles. The only other people on the street are four North Africans hoping to sell counterfeit purses to anyone who might stroll by. That would be me and they take it very personally when I tell them that I don't want a fake Gucci bag.

I've always thought, and this may seem completely off the wall, that I have an immediate connection with many Africans because I spent so much time on the continent. I kick off most encounters with a few words of Amharic, Swahili or Xhosa (though my clicking is not what it used to be) to get their attention. Then I often surprise them when I correctly guess their nationality, usually after I hear their English or French accents but sometimes due to their attire or identifiable tribal scars. And they always seem to get excited when I greet them with a loud "Yo!" or an expansive "Hello!?!"

This group, I'm sure from what little I've heard them say, are from Senegal.

"Why would you leave a nice sunny place like Port Louis to sell bags on a windy beach in Italy?" I ask one of them in French.

"Nobody has any money to buy these bags in Port Louis," he replies, not bothering to compliment me on superpower abilities that enabled me to immediately identify his nationality. "And we don't live there anymore."

"But you can't be making much money here and it must be nerve-wracking to be constantly on the lookout for the *polizia*?" I ask.

Once the topic turns to money and cops my Senegalese acquaintances immediately get suspicious and scurry away.

I perhaps should have questioned the efficacy of my instinctive African connection after an incident that occurred when I lived on rue Béranger in the Marais in Paris shortly after Sonia was born. The dilapidated building across the street from our airy and spacious apartment had been taken over by Congolese squatters from Brazzaville and there were often serious sounding screams inspired by arguments, a rape, a stabbing or too much drinking.

I walked over one night to request some quiet on behalf of my baby daughter and, as I entered the tiny foyer at the bottom of a circular staircase, shouted out my signature "Yo!" But instead of being welcomed, I was immediately encircled by four thugs who were neither intimidated nor worried. Then, as if Jerome Robbins or George Balanchine had choreographed the scene, they all stepped back a few steps. Within seconds a rock solid bag of cement, dropped from above, narrowly missed my head and seemed to shake the building's foundations when it crashed to the floor.

"*Bonjour et au revoir!*" I said with great exaggeration as I beat a hasty retreat across the street.

After the Senegalese beat their retreat, I start reflecting about the years I was based in Cape Town and must confess one lingering regret. During my time as a foreign correspondent in South Africa, I occasionally tested the boundaries of the ludicrous and demeaning apartheid political system. Back then, when there were 'Whites Only' toilets, hospitals and buses, any significant social contact between the races was discouraged and, usually, unlawful. It was considered a big deal when I invited a few African and Cape Coloured friends to my home on Loader Street for alcoholic drinks. Once I even took Coloured journalist Howard

Lawrence into a 'Europeans Only' bar, which probably disturbed him more than anyone else, until we were very politely refused service and asked to leave.

These were hardly revolutionary provocations and to this day I wish I'd been more involved in subterfuge to undermine the hideous white-run regime. I told myself at the time that just reporting on conditions in South Africa was action enough. But in retrospect I feel that not encouraging and actively advocating the overthrow of the government was, though it might have gotten me thrown out of the country or into jail, a sign of collusion, complicity and participation. I wish I'd done more.

Another issue about Africa that still baffles me is why, as I roamed the continent interviewing American ambassadors like Shirley Temple Black in Ghana and scores of State Department officials in the 1970s, I was never approached by the CIA and invited to become a spy. Like many American journalists, I was often accused of being associated with the CIA (and absolutely no one believed me when I denied the charge) but, and I swear this is true, the CIA never asked me to hook up with them and work undercover. I probably, depending on the particular assignment and the money, would have refused but it's always nice to be invited to the party.

Finding the path out of Sestri is, oddly, a challenge. I set off between the idyllic Baia del Silenzio and a backdrop of pastel-coloured buildings only to lose an hour exploring dead-end trails. During my attempt to get out of town, I run into retired history professor Domenico Cattani. When I ask him about the best route to Cinque Terre, he recites the general history of Liguria and describes the train tunnels built along the coast in 1935.

"The old railroad has been converted into a seaside road but I don't think you can walk through the tunnels," he says, adding that he's heard about a path that crosses over the mountains but doesn't know how to reach it. "There's no path right above the coast but someone in town might be able to help you find the right trail through the hills."

"*Grazie*," I say as I head back to the town centre, buy some ice cream and am told to "take a right and you'll find a marked path with signs indicating Riva Trigoso, Moneglia and Déiva Marina".

In Riva, where popular Riva yachts and speedboats of the same name have been manufactured for over a century, I decide to hike/walk/run/sprint through the road tunnels to Moneglia rather than tackle the mountain path. I can't help, both mentally and when I speak to people, contorting that town's name into either Mongolia or Magnolia and no-one is quite sure where I'm heading when I toss out the name to try to confirm that I'm going the right way.

I make it through a few tunnels, but even my fluorescent orange smock isn't bright enough for the Mother of All Tunnels, a 10-kilometre long very dark one-way road with no sidewalks or illumination, except when there's a slit through the rock to let in a soupçon of light. I start walking in the tunnel when the alternating signal turns green but, enveloped in darkness and pushed into the rock by the traffic, I use my flashlight to stop a van after five minutes. This would be a suicide mission if I continued.

"Going to Magnolia?" I ask when a workman stops his pickup. "I'm trying to get to Cinque Terre."

The driver looks a bit befuddled.

"It's crazy to walk here," he says. "Get in quickly."

We continue in total darkness and I'm especially grateful for the lift. It wasn't until a few days later that I found a guidebook that warned "because of the heavy traffic … the winding but scenic provincial road that hugs the coast between Sestri Levante and Moneglia (11 kilometres) is best avoided: the narrowness of the tunnels originally dug for the Genoa-La Spezia railroad line (which was later moved inland) necessitates an alternating, traffic light-controlled one-way system, which can mean long delays, although the magnificent view at the end of the tunnels make the wait worthwhile."

I simply want to add, just in case anyone's stupid enough to think about following in my footsteps, that "the tunnel just before Magnolia is so dark that anyone walking through it will almost certainly not be alive to cherish the light and magnificent views at the end of the tunnel."

Borrowing a line from Odysseus, I tell the driver when we get to Moneglia that "I'll speak well of you as I pass on over the boundless earth."

At the 'new' inland railway station I meet the first English stationmaster, an Englishwoman at that, on the MedTrek. She says there's a well-marked path over the mountain north to Riva and another well-marked trail south to Cinque Terre on the Riviera Spezzina, which gets its name from the town of La Spezia.

I'll return to Riva in the morning but now take the train to Monterosso al Mare, where I head directly from the station to join Elissa and some friends for dinner.

"You're not going to like our room," Elissa says as I feast on pesto a lasagna at Le Pirate. "They gave me the only room without a carpet that's also the only room with a view of the Med blocked by a tree. Apparently dogs aren't permitted in the hotel, although that wasn't mentioned on their website, and they've made a once-in-a-lifetime exception."

"Let's be Zen about it," I tell her. "We're only here a couple of nights. It can't be that bad."

The tree outside the window definitely does obstruct our view but it doesn't make much noise and we get a decent sleep. Then I catch the 8:40 train at the station, which is filled with backpackers riding in both directions to hike the popular local trails, back to Riva and spend three hours hiking over the hills to Moneglia/Mongolia/Magnolia. Once there, I follow the path marked 'Déiva Marina'.

The walk, just above the water, takes me on an up-and-down-through-the-woods-from-village-to-village trek along a hillside covered with Aleppo pine trees, rockroses, lavender, prickly ivy and wild asparagus. I walk downhill from Framura to the coast at Anzo, where there's a statue of a Madonna holding her son atop a rock just a few metres offshore. A bit further along, in Bonasolla, I run into the picturesque Madonna della Punta chapel built into the cliff and in Levanto I see the first sign indicating 'Cinque Terre'. Hikers at the Aqua Dolce camping site give different estimates, ranging from 90 minutes to three hours, about the walking time to Monterosso. Along the way I find a B&B called Mare Mesco featuring a sign that says 'Rooms and Rum' in multiple languages.

I meet solo and group hikers on the trail, mostly Germans coming to Levanto from Monterosso, and am delightfully surprised when the path arrives at the entrance to the Hotel Bellevue.

The next morning I'm the angriest I've been on the entire MedTrek. The Swiss owner of the hotel and I awaken every other guest with a shouting match in English that begins when I, not too politely, chastise her for not putting her 'No Pets' policy on her fraudulent and misleading website.

"You tossed us into a room with no carpet and no view just because of an eight-pound poodle!" I shriek, immediately reminding myself that I skipped my morning meditation session. "You're too arrogant and self-important for Italy, the Cinque Terre and the Mediterranean. Take your tight ass back to Switzerland."

I generally like to avoid these exaggerated and ear-splitting outbursts, which I admit were a frequent occurrence when I was boozing, especially when I'm MedTrekking. But today I'm tempted to huff, puff and blow her house down. She initially tries to maintain an implacable cool, calm and collected we-don't-take-sides-during-a-war Swiss façade by giving me her best the-hotel-owner-is-always-right sneer. At one point her nose is so high in the air that all I can see is the hopefully cancerous mole at the tip of her pointed chinny chin chin.

"You've given us the only room on the entire Mediterranean with a view blocked by a tree!" I yelp, sounding more like a whining jackal than a poor excuse for a human being. "Only a constipated cow would give a rat's ass if a client with a reservation shows up with a tiny poodle. Only a fricking hag, who keeps one room without a view while hoping and praying that someone with a tiny French poodle shows up so she can get some joy by giving them the worst room on the entire Mediterranean, would be bothered by such an innocent and minor transgression.

"I'm going to leave this dump and tell everyone I meet on and beyond the Mediterranean, even in Australia and Argentina, to 'BOYCOTT THE HOTEL BELLEVUE RUN BY THE SWISS BITCH IN MONTEROSSO," I shout. "In fact, I might carry a placard when I hike in the Cinque Terre denouncing this dump and start scribbling anti-Bellevue graffiti with my respected MedTrekker tag."

Not a bad idea, I think to myself. After all, the word graffiti is derived from the Italian *graffiato*, or scratched, so this would be an appropriate place to start. But before I split I've got to push the Swiss hotelier's buttons a bit more so she'll lose her temper and look at least as stupid as I do in front of the befuddled guests coming down for breakfast which, of course, is not served one second before 8am.

"Do you know that your clock is one minute slow?" I say very softly, pointing to the oversized Black Forest Swiss Cuckoo clock mounted on the wall. I know from experience that the best way to outSwiss a Swiss is either by mentioning the time or insulting his/her bank.

That did it. She freaks.

"Go back to America!" she cries as she swipes my credit card. "Never darken my door step again!"

"I will and I won't," I scream, trying to get in the last lick. "But not before I call American Express and tell them to remove that fraudulent room charge and urge them to quit doing business with you. Who wants to have anything to do with a Swiss harpy who can't even set her clock correctly?"

Then I leave, both embarrassed by my immature and disgusting behaviour and pleased by my immature and disgusting behaviour.

I'm so pissed off that I also get into an argument with Elissa and we agree that, unless I never want to see her again, I should take a day off. We check out of my least favourite hotel on the Mediterranean and drive south to citadel-dominated Portovénere where we explore the town and the Gulf of Poets, which gets its name because Percy Bysshe Shelley and Lord Byron lived and wrote here. We walk to the black marbled Church of San Pietro, which was the site of a temple to Venus, or Vénere, before the Christians came along. And we take a boat around the offshore island of Palmaria, the largest of three islands colonised by Benedictine monks that are now among UNESCO's World Heritage Sites. The captain points out a pile of rocks that, he says, "used to be Byron's Cave, where the poet composed *The Corsair*".

I ask for details about Byron's purported swim across the gulf to visit Shelley in Lerici and Shelley's drowning near here in 1822, less than a month before his 30th birthday. One school of thought, I say, is that Shelley was murdered by the British because of the incendiary nature of his verse. That's news to the captain.

Our top floor room at the Grand Hotel Portovénere, a Franciscan monastery in the 16th century, does not have a tree blocking its extraordinary view of the Med and the next morning I take the first ferry back to Monterosso to hike the Cinque Terre. I'd walked the Five Lands once before, from south to north, and explain to Elissa that for MedTrekking purposes it's imperative that I walk the same path in the opposite direction.

"I'll never be able to live with myself if I don't do it the 'right' way," I say. "It could put the credibility of the entire MedTrek in jeopardy."

Elissa may not walk much with me and her career as a private chauffeur is short lived. But, despite our tussle today, she continues to be a prime enthusiast of the MedTrek and my efforts to begin to transform reams of daily diaries into some kind of literary work. Remarkably, perhaps a sign of my own post-divorce growth, she doesn't have a drop of French blood and, among other things, deserves the credit for coming up with *The Idiot and the Odyssey* title.

Elissa's also passionate about her own MedTrek-like project, which is one of the reasons we hit it off almost immediately when she first stopped by my place in Valbonne with our mutual friend Cathy Nolan, a Paris-based journalist.

Elissa and Cathy, both fervent fans of Saint Mary Magdelene and the cult of the Black Virgin, were on their way to visit Magdalene's skull in the bowels of Saint-Maximin's basilica in the Var. Legend has it that Magdalene, after that nasty crucifixion, sought refuge in Saintes-Maries-de-la-Mer in the Camargue before moving inland to preach in Provence. They had booked a room in the house of an ex-communicated Dominican priest who, for 17 years, had guarded the mountain grotto in nearby Sainte-Baume where Magdalene's bones were first found.

Their intriguing odyssey makes my MedTrek look relatively sane.

There are only two other passengers on the 'early' *barca* and we don't pick up anyone at stops in Riomaggiore (it gets its name from the Rivus Major, a river that's now covered over), Manarola, Corniglia or Vernazza (the only village with a real port), which are the other four members of the Cinque Terre. Typically, the boat people aren't sure of the distance by foot from Monterosso al Mare to Portovénere.

"Fifty kilometres," says the ticket seller with some uncertainty. "It definitely can't be done in a day."

My guess is that it's between 30-40 kilometres and will take six to seven walking hours. But after my miscalculation at Mount Portofino, I'm less sure of myself. In any event, my first objective is to hike to the southernmost village of Riomaggiore where I'll meet Elissa for lunch.

I debark in Monterosso where I hit my first bottleneck when some Germans have formed a long straight line to buy the three-euro tickets required to hike in the Cinque Terre National Park.

Why the charge? The ticket stub says it's to support 'a landscape that needs saving'. The Cinque Terre ('*terre*' meant 'villages' as well as 'lands' in medieval days), which UNESCO declared a World Heritage site in 1997 and Italy made a national park in 1999, is one of the most popular places on the planet. Over 1.5 million hikers pay the nominal day fee each year to plod on well-posted trails along the rocky coastline, steep hills and sloping vineyards in the 10,550-acre protected parkland. Seventy percent of visitors are foreigners and most choose to come during the cooler months of April and October.

It's easy to understand the popularity. Visitors discover a landscape with remarkable views of the sea and five picturesque fishing villages, as well as 7000 kilometres of manmade dry-stone walls and terraced fields.

Although the Cinque Terre has been adversely impacted by erosion, the creation of the park has led to reconstruction of dry-stone walls, the planting of new vineyards and the presence of knowledgeable park employees to check tickets and ensure safety for hikers. It has also helped further preserve the difficult-to-access rugged coast with its intriguing geological formations, 11th century religious sanctuaries, 14th century churches, 15th-16th century castles, numerous Genoese lookout towers, storybook houses, very few automobiles and picture postcard perfect panoramic views.

"We want to develop sustainable tourism for this fragile and delicate environment," explains Doriano Franceschetti, a park spokesman who takes me on a tour of a renovated train station and improved walking paths financed by ticket sales and donations.

Personally, I'm all for charging hikers a fee if the funds are used to protect the environment and improve trails and amenities. But I'm happy it's not a pan-Mediterranean phenomenon. I calculate that, at this rate, it would cost me over 5300 euros just for the right to hike around the sea.

Knowing that I've got to meet Elissa for lunch and then hike beyond the Cinque Terre to Portovénere, I'm in speed-walk mode as I begin the uphill march to Vernazza. Still, it takes some time to get around 54 Austrians, each carrying ski poles that widen their physical presence, walking in single file. I don't want to appear to be a rash American in a rush, so I calmly perfect my "*Gruß Gott*" and "*Danke Vielmals*" as I pass each hiker. I chat with one woman, who explains that they're all from the same rural town near Graz, and mention my luncheon date and my effort to make it to Portovénere.

"Halt!" she screams to her compatriots. "Let's take a water break and let this young man get by us all at once. He's meeting someone at The Kissing Path."

Her gang moves to the side and I double-time it past the whole troop. Germans and Austrians make up the bulk of the hikers today but there are groups of Italian school kids and some Americans, who tend to ask me "Is it all uphill?" or "How far is it to …?" But they're easier to pass because they seem to stop every ten minutes for a break.

"How are you able to walk so far?" a woman from Chicago asks when I explained that I was heading to Portovénere.

"Walking's not just physical but also spiritual, emotional and mental," I tell her. "When I walk, I know that I am walking and not doing anything else. I concentrate without concentrating and achieve a sense of calm and ease. And I rarely stop for more than 15 minutes at a time."

"Are you a mystic?" she asks after about thirty seconds.

"Not at all," I laugh. "But I am trying to learn how to walk solidly but leave no tracks in the spirit of Odysseus."

She looks at me like I'm out of my mind.

I run into a shrewd old Italian farmer charging five euros for a glass of locally-made lemon water. I tell him that the last time I was here it didn't cost me anything to munch on plump green grapes that are used to make *sciacchetrà*, a golden-yellow dessert wine. I mention that wine's been made here for millennia and amphorae with 'Cornelia' stamped on them were found in Pompeii. Although I tell him that I've been in Menton for the lemon festival, he doesn't lower the price. Reluctantly, I hand over a bill to support the rural economy.

I'm ahead of most of the morning hikers when I get to Vernazza, the liveliest of the five villages with picturesque *caffè*-smelling bars ringing its port. I explore a maze of narrow cobblestone alleyways before I continue uphill towards Corniglia, the highest Cinque Terre village, where I stop at a perched bar that hangs precariously from a cliff with an out of this world view of the land and sea that's complimented by a soothing scent of lavender, lemon, rosemary and thyme.

I speed walk down the 365 steps to the Corniglia railway station where a sign indicates that the coastal path to Manarola is 'Closed Due To Works'. There are other higher paths but I convince some construction workers that the low path, the one closest to the sea, is the only way I'm permitted to go. "*Permesso piacere?*" I ask. The foreman lets me become the first 'tourist' to walk over a new wooden suspension bridge and I have the path to myself until I arrive in Manarola.

"You jumped over that without blinking an eye!" says an American as I deftly negotiate a climb over the fence blocking the path and almost topple into the sea below.

"I'm walking around the Med and wouldn't get very far if I blinked at this type of deterrence," I reply.

The next stop is the fabled Kissing Path, easily the most popular and romantic section of hiking trails that link the coastal villages. Although even devout Romeos and Juliets would probably not try to trudge the entire trail that connects the pastel-coloured seaside towns, absolutely everyone, from really young lovers to old fools, insists on hiking on Via dell' Amore. It's also known as the 'Street of Love' and includes a 'Tunnel of Love' with enough sentimental graffiti on its walls to put both Byron and Shelley to shame.

After visiting the Kissing Path most people take one of the frequent trains from village to village while more adventurous visitors meander on 60+ kilometres of trails that traverse olive groves, vineyards, orchards and chestnut woods between sea level and an altitude of 550 metres. The eight-hour march on the Sentiero Azzurro runs high above the villages and includes many hilltop chapels and sanctuaries.

The Cinque Terre National Park also includes a 6800-acre protected marine area and after lunch with Elissa I take a quick dive in the sea, swimming without a breath on the bottom for so long that, like Odysseus, I "came up spouting brine, with streamlets gushing from my head and beard".

There's no question that the best view from the water is the sight of yet another smitten couple tenderly embracing on the Kissing Path.

There's a march of 845 steps up the hill from Riomaggiore to the road to Portovénere. I stay on the windy tarmac for a few kilometres because there's little traffic, fantastic sea views, rows of terraced vineyards, endless olive groves and breathtaking steep cliffs. One farmer has a private 'train' that takes him up and down his vertical property on this spectacular stretch of sea that's a twin of the Costa Brava.

Then I make a big mistake. I choose one of the lesser GRs down the hill towards two fabulous sounding destinations, the Menhir du Tramonti and the Fontana di Nozzano. Who could resist a menhir and a fontana in one swoop? Not me!

The map indicates that the GR 4b runs into the GR 4c but within 15 minutes I wind up in a briar patch that tears my shirt and arms to shreds and reopens some of the cuts on my face. By the time I realise that going further is hopeless, I've wasted an hour of daylight. I tumble around in the bushes and somehow make it back to the main path.

Then, like a more mature hiker, I continue on the *Palestra nel verde* through the forest and along the cliffside to Portovénere. This is another MedTrekking must and my sunset arrival is a fitting finale to the Cinque Terre circuit.

The hike into La Spezia the next morning won't be a bramble-and-thorn filled walk like yesterday, according to the receptionist at the hotel.

"It's nothing like the path from Cinque Terre," he says. "You're headed into a naval port."

Pleased to have reached Portovénere, with its 12th century houses and 6th century San Pietro church, I want to make it to La Spezia before accompanying Elissa to Rome and getting her on a flight to Los Angeles. A sign near the hotel says it's only 13 kilometres into town. It's also dark, humid and blustery and as I look across the port to Lerici where a large passenger ship is dropping anchor I don my bright orange smock to light me up when cars buzz by.

I ignore the first drops of rain and take the Degli Scavi Romani through an old Roman village before stopping for a coffee in Le Grazie at 7:30. By the time I reach the pleasure port of Fazzano at 8:30 it's pouring and Elissa has left three messages asking me to abandon the day's march. I take a bus back to Portovénere and wonder if, like Byron, I shouldn't take to the water.

I'm not too dismayed at the delay because I've learned to avoid projecting more than a few steps in advance.

That wasn't the case with Odysseus who was frequently reminded that he'd have a tough time. "Great captain, a fair wind and the honey lights of home are all you seek," Teirêsias said. "But anguish lies ahead; the god who thunders on the land prepares it, not to be shaken from your track, implacable, in rancour for the son whose eye you blinded.' Another time he's told "Your voyage here was cursed by heaven!" Who wouldn't, as Odysseus did, come to the conclusion that "the gods have tried me in a thousand ways"?

I'm not being tried by the gods and unlike Odysseus I've got a book called *Twenty-Four Hours A Day* with meditations that reinforce a reasonable attitude towards the future. One entry says "not to think of the Red Sea of difficulties that lies ahead." I am sure that when I come to that Red Sea, the waters will part and I'm not worried about the logistics of getting to La Spezia when the weather clears.

36. Finding My Marbles on the Etruscan Riviera

"Men's lives are short. The hard man and his cruelties will be cursed behind his back, and mocked in death. But one whose heart and ways are kind–of him strangers will bear report to the whole world, and distant men will praise him." — The Odyssey

Anyone who enjoyed trudging abreast the military facilities in Toulon and around the industrial installations in Fos-sur-Mer, which both blocked access to the sea, will love slogging through La Spezia at the end of summer. The naval, army and air force military base dominating the town's seafront features high fences and intimidating signs that make it clear that it would be worse than fatal to trespass. To top it off there are masses of industrial buildings, a gigantic power plant and hectares of commercial shipping facilities. What environmental masochist could ask for more?

The urban La Spezia trek consists of a half-day view-blocked walk alongside Italy's largest naval dockyard that, though it begins on the pleasant via de Marina in the port of Cadimare, is first a *Zona Militaria*, then a *Marina Militare*. The port, armada, sailors and everything they own is protected by a thick wall topped with razor wire that is high enough to block any snooping. There's also a smelly moat and enough *Divieto di Acceso* signs to intimidate a Mafioso. The booming cargo port and the massive red-and-white electrical plant are equally daunting. The only way to reach the Med is to put a car on a ferry to Corsica, Sardinia or Tunisia.

Yet there are myriad amusements in La Spezia: an indoor bocci ball terrain with rubber courts; German bus drivers sunning in the middle of a wide bike path; families taking their kids to the Arsenal Museum to see a '100 Years of Naval Defence Systems' exhibit; and other folks heading to the Museo Lia, a restored 17th century monastery with over 1000 artworks dating from the Roman era to the 18th century. There are even a few hundred metres of pleasant promenade in the middle of town where boats shuttle passengers to Portovénere and the Cinque Terre. One hopeful sign is a gigantic billboard proclaiming that sections of the military land are being converted into up market apartments. Buy now!

After Cinque Terre, it's humbling to have a dose of the industrial beast to balance the natural beauty. But once through La Spezia proper I figure it should be an easy stroll along the dockyard wall to the resort town of Lerici, the Saint-Tropez-like harbour where Shelley lived.

Unfortunately, I obey a sign that forbids pedestrians to take an overpass that briefly bisects the forbidden military territory and provides cars with a short-cut to Lerici. Instead I spend an hour zigzagging inland past the electricity plant and through a marble quarry until a farmer suggests that I climb to the top of a plateau and follow a path with, he says, "*fantastico*" views of the bay back to Cinque Terre and a little unpaved road that will take me to Lerici.

I pass other locals during the climb. One farmer is carrying a sack of seed weighing at least 30 kilograms without breaking a sweat, another is pushing a wheelbarrow almost overflowing with cement. At the top is a GR that takes me to a village above seaside San Terenzo, where Shelley and Byron were staying shortly before Shelley's death. The sunset spectacle of Lerici, La Spezia harbour, Portovénere, the islands and the sea make this a worthwhile detour.

In Lerici I visit the 13th century castello, rebuilt by the Genoese in the 16th century, before trying to find a room at hotels named after Shelley, Byron and Florida. They're all full on what is officially the last Saturday night of summer in late September. I'm told that the crowds are a national phenomenon because just about everyone in Italy feels genetically compelled to make a final summer's end pilgrimage to the sea.

The walk out of Lerici passes the Restaurante di Golfo di Poeti and I follow an uphill GR to Tellaro, which one local guidebook claims has "all the features of the perfectly preserved, picturesque Ligurian seaside village, complete with church overlooking the sea". Although it's early Sunday morning, a store is open and I ask the saleswoman for directions to Viareggio.

"Viareggio is 50 kilometres from here! You can't walk that far," interrupts a man standing next to me. "Come to my church instead."

After climbing a hill that towers over his church overlooking the sea and some inviting isolated coves, I follow the GR to the tip of Point Bianca, where multiple signs proclaim that the path is 'dangerous' and 'impassable' due to landslides. Oddly, after having been misled by a sign yesterday, I heed this one because local hikers monitoring the GRs invariably know the lay of the land.

Going directly uphill on a briar-and-bramble invaded stone path, I'm serenaded by the heavenly chiming of church bells. In the vista-rich Parco Naturale Regionale di Montemarcello-Magra founded in 1995 I pass an agriturismo farm selling *olio* (oil) and a sign in Italian that proclaims 'Recycling + Not Littering = A Blue Sea'. All just a couple of hours from urban La Spezia.

An official at the tourism office in Montemarcello tells me the town is named after the Roman consul Marcellus, who bested the Ligurians here. He hands me a brochure that contends "Montemarcello has for years attracted high-class tourism and been frequented by prosperous, discreet intellectuals, mostly from Milan." The high-class tourists and intellectuals aren't around this morning but when I stop for tea there's a table of pompous British transplants that seem to be auditioning for roles in *Under The Tuscan Sun Too*. I scram and follow a footpath down to Bocca di Magra, the mouth of the boat-filled Magra River and the border between Liguria and Tuscany.

During the downhill march, I count 16 tankers and cargo ships waiting to drop off or pick up shipments in La Spezia. Then another MedTrek mystery: a speedboat, with a bouquet of flowers placed on the steering wheel, is 'parked' in the middle of an olive grove. Is the boat dead? Is this what the owner wanted done upon his death? Whatever the purpose, it seems a fitting memorial.

The Monastero di San Croce, just uphill from the wide and impassible river, bills itself as a *'case di incontri spirituali'* or a house of spiritual encounters. I try to get a room but, like other hotels this weekend, it's fully booked. I put it on the list for my guided tours when I start taking groups on walks around the Med.

I hike two kilometres along the Magra to a bridge and another two back to the mouth of the river on the other side. From the *bocca* to the *punta* to the *bocca*. Once on the sea, I'm on the Via J.F. Kennedy as restaurants begin to fill with the Sunday lunch crowd.

Tuscany's flat and sandy Versilia district features, as the Michelin guide predicts, "a string of superb resorts boasting fine sandy beaches which slope gently into the sea and are ideal for families with young children". I'm particularly intrigued that there is a red *salvataggio*, a colourful rescue boat equipped with oars and life jackets, every 100 metres.

This is another rich coastal plain created eons ago by the alluvium deposited by streams tumbling down from the nearby Alpi Apuane, which is why this stretch of coast is often called the Riviera Apuane. More recently the mountains have become scarred by the constant excavations of much-demanded Carrara marble at quarries like the Cave dei Fantiscritti and the Cave di Colonnata.

I learn how Italy loses its marble(s) after walking another ten kilometres to the Marina di Carrara. The sprawling Nuovi Cantieri Apuania is filled with slabs of different shaded white-and-red marble stacked like toast and ships, like the *Bothnia Carrier* docked here today, are waiting to load it. The *marmi*, as the Italians call their marble, is not all exported. The Guardia Costiera building is constructed completely of marble and there's a marble monument to marble miners, or marmites if that's what they're called in Italian.

The Commune of Massa advertises its free beaches with one caveat: "Beware Bathing Not Safe For Lack Of Special Rescue Services". They're not lying. There are no *salvataggi* on the sand, though their frequency resumes on the family-filled beaches near Marina di Massa where, at five in the afternoon, the entire populace seems to be strolling next to the Ligurian, Tyrrhenian or Mediterranean Sea.

My 70-euro sea-view room at the Hotel Tirreno in Marina di Massa looks onto a pier extending into the sea. When I open the shutters at 7am, hoards of fishermen are already out, large machines are kneading the sand and the *salvataggi* are being equipped to save the drowning. The sea looks lazy, like she's not quite ready to awaken. In Marina di Torre del Lago Puccini, where Puccini composed most of his operas, scores of industrious bronzed Italian men are preparing the beaches, terraces and lounge chairs for the last gasp of the summer season.

There are absolutely no Italians out at this time of day but dozens of wall-to-wall seaside restaurants like Pirata, Grazia, Sayonara and Café New York seem to expect them to show up for lunch. The most notable event of the morning occurs near some grassy sea level sand dunes when I pass a sign indicating that I'm crossing the 44th Parallel, the imaginary circle of latitude that is 44 degrees north of the Equator and also runs through Oregon, Lake Michigan, Vermont, Maine and Nova Scotia.

Forte dei Marmi, or Marble Fort, is an elegant resort that distinguishes itself by the rainbow of colours used to decorate the cabanas on the sand. Each cabin is a different shade and the beach has a bright and playful red, orange, yellow, green, blue and white hue. Many beaches are private, though no one says a thing as I occasionally trespass on their stone and wood walkways. The sidewalk on the Lungomare di Levante is, practically and sensibly, divided into one lane for cyclists and another for pedestrians. Bicycles are so popular that restaurants tend to have specially designated parking spots for them.

Again the city centres of seaside towns like Marina di Pietrasanta and Lido di Camanta are located a few kilometres inland, which is why the seaside resorts are called "Marina di …" or "Lido di …" I hopscotch over the plentiful jellyfish population as I stroll into Viareggio, which I last visited in the mid-1990s to do a story on a parade that featured a Michael Jackson caricature as the lead float.

The town's landmark gigantic clock is the 4000-kilometre mark on my MedTrek. To celebrate, I have a seafood salad at the Gran Caffè Margherita dominated by a Baroque cupola. As I sip a coffee, I recall that I was in northern Spain to mark the first 1000-K; in Calapiteres, Spain, for 2000-K; and between the Atlantic Ocean and Tangier in Morocco for KKK. I'll still be in Italy 1000 kilometres from now.

I walk six kilometres through the pine forest that is the northern boundary of the Migliarino-San Rossore-Massaciuccoli regional park extending from Viareggio to Livorno. Back on the sea is the first of three or four small marinas and, walking with my shirt off, I frequently ask restaurant owners and lifeguards about the lay of the land between Marina di Pisa and Livorno. There's an overwhelming consensus that I'll be stymied by the two large rivers, the Serchio and the Arno, on either side of the bird-filled Tenuta di San Rossore natural park. When I leave Marina di Vecchiano, there's a single long-necked swan in one of the marshes that seems to be saying "This is one of the few places in Europe where I'm not accosted by man. Leave me alone!"

The Serchio, where one tourist recently drowned, is wide, deep and there's no boat I can hail to take me across. I walk six kilometres inland to Vecchiano and buy a bus ticket at a bar to take me to central Pisa. After getting the ticket and paying for a bottle of San Pellegrino, I politely ask what the time the bus comes.

"That's not my problem," scowls the bartender/bus ticket salesman. "I just sell tickets. Go look at the times at the bus stop; idiot."

This rudeness seems to be an accepted demeanor in Italian bars that sell bus tickets. Or at least bars that sell bus tickets to me. Try to get some information about buses and they go ballistic. This guy's so rude that I'm tempted to insult him, or maybe even hit him. After all, I haven't yet had a fistfight on the MedTrek. Instead, I remember that Athena warned Odysseus to "be silent under all injuries, even blows from men" and Homer counseled to "drop that talk of using fists; it could annoy men".

I ask everyone I meet about prospects of walking through the Tenuta di San Rossore between the Serchio and Arno Rivers. Without exception, they look at me like I'm a village idiot. Don't you know, their eyes say, that no cars are allowed in the regional park, that there are marshes and rivers that will block your path, that it's a former presidential estate, that you're not supposed to disturb the birds and upset the biodiversity, that you'll get lost, that you'll drown, that it's a military restricted area, that you'll be arrested?

In Pisa, a naval base and port before siltation distanced it from the sea, I walk along the Arno, which bisects the town, and visit the municipal tourism office.

"You can arrange a free visit to Tenuta di San Rossore on Sunday and holidays with a minimum of 20 people through the Ente Parco, the agency that runs the entire park," a woman tells me, handing me a brochure about the 24,000-hectare Regional Park Migliarino-San Rossore-Massaciuccoli that includes the 4000-hectare Tenuta di San Rossore. "But you'll be arrested if you go in without a guide and group. You certainly can't hike along the sea by yourself and, even if you did, you'd be trapped between two big rivers."

I walk up the Via Santa Maria, have a quick breakfast at the Hotel Francesco, arrive in the Campo dei Miracoli and enter the Duomo. I sit near the ornate pulpit created by Giovanni Pisano between 1302-1311 and look at the panels evoking the life of Christ. Should I walk where everyone tells me not to or let the birds rest, leave the lakes and swamps alone, not destroy the vegetation and skip a few kilometres of the seaside? In the end, for the sake of nature, I bow to public opinion. And to the Leaning Tower as I head out of town.

The Marina di Pisa, on the southern bank of the mouth of the Arno, has nifty little cabins with fishing nets suspended from wood poles that are accessible by boat. There are a dozen boats fishing near the mouth of the Arno which means, unless everyone is here to sneak into the Tenuta di San Rossore, that there must be some fish.

The first buildings in town are boarded up and the beaches are separated from the sea by a levee. One sign says 'Possibility of strong currents' and a poster promoting an environmental association reads '*Salve il mare con noi*', or 'Help us save the sea'. Another sign, near wall-to-wall restaurants and nightclubs with names like Zara and Marco Polo along the seafront, describes local floral and fauna.

If the sea was lazy yesterday it's dead today. Not a creature is stirring not even, if I can trust the lack of activity offshore, a fish. The boats look like they're stuck in a misty marsh and few of the restaurants and beaches seem to expect any business. There aren't any *salvataggi* or ready-to-jump-in-the-water lifeguards. Watching a bloke stare transfixed at his partner as she sits deep in meditation on the sand is my most social moment until noon, though there are two weird sightings. A pair of high heel shoes tipped with sand dust is standing upright just steps from the waves. Where did she go, I wonder? And, as if to bespeak some economic message, three chairs of varying status are side by side: one is a beach chair with a cloth seat, the other a plain white plastic chair, the last a dilapidated steel chair with plastic webbing that has come apart.

As I approach Livorno, there's also one innovation that I haven't seen anywhere else. Tall sprinklers, fed by hoses from distant faucets, are placed about 15 metres apart to water the sand near the sea. Now that would have baffled the ancient Greeks.

I'm surprised at the size of Livorno, the country's second largest port after Genoa, when it appears in the distance. And even more surprised when I get to it. A fenced-in commercial port dominates the western side of town. Containers are stacked five high, gigantic cruise ships and tankers are loading and offloading, ships are being built and ferries are coming and going to and from Sardinia, Libya and Corsica.

Someone has scrawled '*MERDA*' on the sign at the city limits and it doesn't take me long to understand why. I stroll through the worst odour I've encountered on the MedTrek. How to describe it? Take the smell of that malodorous garbage avenue in Morocco, add ammonia and sulfur, let a thousand bodies decompose for a week, and top it off with some skunk spray. The city's first port, Porto Pisano, was silted up centuries ago and replaced with the new harbor, or the first stages of it, in 1620. It took almost 400 years to create this distinctive smell. Remarkable.

It begins to rain and I don my orange find-me-if-I'm-dead smock. But the sun comes out as I reach the centre of a town some call 'Little Venice'. In another yin-to-yang transition, I'm pleasantly surprised by boat-filled canals, large piazzas, arcaded streets and big parks. There's even an Italglish sign on the sides of buses: 'Citta' In Bus: No smog, No stress'.

The way out of the Piazza Repubblica towards the Etruscan coast, which stretches for 80 kilometres from Livorno to Piombino near the island of Elba, is more to my liking. At this end of the port they're building large luxurious Galaxy yachts, each just a few feet longer than the next. Then the Baracchini Lungomare – which dates from the middle of the 19th century and launched a nationwide trend of seaside gardens, wood chalets and swimming establishments – continues past the Boston Hotel to the Naval Academy, where sailors are nattily dressed in uniforms.

Once past the large stone city 'gates' constructed for Queen Margherita in 1890, swimming facilities consist of both natural and manmade pools, sandy beaches and hundreds of cabanas. Across the street are fashionable turn-of-the-19th-century houses, a football stadium and a hippodrome. In Antignano there's a miniature Abbaye des Lérins proudly situated on a promontory that slightly juts into the sea. My third floor room at the Hotel Universal seems to be floating on water. And just across the street is perhaps the largest baseball stadium in Italy.

I do my laundry in Livorno and eat a *risotto ai funghi* and a *saltimbocca al limone* across the street from the laundromat before returning to the hotel for a soothing sleep to the sound of slapping waves.

Along the sunny promenade, I immediately pass a clump of six competing gas stations. Such competitive proximity, rather rare in Europe, is a MedTrek record. Then I embark on a stupendous stretch of rocky coast that rivals Spain's Costa Brava and France's Esterel with its coves, vistas and seaside villas. The vegetation, including pines and eucalyptus, and the campgrounds, like Il Grande Blu, are also similar to those in France and Spain. Of course there's a genetic connection. These coasts – as well as the Balearic Islands, Elba, Sardinia and Corsica – are all part of the vanished continent of Tyrrhenia, according to numerous academics. They were once one.

This part of the Med is still considered the Tyrrhenian Sea because each town has a seaside street called via di Mare Tirreno. Perhaps to hedge their bets or avoid irritating cartographers, it's often next to via Mare Mediteranno. A railway track parallels the sea, there's a Baroque 18th century pilgrimage church in Montenero and a fantastic storybook castle at 282 Via Aurelia owned by one Sydney Sonnino. One thing Sydney and other rich Italians have done very effectively is block any pedestrian entrance to the seafront by putting their villas, and the long adjoining walls that extend into the sea, right next to each other. Once at the sea, it's difficult to make much headway on the rocks.

This is the Etruscan Riviera, called that after the somewhat barbaric Etruscans who once controlled the region between the Arno in Florence and the Tiber in Rome. The pre-Roman Etruscans, whose powerful empire took off around the 8th century BC, were renowned for expertly working iron, copper, gold and silver mines and usually built their villages on elevated sites with walls of huge stones. They were, at the apex of their power and glory during the 6th century BC, the top of the totem pole. Their domain, known as Etruria, consisted of twelve city-states including Cortona, Perugia, Tarquinia, Veii, Volterra and Vulci.

Historians contend that the Etruscans had a keen sense of town planning, believe the Greeks influenced their art and culture, and tout their skill as artisans who, among other things, created ornate burial urns. Their alphabet has been deciphered and a number of vast burial grounds and excavated villages provide insight into their customs, paintings, pottery and sculpture. They began to fade from the scene around 396 BC when Rome attacked Veii and started exerting the influence of its blossoming empire throughout the Mediterranean.

Remarkable, I think to myself, how I'm continually exposed to the vagaries of history along different sections of the sea. One thing that's always enthralled me about the Etruscans, for example, is a polytheistic belief based on the premise that all visible phenomena are a manifestation of divine power controlled by deities hanging around in the human world. As a kid I always thought that, besides having one high god (which for the Etruscans was the bright sky god Tinia), it would be nice to have individually named gods in charge of things like the moon, the sun, love, war, television, mountains, nuclear power, education, death, hookers and so on down the line. In fact, I think I'll declare Quercianella, the next village on the map, to be the god of MedTrekking. What a smashing name!

Among other things, Quercianella is memorable because of an oddly-named road called Via M. Kaiser Parodi. That's not the only parody here. The town has a *yoghurteria*, the first I've seen in Italy, and someone is pecking on a typewriter, a weird and wonderful sound anywhere these days. On the rocky seashore a young boy, about ten, has created a dozen rock sculptures in various shapes and forms by simply balancing stone upon stone. If there's another Tower of Pisa on the cards, this kid will design it. A few minutes later I see *La Botteghina* driving through the neighbourhood like an ice cream truck, but it's selling fresh fish. What a god!

A sign points towards Nibbiaia, which is such a melodic name that I vow to dub it the god of Scrabble. As I head towards Castiglioncello, yet another great name for a god, I see a sandy beach with 60 empty lawn chairs. Another subject for David Hockney. I pass dozens of luxurious villas until I get to Castiglioncello, which received the *Bandiera Blu Spiaggi*, the Blue Flag Award doled out by the European Union for clean beaches. Then I relax on a restaurant terrace for an hour to nurse an Earl Gray tea during a rainstorm.

I take these storms in stride now. After all, no one's waiting for me, there's no place I have to be. I don't despair or pray, as Odysseus once did. "The storms continued. So one day I withdrew to the interior to pray to the gods in solitude, for hope that one might show me some way of salvation." The weather, like Italians flocking to the coast on the last weekend in September, is impermanent. It will pass.

I have the sandy seashore to myself through Galetta, Rosignano and Solvay, where there's a gigantic industrial chemical complex and a long pier with a tanker docked to it. All of a sudden the sea becomes bright blue, a glaring turquoise tint that I've only seen in the Seychelles. Apparently this is due to the release of calcic water by the chemical plant and, though perhaps toxic, it looks spectacular.

I chat with an Italian I meet on the Pietra Bianca, or the 'White Beach', near the chemical plant. When I tell him I've walked here from Ventimiglia, he says, somewhat awestruck, "*Complimenti!*" A bit later, in Vada, a Moroccan says "*Bravo!*" when he learns that I've walked the north coast of Morocco. This rare burst of appreciation gives me strength to continue to the Marina di Cécina.

Nothing better than an uneventful 35 kilometre day. Once I leave Marina di Cecina, I run into a small seaside resort every eight kilometres. In Marina di Bibbona I stop for a tea and an ice cream sandwich, in Marina di Castagneto-Donoratico I stop for a Coke, and in San Vincenzo I visit the train station. Then I conclude the day with a walk through the Parco Naturale di Rimigliano. Even the monuments, like a tower in Bibbona with the European and Italian flags flying over it, are calmingly low key.

Not that there are no major occurences. I save a little girl's ball from being swept into the sea, throw four beached jellyfish back in the water and tell some Senegalese that by my count there are many more Africans on the beaches today than Europeans. The big event, on a walk that is mainly barefoot on the 50 to 100-metre-wide stretches of beach, is the looming approach of Elba, Napoleon's island of exile that is eerily shaped like his bicorn hat. It's the largest island in the Tuscan Archipelago that also includes Pianosa, Capraia, Giglio, Giannutri and Montecristo.

There are small clusters of Europeans, mainly Germans and German-speaking Swiss, near the marinas, but there's almost no one on the beaches in between. Certainly, nobody except me is marching from one marina to another. The German and Swiss crowd at Riva degli Estruchi are much more attracted by sophisticated campgrounds and hotels. It's refreshing when I see some locals looking for mushrooms in the pine forests of the Rimigliano Park.

Near Baratti I meet a group of 20 American/Canadian cyclists biking through Tuscany on a Women's Quest tour. They're the first North Americans I've spoken to in a week and they can't grasp the idea of a walk around the entire Mediterranean. I head towards Populonia where the sea becomes inaccessible. The local map has dark blue lines indicating 'cliffs' and I take a forest service fire road for ten kilometres through the Parco Archelogico di Baratti Populonia to Piombino. I'm alone except for some woodcutters and a passing jeep with an Archeological Office of Central Italy logo.

In Cala Moreso I'm famished and stop at a calm restaurant in a tranquil cove for a vegetarian couscous and clam spaghetti. Phil Collins' *Another Day In Paradise* is playing, at a low volume, on the sound system and the attractive waitress appears to be settled in her own paradise without a care in the world except me, her only customer. She's remarkably friendly and totally concerned with my comfort and meal.

"Let me know if you want another serving of the couscous," she says when she brings my first course. "Anyone who's just walked over that hill deserves to be treated well."

I'm able to see Elba from my table and ask her, when she brings the just-cooked spaghetti, whether it's worth a side trip.

"One of the great things about Elba is the view you get of our restaurant from the summit of the Monte Capanne," she said. "You can drive around the whole island in a day if you rent a car and a great place to chill is on the beach in Marina di Campo."

"Want to join me?" I ask, almost 99 percent in jest. "I need to practise my Italian."

"I'd love to but then my husband would have to kill both of us," she replies, less than one percent in jest.

"Take her, take her!" jokes her husband/chef, who overhears our conversation when he approaches the table to see what I think of his cooking.

"*Meraviglioso!*" I reply, referring to both his family recipes and his lovely wife.

After I pay the bill I walk through Piombino, past the Salivoli pleasure yacht harbour and to the train station where I have a coffee and chat with a 24-year-old Yugoslav gardener in love with a 21-year-old American student in Florence.

"I just love the way you Americans are able to do anything you want," he tells me in Italian. "Study in Florence, walk around the Mediterranean. That's a luxury most of us will never have."

"Well, stay close to your American girlfriend and you'll probably be exposed to all sorts of amazing choices," I say as I head to the ferry dock where there are frequent and inexpensive ferries to Elba. In another example of American whimsy, I take one to explore Napoleon's isle of exile after finding a room at the Paradiso in Viticcio with a view of the sunset and the sprawling sea.

The next day I learn that Napoleon, who was here between May 1814 and February 1815, hardly lived in penury on Elba but instead had all of the comforts of home. I visit his main residence, the Palazzina del Mulino, where I touch his straw mattress and admire his bicorn hat, in the capital of Portoferraio. Then I drive by the ex-emperor's summer home in San Martino and explore the steep, narrow roads all over the island. It's easy to understand how Napoleon had a chance to regroup and within just a few months regain his self-confidence to flee and meet his Waterloo.

Outside Piombino I trudge past a rusty iron port, some industrial plants and a gigantic ENEL electricity generating facility. It's not even worth trying to get close to the sea. One of the factories, Lucchini Piombino, has a private port that would have cut me off. As would the Cornia River.

Fortunately, the World Wildlife Fund has created a sanctuary, known as the Riserva Naturale Oasi WWF Palude Orti-Bottagone, amidst the marshes and reeds that surround the plant. I don't know how the birds can land amidst all of the towers and wires. And the electricity zinging above them must fry their brains. But at least they have their own oasis.

I pass a group of overweight French cyclists and a campsite full of typically well-equipped Germans. Then, in a nature sanctuary known as the Parco Della Costa Orientale e Della Sterpaia, a sign cautions me to keep things clean and not disturb the wildlife. It's a windy, wavy, blustery, sprinkly day and I again have the beach to myself. The restaurants and surf/sailing schools are now closed for the winter.

I run into Italian families at Camping Tahiti and a pack of Germans staying at a resort called Golfo di Sole. A sign says the hotel has a private concession from the state to operate the entire beach. I sprint, in an effort to avoid a downpour, into Follonica where I stop at the first restaurant to feast on *pennette al salmone*. The *Viale Italia* has cozy looking houses right on the sand and I'm tempted to stay at the Albergo Piccolo Mondo, which is built on stilts at the end of a pier.

Instead I walk past dozens of apartment buildings between Follonica and the packed port of Scarlino, which is the end of the Etruscan Riviera. I call it a day at the Puntone di Scarlino.

I've been told that I can't get around the Punta Ala, a jetset resort with luxurious rural hotels charging big city prices, due to the cliffs, the lack of a beach, private property and no path. Two *carabinieri*, however, claim that it's shorter to walk around the point than climb over the hills. I'll simply have to check things out for myself.

I have no trouble making the 15-kilometre hike from Puntone di Scarlino to Punta Ala on a broad dirt path called Le Bandite di Scarlino, or the Walk of the Bandits. I traipse through a forest, over a mountain and above the sea shortly after sunrise. Besides expansive views of the rocky coast and some secluded sandy beaches, I meet my first family of wild boar on the narrow shaded forest road.

When I first hear the scrimmaging in the nearby brush, I'm startled and jump back, thinking that a wolf is about to attack me. Then, as the noise intensifies, I think it might be a pack of wild dogs readying to tear me apart. I'm pleasantly relieved when I see a compact, tuskless dark grey sow, who looks like she weighs over 100 kilos, confidently stomp across the road followed by four we-don't-have-a-care-in-the-world piglets.

Boar usually live in large groups known as sounders that include sows and their piglets (the males tend to hang out on their own unless they're breeding). So I wait a few more minutes until I'm sure the coast is clear and that the family, which has wandered into the forest, is not a scouting patrol for dozens of their buddies.

I walk adjacent to a piece of land fenced off to 'protect the cultivation of mushrooms and asparagus' before I arrive on the beach approaching Punta Ala which, as its name implies, extends into the Mediterranean in the shape of a wing. Two trademark towers, the Torre Nuova and the Torre Hidalgo, built in the 1500s to guard against attacks by barbarians and other invaders, make me feel very secure. But after a tea near the port, things go awry. I can't find the path along the cliffs and walk in circles for almost an hour. I waste even more time on a golf course in an attempt to reach a forest service road through the mountains. Each time I get close to the apparent path, it seems to disappear. Fata Morgana on the Mediterranean? It's got to be, or else I'm going crazy.

Fata Morgana, as Delphyne explained to me in the Camargue when we were having all sorts of naked and murky visions, is not just a mirage. It's an optical phenomenon frequently due to a temperature inversion and, not unlike an acid flash, it makes objects on the horizon appear to be floating or elongated. Walk along the Mediterranean long enough and you'll see what I mean.

On a combination of rural and urban roads to La Rocchette, not far from Castiglione della Pescaia, I run into two Nigerian hookers in the middle of nowhere. And, no, this has nothing to do with Fata Morgana. They're wearing skimpy black dresses undoubtedly purchased from a streetside vendor outside a discount department store, are adorned with enough plastic jewellery to start a recycling plant and stand with a slouch that would make my chiropractor blanch. They obviously hadn't heard the golden rules: Location, location, location and posture, posture, posture.

"With all due respect, and I don't pretend to be an expert, this has got to be the worst place in the world to try to turn tricks," I say in Italian until my sixth sense kicks in and I realise they're Nigerian and speak English. "There are no truck drivers on this road. You should get back to Livorno where there's a potential clientele."

"Our pimp dropped us here because we weren't getting any customers in Livorno," says one with lips so chapped that I'm tempted to give her my cinnamon-flavoured lip balm. "And before that we weren't doing too well in Florence and Milan. Would you like a blowjob? It's only 20 euros."

I ignore the offer, though I've got to admit the price sounds pretty competitive.

"Maybe it's time to go back to Lagos," I smile before I return to the sea and end the day's outing in La Rocchette where I hitch a ride with a local judge to Castiglione della Pescaia.

37. Marching on Roman Ruins and Meeting Athena

"I must take an oar and trudge the mainland, going from town to town, until I discover men who have never known the salt blue sea." – The Odyssey

The thirty-something-year-old daughter of the owner of a family-run hotel in Castiglione della Pescaia offers to drive me to La Rocchette to resume the MedTrek.

"Who wouldn't want to do a favour for someone hiking around the Med?" Laura rhetorically asks before she enthusiastically describes the coastal terrain that I'll be hiking during the next few days. "That's such a fun and noble pursuit!"

As we drive along the sea, an eerily foggy morning is created by a confrontation between unseasonably warm air and the cold seawater. This local Fata Morgana phenomenon, known as the *caligo*, creates a mist called *calignoso* that gives the seaside a cold, wintry and sinister appearance. But paradoxically I begin to sweat almost immediately when I hike from a promontory topped with a stone villa in La Rocchette to one speckled with prickly cacti on the outskirts of Castiglione. A communal beach clean-up is underway and volunteers are removing debris and raking the sand. One couple with the relaxed but studious calm of Zen monks filters sand as though they have all the time in the world.

Maybe it's the *caligo*, but I get the notion that this could be the day that I stumble either upon the blue pack containing the money and passports that Luke and I lost in Morocco or Odysseus himself. I keep my eyes fixated on the waves, cherish a sea smell complemented by the scent of lavender and, when I reach the Bagno Somalia in Castiglione, stop to admire the castle dominating the town's highest hill.

Keeping my eyes peeled, I continue past my hotel to Marina di Grosseto and Principina a Mare. The beach, just as Laura described it, "resembles the Arizona desert with trees." It's now sunny, the sea's calm and I can see the islands of Elba and Montecristo as I approach the Ombrone River. Laura insisted that "it's impossible to cross the wide and deep Ombrone and the bridge is way upstream." She's absolutely right.

I walk up river for two kilometres along canals and bogs, called *paduli* in the local Tuscan dialect, that are formed by the depressions that trap seawater between the dunes. I watch fish jump, run into a herd of longhorn cattle and meet some wild-looking horses. I don't see any *butteri*, as local cowboys are known, but Laura claims they're straight out of a Sergio Leone spaghetti western.

A wooden information panel tells me about the local feast of fauna and fowl. There are pheasants, owls, egrets, ospreys, geese, herons, kingfishers, flamingoes and ducks, not to mention wild boar and wolves! The flora is equally rich, it says, with water buttercups, yellow iris, sea lavender, and Artemisia.

This alluvial plain was formed in the late Pleistocene Era from sediment deposited by the Ombrone and, according to another informative sign, there was a lake here during Etruscan times until siltation gradually replaced the water with marshes. A Benedictine Monastery was built in 1101 and the Knights of Malta were running the place by 1221. Attempts to improve the lay of the land and eradicate the marshes first got underway at the end of the 16th century when the Medicis and the Dukes of Lorraine created canals and planted a wide variety of trees.

But those efforts didn't prevent the spread of malaria (from the Italian words *mal* and *aria*, or 'bad air') in the 19th century. In fact, it wasn't until 1898 that it was understood that malaria is caused by mosquitoes rather than by the mixture of fresh and salt water in the swamps. The National Veterans' Association managed the land after World War I but it's been privately owned since 1954 and is now considered one of the richest agricultural zones in the country

That night, I return to Castiglione and dine on seafood risotto at La Terrazza di Betti Gabrille on the Corso di Liberta. There's not a whiff of *mal aria*. Nor a lost pack emerging from the sea.

The next day gets underway with three *caffès* and a marmalade croissant at a bar near the port after Laura informs me that the 700-hectare Maremma ('marshy land by the sea') Park on the other side of the Ombrone, which the Michelin describes as a place of "melancholy beauty", is inaccessible to hikers.

"There are marked paths but it's impossible to walk along the beach because cliffs run straight into the sea," she says. "If I were you I'd skip it and take a bus south to Talamone or Orbetello."

Fat chance. Actually I'm intrigued about walking here because a local guidebook describes the area as "once a marshy district haunted by bandits and shepherds". Once I cross the Ombrone and return to the sea, I'm within the boundaries of the Maremma Park. After Marina di Alberese there are seven stone Etruscan towers in the Uccellina Mountains. Although I see a few hikers and groups of Italian kids on a school outing, this is a strikingly isolated stretch of coast.

In an hour I'm away from all of the other day-trippers and, as Laura predicted, I'm stymied by the first cliff, not to mention thick juniper, myrtle and heather bushes. I crawl through the brush and briars over a promontory to a second beach until, a few steps later, I confront a truly insurmountable cliff and head inland on a narrow dirt road.

As I walk away from the sea, I'm on the lookout for a trail running parallel to the Med towards Talamone through the impenetrable forest. But if it's there, I can't find it. Content with stupendous views of the Tyrrhenian Sea and the rolling Tuscan hills, I run into a wolf, a fox, dozens of pheasants and herds of roaming wild deer. The dearth of people, trails and a ban on hunting keeps the Maremma teeming with wildlife, if not bandits or shepherds.

When I finally arrive in Talamone on an inland road, I immediately walk to the edge of the Maremma Park to determine whether I might have missed a route along the sea or over the hills. Apparently not.

"The only way to keep the park pristine is by not giving people an easy way in," a forest ranger explains as he shows me a family of muskrats practicing a synchronised swimming routine in a canal. "But the public does have access to a few marked paths and there are very few complaints. Who wants to argue against preserving nature?"

Beyond Talamone in the direction of Rome is a *passaggio pubblico al mare*, or public walk, that is theoretically maintained by the Commune di Orbetello. As I edge around a five-kilometre bay to the little village of Fonteblanda, the *passaggio* consists of rocks, pebbles, seaweed, debris, and occasional patches of sand. The trail has disappeared.

I cross the Osa River on the omnipresent Via Aurelia and get my first look at an isthmus that connects the mainland to the hump-shaped Promontorio dell'Argentario. I pass dozens of campgrounds, including one named Africa, and after the Albegna River find myself in the town of Albinia, which I initially confuse with Albania. There are signs to the Saturnia thermal baths, one of Italy's best-known spas, but I leave the Strada del Padule and continue on a manmade dike/road that leads to the Argentario promontory. The dike runs through the middle of the Laguna di Orbetello and, halfway across a lake full of fish performing multiple jumps, through the town of Orbetello. This was Urbis Tellus, or the territory of the city of Rome, during the era of Charlemagne, who gave it up in 805. I drop into the Cathedral, built on the site of an ancient Etruscan-Roman temple, and spend an hour online at the Bar Bagianni in the Piazza Garibaldi before enjoying a pizza in the sun.

At the other end of the dike is Porto Santo Stefano and I'm told that there's a road winding around the promontory and the 600-metre high Monte Argentario, as well as a ferry to the nearby Isola Giglio. After a coffee at Il Moresco, I decide to walk to Porto Ercole and hike on the Medside of the isthmus back to the mainland. Scores of cars and hundreds of Italian sunbathers have taken over the sandy beach in Fenigila, where I plant myself in the sand for a 15-minute tanning session, because of the Easter holiday. Beyond Ansedonia, a mini-Saint-Jean-Cap-Ferrat with lots of lovely cliff-hanging villas and the chic Il Pescatoria di Ansedonia restaurant, I take the via delle Mimose to the Torre della Tagliata to see remains of bygone Roman baths.

The Strada di Litoranea continues to Capalbio Marina where I stay at the Albergo del Lago, not far from the offices of the World Wildlife Fund on Lake Burano, part of a 410-hectare reserve founded in 1967. Though there are guided visits, no one is permitted to walk through the park. I stick to the road and admire the swans floating in the canal on the way to Chiarone, a tiny village that's the boundary between Tuscany and the Lazio region, which includes Rome. After lunch, the chef suggests that I walk along the road to Pescia Romana where I can cut down to the sea.

When I reach the marina I hitch back to the nearest train station. I hold a ten-euro bill in my hand but it doesn't interest the Catholic Italians on the way home from church. Two Jehovah's Witnesses pick me up and I gladly give them a ten-euro donation without taking any of their proffered literature. Then I catch a train to Rome to meet up with Luke, Sonia and Elissa for some mundane sightseeing.

The incessant and merciless sirocco wind doesn't just produce rain from the moment Luke and I start walking at Marina di Pescia Romana. It creates an Egypt-like sandstorm that unmercifully pelts us and dramatically slows our pace.

"Consider it a free dermoabrasion," says Elissa when I call her in Rome and describe the bleak walking conditions.

The weather's only one restraining factor. As predicted by absolutely everyone, it actually is impossible to get across the three rivers between Pescia Romana and Montalto Marina. One person who can say "I told you so!" is the shopkeeper who sold us supplies when we arrived in Pescia. I'll always remember him because he called me Luciano which, of course, would be Luke's name in Italian.

"*Scusi?*" I replied. "Why Luciano? Am I lucky?"

It turns out that I resemble his best friend from Northern Italy and that "you both look like Michael Douglas". Then, after we establish that I'm actually an American who looks like his best friend, he concurred with everyone else.

"You won't be able to walk more than a few kilometres without hitting a river that you won't be able to cross," he said. "And it's a very long walk upstream to each bridge."

We reach the first impassable river after only 1.5 kilometres and immediately beat a retreat back through a field where a number of North African agricultural workers are harvesting barley. "You'll just have to repeat the backtracking every time you reach a river," their Italian boss tells us. "You won't get anywhere on the sea until you're beyond Montalto Marina."

When we finally reach Montalto Marina, the sea is so rough and the surf so pounding that, along with the wind and rain and sand, we can't see much of anything on the way to Tarquinia Lido. Somehow, though, we manage to ford river after river without getting too wet, though we have to wallow in quicksand at one point and at another use a discarded bedspring to create a bridge.

Besides the rain and rivers, the blistering sand also slows us down. It gets into our hair, our pores and everywhere but up our asses. I feel like Lawrence of Arabia on a bad hair day. The sun comes out at mid-afternoon but the wind doesn't die down. In fact, it blows my baseball cap into the sea as I leap across one stream.

We're completely unprepared for Marina Velca, which has been flooded twice during the past two years. There's a mini-Katrina scene of destruction with destroyed boats, torn up yards, piles of dirt and furniture in the middle of streets, and homes waiting to be repaired.

"We were flooded because nobody cleaned the bottom of the Marta River and it finally went over its banks," says the owner of the Pegasus Hotel. "I think it's been filling with junk since the Etruscans used this as their main port to rule Etruria."

She assures us, though, that we should be able to ford the Marta "at the mouth, just where it enters the sea" and that, once we do, Tarquinia Lido is just "a few metres away".

"Take this bamboo pole to check the depth just to be sure," she says, handing me a long stick.

The current is so strong, the water so agitated and the waves so high that only an idiot would attempt to measure the depth, much less try to cross the Marta. We return to the Pegasus and head inland to cross the river. When we arrive in Tarquinia Lido, the seaside marina of the inland city founded in 12 BC that is renowned for its Etruscan burial ground and museum, we return to the mouth of the raging Marta and continue to the Helios Hotel.

The peaceful sunset from the small terrace outside our fourth-floor room makes me wonder if the day's wind, rain and pelting sand weren't a figment of my imagination. But we're too tired to do anything more exciting than have seafood risotto in the hotel restaurant and hit the sack. The adverse conditions had to be real.

I let Luke sleep in and take advantage of the quiet morning. I'm exulting in the idea of die-each-night-and-be-born-again-each-morning concept and get this advice from Deng Ming-Dao: "Morning, the time of birth, should not be wasted on a quick breakfast, a hastily read newspaper, and a manic rush to work. It is far better to awake from peaceful sleep, wash yourself, drink clear water, and immerse yourself in the rising energy of the day."

When I finish meditating on the terrace, I look towards Monte Argentario and am energised by the progress I've made.

Luke and I endure, in the company of a sombre German tour group, one of the worst breakfasts of the entire MedTrek – the corn flakes are soggy, the orange juice is watery, the coffee is tasteless, the croissants are hard as rock, the eggs are brown and the fruit hasn't ripened – before we get an early start towards Civitavecchia, the main port serving Rome, on another windy morning. We head towards the Saline di Tarquinia, a natural park along the sea about two kilometres out of town. And this is a serious natural park. A six-foot high fence topped with barbed wire protects the waterfowl in the impenetrable reserve. Great if you're a bird, not so great if you're a hiker.

We walk down a fenced-in road to the park office with the intention of taking one of the many *sentieri* to the sea. But the entry gates are all locked and, after chatting with a couple of park officials, the only option is to backtrack. "Go back 1.5 kilometres and take a left to the sea" were their simple instructions.

Our first obstacle is getting across a dike that looks like it might be swept away by high waves. "It's all a question of timing," Luke says as he surveys the situation. "Go at just the right time and you won't get wet."

I watch the rhythm of the waves, take a run and make it without any problem.

Then Luke follows, but his timing is completely off and he gets thoroughly drenched. I laugh my head off. He doesn't.

We continue along the beach with waves constantly attacking us and frequently have to hold onto the park fence to avoid the water. There are a few more small rivers to cross, but the sun's out and we make decent headway until we reach the Mignone River, when we cut up two kilometres to cross a bridge. By the time we stop at a bar for some *caffès* and a spinach *panini*, our feet are soaked and we both remove our shoes and socks to let them dry in the sun.

It's here, in this nondescript café during an uneventful day that, for some reason, I feel compelled to confess to Luke how absolutely grateful I am that he's spent so much time marching with me in France, Morocco and Italy.

"Damn, this makes me happy, just sitting here with you, completely soaked, as we sip on Italian cappuccinos after battling with the wind and the waves," I smile. "It's so insanely simple, with no bells and whistles, that I truly treasure and appreciate it."

Unlike my own father, who was so typical of his generation, I've never had any problem hugging my son, telling him that I love him, supporting him in his various endeavours, or expressing my appreciation to him for doing stuff like this with me. It's been a delight to see him performing in plays since he was five, accompany him on tours of the film and theatre programs at colleges in the US and England, and encourage him to pursue a career in the arts.

But, as he matures from a teenage boy to a young man, MedTrekking together seems especially profound and I'm particularly maudlin today. I feel like I'm making a deathbed statement.

"I'm not sure you can really understand how much it means to me that you, instead of others who've accompanied me, have become the mainstay companion of this project," I confess. "It's probably normal that, since you're my son, you're my best friend. But having spent so much time doing this with me makes you both a very special best friend and a very special son."

"Well, since we're getting so sentimental, I want you to know how instructive this whole experience has been for me," Luke says as we indulge in an obscenely rich tiramisu. "Today, having spent as much time as possible walking with you, I realise how lucky I am to be sharing something so genuine with someone so important to me."

The *compartimento* of Viterbo becomes the *compartimento* of Roma, a major milestone just before we arrive in the rundown northern side of Civitavecchia. The most remarkable innovation in a place that's been a port since the reign of Trajan is a Pans & Company drive-through *panini* outlet at a gas station that, here anyway, seems much more appropriate than another McDonald's. But we give it a miss and visit the Fort of Michelangelo, which involved creative input from Michelangelo, Bramante and Bernini before it was completed in 1557.

"And these Renaissance artists aren't the only ones who created things here," I tell Luke as we enter the Archeological Museum. "Stendahl was the French Consul in the 1830s and this is where he wrote most of *The Charterhouse of Parma*."

Beyond is Castrum Novum, which was created by the Romans in 264 BC when this was the northern end of their empire. According to a milestone on the Via Aurelia, we're 64 kilometres from downtown Rome. We walk past a number of restaurants built on stilts, pass some upmarket seaside villas and drop in on well-preserved Etruscan ruins on the way to Santa Martinella where we end the day at the Fiume Rio Fiume (rough translation: River River River) just before Santa Severa.

It's a quiet, drizzly morning but the rain has stopped by the time we kick off the hike the next morning. Our goal: get within hearing/seeing distance of the Leonardo da Vinci Airport slightly south of the capital.

We stop to admire the Castelló di Santa Severa, a fortified Roman city built in the 3rd century BC, and learn that this is the end of our beach walk when we encounter an *Armi Missilistica*, or military installation, with constant 'No Trespassing' signs and a serious barbed wire military fence. Back on the Via Aurelia, a building with the marking AURELIA KM 51.75 indicates the current distance to central Rome. We pass a farm that claims to grow "organic crops untainted by fertilisers and chemicals", a gigantic wine-selling warehouse called the Casale Cento Corvi and the Macchiatonda waterfowl reserve, and cross bridges over the Tirreno, the Zambra and the Vaccina rivers.

I mention to Luke that I don't mind walking on a road when there's no option.

"Lao Tsu once said that 'If I have even just a little sense, I will walk on the main road and my only fear will be of straying from it. Keeping to the main road is easy, but people love to be sidetracked,'" I tell him as we arrive in Ladispoli.

The stroll to the sea takes us through an array of interestingly named streets. The outer ones are named after European capitals (Belfast, Parigi, Helsinki, Dublin, Atene, Sofia, Bucharest, Tirana), the next after flowers (camellia, muguet, mimosa, gardenia, hortensia) and those closest to the sea after Italian towns (Roma, Napoli, Palermo and La Spezia). For some reason, the via Kennedy is the name of the street next to the sea.

The waves in Palo Vecchia, which has been abutting the sea longer than almost any village I've passed on the MedTrek, are crashing into the rock wall beneath its two-storey houses and dominating castle. But due to global warming that's gradually raising the level of the Med, a new breakwater is being constructed about ten metres offshore. I certainly wish it had been completed when I try to make a dash around the castle walls and, due to lamentable timing, am soaked by the time I reach La Posta Vecchia restaurant and hotel. It's Luke's turn to laugh as I toss my drenched jeans and socks into a garbage bin and change into shorts.

We walk through the quaint little towns of Marina di San Nicholas and Passe Oscure to enter the commune of Fiumicino and reach Fregene, which is longitudinally south of the Vatican and about eight kilometres north of the airport. We pass a hotel called Gilda on the Beach before catching a bus into Rome with a bunch of Bangladeshis.

I have the same perhaps misguided 'connection' with inhabitants of the Indian subcontinent, which I think is the most interesting place in the world, as I do, or think I do, with Africans. That's news to these guys. They completely ignore me when, trying everything in my book of tricks, I attempt to initiate a conversation in a half-dozen different languages, including the few words of Bangla that I know. These immigrants, who are on their way to Rome to sell sunglasses and other goodies on the street, keep to themselves.

We – Elissa, my kids, their partners and I – take an intriguing tour of Rome based on *Angels and Demons*, one of Dan Brown's 'other' books. The Path of Illumination takes us from the Church of Santa Maria del Popolo in the Piazza del Popolo to the Church of Santa Maria della Vittoria, the Tritone Fountain and other sites of murder and intrigue in the novel until we arrive at the Castel Sant'Angelo. I'm primarily interested in our stop at the Piazza Minerva near the Pantheon, the pagan temple originally built in 27 BC to honour the seven deities of the seven planets.

The Pantheon's been one of my favourite monuments in Rome since I wrote a guidebook to the city in the early 1970s. And Minerva, of course, is the Roman name for Athena, the goddess who aided and mentored Odysseus. It was she whom Homer enabled to shape the finale to *The Odyssey*.

"Conclude it as you will," Zeus told her.

After walking 4401 kilometres around the sea, I'm looking for some guidance. I thrive on all of the physical aspects of MedTrekking and have learned to take the journey a day at a time. I've moved past my divorce in the company of my son and am with a wonderful new woman who supports my midlife project.

But if there's any place to run into Athena and get some additional instruction, this is it.

During his own journey, Odysseus said "After this voyage god grant I find my own wife in my hall with everyone I love best, safe and sound." And Athena told him that he'd finally be able to get a decent night's sleep. "That bed, that rest is yours whenever desire moves you, now the kind powers have brought you home at last."

Of course, she wasn't the only one who predicted what would happen when Odysseus finally made it home to slay the freeloading suitors who'd been pestering Penélopê. Zeus declared "Let him be king by a sworn pact forever, and we, for our part, will blot out the memory of sons and brothers slain. As in the old time let men of Ithaca henceforth be friends; prosperity enough, and peace attend them."

I'm not looking to hear from Zeus, nor do I seek a momentous augury from

Athena. After all, I've made it to Rome and I'm not facing a crisis. I simply wonder, after walking this far around the sea, whether Athena might suggest a change of plans.

I spend 15 minutes wandering around the Piazza Minerva and the Pantheon, which means 'Temple of all the Gods' in Greek, looking for clues. I stare at the Latin inscriptions on the six-metre high sixth century BC obelisk atop Il Pulcino Della Minerva, the marble elephant sculpture sometimes called 'Minerva's Chicken' that was designed by Bernini to illustrate power, wisdom and strength. I translate one inscription on the obelisk, which was brought to Rome by Diocletian for the nearby Temple of Isis, as "A strong mind is needed to support solid knowledge". But that's not the clue I'm looking for.

I enter Santa Maria sopra Minerva, the only Gothic church in Rome that happens to be built over a temple dedicated to Minerva. Nothing there either. Then I go into the Pantheon, where thoughtful Romans used to meet to resolve their problems, and crane my neck to look at the Great Eye in the concrete dome, the only source of light and the very tangible symbol for the sun.

I can't see Athena anywhere, though I recall that Homer wrote "who could see the passage of a goddess unless she wished his mortal eyes aware" and "for not to everyone will gods appear". Maybe I'm not supposed to get a message.

I walk outside and our guide, a young American college student, approaches me. I take a close look at her and remind myself that the gray-eyed guardian-goddess Athena can take the form of any mortal.

"Stranger, you are no longer what you were just now!" I say, stealing a line from Homer in an attempt to make the goddess laugh. She simply smiles, knowingly I thought. Then, as though this was preordained, she speaks.

"You should continue your walk to Aeaea and there, like Odysseus, spend a full year in the land of Circe around Mount Circeo," responds this contemporary Athena wearing Nike's tennis shoes and a Nike T-shirt. "Learn what you can from her as she instructs you about the object of your walk and informs you about your real quest. Only then will you be able to complete your journey. Ask her to turn a pig into a young Labrador to walk with you. Don't walk further until the time is right and then, having completed this 4500-kilometre warm up on your walk, go only to the places that Odysseus passed before completing your journey in Carthage, Tunisia. At that point, you can decide whether you want to attempt to enter Algeria."

I don't bother telling Luke, Elissa or Sonia what I'd just heard. Instead, as our *Angels and Demons* tour continues to Piazza Navonna, I reflect on the implications of spending an entire year near Circe's haunts. Then, after I give the guide a very generous tip (hey, she was a goddess!), I ask my family to join me on a pilgrimage to my favourite spot in Rome.

We enter the Cemetery of the Capuchins on Via Veneto and I guide them through the crypt in Santa Maria della Concezione, a church commissioned in 1626 by Pope Urban XIII. They marvel, as I do each time I come here, at the inventively arranged skeletal remains of 4000 Capuchin monks who died between 1500-1870. Then we all digest the profound passage written on a sign above a row of skulls:

"What you are now, we once were; what we are now, you will be."

The next day I return alone to the Gilda on the Beach Hotel and send a quick email.

MedTrek MileStone #5 – Fregene, Near Rome, Italy

I've made it to Rome after MedTrekking over 4400 kilometres and am heading south towards what the Italians call the Ulysses Riviera to walk on Odysseus' rocks, sit on his boulders and stare at his sea. I'm going to spend a year in Aeaea, about four days walk from here near the jet-set resort of Sabaudia. This is where Odysseus met Circe, the enchantress who turned his men into swine and gave him instructions concerning his voyage to the underworld. I've been led to believe that she'll also have some suggestions regarding the future of my MedTrek.

I'll let you know what I learn after spending 12 months in and around the Parco Nazionale del Circeo and Mount Circeo but today I'm pondering Odysseus' words when he entered the hall of suitors: "You yellow dogs, you thought I'd never make it home from the land of Troy. You took my house to plunder, twisted my maids to serve your beds. You dared bid for my wife while I was still alive. Contempt was all you had for the gods who rule wide heaven, contempt for what men say of your hereafter. Your last hour has come. You die in blood."

I pushed the 'Send' button and then, my head spinning all sorts of fantasies that block out the clatter of a departing airplane, I cross the sand to the shores of the Mediterranean, turn left and take my first step towards Ostia Antica, Nettuno and Monte Circeo. The goal is the path, the path is the goal.

Hiking Addendum

Long-Distance Trekking and A Few Favourite Walks

"Don't let your thoughts carry you away. Come back to the path every moment."-
Thich Nhat Hanh, The Long Road Turns To Joy – A Guide To Walking Meditation

Tackling a long-distance trek on the Mediterranean, or anywhere else, not only requires preparation, training and conditioning to avoid unnecessary aches, pains and injuries. It also demands a balanced mental, physical and spiritual attitude to achieve and maintain the right rhythm to consistently walk more than 30 kilometres, or about 40,000 steps, day after day.

Almost every newcomer who ignores my advice to "hike one day, take one day off" at the outset of a MedTrek walkabout winds up out of action due to blisters, pulled muscles or other minor ailments. Even if you're in a hurry to get around the sea, be prepared to initially take it easy. Start with shorter and slower hikes before slowly slowly (yes, that's two slowlys) increasing your pace and distance. Once you establish your own cadence, a 20-30-kilometre march will be a physical and psychological walk in the park, though many hikers tend to hit a wall between 40 and 50 kilometres.

You are, of course, what you carry. I started the MedTrek with a backpack that seems to get consistently lighter unless I require supplies for long periods away from civilisation, which is frequently the case in countries like Morocco. The most essential item to have with you at all times is, without a doubt, water.

Although the MedTrek rarely roams too far from the sea or populated areas,

I always carry a first aid kit, sunscreen, a poncho, a baseball cap, a map, gloves, a swimming suit, a change of clothes, essential toiletries (meaning a toothbrush, comb and toilet paper), a mobile phone (that's turned off unless I'm making a call) and something to read. A second pair of shoes comes in handy when mine get soaked (yes, falling into the sea happens from time to time) or I get pinched toes. And I prefer to wear a bright red hiking shirt when I'm on this type of outing so I'll be easy to spot if I'm injured or lost.

I frequently establish a base camp where I store my computer, extra clothing, books and other paraphernalia. This tactic enables me to walk almost unencumbered with a small daypack. It frequently necessitates the use of public transport at the beginning or end of the day to reach the start of the hike or get back to my lodging. But I've concluded that the added time, which becomes a relaxing break after a while, beats carrying a 20-30 kilogram pack and looking for a place to stay or camp every night.

Once I get going I rarely stop for more than 15 minutes, even for lunch that usually consists of fresh produce that I buy in the local markets or swipe from the hotel breakfast buffet. Taking more time than that, I find, causes my muscles to tighten and destroys my trekking rhythm. On the trail I often find myself doing pushups, planks or stretching exercises to limber up and stretch while toting a heavy, or even a light, backpack.

After walking for a few days, my taste for rich ingredients and long meals tends to diminish, though I occasionally drop into *chirinquitos* or hole-in-the-wall restaurants for a tomato salad and freshly-grilled sardines. There are usually roadside peddlers, farms or markets selling fruit and vegetables and/or shops with bread and other basics. There are also numerous vineyards offering *dégustation* and a quick wine-tasting stop is a pleasant, inexpensive and energising detour. Almost everyone rewards the walker and no one expects hikers to buy much.

Occasional injuries, as well as a slew of logistical/weather problems, come with the long-distance hiking territory. Don't be surprised or upset when your plans fall apart due to storms, injury, family, work, travel or other obligations. There's always, until that fateful day of your death, tomorrow.

It's invariable that, unless you like detailed planning more than I do, topography and elevation can also spoil your distance calculations and short-circuit your plans. Rivers or marshes that force inland detours are probably the most frequent hazard on the MedTrek and, though I never seem to be capable of following this advice myself, you'll often get in trouble if you don't stick to a blazed path. When I don't have a base camp, I almost never know where I'm going to wind up sleeping until the end of the day. And, yes, sometimes finding a place to crash requires some creativity.

Although it's difficult to get lost (just keep the sea on your left or right), it's helpful to have a map and start the day with a local geography review during breakfast. Also choose the right season for your hike to get both the most favourable weather conditions and lowest prices. Though there's more daylight, summer on the Mediterranean is usually too hot, tourists are omnipresent and accommodation can be difficult to find. I thrive on being out there on mild autumn, winter and spring days.

As I frequently noted, I never walk much faster than the slowest person accompanying me. But while it's enjoyable to hike with companions, it's *de rigueur* and/or fun at certain points, to hike alone. Most people you meet, with the occasional security officer being the notable exception, admire hikers (despite the astonishing stench sometimes produced after a day's sweaty walk) and will help you out with a lift, water, food or any other kind of assistance. I sometimes get myself into trouble but have not yet been assaulted or seriously threatened by anyone I met. Always be flexible and try to maintain a stressless demeanour.

If you wind up at some of the places mentioned in *Walking the Mediterranean* – and I think everyone should stay in a monastery, drop into a nudist camp and sleep on the beach – you won't regret it. And it's a kick to find a cheap hotel on the sea, rent a fairly primitive squat for just a few bucks and, occasionally, splurge if you're really wiped out.

As you've read I prefer to start the hiking day, after a bit of meditation and a hearty breakfast, at the crack of dawn and end it with a nightly bath, with sea salts or oil, followed by a leisurely dinner. I usually offer fellow hikers a massage that combines shiatsu and other techniques I've picked up but rarely, when I'm in hiking mode, do I take time off to enjoy the scores of thallasotherapy centres, reflexology institutes and spas along the Mediterranean coast. However, when I lead tours around the Med, I'll build this into the program.

Here are a few MedTrek hikes, ranging from a day to a few days, that I would do again at the drop of a hat or encourage anyone to take to get acquainted with the varied Mediterranean seaside.

France – The Saint-Tropez Seascape Stroll – two days
The 37-kilometre hike from Saint-Tropez around the Rabiou Point to Cavalaire-sur-Mer has exceptionally varied terrain and uninterrupted contact with the sea. It doesn't take too many steps to appreciate why locals and tourists flock to these expansive beaches, silent coves, majestic capes, solitary lighthouses, jutting rocks and crashing waves to stroll through vegetation that includes eucalyptus, cork oak, pines, chestnuts and full-flowering mimosa. The rhythmical names of the capes – Camarat, Cartaya, Taillat and Lardier – complement the physical beauty. Avoid this hike during the summer due to crowds, heat and prices.

France: The Calanques Cove-to-Cove Constitutional – two days
The 20-kilometre (as the cormorants fly) walk along the limestone *calanques* – with names like Port-Pin, En-Vau, Morgiou, Sormiou and Sugiton – between Cassis and Marseille is absolutely surreal. The white, weathered pinnacles and numerous

deep inlets that marry sea, rock and sky are, if not heaven on earth, the moon on earth. Get a map of the area with detailed descriptions of the coastline and the many trails to avoid getting too lost. Take more water than you think you'll need. The area is frequently closed to visitors during the summer, and when the winds are strong, to prevent fires.

France: The Camargue Marsh Hike – one-three days

Get a detailed map of the Camargue and plot your own 10-60 kilometre excursion into the seductive maze of marshes, sand banks, dikes, canals, lagoons, salt flats and sea inlets. You'll have 800-square kilometres of protected botanical and zoological nature reserve and national park, which the Michelin guide says is "the most original and romantic region of Provence and possibly of France", at your fingertips/footsteps. Stay in the fortified city of Aigues-Mortes and/or Saintes-Marie-de-la-Mer after you've said hello to the Camargue horses, bulls and birds. Prepare to get lost.

France: Barefoot Sand Walking – one-three days

Start off in the canal-filled city of Sète, which is the entry point to the French Med's best sandy beaches, and walk barefoot on the sandbar that separates the sea from the Bassin de Thau. Visit Listel, where a famous 'sand wine' is produced from grapes cultivated between the sea and the Bassin de Thau, and continue walking at least until you reach Le Cap d'Agde's 'nudism obligatory' beach. Then stay, keep going or turn back. The excursion affords lots of opportunities to walk barefoot even if you don't want to take off all of your clothes.

Spain: The Costa Brava Road Walk – one-two days

It's sometimes necessary to walk on a paved road and the stretch of two-lane blacktop from Sant Felieu to Tossa de Mar is the place to do it, especially in the winter when there's very little traffic. Forests and the sea abut the GI 682, a stretch of tarmac so picturesque that it's been proclaimed a European Monument. There are frequent descents to beaches, coves, campsites and resorts, like Rosemar and Cala de Salions. But it's best to stay up high and enjoy panoramas that merit all sorts of superlatives. Don't bother counting the curves between Sant Feliu and Tossa de Mar. There are 365.

Spain: The Captivating Cap de Nau – one-two days

The walk from Xabia to Cumbre del Sol merits, without a doubt, a top rating. The mythical El Mongo Mountain keeps appearing at various angles and there's a great view from the lighthouse at the tip of the Cap de la Nau, the most western of Valencia's capes and a traditional telltale sign for navigators. Enjoy the stroll along the cliffs to La Granadell beach and stop for dips in the numerous swimming holes.

Spain: The Costa Blanca's Inland Sea – two-three days

I would use this walk to promote the MedTrek to potential hikers. It involves a flat stroll through a unique natural setting, the 24-kilometre sandbar that separates the Mediterranean Sea from the placid Mar Menor, between San Pedro de Pinatar and La Manga. That's followed by a 36-kilometre hike from La Manga to Playa El Lastre that mixes demanding 300-plus metre mountain climbs with stupendous views, steep cliffs, wave-battered rocky coves and sandy beaches in a completely stark and isolated natural environment.

Spain: The Cabo de Gata Catwalk – three-four days

The 100-kilometre wild walk from Carboneras through the Cabo de Gata natural park includes some of the most impressive limestone cliffs, rustic coves, unnamed little creeks and sandy beaches on the Mediterranean. If you feel like you're in the middle of a movie set, it's because Peter O'Toole, Richard Chamberlain and other actors have shot films here. The vast Cabo de Gata park often seems devoid of humans and you can count on finding yourself alone on an isolated beach.

Spain: Reaching The Southernmost Point In Europe – two days

Stroll from Gibraltar, once you've seen the tailless Barbary macaques, into Algeciras to kick off the 30-kilometre walk through a natural park to Tarifa at the tip of the Iberian Peninsula. The path parallels the Strait of Gibraltar along sloping green hills occasionally topped with industrial windmills that resemble quixotic stick figures. You're likely to be on your own except for some horses, cows, sailboats and the tanker traffic in the Strait. Beyond the Tarifa lighthouse is the expansive Atlantic Ocean and across the 13-kilometre wide Strait of Gibraltar is the Moroccan coast.

Morocco: Get a Sniff of Tangier – one day

Take a bus, or hire a driver/fixer, to get to the northwestern-most tip of Africa at Cape Spartel and visit the nearby Caves of Heracles and the one-time Phoenician, Carthaginian and Roman settlements in Lixus. Gaze across the Strait of Gibraltar to Tarifa and Spain before walking to Tangier along the hilly Mirador de Perdicaris or on the main road past the king's summer residence. Then explore the city's medina and the art-filled museum in the sultan's former palace before dropping into the Gran Café de Paris or Café Central for mint tea.

Morocco: Moving from Morocco into Spain – one day

The village of Wa Musa sits in the shadow of the steep and towering Jbel Musa mountain, which some believe is one of the two Pillars of Heracles, and a path along the sloped seafront features calming views of the Med, the Strait, Spain and Gibraltar. Walk through down-to-earth seaside villages to the Spanish/Moroccan border at Ceuta/Sebta, one of two Spanish enclaves in northern Morocco. You may have to follow the border fence over the mountain to enter this intriguing Spanish enclave at Fnideq if the soldiers at the seaside refuse you entry.

Morocco: Beyond Jebha to Al Hoceima – about three days

Spend a day walking along the dizzying stretches of the narrow road curving along the coast from Azla, Oeud Laou or Stehat to Jebha. Stay in Jebha, the closest thing to a bustling metropolis in this undeveloped part of the country, for a night before climbing the Pointe des Pecheurs. Then, equipped with supplies for a few days, follow the trail through marijuana fields to Torres El Kala, Bades, the Bokkoyas Mountains and Al Hoceima.

Morocco: From Melilla to the Algerian border – three days

Tour Melilla la Vieja, the old town in 'the European city closest to the desert' that is Spain's second Moroccan enclave. Hike the 40-plus kilometres through Nador to Kariat-Arkmane. Then make the run along the cliff coast through Cap de l'Eau (those are the Spanish-controlled Chafarinas islands just offshore) and Ras Quebdana to Saidia at the Morocco-Algerian border. Drop me a note if they've opened the border or give me a call if, like me, you lose your passport and credit cards in the sea.

France-Monaco-Italy: Three countries in one day

Walking in three different countries – France, Monaco and Italy – within just a few hours is not an everyday happenstance on the Mediterranean. Kick off the day in Beaulieu, enjoy your stroll through the Principality of Monaco and cross the border into Italy after tea in Menton. If you want to add some elevated hiking to the day, the Nietzsche Trail heads uphill from Eze-sur-Mer to Eze Village, which offers some of the best views on the French Riviera.

Italy: An Imperial Meander – one day

Visit the two olive oil museums in Imperia, each tracing the history of olives and touting the fruit as 'the lubricant of the health-inspiring Mediterranean diet', before making the spectacular seaside romp from Oneglia around the Capo Berta to Diano Marina. If I had to invite someone to the Ligurian Med for some civilised, family-style hiking, this is where I'd start. The rocky hillside has been secured by steel 'spaghetti' wiring to prevent a landslide, an old stone house has been charmingly renovated, and there are scores of Italian cyclists, families, kids and older couples strolling on a paved road-sized but closed-to-vehicles path.

Italy: Making it into Portofino – one day

Take off from Nervi, on the outskirts of Genoa, on the omnipresent Via Aurelia and walk through Bogliasco, Sori, Recco (where you should munch on some *fugassa al formaggio*, the pie made with *prescinseua* cheese) and Camogli into the

4680-hectare Portofino Regional Nature Park. Climb the 2000-foot-high Mount Portofino and make the challenging walk up-and-down along the cliffs and coves to Portofino. Stay at the Hotel Splendido, a former 16th century monastery where Richard Burton proposed to Elizabeth Taylor.

Italy: Before, Within and After Cinque Terre – two-three days
Trains running along the coast make it easy to start, finish and/or interrupt a walk in the Cinque Terre, or the 'Five Lands' of Monterosso, Vernazza, Corniglia, Manarola and Riomaggiore. But expand this popular hike (one of the few on the Mediterranean where you'll be charged a fee) by starting in Moneglia to the north and continuing to citadel-dominated Portovénere to the south. The walk is an up-and-down-through-the-woods-from-village-to-village trek along a hillside covered with Aleppo pine trees, rockroses, lavender, prickly ivy and wild asparagus. Don't forget to stop for a snog on the fabled Kissing Path, easily the most popular and romantic section of hiking trails that link the Cinque Terre coastal villages.

Italy: The Etruscan Coast and Elba – two-three days
Start your hike on the Etruscan Riviera, which stretches for 80 kilometres from Livorno to Piombino near the island of Elba, in Castiglioncello. Proceed along the seashore through Galetta and Rosignano to Solvay, where the sea has a glaring turquoise tint that I've only otherwise seen in the Seychelles. Continue barefoot on the sand through Marina di Cecina, Marina di Bibbona, Marina di Castagneto-Donoratico and Santa Vincenzo to Populonia and Piombino. Take the ferry to Elba for a two-day break on the island that once, briefly, housed Napoleon.

Italy: The Ulysses Riviera – one week
To get a taste of what's coming next in *Walking the Mediterranean*, trek for a few days between Rome and Naples. Amble into Anzio, which is rumoured to have been founded by a son Odysseus had with the Sorceress Circe, and visit the seaside archaeological park and the World War II cemetery. Saunter through Sabaudia into the Parco Nazionale del Circeo and climb Monte Circeo, where Odysseus's men were put under Circe's magical spell. MedTrek through Terracina and Gaeta along the Ulysses Riviera, the coastal region named for the legendary journey and adventures of Ulysses/Odysseus, to Pozzuoli and Naples. As dictated by the goddess I met in Rome, I'm hanging around this area for a year. But after just a short time I'm already tempted to take up permanent residence near the alluring ruins of Pompeii in the shadow of Mount Vesuvius.

Acknowledgements

Walking around the Mediterranean is a gas and I owe a huge debt to the gods, earth shifts and other natural and supernatural forces that combined to create and nurture the still-glorious sea. My project would have not been launched without ongoing inspiration from Homer and Robert Fitzgerald's inspiring translation of *The Odyssey*, which I bought when I was in college for $6.95. That was a very small price to pay for a lifelong muse.

I certainly would not have fully appreciated my hiking adventure without meeting hundreds of people on the shores of the sea and being accompanied by a score of companions on the MedTrek path. Each of them, from cantankerous Delphyne to my blossoming son Luke, from the nurse who bandaged my wounds in Morocco to the French woman who gave me a lift near Narbonne, are gods in his or her own right. I still have an issue with arrogant security officials but it would be unreasonable to think that anyone can achieve nirvana after walking less than 5000 kilometres.

A number of publications – including *Boston Magazine, France Guide, San Francisco Books & Travel, Time, The Times of London*, and *Fast Thinking* in Australia – helped defray the costs of this caper by printing various versions of my Mediterranean tale. I also want to thank Russ Collins for posting the French chapters of *Walking the Mediterranean* on his excellent Beyond the French Riviera website (www.provencebeyond.com). And I was delighted to learn that California college student Jamie Coskun got an A for his description of my project.

My octogenarian mother, the indefatigable Helen Stratte, proved to be my most fastidious copyreader and my wife, ace Los Angeles Times blogger/journalist Elizabeth Snead (who gets credit for coming up with the *The Idiot and the Odyssey* title), and daughter Sonia have been extremely patient with my persistence.

Among the many people who read, commented on and critiqued the manuscript at various stages are (and I apologise to anyone I've forgotten) Armando Arorizo, Helen Blythe, Taylor Chambers, Felicia Eth, Melanie Fleishman, Sam Fleishman, Lex Hames, Barry Holmes, Lucienne Joy, Marion Kaplan, Michael Knipe, Andrew Lownie, Ilene Medecin, Francis O'Hara, Alison Prideaux, Deborah Ritchken, Peter Rubie, Mira and Tony Rocca, Gerald Rodgers, Elizabeth Snead, Harry Stein, Jimmy Stewart, Kip Stratte-McClure, Luke Stratte-McClure, Robin and Elliott Thompson, Craig Unger, Vince Tomasso, Jeff Wheelwright and Tara Wigley.

Most importantly, continual encouragement from my publishing team in Australia helped me shape this opus for publication Down Under. Editor, publisher, long-time colleague, friend and fellow-hiker John Keeney provided tremendous insight even before he took the foolhardy financial risk to shepherd the project to fruition. I've invited John, editor Tim Mendham and designer Nick Dale to walk with me in Algeria in return for their invaluable assistance and contributions.

Ever walk onward!

Antibes, France, September 1, 2008

FAST THINKING is the world's foremost magazine devoted to innovation across all walks of life. An original quarterly, Fast Thinking deals with invention and creativity in business, management, science and technology, education, politics, people and life. Based in Sydney, it is now sold in over 30 countries. It's major web portal is becoming a world-wide library of essential links and an archive of relevant articles and blogs.

The FAST THINKING Book Series now has two ranges. The first was Business (Innovation x Ideas), with such titles as "Re-Thinking Innovation" based on the mammoth IBM global survey of innovation, the largest transnational innovation review of companies ever undertaken. The second series, called the Creative Travel Series, debuts with this volume, "The Idiot and the Odyssey".

High quality, complete, book or article manuscripts on creative travel or on innovation in the subjects named above, as well as art, architecture and design, will receive careful editorial review for book, magazine or digital journal publication by our editorial team.

Contact FAST THINKING at fteditor@fastthinking.com.au

Subscriptions, books and other items are available at preferential rates via our web site store at www.fastthinking.com.au.